BREATHWORK AND PSYCHOTHERAPY

Clinical Applications for Healing and Transformation

JESSICA DIBB

FOREWORD BY *Daniel J. Siegel, MD*

Norton Professional Books
*An Imprint of W. W. Norton & Company
Independent Publishers Since 1923*

This book is intended as a general information resource for professionals practicing in the field of psychotherapy and mental health. It is not a substitute for appropriate training or clinical supervision. Standards of clinical practice and protocol vary in different practice settings and change over time. No technique or recommendation is guaranteed to be safe or effective in all circumstances, and neither the publisher nor the author can guarantee the complete accuracy, efficacy, or appropriateness of any particular recommendation in every respect or in all settings or circumstances.

It is highly recommended that you not try any of the Group 5 breathwork practices described in this book without the supervision of a qualified and experienced breathworker, preferably one who has been certified by the Global Professional Breathwork Alliance (GPBA). If you are new to breathwork, it is recommended that you obtain guidance from an experienced breathwork facilitator, also preferably one who has been certified by the GPBA for all breathwork practices. Please also note certain physical conditions with which certain breathwork practices should not be used at all.

The names and identifying details of some breathwork clients described in this book have been changed and any real names are used with permission. Some breathwork clients described, and the transcripts of their sessions, are composites. The author is not a lawyer, and nothing contained in this book should be construed as legal advice. For advice about how to prepare legally appropriate informed consent documents, or for any other legal advice or legal questions related to your therapy practice, please consult an attorney with relevant expertise.

Any URLs displayed in this book link or refer to websites that existed as of press time. The publisher is not responsible for, and should not be deemed to endorse or recommend, any website other than its own or any content that it did not create. The author, also, is not responsible for any third-party material.

Foreword © 2025 by Daniel J. Siegel
Copyright © 2025 by Jessica Dibb

All rights reserved
Printed in the United States of America
First Edition

For information about permission to reproduce selections from this book,
write to Permissions, W. W. Norton & Company, Inc.,
500 Fifth Avenue, New York, NY 10110

For information about special discounts for bulk purchases, please contact
W. W. Norton Special Sales at specialsales@wwnorton.com or 800-233-4830

Manufacturing by Versa Press
Book design by Brooke Koven
Production manager: Ramona Wilkes and Gwen Cullen

ISBN: 978-0-393-71200-1

W. W. Norton & Company, Inc., 500 Fifth Avenue, New York, NY 10110
www.wwnorton.com

W. W. Norton & Company Ltd., 15 Carlisle Street, London W1D 3BS

1 2 3 4 5 6 7 8 9 0

With forever love for my family bookwriting team:

Saul H. Mendlovitz, my father—you inspired bold, expansive visions, taught me to think about creating a world without war, modeled daily personal growth, and tolerantly did the breathing practices until your last breath at 99—the weekend the manuscript was complete.

Martha Mendlovitz Matt, my sister—your inner light of faith in me, our family, and this book, and your prodigious capacity to brighten and nurture everyone's life, was, and is, indispensable beyond words.

Joshua Caleb Dibb, my son—your practical, emotional, and spiritual mentoring and companionship contributes inestimable, irreplaceable value and sustenance for the deep journey of creating and becoming.

Princessa, your beauty, wisdom, and luxuriating being and breathing accompanied this writing, and is a profoundly missed, forever cherished, example of connection, courage, peace amidst change, and unconditional love.

and

The life force, love, and potential that breathes within all beings.

Contents

FOREWORD *by Daniel J. Siegel, MD* — ix
INTRODUCTION — xix
ELEMENTS FOR NAVIGATING THE JOURNEY — xxv

PART I / DISCOVERING

1: The Unifying Language of Breathing — 3
2: Breathwork for Well-Being and Conscious Living — 25
3: The Five Groups of Breathwork — 44
4: The Mystical Science of Breathing, Cellular Respiration, and Conscious Breathing — 60

PART II / PRACTICING

5: Exploring Our Breathing Biographies — 91
6: Optimal Breathing — 102
7: A Breathwork Kit for Whole Living — 145
8: Structural Supports for Breathwork Sessions — 170
9: Components and Processes of Human Potential Breathwork Sessions — 191
10: Inviting Psychological Distress To Breathe: Repairing, Restoring, Re-forming — 248
11: Full-Spectrum Healing and the Evolution of Breathwork — 273

PART III / EXPANDING

12: The Plane of Possibility and Breathwork — 293
13: Authentic Breathing, Authentic Life Urge, Authentic Self — 304
14: Breathing Expanded States of Consciousness — 322
15: Toward a Breathing-Centered World — 348

APPENDIX: Index of Breathing Practices — 351
ACKNOWLEDGMENTS — 355
CREDITS — 363
REFERENCES — 365
INDEX — 385

Foreword
by DANIEL J. SIEGEL, MD

Welcome to an inspirational focus of our clinical work on the fundamental rhythmic process of life—our breathing. In this interweaving of science, practical applications, and poetic, spiritual illuminations on the subjective nature of our lives, you will find a journey that our guide, Jessica Dibb, has cultivated many decades in her searching for various ways to combine health-promoting practices with the world's bodily-based wisdom traditions. In taking in the insights and practical suggestions of her teachings here in *Breathwork and Psychotherapy*, it may be helpful to keep in mind how we come to understand our world in general—and clinical practice in particular—in order to fully integrate this helpful material into clinical work.

What emerges in this wonderful compendium of an approach to something so common in our lives—the breath—is a way of knowing that can be compared to how we might experience and express our encounters with a flower. A flower can be described by poets with metaphors and images, immersing us in the power of language to directly communicate the awe-inspiring beauty of an iris; the magnificence of a hillside ablaze with bloom; the wafting scent of a rose transporting us into memories of times past; the longing that arises, the feeling of nostalgia we cannot quite articulate but can simply feel, fully, in a heartfelt ache; the body leading the way beyond what our brains may be able to conjure up. We immerse ourselves in sensation, in the images that poetic knowing invites us to experience—to imagine.

Yet a scientist's perspective might examine a flower, dissect its components of petal and stamen, study how it varies across the seasons, across species. In science we analyze—"down-break"—the world into its component parts. We can take on new hypotheses, challenge our presumptions, let go of what doesn't work and assemble new, more intricate, more supported proposals on the way the world functions. While even these hypotheses are stories—narratives we construct and coconstruct to try to articulate what may be as close to truth as we can get—they have the added value of being refutable, testable, and modifiable. Hypotheses can evolve with careful scrutiny in the best of cases. We can try to know the flower from the "inside out" as we take it apart and compare and contrast its components across all other flowers. A common *linear* view from science would see part A, B, and C and note how, when added together, they may lead to outcome D and E. In contrast, a *systems* view of science might see these components, yes, but then also add the dimension of the multidirectional influence of components A, B, and C and their mutual influence on D and E. In turn, D and E influence other elements of the system, and the shared flow of that system has what systems science calls "emergence": in which something arises from the components' interactions that is more than merely the components themselves. Systems views embrace the reality of the relationality of components and their interactions as what emerges, much like the notion of synergy: The whole is greater than the sum of its parts.

Returning to a more poetic view of reality, we sometimes directly capture this emergent aspect of our world, perhaps in a way that a scientist might ignore. A scientist may not "see the world that way," or even more than disregard that synergetic, systems, poetic view, linear scientists may even dismiss it as "not real" or "not scientific" or "not even wrong," meaning so off-base it isn't worth even addressing and debating. Could there really be such a divide in how we come to study and know what we think we know?

Consider water. A linear scientist might take water apart, analyze its components as two atoms of the element hydrogen and one atom of oxygen: H_2O. There would be nothing "wrong" with this analysis; it would be simply limiting the scientist's understanding of one property of water: wetness. The property of being wet does not arise from a single molecule of water, it emerges from molecules' interaction with each other, a synergy of their relationality, their relational connection. Wetness is an emergent property of water itself and cannot be understood—nor even sensed—when breaking water down to its constituent parts.

In contrast, a poet might experience the wetness of water and express the subjective sense of that immersion as allusions to the ocean's spray, sensory descriptions of dipping into a tropical coral-lined bay, the chill of being swept into a river beneath a glacier's summer melt. You'd receive these communications and perhaps have a sense—a feeling inside—of these poetic references to water's wonder; feeling them, filling with them, letting them flow over you like the water itself. And this poetic use of language and imagery would be still consistent with the emergent aspect of two atoms of hydrogen, one of oxygen, taken together as a molecule interacting with other such molecules in their collective synergy—in their relationality. There is nothing incompatible between a poetic view and a scientific analysis—especially when we embrace a systems view from science. They are each a way of trying to communicate how we experience and then express aspects of our shared reality.

Jessica Dibb has provided us with a comprehensive, clinically useful, compassionate, scientifically sound and poetically inspiring compendium of wise insights into understanding breathwork and applying it to cultivating health. I suggest that clinicians take on three or four "hats" of identity in this exciting journey. These identities will allow you to use a different way of knowing, a different kind of lens to take in the world, which are quite distinct yet each valuable on its own. Taken together, these distinct identities and their filters of knowing can help create a synergetic way toward knowing breathwork.

One filtering identity is for your own *personal* use, getting familiar with how you as an individual relate to the breath and use these practices for your own health-promoting care. A second identity lens is as a student of approaches to well-being, as a *clinician*, soaking in the insights from decades of practice that our guide has assembled here for our collective benefit. A third identity is that of a scientifically-informed discerning *thinker*, one who can learn from the empirical studies of conscious breathing practice, assembled here in a helpful categorization of five levels of techniques with a wide array of illuminating case examples and immersive practices. A fourth identity lens is as someone who can be open to the poetic expression of a more *spiritual* nature. "Spiritual" here is a term to signify living a life of meaning and connection: meaning beyond merely surviving, connection beyond the boundaries of the skin-encased body. And as my dear friend and colleague, John O'Donohue, would say when we'd teach together on "Awakening the Mind"—we are all "mystics." *What is that?* I'd ask John. His reply: *Someone who believes in the reality of the invisible.* Not all that we believe is true; but what our eyes can actually see is a limited subset of what is real. And in this way, a true scientist must be a mystic.

As we become aware of breathing, we take into our conscious mind the subjective sense of the objectively experienced in-breath with inhalation; we take into awareness the out-breath with exhalation. This process of not just breathing but being intentionally aware of the breath has been shown to have many health-promoting effects in our lives. Why would this "conscious breathing," as Jessica Dibb has called it, be so helpful?

One reason may be that we activate a SIMA process—a "sensory implication of motor action," as we ready ourselves for what will come next on the immediate horizon of the present moment. This is how the brain functions as an "anticipation machine," always readying itself for the next moment. We come to sense the rhythm that following each in-breath is an out-breath—we SIMA the in-breath with an anticipatory representation of the out-breath. Then, *voila*! The out-breath comes. Following every out-breath is an in-breath to come. One possibility is that the brain's SIMA process, as a part of the mirror neuron system, may directly influence our *inner* sense of peace and our *relational* sense of connection. The coherence of matching what we anticipate should come next with what actually arises may be deeply integrative—and this differentiation and linkage may be one aspect of why being aware of the breath is so transformative. As a twelve-year-old patient of mine once exclaimed after being taught a simple breath awareness practice, "I've never felt so peaceful before in my life." Indeed.

A second possible mechanism may be that we balance the two major branches of the autonomic nervous system (ANS) with breath: the parasympathetic activating with the out-breath, the sympathetic with the in-breath. Being aware of breath may help differentiate and link—or integrate—our ANS, and create heart rate variability coherence: a sign of good, health-promoting vagal tone.

A third reason for the health-promoting power of being aware of the breath is that breathwork links the voluntary with the automatic. You'll learn here fundamentals of conscious breathing and ways you can intentionally modify the ratio and cycling of in- to out-breath. Breathing is one of the few processes that is both involuntary (it happens without conscious intention or subjective awareness on its own) and voluntary. Like blinking, we breathe automatically, yet we can also intervene and vary our breathing rhythm. Being aware of breath may help us balance this subcortical automaticity with our cortical intention and awareness.

A fourth powerful possibility becomes clear when we see that the mind's regulatory role involves both monitoring and modifying energy flow. Conscious breathing lets us develop the interoceptive monitoring that research suggests promotes emotional awareness and regulation and enhances empathy and social intelligence. We also learn to modify the energy of breathing as we shape the rhythmic cycles of the breath, a process available at any time of the day! In this way, breath practices can strengthen the mind's capacity for *regulation* by stabilizing and strengthening both our monitoring and our modifying ability.

A fifth of perhaps many more reasons that the skills you'll learn in this book will be useful in promoting well-being in you and your clients is that it builds the three pillars of mind training, which research shows cultivates five physiological changes for health and stimulates the growth of neural integration in the brain. Reducing stress, enhancing immune function, improving cardiovascular health, reducing systemic inflammation by altering epigenetic regulatory molecules, and optimizing telomerase levels to repair and maintain the crucial ends of the chromosomes are each an outcome of this three-pillar practice work. In addition, studies suggest that both structural and functional integration are enhanced in neural networks such as the corpus callosum, hippocampus, prefrontal cortex, and the overall connectome. An integrated brain is correlated with well-being along many measures.

What are these three pillars? Focused attention, open awareness, and kind intention. We train the mind to strengthen these three fundamental pillars. Breath awareness may involve each of these three key elements of what many might simply call "mindfulness."

In my own personal and professional journey (see Siegel, 2007; 2010; 2017; 2018; 2020; 2022), the distinction between being trained as a linear scientist in biochemistry and medicine and the immersion in systems science was an important shift in gathering new insights into the nature of the mind and mental health. For example, in the 2500-year-old view of "mind is what brain does," we can see a whole perspective that our mental lives are determined solely by what goes on inside our heads. While the connection of mind and brain is certainly true, the brain source of mind is likely just one part of a much larger story. How could the rest of the body not be involved in our experience of emotion and meaning—fundamental aspects of our mind's subjective experience? And how might the relationships we have, with other individuals and with all of nature itself, be so important in shaping our mental health?

Addressing these questions led to the birth of the consilient approach of Interpersonal Neurobiology, and it has required blending empirical linear science with the exciting newer views of systems science. By proposing that the mind might actually be an "emergent property" of something that was *both* within the head's brain and in the whole body, and that this "something" was also extending beyond the individual's body and in the relationships with people and the planet, a new scientifically-grounded systems views could be envisioned. These emergent properties might be seen as the mind's four facets: subjective experience, consciousness (that lets you know you are having a subjective experience), information processing (that transforms energy into symbolic processes), and a fourth that serves not just as a description but a working definition: *an embodied and relational emergent self-organizing process that regulates the flow of energy and information.*

This systems' view of the mind as an emergent property of energy flow has been supported by a wide array of empirical studies on the mind, mental health, and mental suffering (see Siegel, 2020; 2022). It also offers another reason why breathwork may be so helpful: awareness of the breath reminds us—brings back to mind—that there is an inner and an outer nature of who we are. We take air into these bodies we are born into; we let the air back out into the larger world. And we are deeply reminded that who we are is not just these bodies; we are interconnected to all that is around us—and we are intraconnected to a larger whole. The breath is a rhythmic reminder of our inner and inter locations, and our intraconnected identity. The breath may seem mystical in that it is indeed, as O'Donohue would have said, "invisible," yet real.

This offering of a definition of the mind as a self-organizing process also has had profound implications for our field of mental health. We can now have a definition of the mind which allows us to take the next step and define what a healthy mind is. In these ways, we can say that mental well-being arises from optimal self-organization. The mathematics of complex systems reveals that this optimal flow of a system regulating its own becoming involves balancing two processes. One is differentiation, the other is linkage, wherein linking does not eliminate the essence of the differences of the components of the system. We can call this balance of linking differentiated parts "integration." With integration, complexity science tells us, a complex system achieves what we can describe with the acronym FACES flow: flexible, adaptive, coherent (resilient over time), energized, and stable (reliable, not rigid). This FACES flow describes a central river of integration, bound on one side by a bank of chaos, the other, a bank of rigidity. It turns out that a broad range of studies supports the notion that integration enables mental flourishing filled with this FACES flow; impaired integration leads to the chaos and rigidity that can be seen as hallmarks of mental un-health (see Siegel, 2017 and Siegel, 2020 for a summary and review).

From this view of integration as the basis of health, and also the notion that consciousness is needed for change, I developed a practice known as the Wheel of Awareness (Siegel, 2018), in which we can experience the integration of consciousness. This is the first of nine domains of integration that serve as a way of organizing a clinical approach to using this view of mind in therapy and in life (Siegel, 2010). The metaphoric wheel involves a rim of the things that we can be aware of; a spoke of attention; and a hub of knowing, of being aware. After surveying tens of thousands of individuals doing the Wheel practice, a surprising finding kept emerging. The subjective experience in the hub, the experience of pure awareness, as compared to what we are aware of on the rim, was often articulated with terms such as "timeless," "connected to everything and everyone," eternity, God, love, joy, home, peace, and clarity. A search in the neuroscience field did not yield any correlates of such experiences and prompted me to explore further into the notion of mind as an emergent property of energy. Physics is the field of science deeply devoted to studying energy and its properties. In a meeting with over one hundred and fifty physicists, those working in quantum mechanics would tell me that "energy is the movement from possibility to actuality." This view then led to a visual depiction of my interpretation of how their ideas could then be correlated with the findings from the Wheel of Awareness survey reports. The shorthand way of summarizing this exciting part of the journey is that there appears to be a direct correlation of being aware to a "Plane of Possibility" derived from the physics notion of a "quantum vacuum," also known as a "sea of potential" and a "formless source of all form." This is a generator of diversity, as it is the quantum vacuum that is formless, yet full of all possibilities that might arise.

The scientific hypothesis that then emerged from the survey of workshop participants doing the Wheel practice and the view of energy as moving from possibility (the Plane) to actuality (what we would call plateaus and peaks on the graph of the mind's energy flow positions) is that *awareness itself arises from the energy position of being in the Plane of Possibility*. We become aware of something that is either a higher probability (a plateau), such as a state of mind or mood or motivation, or an actuality, such as an emotion, thought, or memory.

While it has been uncomfortable at times to find linear scientists arguing against these views, sometimes chasing me down hallways, begging me to "stop talking about energy or quantum physics when discussing the mind," it has also been profoundly liberating to embrace the empirical findings from physics and the insights of the mathematics of complex systems. If mind is indeed an emergent property of a complex system, and it is arising from energy flow within that system, then turning toward the science of energy is, well, a scientific thing to do. It may be a *systems* science that we need in order to embrace emergence. But a quantum physics view also helps us see how we in fact live in two realms of our one reality. One realm is that which was articulated by Sir Isaac Newton over three hundred and fifty years ago: a classic, large-object or macrostate physics view of entities separated in time and space. Another realm is that of small processes, smaller than an atom, like photons or electrons. These units of energy are "probability fields" that follow quantum mechanics. In these quantum equations there is no variable of time; the quantum microstate realm is "timeless." And in this realm the Newtonian, classical physics, notions of separation in time and space do not have meaning. Also, the noun-like entities of the Newtonian realm are quite distinct from the verb-like, massively connected processes of the quantum, microstate realm.

In working with those of various indigenous traditions and in contemplative practices, and more recently religious leaders from a variety of cultures, this hypothesis—that we can tap into pure awareness and feel the connection to a sense of being a larger whole, and also sense the timeless nature of reality—fits well with their teachings, cultivated over thousands of years. It has also helped understand breath practice. It may well be that the conscious breathing that you will learn about in-depth in this book will enable you to access this Plane of Possibility. Each day I do the Wheel practice; I experience that expansive timelessness. There is a dissolving of the sense of being a noun-like entity, separate and alone. As Albert Einstein once wrote, this sense of separation is "an optical delusion of consciousness"—a delusion that practices like the Wheel or breathwork may help dissolve. Said a different way, we live in two realms of one reality, and these practices may help us integrate the classical, large-object Newtonian realm of having a body with the open, timeless, quantum microstate realm of being a verb-like, deeply interwoven set of processes. This integrative state of embracing both realms may be accessed as we immerse ourselves fully in being aware of the breath.

We can remember some of the qualities of this mindful awareness that comes with conscious breathing with the acronym COAL: curiosity, openness, acceptance, and love. Breathwork invites us to bring this COAL state of mind to our lives and to the lives of those with whom we are privileged to be working. We can bring connection and hope to people's lives by helping them connect to the two realms of our one reality. When we realize we are not alone, that we can access this timeless sense of connection by riding the wave of the breath, we help ourselves and others to move life from the repeating patterns of chaos and rigidity of mental distress to the freedom of a more integrated state.

There may be many other fundamental mechanisms that breathwork offers, powerful ways to promote mental health as it creates more interoceptive skills. Breathwork promotes our awareness of the inner life we have in our bodies, and therefore generates more emotional regulation and social connection, increasing our capacity for empathy and compassion. And if that were not enough, the ever-present capacity to breathe consciously makes it an extremely accessible skill to develop. Dive into the practices ahead with your many identities, allowing them to encourage curiosity, openness, acceptance and love to all that may emerge in the journey ahead.

In this wonderful book, you have an invitation to take these various identities—personal, clinical, thinking, and spiritual—and soak in the flow of the book, and of the breath; taking in the poetry of the spiritual dimensions offered here, along with the science and practical clinical insights. Breathe into this work as an interwoven tapestry of these wondrous, distinct, but interconnected strands, and you may find yourself feeling more whole and more empowered, inspired by your new breathwork skills to catalyze the journey to wholeness for others.

References

Siegel, D. J. (2007). *The mindful brain: Reflection and attunement in the cultivation of well-being.* Norton.

Siegel, D. J. (2010). *Mindsight: The new science of personal transformation.* Bantam.

Siegel, D. J. (2017). *Mind: A journey to the heart of being human.* Norton.

Siegel, D. J. (2018). *Aware: The science and practice of presence.* Tarcher/Perigee.

Siegel, D. J. (2020). *The developing mind: How relationships and the brain interact to shape who we are.* Guilford Press.

Siegel, D. J. (2022). *IntraConnected: MWe (Me plus We) as the integration of self, identity, and belonging.* Norton.

Introduction

There is one way of breathing that is shameful and constricted. Then, there's another way: a breath of love that takes you all the way to infinity.

—RUMI

THIS BOOK is offered to every person . . . to every Breather. While reading, hearing, or feeling these words, we are joining 8 billion-plus other people, and we are all breathing together.

The fruition of a birth happens upon hearing the baby's first breath. New parents tend to watch for their baby's every breath. We notice with respect when someone's breathing is becoming more powerful during acts of athleticism, emergency rescue, and courageous participation. Lovers spontaneously mirror each other's breathing patterns, and in the most intimate moments breathe each other's breath as one breath. The last breath is listened for with the utmost tenderness, reverence, fear, or love.

Often, we don't recognize or honor these truths until we experience something that challenges our breathing. We all desire a wholesome, fulfilling, long life—and that will benefit from the support of optimal breathing. In fact, the famed Framingham Heart Study shows that respiratory wellness is a powerfully significant predictor of health and longevity. Indeed, our most important treasure chest exists within our physical chest. Yet somehow the nutrient and medicinal value of breathing is still seen as adjunctive or complementary.

How paradigm shifting it would be for us individually, relationally, and collectively to fully recognize the potential that dwells within this primary driver of life! Fortunately, exciting advances in modern research are now catching up with ancient, often esoteric, wisdom about the remarkable potential for physical, emotional, cognitive, spiritual, and relational well-being within each breath. We each deserve the whole measure of this nutrient and medicine for our own sake, and because the quality of our presence affects everyone around us—affects the world.

The vocations of Breathworkers, psychotherapists, and other healing professionals who work with people's inner landscapes are among the most inspiring in this world and deserve the most cutting-edge transformative tools on the planet. I presented Integrative Breathing at the Psychotherapy Networker Conference six times between 2006 and 2019. Three thousand to 4,000 deeply earnest healers attended those groundbreaking conferences. Two lasting impressions reverberate. First, psychotherapists yearn to relieve people's suffering and support them in manifesting meaningful relationships, vocations, and lives. Second, about 75% of the psychotherapists who participated in the Breathwork workshop reported that Breathwork was their single most transformative experience at the conference—going straight to the heart of what matters most to them.

Visionaries and innovators populate the history of human potential, healing, and psychotherapy, and many have inspired us to reenvision our approaches. Consider the shock waves and innovation that emerged from Sigmund Freud's radical envisioning of the individual's unconscious and psyche. Consider how Carl Jung reenvisioned the psyche, bringing awareness to the collective unconscious, imaginal, and archetypal dimensions in treatment. Subsequent luminaries include Carl Rogers, Murray Bowen, Virginia Satir, Abraham Maslow, Eugene Gendlin, Alice Miller, and others too numerous to name. Today, psychotherapy is impacted by Dr. Daniel Siegel's groundbreaking lens of interpersonal neurobiology, Jon Kabat-Zinn's seminal work on healing through mindfulness, and many other contributors through work in neuroscience, trauma understanding, and emergent psychotherapeutic processes.

We also build on a lineage of cultures who have utilized breathing as medicine throughout time, including ancient Egypt; Shamanic traditions in Africa, Australia, and South and North America; yogic traditions in India; Taoism; and Qigong. Twentieth and twenty-first century pathfinders for breathing include Shirley Telles, Stephen Elliot, Jack L. Feldman, James Nestor, Richard Brown, Patricia Gerbarg, Stanislav Grof, Leonard Orr, Sondra Ray, Patrick McKeown, and others too numerous to name. I am grateful to the community of past, present, and future Breathworkers, psychotherapists, and human potentialists for your caring, courage, risks, and inspiration.

Until recently, the Breathwork field has largely been perceived as merely complementary—even lightweight or too far-out—and adjunctive to mainstream, holistic, and integrative medicine. Yes, Breathwork supports other healing modalities superbly. Yet I and countless others have also observed Breathwork as a primary modality that sometimes cures physical and psychological ailments. Thus, I am inspired to help accelerate public awareness about Breathwork, and the creation of jobs for Breathworkers in hospitals, medical offices, schools, universities, and other public venues. We can envision and build a *human culture that centers breathing*.

My work at Inspiration Consciousness School and Community for over three decades has informed the viability of this vision. We have cultivated a principle and practice of Breathers opening to expanded states of consciousness in classes as short as four hours, followed promptly by trips to museums, malls, hospitals, libraries, and parks to practice integrating in ordinary settings. We then debrief these experiences and address questions and concerns. After an additional immersion into expanded states, participants go to their homes and work as electricians, physicians, teachers, parents, and so on to practice integration through Conscious Breathing.

To help professionalize and expand the Breathwork field, it was exhilarating to upgrade Breathwork facilitator training at Inspiration and develop ethical standards for Breathworkers. I discovered a kindred vision in psychologist Breathworker Jim Morningstar. At the 2001 Global Inspiration Conference, we were given a vote of confidence by 60 Breathwork trainers and Breathworkers from five continents to initiate and codirect a new organization—the Global Professional Breathwork Alliance (GPBA). This organization has become the gold standard for providing ethics and training standards for Breathwork worldwide. Developing a cutting-edge, in-depth program for training Breathworkers at Inspiration, guiding the GPBA, and creating conferences that brought together Breathwork teachers, researchers, and practitioners who were creating powerful applications helped stimulate significant shifts within the Breathwork field, as well as public perception about Breathwork. These experiences have amplified my visions about Breathwork's value to humanity's collective life.

Just when I was fully committing to writing this book and honoring the global groundswell of Breathwork, in 2019 and 2020 we encountered three waves of breathlessness in three pressing issues—health and well-being, equity and human rights, and ecological sustainability and thriving. The breathlessness of COVID-19 induced global awareness of the preciousness of breathing. George Floyd's words, "I can't breathe," became a shot heard round the world—reenergizing movements for racial justice, equity, and related intersectional issues. And unprecedented and devastating forest fires in Europe, Australia, and then the United States erupted, causing toxicity, destruction, and death to plant life, and human and nonhuman animals.

By this time, I had experienced breathing as a fundamental medicine, abundant nutrient, and unifying force for healing and transformation, and a positive force multiplier for individuals, groups, processes, and actions. Breathing is vitally important to everyone, whatever their status, orientation, history, and aptitude. Healthy breathing and Breathwork are supremely natural conduits for health equity, and equity in general. With reverence, I experienced a compelling urge to write about breathing in relation to everyone's value and potential—for every being, gnarly or not, kind or not, saint or sinner. Thus, the Universal Breathing Declaration (see Chapter 15) was born, expressing every Breather's right to breathe safely, optimally, and freely. Dedicated to a world of liberated potential and creativity, the declaration's orientation advocates for optimal physical, emotional, cognitive, spiritual, and social resources for all, and directs attention to healing and transforming challenges to healthy breathing for all, such as illness, social and economic inequity, war, genocide, and ecocide. Breathing is the greatest equalizer—it both symbolizes and acts as a mechanism for harmonious coexistence. Moreover, the right to breathe well is intrinsically interconnected with the rights and well-being of all life and our planet.

This book is a guide and adventure into the heart of healing, transformation, and wholeness. To a great degree, it is a radical statement about the potential for psychological integration; aligned somatic, emotional, cognitive, and spiritual intelligence; coherence; creativity; consciousness; and most of all, love—personally and collectively. May it be a practical, inspirational manual—a sherpa and friend for healing professionals, clinicians, Breathworkers, and every Breather.

To Clinicians: I am touched by your humility, nobility, and commitment to relieving unnecessary suffering and contributing to life optimization. We deserve the most powerful tools and medicine that this oxygen-rich world can provide for our precious, challenging, sometimes scary, and sacred work.

To Breathworkers: With all that breath has bestowed upon us, it is our responsibility to birth a next iteration and generation of Breathwork best practices that can impact humanity significantly, widen and extend the profound pathways we have already forged. Ensuring that Breathwork as a healing art and profession is fully integrated into mental health and social structures will prevent its being marginalized or seen as merely adjunctive therapy. Becoming informed about the full spectrum of human experience—from trauma to enlightenment, from temperament and neurosis to discerning the nuances of consciousness—is essential. Creating and updating theory, tools, research, and literature to expand Breathwork applications beyond relaxation, reset, emotional release, and peak experiences is indispensable.

To every Breather: Pierre Teilhard de Chardin famously said, "Someday, after mastering the winds, the waves, the tides, and gravity, we shall harness for God the energies of love, and then, for a second time in the history of the world, man will have discovered fire." I am humbled and honored to share knowledge and stories about the healing and transformational potential of breathing. *Breathwork is a royal doorway for humanity to shift its consciousness and culture from fear and personality (no matter how interesting and healthy that personality may be) to a culture of love and creativity.*

As we wend our way through the adventure in these pages, I dare hope we will experience unions of science and soul, methodology and creativity, maps and uncharted territory, boundaries and boundlessness, trauma and resiliency, body and spirit, heart and head, and self and other. *I hope we will be inspired to reenvision a humanity that centers breathing.*

In the end, this is all about love. All our efforts are, at core, the desire to love . . . to be loved . . . to be love . . . and to be the creativity to which love gives birth. And breathing is not only what makes all this possible—it is a universal vehicle for its actualization and full flowering.

And we are all breathing together right now.

Jessica Dibb
MARCH 31, 2024
Traditional Lands of the Susquehannock,
now known as Maryland, USA

Elements for Navigating the Journey

NOVEL LANDMARKS

Breathing and Breathwork are fundamentally powerful for physical, emotional, cognitive, and spiritual capacities and well-being. This book elucidates a vision to support Breathwork's rightful place in the canon of human potential—to serve its deep and intrinsic potency to fully emerge into our world. Thus, the words *Breathwork, Breathworker, Breather* (all people), *Breathee, Conscious Breathing* (CB), and *Breathing Practices* are capitalized. Thank you for exploring this vital and seminal territory with us.

NOVEL COORDINATES

Because we are all Breathers, and we need to learn and evolve together, in much of the book, not all, the pronouns *we* and *ours* are used rather than the traditional *you/yours*. *We* is sometimes used for all people, sometimes for clinicians, and sometimes for Breathworkers. We are all in this together—whatever our role—we are breathing together.

NOVEL NOMENCLATURE

- *Breather* = every person.
- *Therapist-Breathworker* = A psychotherapist, psychiatrist, counselor, minister, or other mental health clinician who does in-depth

Breathwork training and integrates Breathwork into their vocation. Also, a Breathworker who does in-depth study and/or training in psychotherapy and psychotherapeutic models and processes for improving individual well-being, the effects of trauma, and mental health—and integrates psychotherapeutic values, wisdom, and experience into their vocation. In the future *Therapist-Breathworker* may be used for graduates of a training that has evolved to meet exemplary standards of both disciplines. For this book, the same term is employed for both orientations in acknowledgment of the depth of the original training, rigor in the secondary training (with possible certification), and sincerity, commitment, and nobility in purpose and professional ethics.

- ***Breathee ("Breathe-ee")*** = A person who is engaging in an individual or group Breathwork session that is facilitated by a Therapist-Breathworker or breathing itself. Opening more fully to the primacy, power, and potential of Conscious Breathing engenders something alluring and respectful about using a term that denotes placing ourselves in the brilliance of *breathing* itself to be guided, taught, and transformed during an intentional session or practice period. Therefore, *Breathee* is a differentiated term from our normal state of always being a Breather.

BREATHWORK AND PSYCHOTHERAPY

PART I

Discovering

ONE

The Unifying Language of Breathing

> *Breathe in without*
> *Breathe out, you're alright*
> *Breathe in with all*
>
> —DEAKIN, "GOOD HOUSE"

WE ARE born wired to breathe...and to love. When you and I emerged into this world, our first action was to breathe...to inhale and exhale...setting into motion everything that we were at that moment, our capacity to love, and our *potential*. We are all united through sharing that initiation—the first breath. With optimal conditions, every cell, instinct, need, desire, sensation, feeling, awareness, and possibility for us was activated in the first breath. Then, in each subsequent breath, our potential is given the opportunity to be energized, nourished, and embodied. Every breath of every person carries this aspiration...to breathe, live, grow, express, love, create, and experience meaning, purpose, and fulfillment.

The true measure of the profound, perhaps never-ending, implications of the first breath and every breath thereafter is still vastly unrecognized and underutilized in our world today. We have an incomparable treasure chest...a comprehensive medicine chest...within our physical chests. Breathing is likely the most important nutrient, medicine, healer, friend, teacher, lover, and partner of our lives...perhaps the ultimate modality for healing and transformation personally, relationally, and collectively . . . and possibly the most essential psychotherapy, human potential pathway, and source for creativity.

This book offers compelling reasons to integrate Breathwork and psychotherapy, and to some extent all healing arts and human potential processes, for individuals and our collective life. It offers methods to utilize and the potential results we can expect for our personal and collective lives.

For all people (Breathers) to garner the knowledge for availing ourselves of masterful Breathwork facilitation, and for clinicians and healers to deliver inspired and effective Breathwork, we need to explore the power of breathing, *Conscious Breathing* (CB), and *Breathwork*. *Conscious Breathing* is any breathing with conscious awareness, or any self-initiated breathing adjustment for a beneficial purpose. *Breathwork* comprises the many formal methods, styles, and applications of Breathing Practices, all of which contain the element of Conscious Breathing. Unparalleled potentiality for healing, personal growth, relationships, and self-actualization can be birthed through CB and Breathwork.

It will assist our exploration of breathing and wholeness to note that the words *aware*, *conscious*, *awareness*, and *consciousness* are used interchangeably in common vernacular. Indeed, throughout time, experts of philosophy, brain science, sociology, spirituality, and so on have continuously questioned, discussed, and argued about what the terms represent. Professor Ram Lakhan Pandey Vimal noted that "about forty meanings attributed to the term consciousness can be identified and categorized based on functions and experiences. The prospects for reaching any single, agreed-upon, theory-independent definition of consciousness appear remote" (Vimal, 2010). This book is dedicated to being as scientifically aligned as possible, without sacrificing Indigenous, traditional, spiritual, experiential, and commonsense wisdom that hasn't been scientifically tested yet. Because there's no consilient agreement about what the terms mean, we trust our reading community's acquired experiential and academic knowledge, and intuition, to comprehend the inferred meaning of each term as it appears; and I, with humility and apologies for any misalignments, am relying on my experiential and academic knowledge, and intuition, to apply the term(s) most aligned with the spirit of what is being conveyed.

The First Breath

Our learning and journey are optimized through appreciating, loving, and experiencing the transformational potential of a single breath—beginning with *the first breath*. Developing awareness and sensitivity about the first breath's significance, as well as every breath thereafter, will support clinicians and Breathers to optimally employ the powerful practices of Breathwork. Practicing Breathwork can support the first breath, as when Sophia, a psychotherapist, did Breathwork sessions for her own personal transformation throughout her pregnancy. During intense labor, Sophia found herself breathing deep, strong, peaceful inhalations, and toning and softly chanting on each exhale. In the birth stage known as *transition*, when most women feel quite challenged and often make considerable noise, she harmoniously met the waves of labor with deep breathing and toning, allowing her body to open gracefully to birth. Her son emerged easily and began breathing without crying. Each breath was peaceful. He seemed relaxed, receptive, and immediately responsive to the welcoming love that surrounded him. His body's extraordinary tranquility and harmony was palpable to everyone.

Breathing's Potential

Every moment is precious. Every breath is precious, filled with potential for living fully—not missing this "one wild and precious life," as poet Mary Oliver reminds us. Speaking, moving, learning, growing, creating, loving, cultivating relationships, and everything that matters requires breathing. Imagine if humanity was fully aware that beginning with the first breath, the quality of each breath can be an enormous determinant for how we inhabit ourselves, appreciate each moment, give and receive love, move through life, and develop ourselves for optimized and actualized living.

The core of our most treasured experiences is the sense of contacting something meaningful, and connecting with ourselves, others, and life. These experiences can be joyous, fulfilling, and preferred; calm, neutral, and sometimes preferred; or painful and not preferred. When we connect to something real and meaningful, most experiences can reveal critical and valuable dimensions of ourselves—and presence with our breathing is a reliable connector and guide.

One colorful autumn day, after her first six Integrative Breathing sessions, Nobu, who loved being alone and usually eschewed human company, decided to walk along a rushing stream that was overflowing after recent rains. He felt his foot contacting the rocky terrain with each step. With the quieting of other human voices, he experienced heightened visceral sensations of breathing. Nobu sat on the stream's smooth, rocky edge, feeling an easy contentment and peaceful coexistence with everything around him. While listening to the rushing water, whistling wind, and rustling leaves, and feeling the cool wet rock on the back of his legs, he continued connecting with each breath. It seemed so simple. He expected that being receptive and calm while experiencing union with his breathing would induce feeling at home with nature. Yet what happened next was completely surprising. Nobu started feeling connected to people in new and remarkable ways. He now sensed their intrinsic right to belong on earth. His heart opened, and he heard himself breathing deeper. Invisible armor seemed to dissipate with each huge sigh.

Engaging with people now seemed appealing, even precious, and he was infused with a fervent desire to give more attention to his loved ones. All of this happened during ordinary sitting. Nobu considered the possibility that learning to breathe consciously with any situation would open more dimensions of himself and life.

Breathe and all you touch is new and real. —Annabel Laity

When Marion's daughter was born with a rare, and serious disease only experienced by 83 people worldwide, her life became a previously unimaginable immersion into devotion. At 6 months, the baby Diana was still in the neonatal intensive care unit and had undergone 11 surgeries. Marion had stretched herself to and beyond capacity, living in the hospital, pumping breast milk round the clock, and struggling to digest vast amounts of medical information so that she could advocate for her daughter's quality of life and help ensure her survival.

Six months into Diana's fragile life, a specific medicine via IV was needed to keep her alive. Fourteen attempts by a skilled medical team to perform a venous cutdown for infusing the life-saving medicine were unsuccessful, and hopelessness pervaded the room. Marion, who had practiced meditation and CB for several years, entered a state of hyper-awareness of both how much she loved her daughter and wanted her to live, and how it seemed her daughter was dying. She remembers it as, "the worst day of my life. I could feel her leaving." Marion chose to stay present with her intense feelings and breathe deeply to get through what was surely coming. Unexpectedly, she thought of one last place to try the needle on her daughter's tiny body. To everyone's astonishment, it worked. It felt like a miracle.

At that moment, Marion felt her capacity to love her daughter unconditionally blossom, her ability to think clearly grow, and her intuition beginning to access new dimensions. These have never diminished. Today, Diana is a beautiful young woman who, while having multiple ongoing medical challenges, lives a meaningful and joyful life.

Breathe and understand that everything is helping you.
—Annabel Laity

Three-Centered Presence and Integration

Through whatever joy, sadness, love, loss, confusion, fear, rage, peace, and creativity we experience, we wish to feel well-being. We likely hope to know ourselves and our feelings, thoughts, and sensations; to feel seen, understood, and valued; to be authentic and fully self-expressed; to experience meaning and purpose; and to participate in enriching relationships. We may desire to feel close to nature and our environment. We may yearn to feel union with something universal—the Divine, a Higher Power, or the vastness of life. Contacting ourselves *as we are* in a given moment or situation, with or without others—without avoiding, controlling, or reacting unconsciously—is essential to experiencing and embodying Presence.

> *Through Love, all that is bitter will be sweet.*
> —RUMI

SOMATIC CENTER

When we are present with our senses, bodily sensations, and physical contact with our surroundings, we are present somatically. In what Eugene Gendlin (1993) terms the *felt sense* of being here, we contact somatic *energy, information, and intelligence*. Bodily sensations are first processed in the brain stem (medulla) and then in higher brain centers. The more somatically present we are, the more fully we experience the millions of sensations lighting up our neural pathways—informing, energizing, and nourishing our life capacities. Somatic presence gives rise to sensations of aliveness and power—building natural confidence and an embodied sense of inherent belonging. The trust this engenders supports our participation in the immediacy of each moment. We can dissolve chronic temperamental or defensive habits such as withdrawing from engagement, controlling, or being aggressive. Natural empowerment arises. We feel the rightness of existing and being infused with energy and aliveness.

HEART CENTER

When we are present with our hearts, feeling our emotions and how we are affecting and being affected by each moment, we are present emotionally. Presence with our emotions and feelings is processed by the limbic system—the brain center circling the brain stem. Opening to the *intimacy* of each moment, we contact emotional *energy, information, and intelligence*. Our capacity to value our individual and relational experiences expands, as does our connection to people, all life, and the world. Our landscape of meaning expands and deepens as we allow ourselves to be developed in enriching ways—even growing from painful and challenging experiences. Greater awareness arises about when and why we feel disconnected. This awareness fosters empathic resonance and compassion for others and ourselves. Thus, we maintain contact with the beauty and value of each moment, which supports attunement and caring for the quality of our relatedness with everything.

HEAD CENTER

When we are present with our awareness of internal or external experiences, however this *awareness* arises—through thoughts, mind chatter, images, sounds, perceptions, or inner quiet—then we are present cognitively. The information needed for perception is gathered in the neocortex—where neurons from different regions of the cortex form large complex networks that underlie conscious awareness. By consciously opening to awareness—with willingness to see and perceive with curiosity—we contact cognitive *energy, information, and intelligence*. We more readily see what is, and what is possible. We develop and deepen abilities to discover, envision, and create. We can more easily access and generate inner guidance. Over time, we can discern causation, possibility, probability, and actuality—while remaining available for further inquiry, nuance, and discovery. Thus, both awareness and vision expand.

Individually, each of these three types of presence is useful and life-enhancing. Consciously accessing them together generates an integrated and whole presence that gathers somatic, emotional, and cognitive energy, information, and intelligence which then contributes to our awareness, relatedness, and participation. At our best, we are present in each moment with *vitality* (sensations and movement), *love* (emotions and relatedness), and *wisdom* (awareness, clarity, and vision).

The neural pathways for mediating both automatic and volitional breathing are deeply embedded in all three aforementioned parts of the brain—the brain stem, limbic system, and neocortex. Thus, breathing is a unifying pathway for integrating somatic, emotional, and cognitive energy, information, intelligence, and dynamism. Conscious Breathing is an optimal mechanism for powerfully changing our brain state, and the fastest way to cultivate *integrated presence*. It is excellent medicine for sensing our body's life force, wisdom, and ability to act; embracing our vulnerable and precious heart's capacity to give and receive; and activating our awareness to experience a larger perspective of ourselves, our situations, and reality.

The brain stem, limbic system, and neocortex are often called the *triune brain*. This concept has served well for holistic approaches to learning, healing, and transformation. Yet since research has now advanced our understanding of the rich connections between regions of the brain, many neuroscientists consider the triune brain concept outdated. Still, metaphorically and therapeutically, it's a worthy descriptor for will, emotion, and rational thinking, and the id, ego, and superego.

Current neuroscience describes three brains—enteric/gut/sensing brain, cardiac/heart/feeling brain, and cephalic/head/thinking brain. These three parts work through parallel distributed processing, meaning they simultaneously contribute to a complex network of interconnected systems. This concept of the brain matches various age-old understandings about how the three centers simultaneously contribute vitality, connection, and awareness for living and functioning.

Studies of the cephalic brain show that it's almost endlessly complex, with over 100 billion neurons (each averaging 10,000 connections) and about 85 billion *glial cells*—the cells that support neurons and optimize the environment surrounding them. The cephalic brain has a comprehensive map of neural connections called the connectome. Yet what connects and unifies the enteric, cardiac, and cephalic brains? Evolutionary insights from neuroscience and interpersonal neurobiology can inform our understanding. Dr. Dan Siegel, cofounder of interpersonal neurobiology, describes *mind* as

> a self-organizing [cephalic], embodied [somatic], and relational [heart] process that regulates energy and information flow in our lives. Then we can see how integration would be the scientifically predictive process beneath optimal living, as linking differentiated parts of a system optimizes self-organization and creates harmonious functioning. We can also see how our mind and the self that emerges from it are created not only in our body and brain, but—equally important—in our relationships with other people and with the planet. (Book Brigade, 2016)

Various nomenclature has been assigned to the three-centers model throughout time. The Enneagram's vernacular is *centers of intelligence*, because being present with each center can engender awareness and wisdom. Applying Dan Siegel's understanding of the mind, we could posit that this intelligence is *awareness of the flow of energy and information*—thus the nomenclature earlier in this chapter of *centers of energy, information, and intelligence*. Moving forward, we will use *centers of energy flow*. This nomenclature was developed by Dan Siegel, David Daniels, Denise Daniels, Laura Baker, and Jack Killen, a working group of scholars studying temperament and wholeness through an Enneagram lens. Fertilized by their insights, as well as time-honored wisdom about the centers, let's call our three-centered interconnected system of functioning, relatedness, and awareness—the **somatic–emotional–cognitive continuum** (SEC continuum). Presence with the entire continuum is **integrated presence.**

Why is CB so potent for cultivating *integrated presence*? First, what drives the SEC continuum, and every life process, is energy. And because breathing is the essential and culminating factor for generating energy (see Chapter 4), optimal breathing is an immediate medium for fostering continual well-being, harmony, integration, and presence. The quality of our perceptions about self, others, and life is impacted by breathing. Second, philosopher and founder of *Focusing* (an internally oriented psychotherapy that directs our attention to somatic knowing or *felt sense*) Eugene Gendlin (1982) noted that "interaction with the world is prior to concepts about the world." Consider the implications of developing our breathing capacity given that breathing is our first and ongoing principal interaction with the world! Third, CB is a consilient factor for our functions and capacities that serve personal growth. It is the underlying pattern and core mechanism of myriad, differentiated brain functions, including drives for self-preservation, connection, and expression, and our search for meaning and comprehending the mystery of life. Breathing is the single most powerful mechanism for integrating all our differentiated capacities. Indeed, to cultivate *integrated presence*, we would be supremely wise to cultivate our understanding, love, and practice of Conscious Breathing. It is likely the single most powerful action each moment for integrating all we are and all we can be—working together harmoniously.

Notably, the beneficial effects of CB are supported by contemporary science. For example, slow deep breathing:

- Helps balance the autonomic nervous system (ANS) by increasing parasympathetic activation (Pal et al., 2004)
- Synchronizes neural structures in the brain, limbic, respiratory, and cardiac systems (Jerath & Barnes, 2009)
- Enhances vagal activation, lowering stress and cortisol levels (Wehrwein et al., 2012)
- Improves cardiovascular function (Chinagudi et al., 2014a)
- Increases antioxidant and melatonin levels (Harinath et al., 2004)
- Supports resilience for stress (Brown et al., 2013)
- Positively impacts heart rate variability in children and adults (Song & Lehrer, 2003)
- Improves childhood cognitive performance (Chinagudi et al., 2014b)
- Builds lung health, which supports cognitive capacities (Venkateswar & Parvathisam, 2022) (impaired lung health is correlated with cognitive decline and dementia; Wang et al., 2021)

The integral nature of breathing, presence, and somatic and psychological integration—and its impact on healing, therapeutic process, and personal development—is evolutionary for healing professionals and those trusting them for safe haven and guidance. The root of almost every issue driving us to seek psychological support dwells in a sense of missed connection—whether that sense is conscious or unconscious, real or perceived—whether the missed connection is with our feelings, thoughts, sensations, loved ones, life, joy, meaning, or purpose. Often, we are experiencing abandonment or rejection of some aspect of ourselves by ourselves or another. Presence can be a remedy for restoring connection so we can heal. Presence is the opposite of numbness, deflection, defensiveness, dissociation, and addictive pathways. Presence, contact, and connection begin to manifest when we breathe consciously.

A SPIRITUAL CENTER?

There's another potential dimension of presence to consider. Throughout time, holistic models often propose components of body, heart, mind, *and spirit*. In Latin, *to breathe* is *spirare*, which is also the root of *spirit*. Indeed, various studies of spirituality, emotional regulation, and physiology are consilient in concluding that CB is beneficial for optimization. Thus, complete models of integrated embodied presence and CB might recognize a *center of energy, information, intelligence—energy flow*—that is spiritual. Whether deeming ourselves spiritual, atheistic, or agnostic, the urge to wonder about, communicate with, and experience the Mystery may be as real and natural as the drive to experience (bodily sensation), connect (heart), and understand (head). Generally, developing this spiritual aspect of self seems to engender qualities like intuition, vision, and feeling oneness with everything. We could call this drive, interchangeably, the God Center or instinct, or the Intuitive Center or instinct.

Theoretically, presence in our Intuitive Center would facilitate contacting the mystery of existence and appreciating our lives from the perspective that there is a unifying life force that transcends and is unbound by space or time. From this vantage point, we may experience ourselves as being created from and loved by the Mystery, being the Mystery itself, or *no self*—that there is *only* the Mystery.

Could biology support the Intuitive Center hypothesis? However speculative, certain facts emerge. Instincts and information circuits that begin in the brain stem receive input from three of our five classical senses—sound, touch, and taste. These and the fourth sense, sight, send information into the brain's relay station—the thalamus—which transmits this information to the cortex, where we become aware of it and create corresponding narratives. Through cortical connections, we then create composites of understanding. Thus, consciousness is an emergent process.

Smell does something different. Bypassing the brain stem and thalamus, it connects directly with cortex and brain parts that create *meaning, memory, and emotion* such that odors and fragrances affect us more immediately and potently. When breathing nasally, we activate movement-sensing olfactory sensory neurons in a thin, porous bony plate (cribriform plate) at the base of the nasal cavity that may synchronize rhythmic activities in the primary olfactory cortex, amygdala, and hippocampus with our breathing. The intimate proximity of these emotional and memory-processing regions to the olfactory sensory neurons likely facilitates ready access to awareness, allowing us to generate more immediate narratives than the other four senses do. The link between smell, breathing, and higher-order awareness is uniquely direct and rapid among the five senses. Might this be a biological vector for the Intuitive or God Instinct?

David Linden, Johns Hopkins University neuroscience professor and author of *The Accidental Mind*, says we could also call the God Instinct, the Science Instinct. He explained in a personal conversation, "Both religion and science start with information fragments, which we are neurologically wired to make sense of by constructing stories; and for the most mysterious things, we develop an Origin Story about life." We might extrapolate that a natural drive toward expanding consciousness and discovering the meaning of life is biologically instinctive. Just as we have, or are, a drive for personal connection, *the God Instinct (the spiritual drive) may be what we are.*

Additionally, we may be driven to create narratives that explain what is missing from the information received through the three centers of energy flow. Much of this information is derived from interoception (unconscious and conscious cognition about interior sensations like muscle tension or relaxation, breathing deeply or shallowly, and fast, regular, or slow heartbeats). Wondering about what the sky is, why people die, and the meaning of life is fed by sensory input, including interoception. Thus, we may be driven to experience spiritual energy flow and create spiritual narratives.

Because consciousness is a continually emergent dynamic, the more present with our SEC continuum we are, the more actively we seek understanding about the larger mysteries of life. The more integrated our presence, the less rejecting we are of any aspect of reality—including phenomena that surface even more questions about life's mysteries.

The urges to inhabit the SEC continuum and contact our spiritual potential emanate through an extraordinary poem by an unknown author. The first stanza imparts the flowering of emotional intelligence; the second conveys cognitive intelligence's expansive possibilities; the third depicts life when somatic intelligence is embodied. Together, these three transmit spiritual dimensions into our lives.

Who Can Tell ...

Who knows what miracles love has in store for us
If only we will have the courage to become one with it?

Whatever we think we know now
is only the beginning of another knowing
Which itself has no end.

And whatever it is we think we can accomplish now
will seem derisory to us
When the powers of our divine nature flower in glory
And act through us.

—UNKNOWN

Thus, without needing to name a spiritual instinct, the SEC continuum gives rise to both pondering the Mystery of life and experiencing the sensations, feelings, and awarenesses of that search. Throughout time, diverse spiritual

lineages have articulated that breathing is the primary portal to spiritual dimensions and the Divine.

- *Breath*, *wind*, and *spirit* are the same word in many languages including *Atman* in Sanskrit, *psyche* in Greek, *spiritus* in Latin, and *nephesh* and *ruach* in Hebrew. In Greek, *psyche* and *pneuma* both connect breathing with life and consciousness. *Diaphragm*, the most essential muscle involved in breathing, is derived from *phren*, which means mind. The intrinsic connection between breathing (human dynamism), wind (dynamism of nature), awareness, and spirit are recognized throughout diverse cultures and times.
- The Sumerians perceived breath and spirit as one. The word *šāru* expressed wind, life, breath, any moving air (as in breathing), or *the last breath* leaving the body.
- Ancient Egyptian art often depicted two gods connected by a trachea, entwined with papyrus and lilies. Though many Egyptologists say this symbolizes Upper and Lower Egypt's unification, another interpretation is that the trachea—the breathing channel—is the unification of material and spiritual reality.
- In India's yogic tradition, the Self, called *Atman*, means "that which breathes." The Upanishad texts say breath is incorruptible. *Prana* describes the universal life force that causes life to grow and thrive. Pranayama—Breathing Practices—was the root and central thrust of yogic practices. *Ayama* means to extend and regulate, so pranayama extends our universal life force through breathing.
- In Chinese philosophy and medicine, the word *Qi* (Ki in Japanese) refers both to cosmic essence and the air we breathe. Qi is also translated as "subtle breath, vital energy, and animating force," and is considered the substrate of existence. We are thought to contain natural Qi at birth; we expend it throughout life and breathing is its primary source of replenishment.
- Taoism uses extensive Breathing Practices. The *Tao Te Ching*, verse 10, says, "When one gives undivided attention to the breath, and brings it to the utmost degree of pliancy, he can become as a babe.

When he has cleansed away the most mysterious sights, he can become without a flaw."

- The Khoisan people in Africa shake the body to activate breathing for entering trances that transmit powerful healing to others. The Zulu tradition uses the word *umoya* for breath and spirit. In *Zulu Shaman*, Baba Credo describes entering a healing trance by meditating on breathing's gentle flow, which fuels energy (*umbilini*) rising through the spine (Mutwa, 1997). In IsiXhosa, one of South Africa's 11 official languages, *umphefumlo* means both breathing and a person's soul or spirit.
- In Judaism, *ruach* means both breath and creative spirit. The word *nephesh* is used to express neck, throat, vital spirit, and personality, and is said to unite with *Neshama* (our divine soul). In Genesis 2:7, G_d blows a "breath of life" into Adam's body of earth and dust, bringing it to life. Breathing continues after the body returns to the ground, when it "returns to the God who had given it." It belongs to God and is God. Thus, Rabbi Shlomo Schachter (2021) says, "Hashem will never be further from us than our own breath."
- The Christian Fathers, the Russian Fathers, and the Jewish mystics believed that breathing was the ultimate way to center the heart in preparation for prayer. Various mystical writings encourage Breathing Practices for engaging the body and psyche's capacities to activate spiritual ability. During Christianity's first thousand years, the Desert Fathers and Mothers, and the Eastern Fathers, had three requirements: correct breathing, ejaculatory prayer, and an experienced guide (Selo, 1954).
- The practice *Shahada* employs breathing to actualize the meaning of the word *Islam*—submission to God—by establishing a rhythm with inhalation and exhalation while reciting the prayer "there is no God, but God." In the Qur'an, 5:110, Allah bestows upon Jesus and his mother Mary the power to perform miracles, saying, "and you create from clay like the form of a bird with My permission, then you [Jesus] breathe into it, and it becomes a bird, with My permission." Thus, the miracle of creating human life, and that human life can

perform miracles, occurs through breathing a divine component that unites spirit and matter.

- The Greek word *hesychasm* means divine tranquility and denotes a foundational Byzantine mystical contemplative prayer in Eastern Orthodox Christianity. "Lord Jesus Christ, Son of God" is uttered while inhaling; "have mercy on me" is spoken while exhaling (Rossi, 2020).
- Sufis (Islamic mystics) utilize breathing rhythms called *habs-i dam*, meaning "keeping one's breath in recollection." Sufis bring attention to God during all activities by feeling breath coming from various body parts, such as the chest or arms, while simultaneously focusing on God.
- Central to various Buddhist teachings is a breathing practice called *ānapānasati*. The Theragatha Verse 548 describes breath awareness as the principal medium of Buddha's enlightenment: "One who has gradually practiced, developed and brought to perfection mindfulness of the in-and-out breath, as taught by the Enlightened One, illuminates the entire world, like the moon when freed from clouds" (Tibetan Buddhist Encyclopedia, n.d.).
- Renowned mystic George Gurdjieff said, "Right exercises which lead directly to the aim of mastering the organism and subjecting its consciousness and unconscious functions to the will begin with breathing exercises. Without mastering breathing, nothing can be mastered" (Ouspensky, 2001).
- Many Native American cultures believe all of life, including the invisible realm of existence, is connected to breathing. This "kincentric ecology" is based on the understanding that "all life shares the same breath," and that the health of all life depends on the health of all breath (Salmón, 2020).
- Over 5,000 years ago, the Australian aboriginal peoples designed the didgeridoo—a powerful wind instrument that uses breathing and the mouth, tongue, cheeks, and diaphragm to create sound. *Circular breathing* is used to play the instrument through both inhalation and exhalation. The Western Australian Noongar people's word *waug* expresses the unity of breath, soul, and spirit.

- The Hawaiian word *ha* encompasses spirit, air, wind, and breath. *Aloha* can be translated as *alo*, meaning presence, and *ha*, meaning divine breath. Thus, in greeting, the presence of divine breath within one other is acknowledged.
- Both the Inuit and Yupik peoples in northern and arctic regions say *Sila* or *Silap Inua* (the source of wind, mind, air, and breath) to describe consciousness, awareness, and the elemental force and creator of everything that manifests through all aspects of nature. *Sila* communicates danger through the volume, rate, quality, sound, and patterns of breathing (early signs everyone can recognize when something is amiss) (Abram, 2018).
- The Baha'i faith teaches that God and humanity share one breath. "I have breathed within Thee a breath of My own Spirit, that thou mayest be My lover" (Bahá'u'lláh, 1857). Because of that essential oneness, diversity can be valued, and progenitors and prophets of all religions are honored. Baha'is believe the one breath's power can create healing, unity, and miracles.

> *Breath is my elder, my ancestor, the eldest and most indispensable force that gives life to material. Before I do anything, before I become anyone, I am breath.*
> —BABA OLUDARÉ, BREATHING WITH ORISHA

Various spiritual traditions refrain from speaking God's name aloud, instead honoring breathing as the name; or offer versions of God's name without vowels so the throat remains open for breathing; or speak God's name in rhythmic cadence with inhalation and exhalation. These orientations of the centrality of breathing to connecting with God elicit optimal probability for intimacy with the Beloved, the Divine. Our awareness is lifted to the incomprehensible sacredness of creation and its emissary—breathing. In an essay called *The Commonwealth of Breath,* cultural ecologist and geophilosopher David Abram writes about this: "Much as I tremble to speak aloud the most sacred name of the holy in my own tribal, Jewish tradition, the four-letter name that—rightly spoken—is not other than the inhale and exhale, the living breath of awareness..." (Abram, 2018).

Breathing consciously, while maintaining awareness that breathing is the breath of the Divine, is a blessing for others and ourselves. Connecting with the Source through breathing increases the likelihood that, like the Divine, we will love all creation because each breath of air participates in incalculable ways with innumerable creations.

> *The worst thing we ever did was put God in the sky out of reach pulling the divinity from the leaf, sifting out the holy from our bones.... The worst thing we ever did is pretend God isn't the easiest thing in this Universe available to every soul in every breath.*
>
> —CHELAN HARKIN, *SUSCEPTIBLE TO LIGHT*

Yet we need not engage, nor believe, the rich tapestry of spiritual teachings about breathing to experience Conscious Breathing's complete contribution to our well-being and flowering. Whatever our philosophical or spiritual orientation—agnosticism, theism, atheism, nature-based, scientific, secular, religious—we are unified through breathing. All animals, except salminicola, breathe and turn oxygen into energy, and all plant life, mushrooms, and mycelium participate in earth's oxygen cycle. We are all held by the same vessel—a constantly evolving and emerging work of art, a creation of venerable nature metamorphosing all living things in each moment through breathing. Oxygen is an abundant substance in the earth's land, seas, and air, and it is the third most abundant substance in the universe. When we breathe we are touching a substance that readily connects everything on earth and dynamically interacts with the entire universe. The implications are profound.

> *He breathed a breath, and knew Its origin lost in the depths of time Before even light lit the universe*
>
> —DAVID TAYLOR, "BREATHE A BREATH"

This abiding, unifying architecture forms unique relationships with everyone. The further we explore this, the more we will discover that breathing is the embodied portal and substrate for all personal and collective experience. Every inhalation partakes of that which holds us. Then during exhalation what is holding us, and *our* holding of it, conjoin to birth something completely new. Each breath is an opportunity for nourishing and developing ourselves, as well as supporting and contributing to everything in the unified field—vegetation, other creatures, land, water, air, and space. There's an ineffable abundance of life, intelligence, and creativity that we can imbibe, build with, and be blessed by.

The personal and collective connection, purpose, and fulfillment yearned for in the inner sanctum of our beings can be actualized through allowing each moment's potency to inhabit us while reciprocally inviting ourselves to live fully into each moment. Conscious Breathing empowers and amplifies this potency and reciprocity. Conscious Breathing propels us toward presence, eventually to live each moment in reference to presence, and ultimately for us to become presence itself.

What would obstruct our ability to be present with these treasures? An enormous factor is our attention being habitually and unconsciously needed or co-opted by unmet and unattended parts of ourselves—including pain, grief, fear, rage, and trauma—that have formulated defensive and compensatory behaviors which prevent us from optimizing ourselves.

Conscious Breathing provides a ready, optimizing, and unifying focal point for bringing attention to our resources, potential, the present moment, and the conditions of our temperament, personal narratives, and embedded memories, emotions, and trauma.

Breathing's Personal, Relational, and Collective Potential

In our neural pathways, breathing precedes language, learned habits, most movement, defensive patterns, addictive patterns, and most trauma. (An exception is the case of prenatal trauma. The field of prenatal and perinatal psychology is growing, and some Breathwork schools address this topic.) Breathing can be involuntary, reflexive, and unconsciously behavioral (Crockett et al., 2016). Simply bringing awareness to breathing opens and amplifies physical, emotional, cognitive, behavioral, relational, and spiritual awareness. Breathing is literally and symbolically the doorway between unconsciousness, awareness, our original unconditioned nature, and the *prima materia*. Consider—CB connects and fuels a communication matrix between awareness and body; inner and outer experience; unconscious and conscious; immediate and future; subjective and objective; personal and impersonal; stillness and dynamism; acceptance and motivation; spirit and matter; form and formlessness. Because CB is the most immediate way to foster integrated presence, at minimum it's a potent doorway to healing and self-actualization; and at maximum, our single most potent nutrient, medicine, friend, healer, teacher, lover, and partner.

Additionally, CB is a medium for relational healing, attunement, and resonance. Conscious Breathing is a sweet, empowering, and surprising modus vivendi through which we can experience and build healthy, creative, meaningful relationships, from seconds-long encounters with a store clerk to decades-long relationships with family, friends, and significant others.

Conscious Breathing is also a game-changing healing modality and engine for social transformation. Our brains evolved, for reasons of safety and security (Slavich, 2020), to identify in-groups in which we belong, and out-groups that may be inadvertently or consciously unwelcoming or hostile to us. That capacity can also ignite division and polarization. It is easy to experience in-group and out-group reactions and responses about different languages, education, socioeconomic status, gender, skin color, religion, age, body types, political beliefs—really anything.

There is only one group of humans we cannot perceive as an out-group— the group of Breathers. We are all Breathers.

Consider the implications. We are all breathing and have a survival instinct to continue breathing. When George Floyd and countless others throughout history say, "I can't breathe," it impacts us viscerally in ways few other words can. We instinctively feel the need for a person, for all people, to breathe. And abundant anecdotal evidence has shown that when people breathe consciously together, many fear-generated divisive orientations begin dissolving. *Imagine our world if we each breathed consciously with diverse groups of people every day in person or online in families, schools, workplaces, faith settings, community gatherings, government offices, creative and theater arts venues, and more!*

The Invitation

Clinicians, Psychotherapists, Psychiatrists, Counselors, Social Workers, Psychologists, Somatic Therapists, and Spiritual Directors, and all dedicated professional healers and caregivers for our psyche and soul growth and challenges—we are in an unparalleled position to integrate Breathwork into treatment and counseling, transforming the world one breath at a time. Exploring new impactful landscapes for mental health and wellness professions can provide immediate and highly integrated environments, guidance, and partnership for awareness, well-being, and love to flow—for individuals, relationships, and the collective. We are endowed with building blocks, including ego; superego; archetypes and complexes; family systems; attachment theory; dream imagery; object relations; and various understandings about self, soma, psyche, and soul. These put us in a seminal and potent position to support well-being through the magic of inspired breakthroughs in the tradition of psychotherapists like Nathan Cummings and Erik Erikson. Integrating psychotherapy and Breathwork, and their science-based, experiential, and spiritual foundations will engender a more expansive wholeness in ourselves and clients. We can embody and offer integration with every breath.

Breathworkers who have already fallen in love with breathing ... who have felt breathing's call, and envisioned wholeness and a unified world ... who have courageously practiced Breathwork so the world is not denied this mighty medicine ... who have midwifed intense emotions and accompanied Breathers on groundbreaking journeys—a deep bow to you. Conscious Breathing's time has arrived, and we have contributed to a vast field of experience, knowledge, and healing. Having illuminated the wisdom pathways of ancient and modern Breathwork to serve the world, it's time for us to robustly integrate Breathwork with the wisdom of other healing professionals and therapeutic modalities. Much evolution awaits through developing more precise and nuanced skills for attending to somas, psyches, and souls. With more comprehensive and refined understandings of the specificities and intricacies of cultivating integrative consciousness, we can become more finely attuned physical, emotional, cognitive, and intuitive vehicles for consciousness and love.

Breathers (everyone) who deserve brilliant, sophisticated guidance, constructed of caring, respect, wisdom, integrity, and innovation, for receiving CB's potency—may this book awaken our understanding of the pan-dimensional landscape of Conscious Breathing and Breathwork so that our previously unrecognized individual and collective capacities may flower. This book intends to endow Breathers with key principles for personal practice and for recognizing quality guidance, co-empowerment, and genuine partnership with trustworthy and skilled Breathworkers/Psychotherapists/Healers.

Breathworkers, Psychotherapists, Healers, all Breathers, let us learn from the master teacher, *Breathing,* and contribute to humanity's shift *from a culture of personality and fear to a culture of love and creativity* for ourselves, each other, all life, and our ecosystem and home.

> *To breathe means to be plunged into a medium that penetrates us in the same way and with the same intensity as we penetrate it.*
>
> —EMANUELE COCCIA, *THE LIFE OF PLANTS*

TWO

Breathwork for Well-Being and Conscious Living

All questions and phenomena of life need to be rethought, re-examined, and re-experienced within the experiential atmosphere of breathing.

—PETRI BERNDTSON

OUR CAPACITIES to sense, feel, and grow begin in the womb. Breathing initiates, maintains, and enhances that sensing, feeling, and growing outside the womb. Because it's our most critical physiological function, our brain will withdraw energy from every other function to maintain breathing.

From our first breath, breathing occurs automatically. We breathe without any conscious effort on our part; yet each cell's vigor and functioning are supported for living. When we breathe consciously, our body's mechanisms for physical functioning, emotional awareness and expression, and cognitive awareness and visioning (the somatic–emotional–cognitive continuum, or SEC continuum) move toward optimization, resonance, and alignment. Conscious Breathing is a gift of nutrients and medicine that keeps on giving.

Indeed, the source of much physical illness and disease is lack of tissue oxygenation; and evidence of reduced oxygen in the body related to transient, acute, and chronic emotional dysregulation is increasingly well-documented. For example, lowered brain oxygen levels (hypoxia) produce hypoxia-inducible factor-1 (HIF-1), a protein linked with major depression and bipolar disorder (Shibata et al., 2013).

Conscious Breathing (CB) is our most immediate, direct action for altering our nervous system and cultivating fertile states for regulation, insight, healing, and integration. Specific Breathing Practices can activate the sympathetic nervous system to energize us when we're hypoaroused or activate the parasympathetic nervous system to calm us when we're hyperaroused. Generally, stronger, quicker breathing increases energy levels for vitality and action, enriching each moment's vividness. Slower, deeper breathing induces relaxation, reduces stress and cortisol levels, accelerates healing, lowers anxiety, generates attunement and compassion for self and others, cultivates relational resonance, elicits meditative states, and heightens creativity (Brown & Gerbarg, 2005a; Chinagudi et al., 2014a, 2014b). CB can balance our parasympathetic and sympathetic nervous systems, generating global neural coherence.

Nevertheless, many doctors report receiving only a few hours to a day of medical school education on the critical function of healthy breathing. Typical medical training covers lung pathologies, rather than lung health. Thankfully, some medical schools now feature units on healthy breathing. The first medical college to recognize the primary importance of healthy breathing and Breathwork was likely the University of Arizona College of Medicine's Andrew Weil Center for Integrative Medicine. Yearly, hundreds of physicians-in-training initially learn by becoming patients themselves, before treating patients—to heal themselves and then heal others. What is the most fundamental component of their training and treatments? Breathwork!

Breathwork is a spectrum of Breathing Practices that enhance physical, emotional, cognitive, and spiritual well-being. The Breathwork spectrum includes simple breathing techniques that encourage relaxation and stress reduction; awareness and mindfulness practices; precise and refined applications that promote specific effects such as physiological and emotional regulation and improved immune functioning; practices that cultivate character attributes and virtues; and intensive breathing processes that access our deepest aspects and potential.

All Breathwork benefits the body, heart, brain, and soul through one or both of two main factors—bringing awareness to breathing and breathing more harmoniously and/or deeply. We can adjust the rate, type, volume, intention, body position, and other internal and external conditions—often to astounding results. Yet it is breath awareness, and becoming more receptive to, and capable of, breathing fully, that engenders the most momentous shifts, expanding our awareness of new capacities and possibilities.

Each breath *offers* abundant potential benefits. Bringing awareness to any aspect of the breath *amplifies* these benefits. Consciously receiving and partnering the *whole* breath—the whole inhalation and exhalation—*exponentially increases* that harvest. Deepening our breathing expands the treasures immeasurably. *Adding informed volitional adjustments* to our breathing's rate, depth, and more can further enhance vigor, functioning, and living. Conscious awareness of the *salient intersections of the unconscious and conscious, and the effortless and volitional,* aspects of breathing abound with thrilling implications.

Practicing Breathwork and consciously breathing ongoingly is possible. We can cultivate skills that allow breathing to be modulated by our life experiences while breathing deeply and fully every moment—through all life's vicissitudes. Every breath then offers significant possibilities for increased health, healing, personal growth, creativity, intelligence, intuition, and connection with others and life. Conscious Breathing opens and invigorates wisdom and abilities for cocreating a wholesome world with others.

We now have enough evidence about the effectiveness of CB and various Breathwork practices to substantiate their inclusion in psychotherapeutic and medical environments and training. Before outlining the full spectrum of these Breathwork practices, let's explore three well-known and respected Breathwork approaches where countless significant benefits have been reported—Coherent Breathing, Sudarshan Kriya Yoga (SKY), and Human Potential Breathwork.

Coherent Breathing

Coherent Breathing, developed by Stephen Elliott, sometimes called resonant breathing, is a practice of five to six conscious, deep, nasal breaths per minute for adults and children over 10. Numerous studies show this practice eliciting emotional and neural regulation (Brown et al., 2013; Gerbarg et al., 2019; Steffen et al., 2017; Wehrwein et al., 2012). Coherent Breathing has likely improved well-being for millions. More instrumented evidence is needed to establish Coherent Breathing protocols for children under 10, however the late, Dee Edmonson, RN, Elliott's research partner (who facilitated over 45,000 Coherent Breath sessions), employed numerous methods to guide children to breathe more slowly, deeply, and rhythmically to good effect.

For most Breathers, five to six breath per minute (called coherence or resonance) pacing seems optimal for autonomic nervous system regulation and healthy heart rate variability (HRV). James Nestor calls this breathing rate 5.5. Some tall Breathers with big healthy lungs may breathe slower for optimization. Some longtime practicing Breathers prefer breathing even slower for maximum benefit.

We will traverse the fascinating origin story of five to six breaths per minute, and open innovative possibilities for individualized optimal breathing rates in Chapter 6. Generally, we know through Breather experience and substantial research that slower, deeper CB can rapidly relieve stress, anxiety, sleep problems, and posttraumatic stress symptoms (Heyda, 2000; Telles et al., 1994).

Dr. Richard Brown and Dr. Patricia Gerbarg contributed considerably to the Breathwork field's overall impact and credibility by expanding our understanding and practice of Coherent Breathing and demonstrating impressive results with diverse populations in the aftermath of traumatic disasters (Brown & Gerbarg, 2010; Brown et al., 2013). For example, they taught Coherent Breathing to 2004 Southeast Asian tsunami survivors. Participants' trauma and stress indices were dramatically reduced after just four eight-hour training days (Descilo et al., 2010). When Brown and Gerbarg worked with 27 heroic first responders to the September 11, 2001, World Trade Center attacks, the participants experienced marked relief from PTSD using Coherent Breathing after years of traditional therapy, pharmaceuticals, and cognitive–behavioral therapy had minimal effect. In just a two-day Coherent Breathing and body movement training, participant scores on the Beck Anxiety Inventory (BAI), Beck Depression Inventory (BDI), and Anxiety Sensitivity Index (ASI) were remarkably lower, and these results were sustained at six months (Gerbarg et al., 2019).

Gretchen Ki Steidle, a graduate of Inspiration's Certified Integrative Breathworker program, founder of Global Grassroots and Circles for Conscious Change, and author of *Leading From Within: Conscious Social Change and Mindfulness for Social Innovation*, traveled to Haiti six days after the devastating 7.0 earthquake on January 12, 2010. She and Barbara Johnson, another Inspiration-certified Breathworker, gathered with nearly 200 displaced mothers and children living in tents and a local orphanage. Gretchen led them in Coherent Breathing (trained by Brown and Gerbarg). With one 20-minute practice, women and children were relaxing, with some falling asleep for the first time since the earthquake a week before.

Sudarshan Kriya

Sudarshan Kriya Yoga (SKY) is a specific sequence and timing of breathing patterns—slow Ujjayi breath (also called *resistance breathing*), fast Bhastrika breath, the chanting of *om*, and Sudarshan Kriya (translated as "cyclical breathing," not pausing between inhalation and exhalation). Out of respect for SKY founder Sri Sri Ravi Shankar, and the precision and nuances needed for optimal results, we refrain from sharing the details of the practice here. For further information, see Brown and Gerbarg's article in the *Journal of Alternative and Complementary Medicine*, "Sudarshan Kriya Yogic Breathing in the Treatment of Stress, Anxiety and Depression," Parts I and II (Brown & Gerbarg, 2005a, 2005b).

Dr. Brown and Dr. Gerbarg's article integrates studies from various sources, validating many reported benefits of CB and SKY. For example, Ujjayi breath enhances parasympathetic activity and increases indicators of vagal tone, respiratory sinus arrhythmia, and HRV. SKY alleviates anxiety, depression, everyday stress, posttraumatic stress, and stress-related medical illness. Positive results are related to slow breathing (two to four cycles per minute), laryngeal contracture, inhalation against airway resistance, prolonged exhalation against airway resistance, and breath holding. The Art of Living Foundation has compiled over 65 studies that show SKY can help:

- Increase deep sleep by 218%
- Increase hormone secretion associated with well-being by 50%
- Decrease stress hormones by 56%
- Decrease depression by 70%
- Reduce anxiety by 44% (Art of Living, 2021)

Human Potential Breathwork

Around the globe, Breathwork methodologies that tap deeply into human potential such as Integrative Breathing, Holotropic Breathwork, and Transformational Breath have facilitated significant physical, emotional, cognitive, relational, and spiritual healing; transformative healing for people with emotional trauma stemming from violence, genocide, war, environmental catastrophe, and ecocide; and profound openings into personal capacities, expanded states of consciousness, and mystical experiences.

Carol Lampman, founder of Integral Breath Therapy, trains therapists to use Breathwork and wrote to me about her work in Israel since the late 1990s:

> The work with Integral Breath Therapy seemed almost magical to those who had been in therapy for years and found only minimal relief. Soldiers who were depressed, physically damaged, and even suicidal reclaimed their zest for life. First- and second-generation Holocaust survivors were healing so fast that it surprised even us . . .
>
> One Israeli soldier, who lost his left arm and severely damaged his left leg in the 6-day war, had been depressed for several years and had considered suicide. His childhood friend, a psychiatrist, urged me to see him, though I was leaving and could only do one session.
>
> I was touched by his pale, drawn face and story of multiple losses. Therapy, medication, and meditation retreats had not helped, and he was reluctant to come. We began breathing and he flashed back to the battlefield. He was continually dissociating, but I kept him breathing. He cried and yelled as his body twisted and turned, remember-

ing the terror. I applied warm packs and kept him breathing and in the present moment.

When the session was complete, his body had relaxed, and he was filled with peace. He felt forgiveness for the doctors that removed his arm against his will. There were tears of gratitude for the many blessings in his life, and he considered a new idea for a business. He looked completely different. Several weeks later the psychiatrist shared that this one session had restored his faith in life. Today, he is thriving with a successful business. He says he learned that everything he needed is only a breath away.

Integrative Breathing is another intensive human potential practice. I was asked to teach and facilitate Integrative Breathing in Estonia in 2004. Estonia regained its independence without any bloodshed from the then Soviet Union in 1991 through its four-year Singing Revolution. Imagine the courage and innovation—and the pain of 51 years of oppression, three under Nazi Germany and 48 under the Soviet Union. The 100-plus Estonians with whom we worked were amazingly vital, yet their lingering trauma was pervasive. They craved healing and growth. The atmosphere was imbued with vibrant life force, and repressed, shackled feelings. This was uncharted territory for them. I was in awe of each participant. Our team of Breathworkers used human potential breathing techniques with men and women who were bound by years of grief, confusion, rage, repression, and trauma—yet were hopeful and excited about new pathways for living. The atmosphere was electric. Within a week, teenagers to elders were laughing, dancing, expressing feelings, crying and laughing, and experiencing vitality and spontaneity they described as completely novel. Some equated a single session of Integrative Breathing to two decades of therapy.

WHAT BREATHWORK DOES IN THERAPY

Kathy Sirota, a psychotherapist and GPBA certified Breathworker shared with me how Integrative Breathing moves people from thinking and talking about experiences to feelings and physicality:

Clients have traditional talk therapy in the first hour and Integrative Breathing in the second hour.... With time, the therapeutic environment's safety, and a willingness to be vulnerable, they begin to accept their contribution to unsatisfying situations.... They reveal to themselves their patterned ways of being that are frustrating them.

In traditional therapy, the client may find this conclusion satisfactory. They leave therapy, feeling empowered to behave differently and create new, more satisfying behaviors. Yet some people find using the new behaviors result in similar frustrating feelings. With Integrative Breathing, the therapeutic sessions don't end—they have just begun.

Now comes the second hour—Integrative Breathing. They have cognitively prepared to go inside. With a deep inhale and a long exhale, they leave behind thinking and talking and move into experiencing deeper, unknown places inside themselves . . .

Then they may notice things: perhaps a sound, body sensation, image, or feeling—perhaps cold feet, ringing bells, a bear coming towards them. They might cry. Clients may see their cold feet are a fear that the childhood message they learned about being unimportant is true. They breathe and unfold into knowing they are precious and deeply loved by God. They might cry through experiencing the pain of loneliness felt since childhood. They breathe and might experience the ringing bells as God calling them to loving connectedness, and that the bear isn't a human-eating bear but is inviting their strength and the warrior within.

Clients are changed by these experiences and know that Being invites them to be their essential nature, to live within the grace of loved, loving, and lovable. They live more in the feelings they've been seeking.... Their minds are guided towards more conscious and loving thoughts and choices.

Breathwork for War Zone Trauma

When war erupted in Ukraine in March 2022, people worldwide responded with compassion, outrage, and love, mobilizing to offer donations, shelter, safe passage, communications, political action, and medical and therapeutic services. Knowing Breathwork's powerful benefits for trauma-healing, Breathworkers within Ukraine, Russia, and countries receiving refugees offered their services and created healing programs.

Within weeks after the conflict began, Mark Walsh, cofounder of the Embodied Facilitator Course, traveled from the UK to Ukraine to facilitate trainings in bomb shelters in Lviv. The initial 10-day training was delivered to 82 trauma educators, first aiders, and Ukrainian soldiers. Mark asked a group of experienced Breathworkers for our suggestions and found that Coherent Breathing, various yogic breathing techniques, and Box Breathing were particularly effective in this traumatic situation. He shared inspiring photos of Ukrainian educators learning Breathing Practices and videos of them singing and hugging. Mark calibrated the teaching for graded exposure to stress while practicing self-regulation—thus supporting resilience. The work has been passed to thousands through Sane Ukraine.

A month into the war, Giten Tonkov, founder of Biodynamic Breathwork and Trauma Release System (BBTRS) joined Nisarga Eryk Dobosz, director of the Integral Body Institute in Warsaw, to create trauma resilience programs for Ukrainian refugees and training for psychotherapists in Poland. Women and children who had been forced to flee and separate from their husbands, fathers, and brothers who stayed to defend Ukraine struggled with "acute trauma, stress, fears, mourning and depression, reinforced by the uncertainty of tomorrow" (Pomagam, 2022).

In the trauma resilience trainings, refugees are taught to locate an inner resource—the place in their body that feels safest and allows movement such as swaying or shaking. Pendulation (alternating attention between tense, traumatized parts and inner safety resources) is used, accompanied by soft breathing. Eventually, they utilize Biodynamic Breathwork's unwinding techniques of deeper breathing—with activation and release alternating with inner resourcing. Sessions conclude with 20 minutes of soft, connected breathing.

> *Tonight we will breathe. Tomorrow we will labor in love through love and your revolutionary love is the magic we will show our children.*
>
> —VALARIE KAUR

Breathe No Other: Breathing Through Othering to Belonging

Conscious Breathing is a personal and connective medium. It is a bio-individualized medicine and nutrient that every Breather deserves for thriving in our world. Breathwork throughout the SEC whole continuum can guide us into transformative and unifying presence with all aspects of self, others, and reality. Thus, it invites us to become present to the suffering and pain created by othering and to become aware of our personal and collective capacity and responsibility for creating a more just world.

Marginalization of any kind is traumatic. It is caused by trauma, and begets trauma. Othering is the product of cultural conditioning, fear, and a lack of integrated embodied presence. The healing of othering and the polarization that creates enemies is one of humanity's ultimate vocations.

This task is particularly challenging because othering tendencies are hardwired in the brain. As we learned in Chapter 1, human brains are designed to recognize to which people we belong, and to which we don't. The binary nature of this discernment creates the perception of safe and familiar in-groups, and dangerous out-groups. When our brain stems sense differentiation, our cortisol levels rise. We prepare for attack and defense, leading to further disconnection and power imbalances (Porges, 2011).

We can create in-group/out-group distinctions between myriad features, traits, behaviors, and orientations. There is only one group I can perceive for which we cannot create a distinction of in-group/out-group—the group of Breathers. We are all Breathers. This remarkable revelation practically becomes a petition that Conscious Breathing and Breathwork's ultimate vocation can and should include the healing of harmful othering.

We leave the love that fulfills us when we put anyone out of our hearts. Because breathing is a unifying language, *breathing together* can dissolve and transcend the primitive brain wiring of in-group/out-group. Experience indicates that people of different skin colors—or any differentiators—who breathe together rapidly experience perceptual shifts away from othering, and experience greater safety in Breathwork spaces to express their feelings about being marginalized. Intentionally creating such spaces can help all of us cultivate greater receptivity and compassion for the internalized trauma in a differentiated group.

INTERSECTIONALITY AND BREATHWORK SPACES

There are many marginalized communities created by othering, which spawns further personal and collective trauma, epigenetic trauma, and transgenerational (inherited) trauma. Some examples:

- Elders
- People with disabilities (hearing, blindness, spinal cord injuries, etc.)
- People living inside prisons (the incarcerated community)
- Religious groups
- LGBTQIA++
- Ethnic cultures that live within a territory with an identified predominant culture, such as Asian and Pacific Islander Americans in the USA, or the Twa in Burundi
- A group that a dominant group identifies as lowest in a caste system
- People with neurodiversity
- The Feminine and/or people identifying as women
- People with medical conditions that affect breathing capacity and require special accommodations

How can Breathwork spaces evolve so that their language, ethics, and practices are inviting, safe, and supportive for these and all marginalized groups? The transformation will hasten as we each develop self-awareness about how we contribute to exclusion, barriers, and suboptimal breathing in each marginalized community. So, let us explore one example—racial marginalization and Breathwork—by hearing some experiences and wisdom of marginalized voices.

RACIAL HEALING BREATHWORK

> *I can hear my brother crying "I can't breathe"…*
> *We ain't gonna stop, until all us free.*
> —ELLISHA AND STEVEN FLAGG, SISTER AND
> BROTHER OF ERIC GARNER, "I CAN'T BREATHE"

Rhonda Magee, a Black woman, and law professor at the University of California at San Francisco, spoke with me in September 2020 when the windows in her Northern California home were shut tightly against smoke due to unprecedented levels of raging forest fires triggered by drought and global warming.* Her 2019 book *The Inner Work of Racial Justice: Healing Ourselves and Transforming Our Communities Through Mindfulness* precipitated requests from people worldwide for her evolutionary thinking and creative practices for healing racism.

Rhonda shared some principles of her work:

> There are the experiences of *I can't breathe* and the way that's showing up, in particular for Black racialized people. It's highlighting the vulnerability of minority populations around the globe, who are disproportionately suffering from COVID, and other indications that we still have these systemic hierarchies tied to our legacies of colonialism, enslavement, and other isms as well. The work I do aims to help us explore and examine racism more effectively, to help us rebirth the human.
>
> There's been a call for a generation around bringing forth new ways of being on the planet and being with each other. I think awareness of breath and body is just so critical. As I say that, I realize I'm

---

* Throughout this book, generally, skin color is not noted when utilizing others' contributions. Race or skin color is noted in this section according to the wishes of contributors to honor intergenerational and cultural experience, trauma, gifts, and knowing.

physically affected by the fire. I can feel the air quality. I literally am feeling it's harder to breathe right now. So, I think... this is very, very real.

The practice is called mindfulness but could be called breathfulness. It's about feeling our presence and sense of aliveness, primarily and foundationally by anchoring on the sensations of breathing, and having that support grounding as we engage in the world.

It is tempting to assert "I *can* breathe" as the cure. Yet as we strive for embodied authenticity, it is central for Breathers to validate their present experience so they can awaken their full potential and possibilities. So many people of color, and other marginalized communities, have experienced the breathlessness of their life force partially or fully choked, beaten, or lynched out of them... by being terrorized, by witnessing other Black, Indigenous, and People of Color (BIPOC) community members being forced into breathlessness... by quieting their breath on the streets, in classrooms, in offices where they don't feel safe. Many rarely feel they can be themselves.

Ayo Handy-Kendi, a Black woman who has been a Breathworker for three decades, facilitates important healing work in two-day experiences called Breath Circles for Race, Diversity, and Gender Healing. White, Black, and Brown bodies come to these groups to share what she calls Transcendence Breath, a human potential Breathwork technique she uses in her Optimum Life Breatheology system of 14 breathing techniques. During Breathwork, Ayo encourages cathartic movements while listening to sacred sounds and drumming. She shared with me that Transcendence Breathwork is used to:

> release subconscious memory, to "wake up" the root cellular trauma of racism, prejudice, oppression, or any woundedness in need of healing. It is an approach that will work with the unconscious, to birth consciously healthy relationships that go beyond the color of our skin to the common humanity within. It's time to breathe away racism and prejudice, using the one tool that connects us all—the Creator's breath of life.

Consciously breathing while carrying significant prior experiences of feeling unsafe to breathe and *inviting those embedded memories into a space to breathe* is vulnerable work. Crying, shaking, frozen affect, raging, yelling, and locked muscles may need to be worked through in safety, with support and validation. It is therefore critical to create Breathwork spaces in which all Breathers feel safe.

One element of safety requires sensitively creating inclusive spaces where Breathers can name their fears, discomforts, and needs, as well as choose not to share. Breathworker Jennifer Patterson, author of *The Power of Breathwork*, identifies with and works with the queer and trans community. She shared with me that she initially felt connected to the practice of Breathwork but disconnected from the space. "There was binary, gendered languaging that felt exclusive and dismissive of the importance of social justice issues being integrated into spiritual settings." She has appreciated finding Breathwork spaces that felt not only accepting, but consciously inclusive.

Another element of safety requires making Breathing Practices accessible for all, which is the mission of Chauna Bryant, a queer Black Breathworker and teacher who shared with me, "Once you know how to do Breathwork, you have immediate self-care accessibility." She encourages Breathworkers to learn from diverse teachers and cultivate openness in Breathwork spaces for conversations about racial trauma and grief. Chauna founded the *Breath Liberation Society,* which provides trainings that include these principles with over 20 teachers of different ethnic and training backgrounds speaking on a variety of Breathwork topics. The *Breath Liberation Society* promotes ongoing continuing education for Breathworkers through supportive community that is ethical and accountable. Breathworkers learn from and respect each other, and meet Breathwork luminaries and elders, both BIPOC and white, who do outstanding work.

Dr. Angel Acosta, a leading Healing-Centered Educator, convened a series of online Breathwork communities "that aimed to provide people with a virtual space to heal from and wrestle with racial trauma" (Acosta & Jimwani, 2020). Over several months, integrated and BIPOC-only groups participated in experimental sessions grounded in Breathwork and the *400 Years of Inequality Project's* framework to process grief and find collective healing.

Dr. Acosta observed themes such as emotional release, heightened mythic material, surprise at the intensity of breathing, and profound connections between personal experiences and the historical timeline. Participants' reflections revealed deep psychobiological responses, connections with the body, insight generation, expanded access to the whole self, a sense of overwhelm, and engagement with racial trauma. Many participants reported crying, and feeling trapped or unable to breathe at times, yet also tapped into their power and agency through Breathwork. They experienced pain, deep connection, and reminders of the interconnectedness of all living beings. Some participants accessed insights about breaking through paralysis toward embodied, empowered action, while others reported access to both the transcendence and embodiment of their soul. Participants also expressed the intense nature of processing current events related to racial injustice, such as incarceration rates, COVID-19, and police brutality.

Dr. Acosta and I facilitated together two racial healing and Breathwork workshops. The first was for about 25 Breathworkers who were all white, reflecting a sad truth in the global Breathwork community. While substantial numbers of BIPOC community members practice Breathwork, the field is still fairly segregated. Participants grieved ways they have unconsciously or consciously denied themselves the richness of relationships with people of color, and have not been conscious allies. They described feeling both rage and love. Overall they felt propelled to address these issues with more energy and drive while also experiencing deep love and peace.

The second workshop was more racially and internationally integrated. The group shared diverse origin stories of fear, violence, and terror, including from Armenia, Ireland, and the US. The rapid and greater softening of defenses and becoming vulnerable was moving, and likely due to the greater diversity and common experiences of fear.

Another Black Breathworker, Kathleen Booker, who works with racially mixed groups, especially with women, passionately shared with me:

> Everybody freakin' breathes—everybody all over the world breathes. Making it black and white belittles Spirit.... The Breath is equal opportunity.... That's the essence of breath... One Love... One Breath. There's enough polarization in the world. Everyone Breathes—we don't need to polarize that!... The breath brings people together. It creates community. It reminds us how we're wired to help one another. Let's not make it black and white. Love IS your Breath, and your Breath IS Love. Your Breath IS Spirit. Spirit IS unconditional Love.... That is an immutable Truth. In every Breathwork session that I lead, the Presence of Love overflows within and from everyone present. Only love is real.

Africa is the origin and cradle of humanity, our DNA, and wisdom and teachings about breathing as the source of life. African spirituality is intrinsically linked to breathing, with ancient African Breathing Practices predating the venerable yogic and pranayama traditions. Baba OluDaré, a keeper of Kikongo and Lukumi wisdom, teaches that the dances and undulating movements of African traditions compel deep breathing and connecting with the healing power of breathing. Baba OluDaré fervently feels that the Black community utilizing Breathwork requires more than de-stressing—it requires reparations from the perspective of breathing. He transmits this into the world as the possibility of #re(s)parations. OluDaré also talks about "respiratory activism," with three goals:

> To reclaim the time, breath and financial assets stolen by trauma, anxiety, stress and racial disparity in Afro-Indigenous communities; [to] reestablish the role of the breath as respiration for healing and wellness, encourage Black-Indigenous communities to breathe for their own wellness, their own communities, their own bodies, their own businesses; [to] encourage essential workers to TAKE the time to stop, rest and breathe deeply. (Bernard, 2020)

Specific practices like Mimi Kàrá (the organic release of sound through moaning, groaning, laughing, crying, sighing, and yelling), and Emi, or soul breathing (full-bodied inhalations to induce complete stretching and mobilize energy), have roots in ancient African wisdom. The colonization and appropriation of these practices by white Eurocentric culture have diminished their depth and sophistication. However, like Baba OluDaré, other wisdom keepers are working to preserve and share the beauty, essence, and power of Breathwork in the African Indigenous traditions.

For example, in South Africa, physician and Breathworker Ela Manga has partnered with African Indigenous wisdom keepers. Together they have developed *Pneumanity Breathwork* that invites breathing down to cellular mitochondria because mitochondrial DNA is what connects us all; it's inherited from, and only from, maternal ancestry beginning with "Mitochondrial Eve," a woman who is said to have lived in Africa approximately 200,000 years ago (ScienceDaily, 2010). Pneumanity Breathwork has seven guiding principles including, Ubuntu—the powerful universal truth "I am because we are"—and sees breathing as embodied Ubuntu.

The Breathwork field must be accountable for its contributions to maintaining systemic marginalization, trauma, and social injustice and elevate Breathwork to dissolve systemic harm. With this recognition I received supported from The Shift Network to create the panel, *A World of Unity, Equity, Empowerment, and Love for ALL: Breathwork for the Ending of Othering* for the Breathwork Summit 2022. I invited Angel Acosta, Chauna Bryant, Baba OluDaré, and Jennifer Patterson and the discussion surfaced four essential remedies.

Breathworkers can study, honor, and teach about African origins of Breathwork, thus empowering African descendants.

Breathworkers should maintain awareness that the spiritual teaching of having no identity can engulf the lived and nuanced life experiences and identities of Breathers, causing them to be inauthentic or dissociative during Breathwork.

White, Black, and Brown-bodied Breathworkers should strive to coteach in the same space about Breathwork. Often Breathworkers of color are only asked to teach about marginalization and oppression in Breathwork.

In group sessions, Breathworkers can name issues of race and suffering alongside other issues that may emerge, even when the group is all one race.

The power and wisdom of Breathwork teachings are spreading into marginalized communities throughout the globe. All these communities deserve their own exploration about Breathwork and healing oppression, marginalization, and othering. Change accelerates the more we each develop self-awareness about our contributions to exclusion and barriers in each community. Any suffering is our suffering. Breathwork propels us to go inside to undo the othering of ourselves and every Breather. Perhaps, then we will breathe with each Breather and truly listen to what they need.

May Breathwork birth a global culture in which everyone breathes with mutual respect, collaborating to build a world we relish together in which we all thrive.

> *Breath is a divine decision that God made ... breath is sanctified, breath is sacred. And to take breath away from another man is to defy God.*
>
> —REVEREND AL SHARPTON, GEORGE FLOYD FUNERAL EULOGY

Breathwork? Breathplay?

Because the term *Breathwork* may evoke the sense of hard work, the word *Breathplay* has occasionally been suggested. Alternatively, some styles are named *"Whatever" Breathing.*

Breathwork naturally and powerfully accesses our highest calling—the call to be whole human beings bringing love, wisdom, and presence to each moment—*love activists*, whatever our other vocations.

Wishing to play is most prevalent in children. As we mature, the wish for purpose and contributing to life becomes more prominent. If we're fortunate, and purposeful, devotion to our vocation can be fulfilling, yet challenging. Similarly, tending to loved ones' hurting bodies, hearts, minds, and souls, sometimes for years, can feel daunting and exhausting, as can giving prolonged focused attention to a cherished art or science project. We usually discover it's worth it; cultivating ourselves as instruments for a purpose—a vocation—is love in action. Within work, there's expansive room for play. We can experience work as a great play of existence, play of life forms, or creation's play.

Breathwork heals and transforms our suffering to support ourselves, loved ones, and the world. Breathwork cultivates our bodies, hearts, and minds so we can awaken and embody our highest potential. Thich Nhat Hanh says, "You cultivate the flower in yourself so that I will be beautiful. I transform the garbage in myself so that you will not have to suffer" (2005). During the COVID-19 pandemic cultures around the world realized that Breathers who transport goods, stock shelves, do plumbing, clean and sanitize, nurse, heal, and so forth, are *essential workers*.

Breathwork is essential, and Breathworkers are essential workers. Though I *played* with the notion of Breath*play*, I experience Breath*work* as a high vocational call for humanity, and have chosen **Integrative Breathing** (a verb), or **Conscious Responsive Breathing** (Chapter 11) to reflect the dynamism and ever-changing inner and outer conditions of breathing. It's a dazzling concept to consider making *Breathing* itself a *field* that spans automatic breathing to human potential breathing.

Breathworkers Rabie Hayek, Petri Berndtson, Jim Morningstar, and I cocreated a professional definition of Breathwork, that was adopted by the Global Professional Breathwork Alliance, the International Breathwork Foundation, and numerous Breathworkers and schools.

> **Breathwork:** The experiential field of study and practice that encompasses a variety of breathing techniques utilized individually and in groups to cultivate self-awareness and the enhancement of physical, emotional, cognitive, or spiritual well-being.

> **Breathworker:** A practitioner of one or more types of Breathwork who facilitates others in utilizing breathing techniques for self-awareness and for the enhancement of physical, emotional, cognitive, or spiritual well-being in an individual or group.

We live most life whoever breathes most air.
—ELIZABETH BARRETT BROWNING

THREE

The Five Groups of Breathwork

Listen, are you breathing just a little, and calling it a life?
—MARY OLIVER, "HAVE YOU EVER TRIED
TO ENTER THE LONG BLACK BRANCHES,"
NEW AND SELECTED POEMS: VOLUME ONE

BREATHING PRACTICES can be grouped according to five primary orientations: relaxation, awareness, therapeutic interventions, character building, and cultivation of our potential (Figure 3.1). The Breathing Practices are identified with the group that most closely aligns with their principal intents, and experiences Breathers commonly report when practicing. While each group has a predominant aim, practices can stimulate multiple orientations concurrently, even all five, depending on Breather experience and Breathworker skills. A simple example is Bumblebee Breath, a favorite of children. This practice, while mostly relaxing and regulating (Group 1), can also elicit awareness of our internal state (Group 2), reduce state anxiety (Group 3), and develop the sense of delight or feeling empowered (Group 4).

Let us deepen our breathing and begin exploring how various types of Breathwork can serve our life journeys.

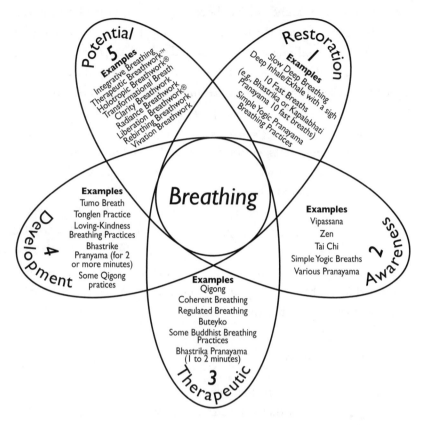

FIGURE 3.1: Five Groups of Breathing Practices
Jessica Dibb. Image created by Altruce Poage.

Group 1 Breathing Practices: Relaxation and Resetting

Group 1 Breathwork has a plethora of time-honored practices that generally induce relaxation and reduce physical and emotional stress. The practices can involve directing breathing and attention to bodily tension; saying something internally or aloud; generating releasing sounds; movement; or visualizing colors, shapes, or scenes. Most Group 1 practices use deeper than normal diaphragmatic inhalations through the nose—slower for calming, and faster for energizing. Exhalations are almost always relaxed and slow, and induce letting go, sometimes with open mouth and intentional sighs or sounds such as humming, toning, groaning, or shouting. Slow, focused breathing activates parasympathetic activity, lowering heart rate and blood pressure which stimulates the relaxation response, engendering well-being. Group 1 practices can be customized for individual needs; some Breathers discover unique personal ways of breathing that elicit relaxation. Though Group 1 practices are usually simple, they can also help ease fear, aggressive behaviors, PTSD symptoms, and anxiety, including about tests, performances, and dental procedures, as well as reduce depression in Breathers with serious medical issues (Aideyan et al., 2020). Two examples follow.

RELEASE OF TENSION BREATH

We generate long, slow, quiet, deep inhales, then say one long "ha" out loud, or shorter "ha"s as many times as needed to complete each exhalation. Practice at least 3 breaths or up to 3 minutes.

EQUANIMITY BREATH

With each long, slow, deep inhalation, we stretch our arms upward. With each long, slow, deep exhalation, our arms slowly make a big circle as we lower and stretch them to the sides and let them float down to our hips. Practice at least 3 breaths or up to 3 minutes.

> *Breathing in, I calm my body.*
> *Breathing out, I smile.*
> *Dwelling in the present moment*
> *I know this is the only moment.*
> —THICH NHAT HANH, *BEING PEACE*

Group 2 Breathing Practices: Awareness and Mindfulness

Group 2 Breathwork elicits conscious awareness and builds capacity for focused attention and experience of the present moment. Dwelling in present awareness (mindfulness) can also be effective for reducing depression, anxiety, and general stress.

Breathing is the critical component of mindfulness, as shown in a forthcoming study by Jack L. Feldman, distinguished neurobiology professor at UCLA. After the breathing rates of mice were regulated and reduced for 30 minutes per day for four weeks, they were much calmer in fear-inducing situations than a control group, thanks to slow breathing influencing the amygdala. Mindfully meditating mice! Breathing slower over time benefits the amygdala, the center that most controls fear responses (Yackle et al., 2017). Neuroscientist Andrew Huberman also found that Breathwork substantially boosts mood and reduces anxiety better than mindfulness meditation without breath awareness (Balban et al., 2023).

Group 2 practices invite awareness to various facets of our experience of the present, such as internal and external body sensations; emotions and thoughts; impulses and reactions; sounds, sights, smells, tastes, and feeling our inner and outer environment; and an expansive *Big Mind* perspective of self and reality. Vivid participation in each moment frees energy and attention that was focused on avoiding certain experiences. We can inhabit whatever we're experiencing more fully.

Enhanced interoception (sensing the body's inner states such as muscle tension, heart rate, breathing quality, etc.) can also open insightful, intuitive awareness of ourselves, others, life, and spiritual dimensions. Interoception can play vital roles in emotional healing because physical sensations bring awareness to the emotions that create them. Problem-solving abilities, concentration, perceptual awareness, and intuition (somatic, emotional, cognitive) can be strengthened.

Jack Kornfield's guided Vipassana meditations, Zen Breathing as described by Dr. Andrew Weil (n.d.), and Dr. Mark Bertin's Mindfulness Breathing Practices (Bertin, 2017) are wonderful Group 2 practices. Two additional examples follow.

VIPASSANA

Frequently taught during 3- to 10-day silent retreats with instructions on mindfulness and alternating periods of sitting and walking meditation, Vipassana focuses on transformation through self-observation. Watching the fluid nature of thoughts, feelings, emotions, and judgments teaches us to accept the ups and downs we experience inwardly and outwardly, eliciting greater freedom and ease. Although teachings and techniques vary, Vipassana students are generally guided to bring full attention to each inhale and exhale. Focus can be on somatic sensations, emotions, thoughts, or all three.

SIMPLE MINDFULNESS BREATHING PRACTICE

Wherever we are right now, we **are** breathing. We can send attention toward our breathing—the movement of our chest or belly, the feeling of air moving through our nose or throat, and other sensations that arise in our bodies through breathing. Our beautifully alive minds may naturally wander away from these sensations. When we notice our attention wandering, we can gently and kindly return our awareness to breathing. When we are drawn toward something other than breathing—an itch, a sound, a movement outside, a memory, fantasy, desire, fear—we can gently and kindly notice it, and then return our awareness to breathing. We give ourselves a time to do nothing else but breathe. Breathe, notice, breathe. We can practice three mindful breaths for a quick reminder of presence any time. A minimum of 3 minutes is recommended for regular practice, and many Breathers practice for 20 to 60 minutes, or more.

> *Breathing is massively practical. It's meditation for people who can't meditate.*
> —BELISA VRANICH

Group 3 Breathing Practices: Healing and Therapeutic

Human beings want to feel healthy and whole, and to heal suffering in themselves and others. Group 3 Breathwork practices are specific applications, many evidence-based, that utilize various breath rates, volumes, sequences, positions, movements, and placements of attention for assisting with physical dis-ease, emotional congestion and expression, pain, anxiety, confusion, trauma, and general dysregulation—sometimes very precisely. Group 3 includes practices for preventing, supporting, and curing respiratory illnesses, as well as aids for sleeping, temperature regulation, blood sugar regulation, and more. In general, Group 3 Breathwork helps heal dysfunction, regulate systems, and optimize functioning, physically, emotionally, and/or cognitively. Two examples follow.

COHERENT BREATHING

Coherent Breathing, founded by Stephen Elliott (Elliott & Edmonson, 2006), as we learned earlier, is a method of conscious, deep breathing through the nose at a pace of five to six breaths per minute for adults and children over 10 years. Stephen was inspired by British physicist Maxwell Cade's vision for embodying master Zen meditator brain states throughout daily activity—what we call throughout this book *embodied integrated presence*. Stephen found the optimal breathing rate for eliciting the pattern is 5.1 breaths per minute (.085 hertz). For typical adults, six breaths per minute had already been recognized as the nominal resonant frequency that maximizes respiratory sinus arrhythmia (RSA)—the heart rate variations that increase during inhalation and decrease during exhalation (lowering blood pressure and stress, and impacting mood positively; Chaitanya et al., 2022). However, Stephen found that 5.1 breaths per minute produces meditative states within 8 to 12 minutes, even without meditation knowledge.

Research shows that Coherent Breathing helps with stress, anxiety, and insomnia (Cuncic, 2020). Coherent breathing doesn't involve changing the volume of air filling the lungs; it slows inhalations to 5 to 6 seconds, with matching 5- to 6-second exhalations. In essence, it intercepts autonomic nervous system breathing by altering typical breathing durations. Recordings of timed sounds (tinkling bells, soft drumbeats, or ocean waves) can guide inhalation and exhalation timing. Stephen Elliott's *Respire 1* is a widely used recording (Coherence, 2004).

BUTEYKO BREATHING

Introduced by Doctor Konstantin Buteyko, Buteyko Breathing is a complementary physical therapy that treats asthma, anxiety, and sleep disorders with breathing exercises. Nasal breathing and breath holding are used to normalize breathing volume and induce relaxation, decreasing the depth of the breath and relaxing the breathing muscles. Breathers learn to breathe low in the diaphragm with lateral expansion and relaxation of the lower ribs, and utilize various respiratory rates for therapeutic effect. Gentle, light, and soft nasal breathing opens blood vessels, and more oxygen reaches tissues and organs. Patrick McKeown, author of *The Oxygen Advantage*, teaches that Buteyko Breathing's principal goal is optimizing everyday functional breathing through techniques that:

- Enhance the amount of oxygen delivered to cells and tissues.
- Optimize the blood's carbon dioxide pressure.
- Slow high respiratory rates.
- Increase everyday tolerance for air hunger (Chapter 6) and decrease fear of breathlessness related to panic disorder or asthma attacks. Research participants with asthma reduced their steroid use by 50%, while the control group's steroid use was unchanged (McHugh et al., 2003).

The following Buteyko exercise can improve panic disorder, high anxiety, or severe asthma, either during an episode or recovery. Practice for 10 minutes, six times daily, or even *every hour*. This technique can also help calm an agitated mind and is useful for beginning meditators.

BREATHING RECOVERY SITTING PRACTICE

1. Breathe in and out normally through the nose.
2. After exhalation, pinch the nose closed for 5 seconds.
3. Breathe normally for 10–15 seconds.
4. Repeat these three steps for 10 minutes.

> *The mind is the king of the senses and the breath is the king of the mind.*
> —THE HATHA YOGA PRADIPIKA,
> TRANSLATED BY B. K. S. IYENGAR

Group 4 Breathing Practices: Human Development

Group 4 Breathing Practices help Breathers develop beneficial human qualities and attributes, and become more integrated and actualized. These practices develop qualities such as kindness, compassion, empathy, integrity, resilience, attunement, joy, courage, strength, groundedness, non-attachment, equanimity, faith, clarity, love, empowerment, and—so vital to us—relatedness, connection, and intimacy. Two examples follow.

TONGLEN (A BUDDHIST PRACTICE)

Tonglen practice offers an opportunity to broaden the scope of our personal reactions to pain, illness, and suffering in ourselves, others, and the collective to a more expansive empathy, compassion, and responsiveness for the suffering in anyone and everyone.

Let us breathe in our own pain, confusion, anxiety, imagining this as thick, tar-like smoke. Breathe out light, brightness, and well-being. Expand awareness to include the suffering of one person. Breathe in this pain as the thick dark heaviness; breathe out as ease and acceptance. As we practice, we allow compassion to expand even further, to our family, friends, country, the world—including those perceived as enemies, those holding opposing beliefs and principles. We hold a vision of their wholeness, breathing in their suffering and breathing out their essential nature. (A Tonglen session can focus on the suffering of ourselves, another, a group, or the entire world.)

MIRRORING BREATH (TAUGHT BY JACK KORNFIELD)

We choose someone with whom we are willing to partner in a relational practice. Making eye contact, we silently acknowledge each other. One partner lies or sits in a relaxed position, and the other partner sits respectfully next to them. The relaxing partner closes their eyes and breathes naturally. The sitter observes the Breather's abdomen, matching their breath rhythm, allowing whatever emotions and sensations arise, and witnessing and holding them with respect for 5 minutes, or up to 15 or 30 minutes. Both partners open their eyes after the agreed duration, silently acknowledge each other, and switch places without talking. The practice repeats with roles reversed (Kornfield, 2013).

Group 5 Breathing Practices: Depth and Human Potential

The Intensive Breathing Practices of Group 5 Breathwork can access our most profound potentials—the gift of our authentic, unconditioned self, which some refer to as *Essence*, or *Soul*. The term *psychospiritual* may apply, though more accurately these are soma/psycho/spiritual and biopsychosocial processes.

These methodologies fairly reliably open expanded dimensions of human experience that engender awe—often called mystical, shamanistic, nonordinary or expanded states of consciousness, holotropic, pure consciousness Events, and even enlightenment. The nineteenth-century psychologist and philosopher William James, who found various ways to experience self-transcendent states, clearly came to see breathing as the origin of awareness and consciousness:

The "I think" which Kant said must be able to accompany all my objects, is the "I breathe" which actually does accompany them. Breath is the essence out of which philosophers have constructed the entity known to them as consciousness. (James, 1912)

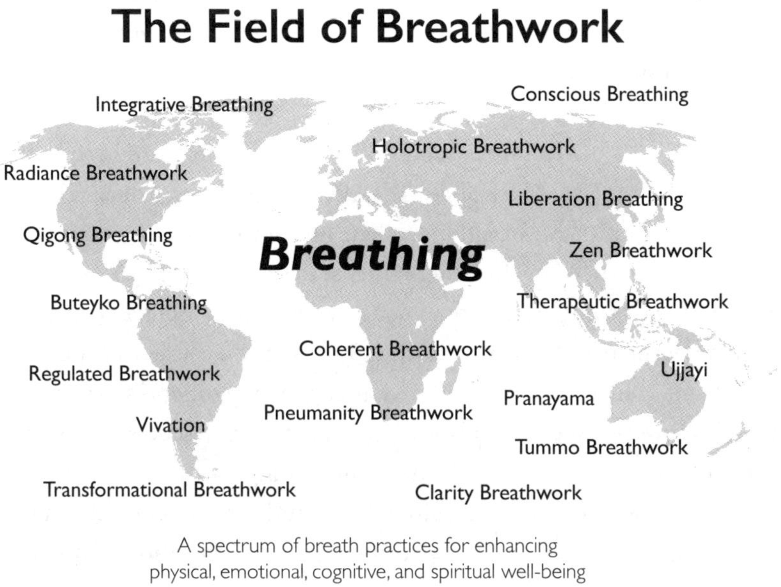

The Field of Breathwork

- Integrative Breathing
- Conscious Breathing
- Holotropic Breathwork
- Radiance Breathwork
- Liberation Breathing
- Qigong Breathing
- **Breathing**
- Zen Breathwork
- Buteyko Breathing
- Therapeutic Breathwork
- Coherent Breathwork
- Regulated Breathwork
- Ujjayi
- Pranayama
- Vivation
- Pneumanity Breathwork
- Tummo Breathwork
- Transformational Breathwork
- Clarity Breathwork

A spectrum of breath practices for enhancing physical, emotional, cognitive, and spiritual well-being

FIGURE 3.2: Some of the Breathing Practices being taught throughout the world on all continents—even Antarctica!
Jessica Dibb. Image created by Sharon Elsberry and Sarah Van Sciver.

Group 5 Breathworkers with scientific backgrounds have observed that prolonged, voluntary, deeper, and faster than normal breathing appears to induce transient hypofrontality, where the neocortex is downregulated; more energy, neural activation, and attention goes to the brain's limbic regions; and gamma brain waves are enhanced. Transient hypofrontality and its benefits have been correlated to expanded states of consciousness, including those induced through meditation and Conscious Breathing (Rhinewine & Williams, 2007).

Group 5 Breathwork is supported by the other four groups. Employing targeted therapeutic techniques from Group 3, for example, can stabilize mental and emotional regulation. Specific human qualities developed through Group 4 practices can help cultivate capacity for doing inner work. It's widely reported that Group 5 Breathwork practices surface information from both our conscious and unconscious mind; grant greater access to emotions, including those cellularly embedded; and bring awareness to nonordinary or expanded states of consciousness (Aideyan et al., 2020).

Each Group 5 Breathwork school and technique tends to have its own focus and methods. Most often, Breathers begin lying down. They are invited to relax, bring attention to their interior self, and breathe deeply and continuously. Many Breathers enter states of expanded consciousness by simply breathing deeper than usual while maintaining a normal rate, with some increasing their breathing rate as the experience intensifies, much like women in labor. This is what I and many other teachers recommend. However, there are also many teachers and schools that suggest breathing faster than normal from the beginning.

Almost every Group 5 Breathwork method recommends continuous breathing (breathing without pausing between inhalation and exhalation, and vice versa), often called Conscious Connected Breathing (CCB) and sometimes called cyclical breathing. Deeper than normal inhalations followed by relaxed exhalations, characteristic of CCB, gained scientific support by Spiegel, Huberman, and colleagues. Their 2023 study showed that *cyclical sighing* is the breathing technique most effective for positive mood, anxiety reduction, and long-term state changes when compared to Box Breathing, cyclical hyperventilation (fast breathing periods alternating with slow breathing or breath retention), or Mindfulness Meditation. Cyclical sighing is done by inhaling nasally a little deeper than usual; then pulling in a second segment of breath on that same inhale; and then sighing out a prolonged exhale through the mouth (Balban et al., 2023).

Four general breathing approaches can be utilized variably for Group 5 Breathwork:

- Breathing at normal rates, yet deeper with some effort on the inhales and completely relaxed exhales.
- Breathing deeply at slower than normal rates with attention on particular features such as completely relaxed exhales or relaxing the jaw and breathing through the mouth.
- Breathing at faster than normal rates, usually with gently efforted inhales and relaxed exhales. However, some schools teach rapid, forceful inhales and/or rapid, forceful exhales. Accelerated breathing rates with relaxed exhalations can more readily activate both sympathetic and parasympathetic pathways and accelerate integration when combined with awareness. Concerns are regularly expressed that this method could lead to respiratory alkalosis or hyperventilation through overbreathing. Yet researchers, therapists, and Breathworkers regularly observe that when accelerated breathing is voluntary, the dysregulations and imbalances associated with involuntary overbreathing don't occur (Eyerman, 2013), or lead to important emotional expression, insights and memories.
- Breathing deeper than normal at natural breathing rates initially, which can then fluctuate between slow and fast rates many times during a session.

When Breathers begin breathing rapidly as emotions and memories arise, often movement only occurs in their chest or upper chest rather than around the diaphragm. My colleague and friend Shirley Telles, PhD (arguably the foremost yoga and breath researcher in the world, with over 260 publications) and I hypothesize it's because the body's natural intelligence may not want to overbreathe, yet wants to continue experiencing something intense and internal. The breathing knows what to do. Shirley teaches that overriding that impulse and forcing ourselves to breathe deeper fast diaphragmatic breaths for long periods—which could deplete our carbon dioxide—repeatedly over time could reduce our carbon dioxide sensitivity and heighten air hunger and anxiety patterns (Telles, 2023).

Whatever methodology is employed, the goals are similar—accessing potential and deep resources; creating and holding space for whatever physical, emotional, cognitive, or spiritual healing is needed for actualizing potential; and cultivating internal conditions that support extraordinary physical, emotional, cognitive, and spiritual capacities. Two primary orientations are used:

1. Breathees enter Group 5 Breathwork without a focus or goal and attend to whatever arises during the session. This method often reveals previously unrecognized somatic phenomena, such as jaw or belly tightness, or bodily numbness, and it can access the unconscious. Soma and psyche structures can be developed that support living with more spontaneity and trust in meeting changes, challenges, and the unknown. Breathing with an open-ended orientation, without tweaking, is our most fertile doorway for contacting and understanding the defended self and experiencing our authentic self.
2. Breathees focus on specific physical, emotional, cognitive, or spiritual issues such as transforming shame, relationship challenges, engaging a problem, anger at the Divine, and so on. Anthony Abbagnano calls this orientation *Applied Breathwork* and uses it extensively at Alchemy of Breath Academy. He shared with me in conversation:

> Identifying the issue, like forgiveness, clearing the ancestral lineage, or turning a relationship around, and bringing breath to it, moves the mind out of cyclical patterns and yields data not available otherwise. Intention can build pathways of hope, possibility, and vision when dealing with depression, anxiety, or trauma. Experiencing how focusing helps, brings empowerment.

Group 5 Breathwork is exceptional in its capacity to elicit emotions, expression, memories, and expanded states of consciousness. Dr. Mary E. Blue, neuroscientist and certified Breathworker, theorizes that Group 5 Breathwork practices in particular have "the potential to help 'normalize' or establish new connections" by consciously engaging two major limbic circuits responsible for unconscious and drive-related functions with areas of the cortex involved in more conscious functions. In our discussions she shared:

> Perhaps when memories are recovered in Breathwork sessions, because the person is cognitively engaged in breathing consciously, the "memory" can be understood in a more adult way. Likewise, the olfactory and gustatory (taste) systems are highly connected to amygdala and hippocampal circuitry and could account for the odors and tastes that people may experience and the associations we often make with certain odors and memories.

Group 5 Breathwork can quickly make Breathees aware of dissociated somatic sensations, disowned or suppressed emotions, memories we've put out of our conscious awareness, and recognitions and insights we've hidden from any time in our life. With guidance from well-trained Therapist-Breathworkers, the emergence of these memories or feelings can be met with the awareness and resources of our adult selves.

Expanded states of consciousness frequently arise in Human Potential Breathwork. A 2024 study concluded that CCB, which is the basis of most Human Potential Breathwork, occasioned beneficial spiritual and consciousness states as well as or better than doses of psilocybin (Bahi et al., 2024). (Chapter 14 contains more detail about Breathwork and psychedelics.)

Expanded states of consciousness and emotional release often include bliss. Bliss is wonderful, and here's to feeling more of it! However, we can become addicted to expanded states and emotional release in Breathwork, chasing bliss as the goal, similar to extreme sport athletes becoming addicted to flow experiences and generating flow hacks to enter the zone. Bliss states usually include considerable dopamine releases. For both athletes and Breathees, one danger of addiction to bliss states is that it can obfuscate deeper possibilities within flow and the potential to elicit a greater nuance, sophisticated personal development, self-awareness, self-knowledge, and self-actualization. We will explore many variants of expanded states and how to integrate them throughout this book.

Shirley Telles and her team examine Sanskrit verses of ancient yogic texts syllable by syllable for meticulous translation. They found that in ancient times, yogis and rishis did conscious volitional overbreathing, to the point of washing out carbon dioxide and suspending breathing in order to evoke unusual sensations and focus completely on what they were feeling, seeing, and hearing (Telles, 2023). This phenomenon happens in Group 5 Breathwork; after breathing very deeply for a while, breathing may spontaneously cease for up to several minutes and we may consciously or unconsciously focus immersively on internally arising phenomenon.

Scores of Breathwork practitioners, organizations, and schools use various orientations and emphases in facilitating Human Potential Breathwork. These include: Integrative Breathing (as facilitated at Inspiration Consciousness School), Therapeutic Breathwork (as facilitated at Transformations), and other styles such as Clarity Breathwork, Biodynamic Breathwork, Holotropic Breathwork, Liberation Breathing, Source Breathwork, Rebirthing, and Transformational Breath.

The potency of these techniques was a primary factor that prompted the formation of the Global Professional Breathwork Alliance (GPBA), which established training standards and ethics for this level of Breathwork across orientations. To find GPBA Certified Professional and ethically compliant Breathworkers and schools go to breathworkalliance.com.

Every way of breathing is a way of being.
—MARK WALSH

A Breathee Using All Five Breathwork Groups

Ava shares: I thought I'd never feel free of the thoughts and sensations that plagued me from sexual abuse I suffered in my home from ages 7 to 12. I thought the best I could do was manage them more confidently and calmly. Doing breathing in yoga classes piqued my curiosity to learn more, and I now use practices from all five groups. Group 1 practices induce immediate physical and emotional tension release. Group 2 prac-

tices help me make peace with my body in ways I couldn't for most of my life. Coherent Breathing from Group 3 helps me process and integrate both good and bad experiences. Group 4 Breathing Practices help me feel more capable, empowered, and resourceful. Integrative Breathing (Group 5) has helped me express and release huge amounts of repressed emotions. Sometimes I move so deeply into the energy and vibrancy flowing through me during Integrative Breathing that I no longer identify with the abuse. Many days, I never think about abuse. My life is about moving forward.

> *She had a revolutionary idea: she would make more time for life's truly important things. First on the list: breathing.*
>
> —AMY RUBIN

FOUR

The Mystical Science of Breathing, Cellular Respiration, and Conscious Breathing

Cowritten with Dr. Mary E. Blue

MANY BREATHERS, Breathworkers, and psychotherapists have deep curiosity about the scientific basis for the miraculous nature of breathing and Breathwork that we have been discovering. Understanding these physical processes can help maximize Breathwork's benefits; identify appropriate applications; and validate its physical, psychological, spiritual, and philosophical effects.

Breathing—the physical act of moving air in and out of the lungs, and respiration—the biochemical process of converting air into energy, are interconnected processes that connect us, via the electrons we exchange, with all life. Breathing is magnificent—wonderfully simple in its largely automatic functioning, while utilizing fantastically complex physiological mechanisms that generate myriad impacts on the body and brain. Conscious awareness and specific physiological engagements with breathing can create awe-inspiring physiological effects. Most books on Breathwork now include some science, usually focusing on a few aspects like anatomy, heart rate variability (HRV), or sympathetic/parasympathetic processes. This chapter is an attempt, perhaps lofty, to deliver basic understanding about 12 physiological effects of breathing, with an even more lofty goal of contemplating all 12 functions working together to expand our appreciation for breathing's power, intelligence, and magic.

We have rigorously ensured that the scientific information presented here is from evidence-based, peer-reviewed research. These 12 breathing vectors are explored: cellular respiration and energy exchange; respiratory anatomy; gas exchange and filtering; pH; brain anatomy; neurotransmitters; sympathetic, parasympathetic, and brain stem; the vagus nerve (VN) and the polyvagal response; HRV; brain waves; microbiome and exposome; and Conscious Breathing (CB). The final section integrates all 12 processes during inhalation and exhalation.

Enjoy the beauty and illumination of this science-based journey into breathing.

Cellular Respiration and Energy Exchange

Oxygen becomes present within us mostly through breathing, and it's the culminating factor in generating energy for us to live and act. Thus, if mind, awareness, and consciousness are, as Dan Siegel proposes, the flow of energy and information... and energy flow is the integrating factor that unifies instinctual, relational, and cognitive information and functioning... and breathing generates that energy, then some understanding of the biological mechanisms that facilitate breathing and its production of energy could empower our use of Breathwork for awareness, integration, and wholeness.

Energy is embodied through electrons, which drive both the fueling and functioning of bodily processes. Cellular respiration requires transferring electrons between our molecules, enabled by oxygen flow. When oxygen moves into our cells' mitochondria—the powerhouses that ultimately manufacture energy in a molecule called ATP (adenosine triphosphate)—electrons from sugars move gradually, like an electrical current, through the electron transport chain (ETC) toward molecular oxygen, releasing energy (ATP) at the end. To maintain cellular homeostasis when energy levels are high the ETC slows, and when energy levels are low the ETC speeds up.

During inhalation, oxygen journeys through our lungs into our blood where the protein hemoglobin transfers oxygen to other tissues/cells for cellular respiration. Oxygen is the culminating electron acceptor in our internal ecosystem, producing the energy for life. Some unicellular organisms, like bacteria, archaea, some viruses, and perhaps some loriciferans, thrive without oxygen, tending to use metals to share or "dump" their electrons to conduct electricity quite well. However, increased levels of complexity in multicellular organisms require oxygen because it's a more efficient energy producer. Thus, as oceanic and atmospheric oxygen levels increased, life forms and their evolution exponentially expanded.

> Oxygen is a highly responsive element that is eager to experience—including experiencing electrons!

Breathing Anatomy

Each breath in (inhalation) fills our lungs with about 500 ml (about 2 cups) of air, weighing about 0.022 ounces. Breathing out (exhalation) releases the same amount of air. Both inhalation and exhalation utilize the mouth, nose, pharynx (throat), larynx (voice box), trachea (windpipe), lungs, diaphragm, ribs, and intercostal muscles.

The diaphragm is a thin, curved skeletal muscle separating the abdomen and chest. In front it attaches to the triangular section at the bottom of the sternum (xiphoid process) and the costal (front wall) surface of the lung, on the sides to the bottom two ribs, and in back to the lower spine, in an overall dome shape with the dome's top reaching upward. During inhalation, the diaphragm contracts, flattens, and moves downward—gently moving and massaging our internal organs, and increasing our chest cavity space for lung expansion (see Figure 6.1). The muscles between our ribs (intercostal muscles) also enlarge the chest cavity by contracting and pulling the rib cage upward and outward during inhalation. The increased space allows lung size expansion, inviting in air. During exhalation, the diaphragm and intercostal muscles relax, the chest cavity reduces, and our lungs deflate like a balloon releasing air.

To protect the lungs, nasal hairs and microscopic hairs (cilia) in the air passages filter out large particles from air. Cilia can be damaged or even eliminated by stressors like cigarette smoking and air pollution (Cao et al., 2020). When debris in the air like viruses, pollutants, dust, bacteria, and allergenic substances get past the filtering system, mucus produced in the trachea and bronchial tubes helps us either cough them out or swallow them. Constant breathing puts us in contact with air, gasses, and components of life in our physical environment—both healthy and unhealthy.

Air enters through the nose and/or mouth, moving through the pharynx (throat), larynx (voice box), and trachea (windpipe) into the lungs. Interestingly, both biologically and metaphorically, the two lungs are asymmetrical, with the right lung having three lobes, whereas the left has two. The right lung is slightly shorter than the left, making room for the liver; the left lung is smaller, with a little notch to make room for the heart where the third lobe would be.

The trachea (windpipe) is the entrance to the lungs. Beginning at the back of the throat, it runs behind the sternum (breastbone) and divides into two channels (bronchi), with one channel (bronchus) entering each lung. Each bronchus divides into branches called bronchioles, each division becoming narrower and shorter. The whole system remarkably resembles a tree's complex root system. Near the trachea, the smooth muscle of the thicker bronchi is supported by cartilage that prevents collapse. As bronchioles get smaller, cartilage proportions gradually decrease until there is only muscle. After about 16 divisions, deeper in the lungs, little sacs (alveoli), about 0.3 millimeters or one hundredth of an inch in diameter, appear on bronchioles, with concentrations gradually increasing until each bronchiole culminates in clusters of alveoli. There are approximately 500 million tiny alveoli! If the lung tissue were spread into a thin homogeneous layer, it would be about 70 square meters—about one quarter of a tennis court!

Incredibly bouncy lungs!

Gas Exchange

Nearly every bodily function—digesting food, thinking, running—requires oxygen and produces carbon dioxide (CO_2). Therefore, air we inhale has higher concentrations of oxygen and lower concentrations of CO_2 than air we exhale. The primary function of the lungs is gas exchange—O_2 is absorbed from air into our blood and CO_2 is released into the air.

The lungs' magic of infusing and energizing the bloodstream with oxygen from air, then filtering CO_2 from the blood and transporting it outside where it nourishes plant life, occurs in the alveoli. During inhalation, oxygen passes through alveoli walls into capillaries, where it binds with hemoglobin in red blood cells. Red blood cells transport the fresh oxygen to the heart's left side, where it's pumped throughout the body's arteries, arterioles, and capillaries, facilitating rapid exchange between blood and tissue. Deoxygenated blood is pumped through veins to the heart's right side, and then the lungs, where CO_2 moves through alveolar walls to be exhaled.

INHALED AIR	EXHALED AIR
78% nitrogen	78% nitrogen
21% oxygen	16% oxygen
1% inert gas such as argon	1% inert gas such as argon
0.04% CO_2	5% CO_2
little water vapor	saturated with water vapor

Factors like humidity, altitude, and deep breathing capacity may shift these concentrations.

Breathing is a powerful, intimate exchange with our life conditions!

pH

Bodies need a precise and constant balance of both alkaline and acidic components (called pH or acid-base balance) to perform myriad, complex functions. Even minor deviations from normal pH can severely affect organ function. Efficiency and optimization of gas exchange during breathing is a principal way to rapidly control pH.

Respiration controls pH by regulating the amount of carbonic acid

(H_2CO_3) that is formed from CO_2 and water (H_2O) in our blood. The enzyme carbonic anhydrase in the lungs reverses the reaction, turning H_2CO_3 into CO_2 to be exhaled. Chemoreceptors in the aortic walls and carotid arteries will note excess blood CO_2, generating more carbonic acid to lower the blood's pH (making it more acidic) and signaling the brain stem, which immediately instigates faster and deeper breathing (respiratory compensation) to expel more CO_2. Extremely acid pH can cause symptoms like nausea, vomiting, headache, confusion, fatigue, and in severe cases kidney distress, chronic pulmonary obstructive disease (COPD), pneumonia, heart failure, or coma.

When blood has insufficient CO_2, pH rises (becoming more alkaline), respiration slows, and the kidneys absorb excess bicarbonate. Alkaline pH can be volitionally induced by increasing relaxed exhales, pausing after each exhalation, and even pinching our nose so CO_2 levels can build. In acute cases, breathing into a bag can build CO_2. Extreme alkalinity can cause dizziness; lightheadedness; confusion; numbness or tingling in the face, hands, or feet; muscle spasms (tetany); and nausea and vomiting.

> Breathing supports elegant interplays
> of balance and complexity!

Brain Anatomy

The nervous system anatomy is divided into two parts—the central nervous system (CNS) and the peripheral nervous system (PNS).

The CNS includes:

- The spinal cord and brain (brain stem, cerebellum, thalamus, forebrain), which are composed of neurons and glial cells. Typical neurons consist of a nucleus or cell body, dendrites, and an axon. Dendrites receive information coming from other neurons, and axons transmit signals to connected neurons.
- Neurons talk with one other at synapses, microscopic gaps where

neuronal axons communicate (presynaptic site) via electrochemical transmission with dendrites (postsynaptic site) of another neuron.
- Glial cells form networks surrounding neurons and neuronal processes. Three major types of glia are astrocytes, which directly surround neurons, support neuronal metabolism, and prevent neuronal overexcitation; microglial cells, which clean up neural cellular debris, perform immune surveillance, and participate in neuroinflammatory processes; and oligodendrocytes, which myelinate axons in the CNS for faster communication between neurons and targets. Astrocytes likely facilitate breathing through metabolic support of rhythm-generating cells in the brain stem that detect hypoxia (low oxygen) and CO_2 levels. "Exploring astrocytes' role could inspire new understandings of respiration and health" (Del Negro et al., 2018).

The PNS includes:

- Sensory receiving cells from the body's muscles, skin, and mucous membranes (somatosensory), ear (hearing), nose (smell), and tongue (taste). (Due to its embryological origin, the eye [vision] is part of the CNS.)
- The autonomic nervous system (ANS) that controls activity of smooth muscles, glands, viscera, blood vessels, and the immune system. It's divided into sympathetic and parasympathetic systems acting reciprocally with each other and with other tissues and organs. The sympathetic nervous system (SNS) arises from neurons in the thoracic (mid) and lumbar (lower) regions of the spinal cord, while the parasympathetic nervous system (PSN) arises from sacral (base) spinal cord and brain stem neurons.

Following the order of brain development in utero, science generally defines the major brain areas as:

- The brain stem (the medulla, pons, and variably, the midbrain).
- The diencephalon (largely the thalamus and hypothalamus).
- The forebrain (basal ganglia that facilitate action and motivation, the

hippocampus that encodes memories, the amygdala that processes fear and threat assessment, the olfactory bulb for smell which provides critical information for all these processes, and the cerebral cortex [neocortex] that is responsible for conscious perception and action).

All nervous system components impact each other!
Breathing brings unity to all aspects of ourselves!

Neurotransmitters

Neurotransmitters are chemicals used to mediate communication between neurons and target cells in muscles, glands, or other nervous system cells. Sensory receiving cells in the skin, nose, tongue, ear, eye, and muscles utilize the amino acid glutamate to excite their target neurons in the CNS. Glutamate also excites neurons within CNS circuits in the processes of breathing, learning, memory, and plasticity, the brain's ability to change or adapt to change. Other amino acid transmitters, gamma-aminobutyric acid (GABA) and glycine, inhibit or de-energize neurons locally within a specific brain region and modify the degree of excitation. Respiratory circuits principally use these amino acid transmitters.

The monoamine neurotransmitter acetylcholine (ACh) is released at the neuromuscular junction, leading to contraction of muscles (for breathing: diaphragm, intercostal, and abdominal muscles). ACh also is the major neurotransmitter used in the ANS, where it facilitates the actions of different glands and viscera. Monoamine transmitters modulate respiratory circuits and impact respiratory control. They include the catecholamines (epinephrine, norepinephrine, dopamine) and serotonin.

- Epinephrine (adrenaline), produced in the adrenal gland, can increase blood sugar levels, heart rate, and the degree of heart contraction (contractility), and mediate smooth muscle relaxation in airways to improve breathing.
- Norepinephrine (NE) acts as a hormone in the SNS ganglia, located close to the thoracic and lumbar spinal cord. When the body needs to respond immediately, these ganglia stimulate release of NE

from the inner part of the adrenal gland into the blood. NE then causes constriction in blood vessels (vasoconstriction), leading to increased blood pressure, which in turn increases the rate and depth of breathing. NE-containing neurons in the midbrain (locus coeruleus) are exquisitely sensitive to CO_2 levels, and their activity increases during inhalation and decreases during exhalation (Melnychuk et al., 2018). Indeed, NE modulates neuronal and glial function to maintain optimal brain function and alertness.

- Dopamine (DA) inhibits NE release and dilates blood vessels. DA affects ventilation, pulmonary circulation, bronchial diameter, lung water clearance, and sensory pulmonary nerve modulation. DA benefits breathing by improving respiratory muscle function and preventing or minimizing fluid retention or swelling (edema). Bringing attention to breathing in meditation practices increases DA release in basal ganglia (Kjaer et al., 2002). However, too much DA inhibits ventilation (Ciarka et al., 2007).

- Serotonin (5-hydroxytryptamine) performs multiple actions. In the body, 95% of serotonin is likely produced in the gastrointestinal (GI) tract (O'Mahony et al., 2015), making it the principal neurotransmitter in the enteric nervous system. Brain stem clusters of serotonergic neurons form specific raphe nuclei, whose axons form extensive networks throughout brain structures like the hypothalamus, basal ganglia, hippocampus, cerebral cortex, olfactory bulb (involved in smell), and brain stem nuclei. This widespread innervation pattern reflects serotonin's multiple actions on mood, appetite, sleep, and cognitive functions like learning, memory, and depression (Perreau-Linck et al., 2007). Serotonin also affects ANS circuits linked to breathing, especially CO_2/pH balance. During seizures, when respiration is diminished, the firing rate of serotonergic neurons that modulate respiration declines markedly (Zhan et al., 2016). Serotonin is structurally like LSD, psilocybin, and mescaline (Johnson, 2019), and hallucinogen administration leads to altered states of consciousness sometimes experienced in Breathwork sessions.

Gratitude for neurotransmitters!

Brain Stem, Sympathetic, and Parasympathetic Control of Respiration

Typical inhalations involve active diaphragm and external intercostal muscle contractions, followed by their passive relaxation during exhalation. Between inspiration and exhalation is the postinspiration (PI) period, which normally occurs except during sleep or anesthesia. Postinspiration periods support vocalization, when expiratory airflow is precisely regulated by the diaphragm, upper airway muscles, and vocal cords to produce sounds. Speaking becomes more difficult with high metabolic demand during active expiration—with breathing speeding up and thoracic and abdominal muscles actively expelling air.

Breathing control utilizes two processes—rhythm generation and pattern generation. Rhythm-generating mechanisms control breathing frequency while central pattern generators regulate lung volume and coordinate activation of upper airway (nose, mouth, throat) and respiratory pump muscles. Rhythm and pattern generation can be separate or interdependent, with breathing rhythm manipulations affecting pattern generation and vice versa.

The respiratory cycle's main driver and central pattern generator is the "inexorable" preBötzinger Complex (preBötC) (Feldman et al., 2013; Del Negro et al., 2018 [Figure 4.1]). The preBötC activates brain stem clusters of inspiratory neurons (premotor nuclei) that stimulate inspiratory motor neurons (peripheral cranial and spinal cord nerves) that contract inspiratory muscles. The preBötC sends axons to other premotor neurons in the medulla that directly or indirectly drive inspiratory pump and airway resistance muscles, and inspiratory cranial nerve XII neurons (Yang & Feldman, 2018). Recent studies indicate that preBötC neurons modulate parasympathetic neuron and sympathetic vasomotor neuron activity in the heart, generating heart rate and blood pressure oscillations in phase with respiration (Menuet et al., 2020).

During PI, diaphragm muscle contraction lengthens, and larynx muscles at the top of our throat move toward our body's midline, preventing lung deflation. The PI benefits gas exchange by increasing the time air spends in the lungs, while decreasing the likelihood of airway collapse

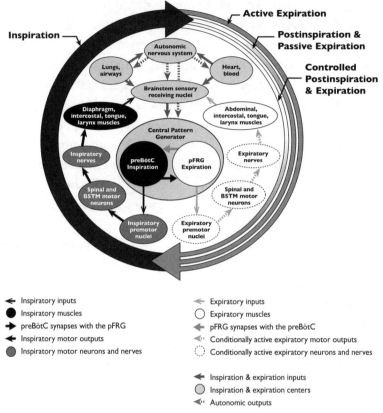

FIGURE 4.1: Respiratory Cycle: Organs, Brain Centers, Connections. Inspiration is the consistently essential phase of the breath cycle, whereas expiration can be variably active or passive. The central pattern generator for inspiration, which drives each breath, is the preBötzinger nucleus (preBötC). The preBötC receives inputs from various organs and systems involved in both inspiration and expiration, including the inspiratory muscles and the autonomic nervous system (ANS). It sends outputs to inspiratory premotor nuclei, brainstem (BSTM) motor and spinal neurons, and nerves that activate inspiratory muscles. After inspiration, there is often a postinspiration (PI) period followed by passive exhalation, where the inspiratory muscles relax. When expiration becomes active, the parafacial respiratory group (pFRG) is activated, exciting expiratory premotor nuclei, BSTM motor and spinal neurons, and nerves that contract expiratory muscles. Conscious control of breathing can extend the PI period.
Jessica Dibb and Mary Blue

by promoting smooth, nonturbulent expiratory airflow (Del Negro et al., 2018). Modulation of airway resistance (i.e., the degree to which resistance to airflow is impacted by turbulence and airway diameter) during PI facilitates coughing, swallowing, and vocalizing safely (Del Negro et al., 2018).

While expiration is normally passive, with increasing demand for oxygen during exercise, at high altitude, or during SNS activation, expiration becomes active. Active expiration is also required for voluntary and emotional actions like laughing, crying, and playing musical instruments. The parafacial respiratory group (pFRG; also called the retrotrapezoid nucleus) in the brain stem drives active expiration during increased metabolic need and REM sleep (Del Negro et al., 2018). Rhythmic bursting of pFRG neurons activates brain stem expiratory premotor nuclei that stimulate spinal cord expiratory motor neurons that contract abdominal (expiratory pump) muscles and internal intercostal muscles that aid expiration.

Centers located above the brain stem control intentional or volitional activities where breathing is involved in speaking, breath-holding, conscious hyperventilation, and emotions like crying, sighing, and laughing. Feedback from stretch receptor neurons senses and regulates the contraction and expansion of airway smooth muscle, affecting breathing too. When lungs inflate, lung stretch receptors inhibit preBötC activity, concluding inspiration, and pFRG neurons are excited, leading to expiratory muscle contraction. Conversely, when lungs deflate, the preBötC is again excited and the pFRG is inhibited (Feldman et al., 2013).

> Breathing energizes a sophisticated community
> of communication and resource sharing!

The Autonomic Nervous System

The ANS regulates the body's unconscious actions, including cardiac and pulmonary breathing rhythms, with the SNS and PSN working together. It supports optimal breathing practice to know that **SNS and PSN are both operating at all times,** even when one is dominant. The SNS facilitates an initiating energy that prepares for engagement with internal and external actions, including actively thinking, navigating stress, and perceived and real threats to survival. When the SNS is dominant, heart rate increases, bronchial passages dilate, blood pressure increases, and goosebumps and sweat appear, while nonessential activities like digestion are dampened. The SNS supports inhalation. Boosting and optimizing SNS functioning, flexibility, and energy supports inspiration, increases energy, increases mental alertness, helps handle emergencies, and more. The SNS can be activated by:

- Inhaling and exhaling orally
- Breathing faster than normal, nasally or orally
- Generating longer inhalations than exhalations

In contrast, the PSN facilitates gathering energy for nourishment, restoration, and maintaining well-being. Boosting PSN activity lowers heart and respiration rates and increases digestion. Enhancing PSN energy can help us release stress, be present to ourselves and others, digest, improve cardiac and respiratory functioning, reduce anxiety, and increase vagal tone. The PSN can be activated by:

- Inhaling and exhaling nasally
- Breathing slower than normal, nasally or orally
- Generating longer exhalations (optimally twice) than inhalations
- Sighing, humming, or singing when exhaling

The autonomic nervous system—a matrix for safety, homeostasis, and well-being in action and rest!

The Vagus Nerve and Polyvagal Response

The vagus nerve (VN; *vagus* means wandering in Latin)—the 10th and longest cranial nerve—is the principal motor component for PSN activation. Yet that only accounts for 20% of its neurons; the other 80% are primarily sensory neurons that transmit thoracic and abdominal cavity information to the brain, a process called interoception. The ears, larynx, esophagus,

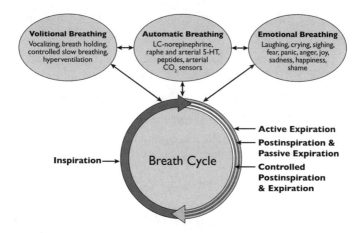

FIGURE 4.2: Types of Breathing and Modulators. Volitional breathing (bringing awareness to the breath and controlling the rate of respiration and activities such as vocalizing); automatic breathing modulators such as neurotransmitters and their receptors along with cardiac, respiratory, and autonomic sensors; and emotional breathing (laughing, crying, sighing, and other emotions) reciprocally affect the breath cycle and breathing behaviors.

Jessica Dibb and Mary Blue

bronchi, diaphragm, heart, stomach, intestines, and other organs send interoceptive information to the VN, which sends it to the brain.

In terms of breathing, the VN provides the major sensory input from the lungs, trachea, glottis, tongue, pharynx, and larynx to the brain. VN sensory neurons monitor airway stretch and inflation, dust, pollen, food, and mechanical force, and so on (Prescott & Liberles, 2022). The VN sends its sensory input to the medulla (brain stem sensory receiving nuclei), which in turn travels to the preBötC. The VN also carries information about gas exchange and blood pressure from chemosensors and baroreceptors and for maintaining optimal lung volumes.

Behavioral neuroscientist and developmental psychophysiologist Stephen Porges proposed the Polyvagal Theory to explain how the VN mediates our body's stress response. Though scientific evidence for the Polyvagal Theory does not meet rigorous scientific criteria for this chapter, we include it here because its framework has proven tremendously beneficial clinically. According to Polyvagal Theory, the dorsal vagal complex (DVC) is a phylogenetically older branch, meaning it has an older evolutionary history (think reptiles, amphibians, etc.), and the ventral vagal complex (VVC) is a more recent evolutionary development consisting of myelinated nerves that provide faster responses. The DVC is connected to vital organs below the diaphragm like the intestines. Under severe stress, it activates the primitive freeze response. The VVC is connected to organs above the diaphragm like the esophagus, bronchi, larynx, and heart, as well as facial muscles. It influences social engagement and the release of oxytocin, and mediates feelings of connection and well-being.

The Polyvagal Theory suggests that the VN exerts braking action on these parts of the body in response to physical and psychological stress. The brake is activated to recruit the PSN to maintain or restore homeostasis—cortisol levels decline, heart and respiration rates lessen, and relaxation is experienced. The brake is deactivated when the SNS takes charge—epinephrine (adrenaline) and NE are released, heart and respiration rates increase, and fight-or-flight survival mechanisms are activated.

Vagal tone refers to VN activity. Because the VN affects breathing, and information travels both ways in the VN, breathing consciously may increase vagal tone. Changes in heart rate variability (HRV) associated with breathing (respiratory sinus arrhythmia) are parasympathetically (vagally) mediated when breathing rates are in typical frequency ranges. A study (six participants) in which breathing rates varied during PSN and SNS blockades showed that HRV changes occurring during slow-paced breathing were essentially vagally mediated (Kromenacker et al., 2018). Bringing awareness to breathing activates the insula and cingulate cortex, reducing sympathetic activity (Strigo & Craig, 2016). In this way, CB can lighten some limiting or defensive behaviors of the SNS. Through respiratory biofeedback, slow breathing techniques will increase VN activity and enhance relaxation, which helps explain Breathing Practices' overall benefits for health and well-being. HRV and higher brain centers come into play to elicit beneficial consciousness shifts.

Breathing wants us to feel well!

Heart Rate Variability

Heart rate variability is the fluctuation in time intervals between heartbeats. The more optimal our HRV, the more readily we can engage with life. A less optimal HRV suggests a higher than optimal stress response and a lower-functioning or dysregulated ANS. Generally, a greater amount of HRV correlates with higher health status, resilience, lower risk of future adverse events, and better self-regulatory capacity. Lower HRV usually translates into depletion, lower resilience, and poorer health (Appelhans & Luecken, 2006). Optimal HRV is age-related. Healthy people have more HRV when young, which decreases with age.

The capacity to flow harmoniously and adjust readily from arousal to rest, rest to focus, focus to imagining, imagining to concentration, concentration to playing, playing to meal preparation, meal preparation to listening to a friend or partner's fears, and responding in emergencies, demonstrates presence with life's changes. A healthy HRV helps us be adaptable, resilient, and able to self-regulate. We can process our emotions more easily and pay attention to what matters. HRV is a helpful, inspiring metaphor and measure for journeying toward wholeness and well-being.

Rollin McCraty and colleagues at HeartMath Institute have demonstrated HRV's contribution to breathing processes and practices, and vice versa, by studying coherence in various psychophysiological contexts. Their findings indicate that "coherence within and among the physiological, cognitive, and emotional systems is critical in the creation and maintenance of health, emotional stability, and optimal performance" and that "the heart, as the most powerful generator of rhythmic information patterns in the body, acts effectively as the global conductor in the body's symphony to bind and synchronize the entire system" (McCraty et al., 2009).

Studies at HeartMath, Harvard, and other research facilities consistently show that HRV is optimized when breathing about six breaths per minute (Coherent Breathing), though wider ranges of four to seven breaths per minute apply for some people. I recommend studying HRV in relation to self-regulated breathing to further maximize its benefits.

Breathing endows us with grace and grit!

Brain Waves: Reflections of Neuronal Activity and Coherence

For brain, heart, and respiratory activity to function coherently, neural activity needs to be stable and coordinated to receive, transmit, learn, and remember information. Brain centers that control these functions must synchronize their activity so that needed information from various sources can be processed and perceived together in the present. Fragmented information bits are joined and organized into coherent activity that presumably underlies conscious experience.

The electroencephalogram (EEG) records large-scale electrical neural activity, offering windows into the macro-scale organization of coordinated activity of different brain regions. For example, a single scalp electrode records the electrical activity of 100 million neurons on average (Nunez et al., 2015)!

Distinct frequency ranges, called brain waves, are observed in different brain states (Nunez et al., 2015) and based on neuronal cell firing frequencies ranging from 1 hertz (Hz; one neuron firing once per second) to 100 Hz. Our state of awareness changes the frequencies:

- **Delta** (0–4 Hz): Delta wave states are associated with slow-wave sleep (deep non-REM sleep) and the generation of empathy, healing, and regeneration while external awareness is suspended. Delta can also be accessed through meditation, breathing, and other practices.
- **Theta** (4–8 Hz): Theta wave states are associated with daydreaming and REM sleep, deep meditation, and inward focus. Theta states elicit vivid visualizations, great inspiration, profound creativity, and exceptional insight.
- **Alpha** (8–12 Hz): Alpha wave states are associated with free-flowing thoughts, calmness, and relaxation.
- **Beta** (12–16 Hz): Beta wave states are associated with normal wakeful states where attention is outwardly directed.

- **Gamma** (40–100 Hz): Gamma wave states are associated with cognitive functions, learning, and memory (Malik & Amin, 2017).

Global (whole-brain) EEGs show synchronous activity occurring when all frequency bands fire together. Awareness arises when specialized neurons, called intralaminar and medial thalamic nuclei (involved in higher-order functions such as arousal and consciousness), fire synchronously with enough other neural cortical networks. Deep within the brain, the thalamus plays an important monitoring role. Research shows slow breathing activating the thalamus and increasing breathing volume (Critchley et al., 2015). Thalamic activation is associated with degrees of felt breathlessness, suggesting that respiratory sensory information is gated by the thalamus (Chan et al., 2018). Studies have shown that CB may improve depression and improve mood by mediating changes in thalamic GABA levels (Streeter et al., 2020).

Breathing activates waves of consciousness!

Microbiome and Exposome

THE MICROBIOME

The human microbiome is composed of trillions of microorganisms that live on and in our bodies. Healthy human functioning is so dependent on these microorganisms that we're a supra-organism—one part human cells and one part nonhuman microorganisms, coevolving over millions of years.

The main communities of microbiota connected to breathing live in our respiratory and GI microbiomes. These two systems, and respective microbiomes, are intricately interconnected. Both are linked to respiratory health (Enaud et al., 2020). Reciprocally, GI and respiratory systems oxygen levels reflect the health of microbial communities within them (Ashley et al., 2020).

The GI tract includes the mouth (used in breathing sometimes), esophagus, stomach, small intestine, and large intestine. An imbalanced gut microbiome underlies wide ranges of illnesses including irritable bowel syndrome, inflammatory bowel disorder, colorectal cancer, obesity, tuberculosis, type-2 diabetes, cardiovascular disease, and even some psychiatric illnesses (Forsythe et al., 2016). Imbalances in gut microbiomes are linked to multiple lung disorders and respiratory infections, including asthma, COPD, pneumonia, cystic fibrosis, and lung cancer (Rapozo et al., 2017). Conversely, respiratory tract illnesses have been linked to gut microbiome composition changes. Specific crosstalk between gut microbiota and lungs is called the gut-lung axis.

Healthy lungs contain dynamic ecosystems of microorganisms, mostly along the upper respiratory tract's (URT) inner lining. Lung microbiome disturbances can produce asthma, allergies, interstitial lung disease, lung cancer, cystic fibrosis, and respiratory infections like pneumonia and tuberculosis (Hand et al., 2016). There's no real barrier between the air and the innermost lung, so lungs are constantly exposed to new microbes from outside through microaspirations of URT content and through mucus. Healthy lungs constantly clear unwanted debris through coughs, mucus, and cilia, and the alveoli are lined with surfactant that prevents some bacteria from reproducing, thus maintaining a relatively steady community of lung microorganisms.

While the lung microbiome consists of microbes derived from the mouth and throat, the nose microbiota is more insular. The mouth-lung axis is so strong that imbalance of the oral microbiome is linked to COPD onset and progression (Mammen & Sethi, 2016). It's already clear that balanced gut and respiratory microbiomes promote respiratory health and our ability to breathe well (Lloyd-Price et al., 2016).

Our microbiome compositions are shaped by intrinsic factors (age, race/ethnicity, gender, and genes) and extrinsic factors (diet, exercise, geography, antibiotics/prebiotics, and microbiota of close contacts, including pets). Also, microbes are present in utero. Through vaginal delivery and breastfeeding, babies' microbiomes are initially shaped by their mother's. Through touch, breathing, and food ingestion, babies continually absorb new microorganisms. Children's microbiomes start to stabilize by age three, becoming a unique, ever-changing microbial fingerprint that accompanies them through life.

THE EXPOSOME

In 2005, Dr. Christopher Paul Wild recognized the health impact of total environmental exposure—from conception throughout life—and named it the exposome. Exposome research may become as significant as human genome research. Wild identified three factors contributing to our unique exposome:

- The eco-exposome—external environmental stressors like climate, traffic, urban and green spaces, bug spray, brake fluid, skin creams, and so on.
- Our biological receptors, which include genetic and epigenetic pathways.
- The endo-exposome—internal and DNA impacts from nutrition, physical activity, hydration, smoking, and so on.

Several studies show significant correlation between stress, poor-quality exposome, and decreased lung function. Prior studies show that "pulmonary development in childhood is a key determinant for long-term respiratory function" and "low peak lung function in early adulthood is associated with a higher prevalence of respiratory, cardiovascular, and metabolic abnormalities in later life, and premature death" (Agier et al., 2019). Healthy breathing can have positive effects metabolically and epigenetically, so we can imagine that CB throughout life would positively benefit our health (Agache, 2019).

> **Breathing cultivates relationships with internal and external universes of trillions, maybe quadrillions!**

Conscious Breathing

CB has potent therapeutic, healing, and transformational effects:

- Engages and/or balances parasympathetic and sympathetic activity that favors deep relaxation and anxiety relief.
- Modulates serotonergic tone that impacts the brain stem centers, setting respiratory rate and action, and modulates hippocampus and amygdala activity for memory retrieval and emotional response.
- Facilitates HRV and coherence, thus enhancing neural synchronicities in higher brain centers involved in cognition.
- Enhances the somatic–emotional–cognitive continuum (SEC continuum) integration, improving overall well-being.

CB is linked to processes like attention, memory, and perception:

- Spontaneous breathing activates motor areas of the cortex involved in planning, initiating, and organizing movements. Bringing attention to breathing enhances activation in these motor regions as well as parietal and medial frontal gyrus regions that are involved in spatial reasoning and attention (Šmejkal et al., 1999).
- When attention to the rate of respiration is tied to a sound, parietal and temporal cortical areas that are involved in speech perception are activated (Šmejkal et al., 1999).
- Deepening or speeding up breathing leads to preferential activation of prefrontal cortex and striatum, areas of the brain involved in planning voluntary movements and associated with diaphragm contraction. These changes occur during inspiration (Evans et al., 1999).

Interestingly, increased rates of breathing and shorter inspiration periods are observed in participants who perform a cognitively challenging task (Evans et al., 2009). In this group, brain regions showing more activation compared to the spontaneously breathing group included the brain stem and limbic regions. The activation was directly tied to the respiratory cycle, and all regions activated were connected to respiratory centers in the brain stem. The ACC, which is involved in limbic cognitive functions like impulse control, decision making, emotion, and empathy, was activated more strongly and synchronized exquisitely with breath onset in the experimental group. A serotonergic nucleus in the medulla, the raphe magnus nucleus, also showed greater activation. The raphe magnus receives projections from the amygdala and insula and has a direct link to breathing (Besnard et al., 2009). This is significant as it provides evidence that the process of attention affects breathing and engages serotonergic control of respiration.

A real appreciation for the significance of the effects of breathing on conscious processes is emerging thanks to studies showing how respiration is regulated in set rhythms that engage the cortex and subcortical structures. EEG investigations have demonstrated mutual features in respiratory and brain networks underlying cognitive function, like attention, memory, and perception. One of the strongest linkages between respiration and memory is in the olfactory (smelling) system. We experience this direct link when a familiar odor elicits a memory or emotional response. This makes intuitive sense since breathing air through the nose excites olfactory receptors in the nostrils, and respiratory frequencies in the olfactory system occupy the same theta wave form as the hippocampus, which is important for encoding and retrieving memories (Heck et al., 2019).

When breathing is synchronized with input from the five senses, especially smell, a sequence of brain wave amplitude (heights of the waves) changes take place one after the other, creating "meaning-dependent cortical activity patterns," like pictures in a film that are associated with memory and learning (Heck et al., 2019). From this we can hypothesize that during CB when at least one if not more of the five senses is activated, we have greater access to imagery and memories, and arguably imagination.

Intracranial electroencephalogram (iEEG) recordings confirm that the coupling of respiration with brain wave activity is strongest with nasal breathing. This entrainment occurs during inhalation and dissipates during exhalation. Likewise, nasal breathing improves accuracy in cognitive test performance during inspiration. This coupling is lost when breathing is diverted solely to the mouth. However, importantly, breathing that is both nasal and oral exhibits responses like those of only nasal breathing (Zelano et al., 2016).

The iEEG studies also show:

- Bringing awareness to breathing creates greater coherence in brain wave and respiratory activity in motor, parietal, prefrontal, and limbic regions where coherent activity predominates in gray matter (mainly neurons), rather than white matter (mainly axons connecting neurons) (Herrero et al., 2018).

- With voluntary increased respiration rates (or hyperventilation), iEEG activity exhibits larger amplitudes and faster frequencies that are more strongly in sync with the respiratory rhythm than during spontaneous breathing. This coherence dissipates when breath returns to the normal rate (Herrero et al., 2018).
- Areas of the brain showing the greatest iEEG-breath coherence during fast breathing are frontal and superior temporal cortex, insula and amygdala, areas that also showed coherence during breathing at the normal rate, but the magnitude of the coherence increased with rapid breathing.
- The caudal medial frontal cortex, involved in executive function, is unique because it's recruited only during fast breathing. This finding along with MRI imaging results showing medial frontal gyrus recruitment with volitional control of breathing provide evidence that these regions, which support our highest cognitive functions like complex thought and executive control, are more fully engaged when breathing with awareness.
- Increased coherence in the insula is notable as the insula is pivotal in interoception (experiencing internal bodily sensations, including the perception of pain and pleasure, touch, and taste). Greater synchrony in the insula may support being present and having greater awareness and consciousness.
- The stronger coherence in amygdala activity with rapid breathing is consistent with increased respiratory rates in high-anxiety states. Possibly, voluntarily increasing the respiratory rate engages the alertness factors without anxiety.
- Accuracy in the performance of a task that involves bringing attention to the breath or inward attention to breathing is associated with increased iEEG-breath coherence in limbic regions including the anterior cingulate (ACC) and premotor cortex, insula, and hippocampus.

These findings are concordant with those in fMRI studies demonstrating stronger breath-neural activation in the ACC, insula, and hippocampus during the performance of a cognitive task and may account for the enhanced interoception in people practicing meditation or mindfulness. In terms of Breathwork, we note that hippocampal activation supports memory retrieval (Farb et al., 2013; Tang et al., 2010).

In summary, spontaneous breathing impacts neuronal circuits throughout the brain, driving specific neuronal circuits depending on the task. Controlling respiration by volition or attention shows coherent activity in overlapping yet distinct brain areas involved in each activity. This respiratory control links respiration and brain activity—with breathing rhythms being an organizing principle for cortical brain waves.

These results provide insight into possible brain mechanisms involved in therapeutic breathing experiences. In terms of Breathwork that induces memories, emotional expression, and expanded states of consciousness (Integrative Breathing, Therapeutic Breathwork, Holotropic Breathwork, Transformational Breath, etc.), the brain mechanisms engaged aren't fully known. Some possible factors emerge from studies on breath awareness, faster than normal breathing, and differentiations in brain waves and coherence. As more scientists personally experience this class of Breathwork, we hope they're inspired to explore physiological and neural mechanisms underlying their experience.

All Together in One Breath

We now have a wondrous opportunity to breathe with expanded awareness of the splendor, intelligence, and miraculousness of each breath. From a single organ or muscle's involvement in breathing ... to sophisticated communication and coherence in our anatomy and breathing processes ... to each breath's primordial force ... to the universe of communities of trillions, maybe more, of interdependent life forms within us—one breath is a profoundly multidimensional, psychedelic, intelligent, embodied experience.

Experience feeling, sensing, conceptualizing, imagining, and visualizing ALL 12 dynamics in each precious breath!

Breathe slowly and deeply while reading and experiencing . . . spontaneous (automatic) breathing. In each inhalation:

- The inexorable preBötC—breathing's central pattern generator—in the medulla, stimulates respiration and receives critical information about breathing muscles, airway conditions and activity, energy needs (ETC activity), current CO_2/O_2 balance, blood pressure, and cellular oxygen needs. The preBötC activates the brain stem inspiratory premotor nuclei that energize cranial and spinal cord neurons to contract the diaphragm and external intercostal muscles, opening the chest cavity for the lungs to expand and inhale air . . .
- Air moves through nasally and sometimes orally (nasally creates more nitric oxide to aid oxygen absorption), to the trachea, bronchial tubes, and lungs—contacting the microbiota lining these surfaces . . .
- Air (generally 78% oxygen, 21% nitrogen, 0.04% CO_2) reaches the alveoli where gas exchange oxygenates capillaries and hemoglobin proteins transfer oxygen (the culminating electron acceptor) to tissues for cellular respiration . . .
- Cardiac chemoreceptors constantly monitor CO_2 level, adjusting alkaline/acid (pH) levels to maintain physiological body homeostasis with our organs . . .
- Meanwhile, neurotransmitter acetylcholine facilitates diaphragm and intercostal contraction; epinephrine mediates airway relaxation of airway smooth muscle; NE supports blood vessel changes, affecting breathing rate and depth; DA enhances respiratory muscle function; and serotonin receptors within the brain moderate our felt sense of breathing and associated memories . . .
- Autonomic control engages: the SNS dilates our bronchial passages and energizes other processes; the PSN promotes relaxation, so we benefit from breathing effects . . .
- The VN receives signals with the ears, larynx, esophagus, bronchi, diaphragm, heart, stomach, intestines—modulating their activity

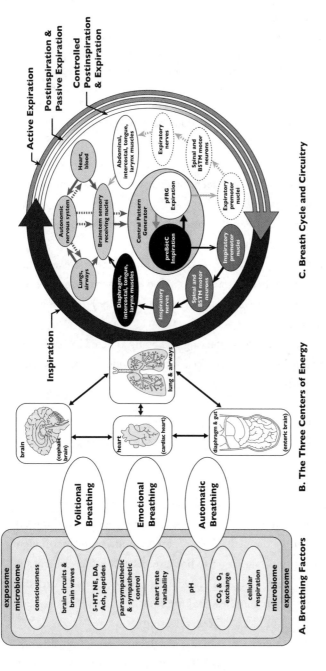

FIGURE 4.3: Putting It All Together in One Breath: Awareness and Being. A. Each breath is influenced by a continuum of factors from cellular respiration to consciousness, all affected by the microbiome, exposome, and whether breathing is voluntary, emotional, or automatic. B. Integrating the head, heart, and belly centers of energy allows for fully embodied breaths. C. The preBötzinger nucleus (preBötC) drives inspiration. After inspiration, there is often a postinspiration (PI) period followed by passive relaxation of the inspiratory muscles. More forceful breaths activate the expiratory muscles. Conscious control can extend the PI and exhalation phases of breathing.
Jessica Dibb and Mary Blue

while affecting and being affected by cortisol levels and mood and presence quality ...

- HRV supports by generating physiological, emotional, and cognitive coherence for presence and action ...
- Gamma, beta, alpha, theta, and delta brain waves are affecting and being affected by awareness, mood, and activity, coalescing all we experience (even fragmented information) into coherent perceptions ...
- The amazing thalamus is affecting and being affected by breathing, creating global coherence in networks that underlie consciousness (whether awake, asleep, etc.) ...

There may be a brief PI period in which the diaphragm and larynx muscles maintain lung inflation and airway expansion to promote smooth airflow. In each exhalation:

- The energy created through inhalation transfers to cells and tissues for cellular respiration, and CO_2, produced by aerobic respiration, is expelled from the cells. Aortic, carotid bodies, and brain stem chemosensors send messages to brain stem centers that control spinal cord neurons—relaxing the diaphragm, external intercostal, tongue, and larynx muscles, making the chest cavity smaller, and deflating the lungs like a balloon releasing air ...
- With vigorous exercise or increased metabolic need, high altitude, or REM sleep, the pFRG is activated, and rhythmic firing of its

neurons sequentially activates brain stem and spinal cord motor neurons. Abdominal (expiratory pump) and internal intercostal muscles contract so we actively exhale and blow out air...
- Air (generally 78% oxygen, 16% nitrogen, 4% CO_2 and saturated water vapor) moves through the bronchi to the trachea and through the nose and/or mouth, impacting and being impacted by microbiota on their surfaces...
- Cardiac chemoreceptors and baroreceptors constantly monitor CO_2 levels and adjust alkaline/acid (pH) and pressure levels to maintain physiological homeostasis with our organs...
- Neurotransmitter acetylcholine facilitates abdominal and laryngeal muscle contraction; epinephrine mediates airway smooth muscle relaxation; NE supports blood vessel changes, affecting breathing depth and rates; DA enhances respiratory muscle function; and serotonin receptors moderate our felt sense of breathing (and associated memories)...
- Autonomic control engages: the PSN extends exhalation duration, and sighing or toning—promoting relaxation and limiting SNS escape mechanisms...
- The VN slows respiration rate, prolonging exhalation and promoting relaxation responses...
- HRV supports by generating physiological, emotional, and cognitive coherence for presence and action...
- Gamma, beta, alpha, theta, and delta brain waves are affecting and being affected by awareness, mood, and activity, coalescing all we experience (even fragmented information) into coherent perceptions...
- The amazing thalamus is affecting and being affected by breathing, creating global coherence in networks that underlie consciousness (whether awake, asleep, etc.)...

And, when we breathe consciously, particularly with slower and deeper breathing, all the automatic breathing phenomena occur and we activate the PSN—increasing vagal tone and HRV, enabling us to let go and relax. CB optimizes our serotonergic, noradrenergic, dopaminergic, glutamatergic, and GABAergic neurotransmitter levels, and synchronizes our gamma and theta/delta waves for retrieving memories, understanding our emotional responses, and engaging complex thought and executive function processing.

Conscious Breathing—gateway to optimal
functioning and elevated states of consciousness!

PART II

Practicing

FIVE

Exploring Our Breathing Biographies

> *To be alive in this beautiful, self-organizing universe—to participate in the dance of life with senses to perceive it, lungs that breathe it, organs that draw nourishment from it—is a wonder beyond words.*
>
> —JOANNA MACY, COMING BACK TO LIFE

CONSIDER WHAT our lives and world could be if we all experienced attention and reverence for our first breath from those at our birth. What if our parents had learned to generate oceanic sounds in their breathing as the earliest sounds in our ears? Envision the effect on us if our parents had frequently and intentionally breathed with energy and purpose while holding our growing infant bodies. Consider how are lives would feel if during our youth we were taught ways of breathing to regulate, calm, connect, and energize. Then we would likely have significant awareness of the sensations and quality of our breathing as it accompanies us through the experiences and learning in our precious unfolding life. This invaluable wisdom would support conscious, somatic contact with the invisible interiority of our psyche, soul, and essence—and also enhance our attunement with others.

Most of us did not have those optimal breathing experiences. Yet at times we have become aware of our breathing in moments of excitement, joy, loss, fear, tragedy, triumph, sensuality, or when in contact with nature, earth, air, water, and fire. Gathering these *breathing memories* and tracing the origin and logos of our relationship with breathing is a powerful entry point into Breathwork, particularly if we want to experience ourselves fully and live authentically. Conscious appreciation of, and visceral contact with, the intrinsic support and wisdom in each breath is a force multiplier for our personal growth.

A breathing biography is an intimate meeting with ourselves, our beliefs, judgments, and hopes, as well as our pleasurable, painful, and transformative memories. Ultimately, no matter what ups, downs, triumphs, or tragedies are part of our breathing biography, we can discover a new, powerfully felt throughline of our worthiness and resilience throughout our lives. Breathing biographies surprise us with immeasurable gifts.

The end of this chapter contains questions to assist us in creating a breathing biography. As an example of the range of experiences for remembering our breathing—and to learn how and why I discovered Breathwork—I offer some portions of my own breathing biography.

To Love, to be Loved, and ultimately to be Love itself . . . in the first memory of my life, I have a visceral sense of seeing and knowing that every person's essence wants this experience of love.

This visceral sense includes awareness of the love within each person wanting to express itself in original ways. Everyone has gifts like unique musical instruments, arising from love to deliver newly born sounds to life while harmonizing with all the other sounds and enhancing them. From athletics to art, from painting to plumbing, from loving children to research—the list is infinite. Love, in its various forms of expression, is a creative force and a manifestation of the Source of energy and matter. Everyone is a part of the momentum of love and creativity.

I saw, and still see, a bubbly effervescence within each person's gifts—an ebullient wish, often secret, for these capacities to flow into our world and contribute to life. Yet it appeared that these capacities were often trapped, partly blocked, or lacked what was needed for growth. I felt, and still feel, sad—with continued hope that our love and wholeness can be liberated.

I remember searching for *the key* to unlock these capacities in my family, friends, and everyone. As a child, I tried being loving, kind, and supportive. I loved showing people new possibilities—wishing it would make a difference. It can hurt our hearts when people don't seem open to alleviating their suffering and becoming self-expressed. It hurt mine.

The summer I turned five, my family rented a magical old farmhouse on a dirt road high in the wilds of a New Hampshire mountain. Amid that epic experience, my mother brought me to an outdoor Royal Danish Ballet performance as a birthday surprise. I remember gasping as beauty, design and love created together. My breathing quivered rapidly, high in my chest, creating sensations of levitating. I was mesmerized. Under a starry summer sky, it seemed that this beauty could heal an ailing world. I was now on fire to become a dancer.

Fortunately, my parents, brilliant intellectuals and social activists at the University of Chicago who were friends with luminaries like Eugene Gendlin, Saul Bellow, Erving Goffman, Elaine May, Mike Nichols, and Edward Hirsch Levi, supported almost everything I wanted to do. My mother found a ballet teacher and devotedly brought me to every class. I loved ballet ardently; my chest would lift, my breathing would heighten, and my body would fill with joy. At age 12 I danced my way to New York. Within six months, I joined 30 girls chosen from 500 to dance at Lincoln Center with England's Royal Ballet and Russia's Bolshoi Ballet in the *Nutcracker*, *Ballet School*, and *Sleeping Beauty*.

One Sunday afternoon when I was 13, a seminal experience of my breathing life occurred in the large, cloistered garden of the Academics and Arts school where I lived. The enormous five-story building was basically empty that day with only about 15 other residential students. As I wandered into the courtyard where spring flowers and leaves were blossoming, my soul filled with beauty and my body with joy. I began to dance—running, leaping, and twirling to sections of flowers, waving my hands over them with love and ecstatically sweeping my arms upward into the sky to invite and celebrate their abundance. I wanted to ensure everything in the garden was loved, celebrated, and supported in growing, including the birds, insects, and stones. I know now that I had entered a flow state and was experiencing extraordinary energy, bliss, visual acuity, and expansive love for almost 30 minutes. I was not aware of my breathing *until* I was moving my hands from some flowers toward the sky and my gaze passed a third-story window with the other 14 residential students looking on intently—many clearly laughing at me. Along with hot flushing, rapid heartbeats, and shaking legs, my lungs seemed to seize. I could barely breathe. I did not want to dishonor the plants nor the magic of this special, sacred experience, yet neither did I want it ridiculed. Slowly, I turned the other way—as if I had not seen anyone—and continued dancing with far less exuberance. Gently, I worked my way into sitting down, seemingly serene. Internally though, my breaths pumped about every two seconds and my rib cage hurt. I waited until my schoolmates drifted away, and then cried softly, feeling a burning soreness as more air entered my lungs.

Other experiences also affected my heart, awareness, and breathing in joyful or painful ways. At age 11, I was besotted with King Arthur and the Knights of the Round Table, where every person's contribution counted. At night I would sneak flashlights into bed and read Arthurian tales beneath the covers, accompanied by breathing sounds and the physical sensations of keeping still.

My parents inspired me when they almost single-handedly racially integrated the school system in our little Massachusetts town. When Black children from Roxbury stepped down from buses at Cohasset High School, I felt exhilarated, yet the body and facial tension in all of us—Black and white—was palpable. We seemed to be holding our breaths or breathing shallowly. I often wish I could return to that moment to breathe more deeply and be more present.

Footage of civil rights marches, images of young men returning from Vietnam—no longer breathing in body bags—and Vietnamese women and children choking from battle smoke erupted onto television screens and newspapers. I could barely breathe when there was a protest march, unless I slipped out of school to join. On the streets I could chant, shout, and breathe better. I was pierced by the awareness of tension, unexpressed potential, and feelings of suffocation that permeated many people and communities. At that age, I didn't consciously name it *restricted breathing* or *breathlessness*. Yet breathlessness is visceral in many memories concerning war, racial injustice, poverty, and the objectification and minimization of women, the feminine, and myself as a girl.

By age 15, I realized that only modest percentages of people would appreciate ballet; also ballet didn't directly impact all the suffering I saw. Continuing the search for a *universal key* for peoples' well-being, love, and creativity, I left traditional education for a few years. Mainstream schooling seemed fine if one loved reading and studying as I did. Clearly it wasn't a happy experience for countless others—including some close friends. I became part of a student-run high school in an abandoned storefront in New York City's Upper West Side. At the Elizabeth Cleaners Street School, students created our own classes and hired Columbia and NYU graduate students, our parents, and their friends to teach. I loved the curriculum's breadth that included physics, women's and men's liberation, Guerilla Theater, carpentry and plumbing, urban ecology, comparative religion, community law, and painting. Random House published our book, *Starting Your Own High School*.

During this expansive time, I discovered and started practicing Kriya Yoga. Every day for 5 years, I practiced eight hours of pranayama (yogic breathing), meditation, and asanas (yogic postures). I learned Breathing Practices to energize myself, warm my body, concentrate and focus, stabilize my nervous system, sustain inner calm, and induce sleep. To this day, I almost always fall asleep within 1 to 3 minutes of lying down. I benefited from a plethora of discoveries, yet eventually realized that yoga's tenets, practices, and culture would not universally appeal to everyone.

Having experienced how body states, emotions, and awareness affect each other, I knew the benefits of holistic approaches for well-being were decidedly transformative. I was inspired to prepare for medical school, become a physician, and support people through holistic healing and breathing.

Three intriguing breathing experiences transpired over the next few years. At 17, yearning to get into medicine, I obtained a hospital nursing assistant position by writing "18th year" instead of "17th"—which *was* technically the truth. Hospital work was exhilarating. Noticing many patients on the surgery floor (not ICU) developing respiratory illnesses shortly after surgery, I wondered about deep breathing for prevention. So each morning, I gathered small tubes from medical supplies and attached surgical gloves with rubber bands. I told each postsurgical patient about our simple experiment to prevent postsurgical respiratory illness by blowing up glove balloons three times daily and walking a little faster than they might do alone—twice within eight hours. The nurses smiled happily as we glided through the halls with IV poles, and inflated the glove balloons larger and larger each day. After a month, the hospital noted a near cessation of postsurgical respiratory challenges. The medical staff granted additional time and provisions for me to continue practicing as the hospital's *breathing angel*.

During my third year of college, I gave birth to a wonderful son. Hearing the hospital midwives and doctors saying they expected a natural birth—thanks to my deep breathing and relaxation—provided delightful respites during the 63-hour labor. Yet one doctor kept urging a C-section. Deep, slow—and fast—breathing empowered my intuition to kindly refuse that C-section, and Joshua was born weighing 10 pounds, 5 ounces. Conscious Breathing guided the day.

During senior year the lab for biology and ecology was on the sixth floor. To study relationships between volume, speed, exertion, and recovery, the professor requested people to run up the five flights of stairs as quickly as possible, then breathe into a breath meter. I had turns as both researcher and participant. The team requested I run up the stairs again because I recovered better than the athletes. Were the readings mistaken? I ran again with almost identical results. The intrigued team issued a third challenge. Yogic texts attest that deep breathing builds confidence, so I did a third time. Similar results.

Several doctors encouraged me to attend medical school. I loved medical settings and enjoyed noting symptoms, behaviors, and clinical markers whose effects and relational synergies weren't acknowledged. Yet mainstream medicine no longer seemed a sufficient key for unlocking love and creativity in everyone. Also, caring for two-year-old Joshua was paramount and time-sensitive, making the long hours of medical school unimaginable.

Amid that dilemma, I became clinically depressed and unable to feel any emotion. Each night, awakening the next morning seemed impossible—my life force felt almost nonexistent. I truly didn't care and wasn't even scared about it.

Solely for my son's sake, I sought help and found psychologist Jason Doty, who listened, then said, "We're going to try Breath Awareness Therapy"—his name for Group 5 Breathwork practices. After five physically and emotionally beneficial years of yogic Breathing Practices, I thought this would be similar. However, in the first session I experienced what, for so long, I had hoped was possible for everyone. As the session concluded, I opened my eyes, utterly astonished why the whole world wasn't doing this. Once again, I had discovered fire—this time through breathing the air we *all* breathe. I experienced myself as electrical energy and felt boundless love infusing me and everything. I saw atoms dancing in the air and experienced new dimensions of aliveness and belonging. I realized that ***our own breathing is a universal key!***

The clinical depression *completely* dissolved in that session. It felt miraculous, and I didn't expect more in the second session. However, as air flow intensified, my throat became exceedingly sore. From age five until that Breathwork session in my early 20s, I had chronic tonsillitis with 104-degree fevers, requiring large amounts of antibiotics, twice a year like clockwork. I remember thinking maybe I was getting tonsillitis again. Group 5 Breathwork guides us to be present with whatever arises and trust the expanding healing energy. Thus, with Jason's guidance, I breathed *into* the sore throat.

Suddenly, I burst out crying about my parents' frequent emotional conflicts during my early childhood. I became aware that the sore throat in the session was the emergence of chronic repressed pain about what I wanted to cry out to my parents at age five. First, the powerful, deep breathing generated vigorous energy to speak the suppressed words aloud to my parents. Next, it attended to healing the sore throat, which was accomplished within a few breaths. At the time I knew the session was about loving my younger self and empowering emotional expression and communication. One year later I realized, with awe, that my usual cases of tonsillitis had not materialized. That was several decades ago. I never had tonsillitis again.

Physical symptoms, depression, and grief were healing through Breathwork. Experiencing more connection to myself and others, I felt more authentic and present. I was intrigued. For the next 5 years, I consciously breathed during everything I did, and therefore quickly noticed whenever I began breathing shallowly or holding my breath. I discovered these constrictions were oftentimes induced by blocked emotions or unconscious fearful thoughts that I could now breathe with, understand, and release, which was accelerating my healing and growth.

Consciously breathing through life's activities and vicissitudes engendered more flexibility, flow, focus, and creativity, and enhanced all experiences—including work, communicating, cleaning, lovemaking, and reading. For example, I wanted to prepare food more creatively and share its nourishment, intelligence, and essence. So, while laying out ingredients to make something, I would breathe deeply, generating vitality that flowed from my chest into my arms and hands. This vibrance coursed through me as love and appreciation for the food, the human or nonhuman animals receiving the food, and whoever or whatever contributed to creating the food. And by consciously breathing during food shopping, I could simultaneously assess ingredients and their cost-benefit ratio, feel love for my family, be present to any grief or confusion I might have, appreciate the food's sacredness, and connect more intentionally with the store staff.

I became enamored with discovering ways Conscious Breathing (CB) could strengthen the embodiment of differentiated aspects of consciousness such as compassion, empowerment, inner guidance, and boundlessness. Cultivating these qualities through perception and awareness, while consciously breathing, stimulates greater embedding of the experience in the brain and body. I experienced CB eliciting *flow* states that produced new insights during ordinary activities. By consciously breathing, I was more present to outer phenomena and internal experiences simultaneously, including liminal and mystical dimensions. Each breath can hold nuances of our experiences (e.g., emotion, reactivity, discernment, smell, sound)—while simultaneously contacting archetypal, imaginal, and spiritual awareness. Breathing reflects the micro, macro, and infinite.

The more I practiced, the more life opened into a kind of consciousness parkway, with an ever-increasing number of lanes traveling together synchronously—and I was in each one. The ordinary was mystical, and the mystical was guidance for what action to do in responding to each moment. To this day, whenever I breathe consciously, these orientations emerge, with new insights regularly dawning.

About 20 years later, long after becoming a Breathworker and facilitating about 20,000 Breathwork sessions, I was admitted to ICU with a previously unrecognized life-threatening genetic condition. In excruciating pain, with my life in peril, part of me wanted to join my beloved younger sister who had died from breast cancer 2 years earlier and lived with me for her last 3 years. Though Jamie was a soulmate, and our spiritual connection tangibly persisted after she passed, minutes after her last breath a silent agonizing scream had erupted within me and it had never fully stopped. Being even closer to her was tantalizing, and I was in extraordinary pain, so staying alive was the most demanding work I'd ever undertaken. Yet I would not leave my now teenage son.

Several hours into this trial, I was stunned when the kitchen delivered dinner because eating seemed absurd. However, "neurons that fire together wire together" (Shatz, 1992). For 25 years I had practiced breathing deeply three times before receiving nutrition, to remember that breathing is our most essential nourishment. Despite being indescribably weak and half out of body, when I saw the hospital food my body breathed deeply three times.

Immediately, I reconnected with my faint life force. Breath by breath it blossomed into strength. With each breath, I gripped the bed rails and intoned, "I cannot leave Joshua. I have to stay."

It took 10 hours to inhabit my body fully as each conscious breath dissolved the desire to leave. Each breath tenderly held the grief about Jamie. Each breath reminded me about my commitment and love for Joshua. And so, I returned to my body and remained. When I asked my doctor why this condition flared up two decades later than for other family members, without hesitation he said, "It's all the breathing you do."

The journey from my first encounters with Conscious Breathing to intimacy with breathing was not a shallow discovery. My love and appreciation for Breathwork and its power for humanity comes from genuine curiosity, being a beginner over and over, referencing tomes of knowledge, and committing to something that will continually transform me. Breathing awareness has enabled greater presence with my interior landscape—my potential, shadows, patterns, needs, and visions. Each conscious breath supports my presence with whatever emerges, grows, sustains, deconstructs, and releases in my personal life and in our collective. Each conscious breath fosters more creative response and participation—with greater peace, wisdom, and love than the breath before. *And I am breathing with everyone right now.*

Breathing Biography Guidance

Writing a breathing biography may take time. We may think we haven't felt our breathing much. We may need to read the questions below many times, allowing the memories of our sensations and our breathing lives to emerge slowly and organically.

We can write or record our breathing biography. If so inclined, we can add drawings, paintings, music, or movement. Consciously breathing while writing may reveal more breathing memories and amplify our perceptions. We may fill with emotion. We may smile, laugh, cry, groan, shout, or sing! It is beneficial to pause often and breathe deeply. Therapist-Breathworkers should create their own breathing biography before guiding others. The following questions may help access the breadth and depth of our breathing memories.

- What inspired you to learn about breathing and Breathwork?
- In your life, when have you noticed any of the following experiences, including sensations, emotions, thoughts, or insights that accompanied them?
    - *Breathing deeper, heavier, or faster than normal*
    - *Breathing lighter or shallower*
    - *Unconsciously or consciously holding your breath*
    - *Breathing slowly and deeply and feeling more peaceful, relaxed, or energized*

- *Breathing differently than normal when feeling fear*
- *Breathing in energizing ways*
- *Breathing when laughing or crying*
- *Breathing during illness or medical procedures*
- *Breathing during play or sports*
- *Breathing when feeling wonder, joy, excitement, or awe*
- *Breathing during intimate moments*

- During your life, have you had any experiences of impaired breathing caused by outside forces, such as environmental factors or other people? If so, do you feel your breathing, body, psyche, or soul was impacted? How? Breathe deeply now and extend compassion to yourself, and acknowledge your innate resilience that continued to breathe afterward.
- When do you remember intentionally breathing deeply, on purpose? What was the purpose?
- What have you learned about breathing throughout your life?
- What Breathwork experiences have you had?

What are your hopes, goals, intentions, and visions for your breathing life?

SIX

Optimal Breathing

In this very breath that we take now lies the secret that all great teachers try to tell us.

—PETER MATTHIESSEN, *THE SNOW LEOPARD*

THE QUEST for *breathing optimally* aligns with becoming our most regulated, authentic, optimized self; imbibing the most important physically and emotionally healthy elements for well-being and functioning; and, contributing to life with energy, harmony, empowerment, wisdom, creativity, and reciprocity.

Learning about and practicing various elements, components, factors, and dynamics that contribute to optimal breathing invites an infusion of awareness that every breath is a psychophysiological process—wherein physical mechanisms and changes affect our emotional and mental state, and vice versa. This reciprocal relationship between breathing physiology and emotive control is well established and beyond dispute. Studies tracking and confirming the reciprocal relationships between breathing physiology, emotive control, state changes, and external factors are also proliferating.

What constitutes optimal breathing is highly individualized—determined by numerous physical, emotional, cognitive, and spiritual factors, which include influences of temperament, personal narrative, relationships, health, environment, and collective events. Dr. Shirley Telles agrees. For example, she views too much focus on standardized breathing rates as detracting from breathing's innate and full healing power.

Further, Shirley's scholarship with ancient texts reveals that historically, *yoga was an art and science of breathing.* In our conversations, Shirley confirmed what I learned through practicing Babaji's Kriya Yoga. The postures (asanas) primarily practiced today were a small portion of yoga—certainly not the emphasis—and the physical asanas developed in ancient India weren't intended as exercise or physiological wisdom. Instead, when people doing breathing, meditation, and consciousness practices experienced higher states of awareness their bodies spontaneously flowed into various postures. These positions were noted and practiced by others who wanted to grow spiritually; yet the original power and transformation arose from breathing. The ancient connection between Conscious Breathing and expanded, wise, emergent consciousness substantiates the sagacity of cultivating a flexible, expansive, and nuanced approach to determining optimal breathing in each individual breath of each Breather.

In this chapter we explore physical contributions to optimal breathing, all of which impact emotional and cognitive states. In Chapter 13 we adventure into psychospiritual terrains of optimal and authentic breathing. The theories, guidelines, and practices in every other chapter also contribute to discovering our bio-individualized and constantly changing optimal breathing.

Learning about, and practicing, some structural processes of Conscious Breathing (CB) and Breathwork expands our knowledge about the vast array of optimal breathing factors; intervenes in unconscious, unhealthy, breathing habits; and strengthens our overall breathing capacity. This information aids Breathers and Therapist-Breathworkers in being breathing-informed when engaging in Breathwork. Additionally, practicing the following principles and processes helps engender breathing experience and acuity for Breathers and Therapist-Breathworkers to become internally guided during Breathwork.

Physical Components of Optimal Breathing

THE DIAPHRAGM

The diaphragm is our most important muscle for significantly affecting our health. Understanding, appreciating, and being able to physically sense our diaphragm monumentally enhances breathing and its physical and emotional benefits. As we learned in Chapter 4, during inhalation, the diaphragm contracts, moving downward and flattening—enlarging the chest and creating a vacuum, so as we inhale air, the lungs can expand. During exhalation, the diaphragm relaxes and forms a dome shape, up into the bottom of the lungs and ribs; working like bellows that help the lungs expel air.

THREE KEY DIAPHRAGMATIC BREATHING PRACTICES

1. Releasing tension and embedded trauma: Gently massage along the bottom rib while breathing deeply and holding tender and tense places until they soften. We can stretch our spines upward, giving the diaphragm greater room and interrupting passivity patterns. Actively expanding and contracting the diaphragm while doing yogic postures that gently twist our spine and abdominal areas creates more flexibility.
2. Increasing diaphragm flexibility and strengthening its motility and resilience: Research demonstrates that bringing attention to muscles in motion, or merely thinking of muscles moving, activates muscle fibers more than exercising without focusing on the muscle. When attention is placed on muscle contraction, the quality is enhanced, a phenomenon called the mind-muscle connection (Calatayud et al., 2016). Placing attention on our diaphragm—the primary respiration muscle—while breathing will strengthen it. Making tones (singing or chanting) brings muscle attention to our diaphragms, throats, and lungs. We can also create our own exercises.

3. Experiencing full-bodied diaphragmatic breathing: Placing one hand on our chest and one on our abdomen, we breathe as usual. Initially our breathing may remain similar to our default automatic (unconscious) breathing pattern. Eventually, simply bringing awareness to breathing transforms our breathing towards well-being. During inhalation we can notice whether our belly is expanding for optimal diaphragm contraction. Is our rib cage expanding to the sides and to the front and back? Is our chest rising during inhalation? For optimal breathing the belly rising precedes the chest rising. If one hand isn't moving, or we feel constriction, this will change as we practice.

- *With hands still on chest and abdomen, we focus solely on our abdomen. Breathing nasally (if possible) for a few breaths to a few minutes, we explore and invite our abdomen's expansion during inhalation, and relaxation during exhalation. By refraining from our chest (and upper hand) rising, our diaphragm is exercised more fully. Our body will love the increasingly efficient physiological progress, even if it is a bit uncomfortable initially.*
- *Now we focus solely on our chest. Breathing nasally (if possible)*

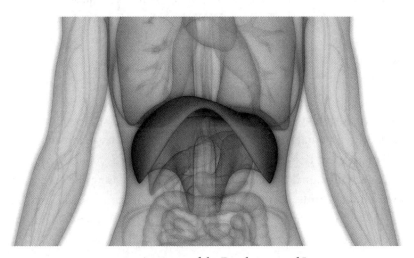

FIGURE 6.1: Anatomy of the Diaphragm and Lungs
"Respiratory System Anatomy and Physiology," magicmine / Alamy Stock Photo

for a few breaths to a few minutes, we explore and invite chest expansion in all directions, allowing our shoulders to rise a little as inhalation ends. Our chest expands through our lungs filling rather than puffing out our chest.
- Now we focus for a few breaths to a few minutes on both abdomen and chest—abdomen rising first, then chest—during inhalation. During exhalation our chest relaxes, then our belly.

Psychiatrist Alexander Lowen, founder of bioenergetics, taught that releasing diaphragmatic tension, even during sleep and orgasm, can optimize health, pleasure, and well-being and facilitate powerful excitation to flow throughout the body (Lowen, 1975, 1988). And, while consciously working with inhalation is most proficient for healthy breathing and correcting maladaptive patterns (because healthy exhalations are usually passive and relaxed), strong, flexible diaphragms will naturally lengthen our exhales, increasing the air volume being expelled. One reason this is important is because during exhalation we release about 3,500 different organic compounds and most environmental pollutants we breathe. Citing a study from *Annals of Allergy, Asthma and Immunology* (Popov, 2011), James Nestor, author of *Breath* (2020), notes that we exhale pollutants, pesticides, chemicals, and engine exhaust, and "when we don't breathe out completely, these toxins sit in the lungs and fester, causing infections and other problems."

Consequently, we benefit from purposefully strengthening our diaphragm as well as releasing its tension. First, we can lie on our back, initiate deep diaphragmatic breathing, and then place a comfortable weight (one or two pounds and gradually increasing) on our abdomen, which will require exerting force to fully expand our belly. Second, we can contract our abdominal muscles after exhalation, increasing the amount of exhaled air. Third, placing our hands under our rib cage and pressing on the abdomen during exhalation increases diaphragmatic relaxation. These interventions increase the diaphragm's bandwidth.

TONGUE AND MOUTH PLACEMENT

Practices such as yoga, Qigong, and Tai Chi suggest specific tongue placements during breathing and movement exercises in order to reduce air exiting orally and to circulate more Qi (life energy) within the body. There are three common positions:

1. Placing the tip of the tongue somewhere on the mouth's roof between the top of the upper teeth and the uvula (the small piece of tissue dangling from the back of the throat). Placing the tongue further back than the teeth involves gently rolling the underside of our tongue along the roof.
2. Placing the entire tongue along the mouth's roof.
3. Consciously relaxing the tongue on the mouth's floor.

Other notable positions include both sides of the tongue curled up toward the center as in Sitali Pranayama for cooling, or sticking the tongue straight out of the mouth, with mouth wide open (lion pose).

Generally, an elevated tongue touching the roof of the mouth opens nasal passages and respiratory airways more, making nasal airflow quite efficacious. Medicine and dentistry increasingly note how tongue positions during childhood and beyond impact airway passages, nasal airflow, and even bone growth, and jaw, cheek, and eye socket density (Eric Davis Dental, n.d.). One study showed benefits with the tongue elevated to the mouth's roof instead of the floor (Schmidt et al., 2009), and another that chewing stimulates stem cell release, which intensifies bone growth and density, and supports good breathing (Nestor, 2020).

Many yogic traditions describe *nectar* releasing from the pituitary gland into the back of the throat through breathing into higher states of consciousness. This nectar is said both to come from higher states of consciousness and to produce them. To support swallowing the nectar rather than allowing evaporation through lips or open mouths we can place our tongue on the roof of our mouth, varying from the tip of our tongue on the top of our top teeth, to rolling back the underside of the tongue along the roof. Some Breathers can eventually reach the nasal cavity with their tongue (an advanced technique called kesari mudra which can take years to attain.) We begin with whatever is comfortable. Over time, without straining we may stretch our tongue further back.

In terms of integrating mystical wisdom and science, we might wonder whether swallowing the nectar has biological implications. Indeed, the results of a randomized controlled study showed that 20 minutes of yogic Breathing Practices (pranayama, Breathwork Groups 2 and 3) increased salivary nerve growth factor production—a neurotrophin that may play significant roles in cognition and slow the progression of Alzheimer's disease (Allen et al., 2011). Another study showed pranayama practices reducing proinflammatory protein levels and increasing tumor suppressor proteins (Twal et al., 2016). Yogic Breathing Pranayama powerfully affects biologically important molecules in saliva, indicating biology and mystical experiences working in tandem.

Obviously, we should refrain from clenched teeth. Most breathing guidance recommends slight spacing between the upper and lower teeth, with lips gently closed to support nasal breathing and unobstructed airways. Some Breathing Practices encourage teeth slightly wider apart during inhale than exhale, and others the opposite. Teeth position can be important during yogic breathing techniques in which sacred sounds (syllables) are induced within breathing—for instance, the three syllables of the Sanskrit mantra *Aum*, which are *ah, e,* and *yim*. Sounding syllables within breathing (not spoken words) requires adjustments in the tension of our glottis (the elongated slit between vocal cords that closes to protect our airway when swallowing), and variations in mouth space by slightly opening and closing our teeth.

No one placement of the tongue, teeth, or glottis always works for all Breathers. Virtually every tongue, mouth, and teeth placement abounds with therapeutic benefits if practiced with understanding and purpose. However, unconscious mouth breathing—when the mouth hangs open, or the tongue hangs outside the mouth or is slack against the bottom—is almost never useful.

One widely practiced ancient yogic breathing technique, *Ujjayi Pran-*

ayama (Ocean Breath) uses slow breathing, glottis adjustment, purposeful tongue placement, and teeth slightly apart to induce parasympathetic activity that supports restfulness and rejuvenation. Ujjayi concentrates breathing sensations and gently force to massage the back of the throat, eliciting a soothing oceanic sound (Shah, n.d.).

UJJAYI PRACTICE

1. Learn to voluntarily contract the glottis, which creates slight resistance to air flow and intensifies the breath's impact on the throat. Four methods:
    a. Lightly touch the front of the throat and mimic sipping through a straw, feeling how the throat tightens.
    b. Speak a sentence aloud, then whisper it, noticing how the throat constricts slightly for whispering.
    c. With wide-open mouth, blow with enough force to blow out candles or create fog on a mirror. The throat sensations are the glottis contracting.
    d. With an open mouth, exhale while whispering "HA" and being aware of the throat's position. Try making the same sound during inhalation. After some breaths, try it with closed mouth.
2. Place the tongue on the roof of the mouth (tip of the tongue at the top of our teeth, or gently rolling the tongue back further) with the mouth and lips closed.
3. Now constrict the glottis.
4. Breathe nasally, slowly and deeply, with approximate equivalent time of inhaling and exhaling.

With the glottis contracted, it should feel as if we are breathing through our throat—not the mouth or nose. We will feel and hear an *oceanic sound* and can intensify the sound by lengthening the exhalation, which increases lung pressure. Yet optimally the sound should arise effortlessly, without trying to transmit its energy or make it audible to others (possibly triggering vanity).

THE BACK OF OUR BODY

For both physiological and psychological (psychophysiological) reasons, bringing awareness to the back of our heads, necks, and torsos during Breathing Practice accelerates healing and transformation. We know that where attention goes, neural wiring flows, muscle growth increases, and immune response is optimized. Our spines are the *backbone* of engaging and thriving in life, and the supersonic communication highway between our body and brain. Placing attention on spinal oscillations and wave motions during breathing invites the spine to both contribute to, and benefit from, breathing. Yet we tend to primarily focus on the front of our abdomen, chest, throat, and face.

We can be ingenious at deceiving others and ourselves about our needs, motivations, traumas, and hopes. Our experiences and memories are encoded in neurons throughout our three-dimensional bodies. A groove in a vertebra or a muscle on the back of the neck may contain critical information and parts of self that need release or development. We may contain bubbles of forgetting about feeling hurt, shame, hatred, rage, unworthiness, or trauma. What treasures can emerge with attention to the parts of our bodies we present less often to others—parts less connected to our self-image? Front to back awareness of the entire thoracic, abdominal, and pelvic cavities, as well as the neck and head, helps us receive CB's total psychophysiological benefits.

UNIFYING OPTIMAL BREATHING PRACTICE

When we breathe optimally, inhales and exhales are perfectly paired to support free-flowing life force.

1. Breathing nasally (unless mouth breathing is needed), we deepen and slow our breathing. During inhalation, we bring attention to our entire abdominal cavity (the skin, muscle, viscera, and spine), relaxing our jaw, with our upper and lower teeth spaced slightly apart, with lips gently and completely closed. Allowing our abdomen to expand,

we bring attention to the diaphragm to activate the mind-muscle connection, enhancing the diaphragm's movement and strength.
2. As inhalation continues, we place hands on each side of our rib cage—inviting the ribs to expand horizontally, and forward and backward. We can also expand our ribs vertically up toward our chest and down toward our pelvic floor.
3. Toward the end of inhalation, we place a hand on our chest to welcome it rising and expanding, with our shoulders naturally lifting without strain. We extend our awareness from the front and center of our chest to the corresponding locations straight behind on our spine and ribs. Our belly may lean forward, our back may naturally arch a bit, and our tailbone may tip back slightly (Vranich, 2016).
4. As inhalation culminates, we may, without straining, sip in even more air and feel our throat expand, helping increase air volume and respiratory resiliency.
5. Exhaling nasally (unless mouth-breathing is needed), our shoulders relax and our chest softens. Our jaw remains relaxed, while our teeth may move slightly closer without fully touching.
6. Continuing exhalation, our rib cage can relax and move inward. Our hands can gently squeeze our rib cage to encourage intercostal muscle relaxation and deeper release.
7. Toward the end of exhalation, we invite our expanded abdomen to soften, relax, and move in. We contract our belly, slightly and softly relax any arch in our back, and bring the tailbone back to center.
8. During the whole practice, we may place the tip or whole of the tongue on the roof of the mouth in one of the positions described above, bringing awareness to full nasal breathing and naturally lengthening exhalation.
9. Movement that facilitates breathing is helpful. Breathing into new, uncomfortable, or energetic sensations during practice can induce spontaneous movements, supporting easier and expanded breathing. Movements include:
    - *Adjusting positions to enable deeper breathing*
    - *Trembling, vibrating, or shaking*
    - *Stretching*

- Contracting and relaxing muscles throughout the body
- Rocking or rotating

10. Pelvic floor muscles (PFM) can support optimal breathing. Relaxing the PFM aids the diaphragm's downward motion, boosting inspiratory flow. During exhalation or coughs, the PFM join with abdominal muscles to facilitate diaphragm relaxation and upward motion. Consequently, both strengthening and developing the ability to relax the PFM and abdominal muscles can help optimize respiratory functioning (Park & Han, 2015). The most studied (and proven) method for strengthening the PFM is Kegel, an exercise that contracts and relaxes the pelvic floor. We identify the PFM and contract them by simultaneously squeezing and lifting for up to 10 seconds, followed by relaxation. Ten to 12 repetitions three times per day is recommended (Sonnier, 2021). We should exhale during the PFM's contraction as opposed to exhaling during relaxation, which may initially feel counterintuitive.

BREATHWORK POSITIONS

Body position can impact the degree of respiratory efficiency (Katz et al., 2018). The word *carriage* invokes the more refined nuances of posture—and, in terms of breathing, how positions affect oxygen and life force flowing to each molecule of the body and psyche, from our bones to our souls. Engaging different body positions during Breathwork facilitates strengthening diverse muscles, unwinding muscle and skeletal patterns that inhibit breathing, and exercising and enhancing ligament and tendon mobility to further optimize breathing. Lung health, medical conditions, fitness, and our life stage are important considerations. The following positions are applicable for optimal breathing and all Breathwork methods in this book.

Standing or sitting with a relatively straight spine. Numerous wisdom traditions and holistic modalities champion the benefits of straight spines for facilitating energy flow psychospiritually and cerebrospinal fluid flow physically. Yet severely contracted muscles, tendons, and ligaments from sitting, slouching, lack of exercise, chronic mouth breathing (causing hunched shoulders and jutting chins), and chronic injuries or illnesses may induce significant discomfort when we attempt to straighten our spine. While there can be merit in rising to the occasion and forcing ourselves to straighten our spines, a straight stiff spine is counterproductive. Consequently, for maximum benefit it's wise to adopt positions that maximize feeling, and energy and information flow, throughout our bodies. We can find positions that support our pelvis and lower back while the upper back is *relatively straight*. Over time, we will sit and stand straighter because Breathwork will unwind tense, contracted, stiff, sluggish, listless, and dispirited parts of our body.

Seated in chairs with feet flat on the ground, or sitting cross-legged on chairs or the floor. Most Breathers sit cross-legged on chairs or the floor for Breathwork Groups 1–4. The spine can be relatively straight without straining, supporting pelvic looseness and mobility around the spinal cord. Our spine rising buoyantly out of the pelvis can feel like a ribbon connecting the sky to the crown of our heads, with shoulders back as in energized, standing positions. Sitting on a pillow or placing one just under the base of the spine can elevate the pelvic floor and the spine, adding buoyancy, making it easier to generate a relatively straight spine.

Standing, legs comfortably shoulder-width apart, knees slightly bent. This familiar position allows play with our spine and shoulder mobility during breathing. We become more aware of our posture, how it might be improved, and ways to lengthen our spine or inhibit any tendency for scrunching or shortening.

Lying on our backs. Our spine is automatically relatively straight when supine. Lying without a pillow is optimal if comfortable; however, pillows should be used to alleviate neck, back, or head strain. Placing pillows under our knees or bending our knees with feet flat can relax the lower back, psoas muscle, pelvic floor, and diaphragm, freeing our attention to more easily engage the diaphragm and abdomen. A supine position can release bodily tension while maintaining connection to our spine, and strengthen the intercostal and thoracic muscles as they oppose gravity to expand the lungs. This position is not recommended for respiratory challenges like COPD unless lung functioning has improved through practice.

Lying on our stomach or crawling position on hands and knees. This position maintains a relatively straight spine while learning how much our lungs can expand as gravity partners them during expansion. Medical staff often put Breathers with lung challenges in these positions. Breathees with lung challenges may lean over to breathe more effectively during Breathwork sessions.

This position can connect us with earth, ground, our inner ground, home, and our instinctual capacities. Conversely, if we want to keep a secret, hide, or have more control, our belly contacting the ground can feel safe until we feel ready to open. Outdoors, this position helps us experience ourselves as part of nature.

Lying on our side. Many Breathers love this position's physical and/or emotional comfort. It creates safety for exploring sensations, emotions, memories, images, and birth memories. There's an obvious womb connection, thus we may position this way spontaneously when passing through intense emotions or opening into a new emergence. Breathees lying on their side next to Therapist-Breathworkers, can experience autonomy and intimacy simultaneously.

However, this position may also restrict breathing, so Breathees sometimes use it unconsciously to reduce sensation, feeling, or relatedness. Side-lying can reduce forced vital capacity of the lungs, with one study showing that left side lying reduces this capacity more in Breathers 50-plus years (Manning et al., 1999). Medical conditions may require someone to use this position. Otherwise, I usually only recommend conscious side-lying for short periods of therapeutic impact.

Squatting. Breathwork while squatting can benefit our immediate respiratory functioning and overall respiratory well-being. Squatting improves lung function by optimizing gas diffusion from our lungs to blood. Some Breathers, particularly children, spontaneously squat during respiratory distress (Jeon et al., 2018), immediately increasing oxygen concentration and reducing carbon dioxide. Additionally, squatting strengthens the gluteus maximus muscle and thighs, can stabilize the lumbar region, and provides resistance dynamics—all of which can contribute to enhanced lung function. (Hackett, 2020). Alternatives are: sitting on a chair with knees at 90-degree angle, elbows on thighs, leaning over; squatting with hips and buttocks against a wall, leaning forward; and sitting on a pile of pillows on the floor, leaning forward.

Cervical alignment. Heads leaning forward while sitting or lying with many pillows can prevent full breathing, and induce psoas spasms and pelvic rotation which adversely impacts the diaphragm's capacity. The psoas muscle connects the diaphragm to the femur; therefore, tight psoas muscles send information that mobilize fight or flight. Dysfunctional breathing ensues which expresses itself uniquely in each individual (faster, shallow, constricted, etc.). When breathing slows, feedback goes to the psoas that we are safe. When the psoas or breathing is dysfunctional or unregulated, it adversely impacts the other. Conversely, when one becomes coherent and regulated, it positively impacts the other.

Movement—position in motion. Movement opens areas of growth—like extrapolating lines in calculus to generate three-dimensional areas. Breathwork can sometimes mobilize greater effects through walking, dancing, shaking, free flow, running, yoga postures, Tai Chi, Qigong, and more—*if they are not distracting from the breathing.*

Ambulatory Breathwork. Breathwork while walking, especially outdoors, is fantastic for grounding, flexibility, empowerment, coordination, and integrating CB into daily life. Practicing barefoot can be enlivening. Preliminary studies show improved sleep, well-being, and reduced pain—possibly thanks to contact with the earth's electrons (Chevalier et al., 2012). CB can heighten the positive impacts of walking, and walking can enhance breathing. They form a reliable, emotionally safe partnership for practicing breathing and integration, and amplify embodied feelings of belonging.

Eye positions. Eyes move and assume positions in connection to information flow, memory, and awareness. EMDR Therapy utilizes these powerful pathways to free physical and emotional patterning tied to trauma. Resonant with EMDR, a Breathee's eyes often move around spontaneously under closed eyelids during transformational moments in Breathwork. Attention to eye movement and position—closed, open, gazing softly, focusing, scanning, or being expressive—reveals fertile information during Breathwork.

Increasingly in the twenty-first century, our eyes are stressed, contracted, and progressively inflexible from focus on small areas—in particular screens—for unnaturally long periods. Closing our eyes doesn't relax the lens—we need to look into expanses (Kelly, 2021). Historically, humans frequently and naturally looked at expansive landscapes and unobstructed horizons. Therefore, before and after Breathwork it's ideal to scan the broadest horizon possible from outside or through a window—moving our eyes back and forth slowly and gently for several minutes while breathing deeply.

Closed eyes enhance most Breathwork because the interior self is emphasized. Some Breathers like blindfolds. Occasionally, open eyes support attention on the interior self. We can also open and close our eyes resonant to various experiences and needs.

Opening our eyes after Breathwork is a fertile moment. Bringing awareness to how our closed eyes feel in response to inner shifts, then maintaining those sensations with open eyes, CB, and silence for several minutes, enhances integration.

Types and qualities of body positions are innumerable. Indeed, when we allow spontaneous movement—which we explore in Chapter 9—infinite numbers of micromovements and permutations are possible.

Embracing Air Hunger to Experience Air Fulfillment and Joy

We're designed to breathe easily with normal carbon dioxide levels; therefore, we aren't usually conscious of air hunger. Various physiological and/or emotional conditions can cause air hunger—the real or imagined sense of not getting enough air. Air hunger is a primal sensation, a compelling urge to breathe when breathing is dysregulated.

Peter Litchfield, respiratory psychophysiologist and president of the Professional School of Behavioral Health Sciences, continually reinforces that breathing is psychophysiological and, therefore, air hunger is as well (Litchfield & Reamer, 2022). Emotions can stir or be caused by air hunger sensations that induce behavioral changes. A Breather may feel there isn't enough air in a small space and behave accordingly, while others in the same space don't feel air hunger. Several trailblazing *pulmonauts* (a phrase James Nestor conjured), including Buteyko, McKeown, Olsson, Litchfield, and Nestor, offer compelling explanations for air hunger and methods for reducing CO_2 sensitivity.

Carbon dioxide is like compost for well-being; it is necessary for regulating extracellular fluids (blood plasma, lymph, cerebrospinal fluid, and interstitial fluid) and it's indispensable for stimulating physiological impulses to breathe. Carbon dioxide is also a medium for relatedness with the venerable plant world—we offer them CO_2 and they offer oxygen to us.

When emotional or behavioral reactions to breathing result in air hunger, Breathwork mitigates those patterns by fostering healthy respiration and stabilizing CO_2 concentrations. A transitional period may include increasing our tolerance to CO_2 (reducing sensitivity to CO_2). We may have become conditioned to depleted CO_2 through overbreathing or blowing out exhales in response to emotional triggers. Emotions don't lower CO_2 concentrations. Learned breathing reactions to emotions take over breathing for control—resulting in compromised chemoreflex regulation and breathing out of sync with respiratory requirements.

Decreasing physical and emotional sensitivity to air hunger is one of the best ways to foster nasal breathing and slower breathing. Science shows that nasal breathing and slower breathing contribute to emotional and physical health and restore healthy CO_2 concentrations (Brown & Gerbarg, 2005a).

We can establish our base CO_2 tolerance using Dr. Konstantin Buteyko's wonderful process with a timer that measures seconds.

1. Sit comfortably, without crossed legs, with normal nasal breathing, without trying to breathe deeper, for 5 minutes.
2. After a normal exhale, pinch the nose with the fingers to stop breathing, without mouth breathing.
3. Immediately begin the timer and hold the breath until feeling the first definite desire to breathe—an urge to breathe, or involuntary contractions in the throat, stomach, or breathing muscles.
4. Note the number of seconds at that point and commence breathing again. Breathing should be normal. Needing a huge breath rather than a calm breath means we've held our breath too long (McKeown, 2020).
5. The time between holding our nose closed and feeling an urge to breathe is a *control pause* (CP).
    - CP of 40–60 seconds indicates healthy breathing patterns with

excellent physical endurance.
- *CP above 25 seconds indicates breathing is functional.*
- *CP of 10–20 seconds indicates significant breathing impairment and poor tolerance to physical exercise.*
- *CP under 10 seconds indicates severe breathing impairments with very poor exercise tolerance and chronic health problems.*

The goal is to reach 40 seconds. If CP is the normal range (20–40 seconds), it helps to increase physical exercise, beginning with walking and working towards more strenuous forms. Buteyko recommends walking while holding one nostril closed to build air hunger tolerance. Every 5-second increase in our CP will enhance our exercise capacity and well-being (McKeown, 2020).

Ultimately, the linchpin of breathing for optimal regulation is working with breathing as a psychophysiological medium and understanding its impact on cellular respiration. While slowness and nasal breathing can extinguish fears about getting enough air, so can any kind of CB, including breathing rapidly. *Any technique that reduces fear lessens the urge to take control of breathing.* Also, practicing inhaling as soon as we've finished exhaling and exhaling as soon as we've finished inhaling can ameliorate breath hesitancy and aid us in meeting emotions, fears, or reflex sensations we've been avoiding. Reducing tension and allowing full breathing, rather than trying to seize or force full breathing, may be the ultimate medicine for optimal cellular respiration and restoring trust in our breathing.

Resetting our physiology to attain normal concentrations of CO_2 is also metaphorically and psychodynamically a pathway for embracing our fears and shadows, discovering the hidden gold within, feeling the joy of life force, and *loving* breathing and life more deeply.

Overbreathing and Underbreathing

Mismatches between breathing mechanics and cellular respiration are most often due to overbreathing or underbreathing. **Overbreathing**, usually the result of blowing off too much CO_2, is frequently stimulated by low

CO_2 tolerance. Overbreathers often feel they can't get enough air through nasal breathing. Consciously or unconsciously, they breathe more quickly and/or deeper to alleviate air hunger. Though physical or medical conditions may be present that prevent getting enough oxygen, the root of daily overbreathing is usually related to behavior.

Overbreathing depletes CO_2. Too much emphasis on the exhale (sometimes we even blow) siphons off excessive amounts of CO_2. Overbreathing usually occurs through mouth breathing, yet can happen with nasal breathing. Overbreathing for extended periods, or chronically, dysregulates pH, causing corresponding physical, emotional, cognitive, and behavioral imbalances. Overbreathing can also induce anxiety, poor cognition, inability to focus, jaw malformations in growing bones, sleep deprivation, nightmares, paranoia, and more (Kahn et al., 2020).

This Buteyko practice, shared by Patrick McKeown in a personal conversation, shifts overbreathing, dissolves air hunger, and invites lighter breathing, so we meet air hunger sensations with more awareness.

> Place one hand on the belly and the other on the chest, breathing through the nose only and keeping the chest still, while allowing the belly to move in and out slightly with each breath. Gradually allow in less and less air, perhaps even to feeling we're barely or not breathing. We can remain in this light breathing for as long as comfortable, or up to 3 to 7 minutes. When there's increased moisture in our mouth, and warmth throughout our body, the body is utilizing oxygen better and there is improved blood circulation.

Patrick says we needn't be concerned about diaphragmatic breathing here: "If you're already doing so, then great. If not, fine. Concentrate on slowing, quieting and softening the breath. The objective is sustaining tolerable air hunger for 3 to 5 minutes."

Underbreathing is characterized by a lack of vitality in breathing or shallow, inefficient breathing, usually resulting in excess CO_2 (depressing the urge to inhale) and low oxygen simultaneously. It can be caused by medical or physiological conditions, yet is more often caused by conscious or unconscious fears that breathing deeply will stir up unwanted emotions or trigger air hunger. Consequently, we may pause longer than optimal before inhaling (reducing oxygen intake); inhale too quickly with small, exaggerated, and forceful inhales that cause oxygen insufficiency; or not exhale sufficient CO_2 to trigger the urge to inhale. Underbreathing for extended periods, or chronically, can lead to fatigue, shallow breathing, shortness of breath, low mood, depression, lack of motivation, confusion, headaches, and even seizures.

The more buoyant our breathing, the more we engage life force and emotions. We meet breathing hesitancy with awareness and reduced fear.

Two practices for repatterning underbreathing:

1. Inhale very softly, with slow, gentle, relaxed exhales. We can softly lengthen each inhale and exhale, until we're almost squeezing air out of our lungs, yet not forcefully. We exhale slowly and thoroughly empty the lungs.
2. Placing one hand on our belly and the other on our chest, we breathe nasally (if possible), bringing attention to the point between exhale and inhale. When our belly is fully relaxed and emptied, we invite its expansion with immediacy, yet gentleness, followed by expanding our rib cage, and then chest. Once we sense expanded dynamism and continuity (lack of breath hesitancy), we breathe this way for 10 breaths, or 3 to 7 minutes. Increased physical energy indicates greater life force and reduced fear.

Connected Breathing and Breath Retention

CONNECTED BREATHING

It's invaluable to learn to recognize the moments when we stop breathing, tense our breathing, or lazily pause. Optimal breathing barely pauses between inhalation and exhalation, or between exhalation and inhalation. Healthy babies' breathing is lively, with a toned reflex, even during calm breathing. The inhale is full and sufficient, and when it culminates the body wants to exhale. The exhale is efficient, and when it is complete the body wants to inhale.

Conscious Connected Breathing (CCB) is essentially breathing without pause or gaps between inhalation and exhalation, or exhalation and inhalation. Some call this circular breathing, yet it's not the circular breathing musicians use.

The psychological implications of CCB are astounding. Breathing, as our first act, basically becomes the primary neural substrate for everything we experience. Breathing is a physiological message to the brain that we're alive. Thus, consciously breathing 100% of the time transmits a message to our soma and psyche that we're willing to be 100%—*fully*—alive!

Many patterns of unhealthy breath holding, shallow breathing, or other breath dysregulations happen because of fear, trauma, and suppressing our life force. Conscious Connected Breathing promotes healthy inhalation, which activates the sympathetic nervous system, and healthy exhalation, which activates the parasympathetic nervous system.

Qigong and other time-honored wisdom traditions also acknowledge the importance of connected breathing—letting one breath flow into the next without pause. Qigong and Taoist Breathing Practices are designed to support our breathing in harmonious relatedness with nature—and nature is dynamic. Even calm and apparent stillness are dynamic. Something is always moving.

Anxiety—characterized by rapid breathing and forcefully blown exhalations—decreases CO_2 levels, inhibiting energized inhalations. CCB's key is a relaxed exhalation, whether breathing quickly or slowly during Breathwork or life. Relaxed exhalations balance the autonomic nervous system, calm us, and expel and retain the right amounts of CO_2 so that inhalation is energized.

To strengthen our capacity for CCB, we can practice from 1 to 20 easy, connected breaths, several times daily. We invite ourselves to relax and exhale as soon as we inhale completely, and to initiate and welcome an inhale as soon as we finish exhaling.

Frequent practicing of CCB can reveal unconscious, maladaptive psychophysiological patterns. Do we tend to pause and hold our breath after inhalation, or before inhalation? At both points or neither? In broad terms, hesitancy to inhale is fear about what will happen next and our capacity to meet it, or sadness about our lives. While experienced Breathers can delay exhalation to hang out in expanded consciousness, unconsciously delaying exhalation usually indicates fear about letting defenses down or beliefs that we're toxic or shameful. By sensing rough patches during any part of inhalation and exhalation—tension, constriction, or lack of movement in the abdomen, rib cage, or chest—we may bring awareness to internalized shame, hurt, grief, anger, fear, and trauma.

BREATH RETENTION

Breath retention or conscious breath holding, common in yogic traditions, can be practiced for specific purposes, therapeutic corrections, and developing body mastery. Benefits include:

- Developing resilience for challenges where physical resources are suboptimal.
- Gathering internal energy for focus, attention, strengthening resolve, and so on, and retaining energy to heighten life force.
- Retraining our lungs to transform patterns of oversensitivity and reactivity—for example, improving asthma control and developing resiliency (McHugh et al., 2003).
- Developing lung and body strength for heroic activities or extreme sports that require substantial stamina.
- Developing capacity to stabilize expanded states of consciousness.

Conscious breath retention isn't the same as unconsciously holding our breath, which often arises from fear, depletion, shock, or habit, and may manifest from unexpressed or unintegrated grief, anger, fear, need, and memories, or repressed joy and love. Unconscious breath holding can irritate our lungs and cause light-headedness, anxiety, and elevated blood pressure (Medical News Today, 2023).

Many hold their breath when feeling elation. Breathing deeply and continuously through life's joys creates new reservoirs for more delight and jubilation. For instance, learning how to breathe deeply and continuously through orgasm leads to more sensation, pleasure, vitality, intimacy, and full-bodied experiences.

Some aficionados of CCB may rail against conscious breath-holding techniques. However, orienting the word *holding* as the way we *hold* a beloved, we can view breath holding as *breath savoring*—retaining breath to experience and receive every garnish—knowing it delivers magnificent potential, whether it's amplifying our life force or rescuing someone from drowning. Holding our breath from fear, habit, or conditioning is not holding anything consciously. Being present and cherishing breathing—*breath savoring*—births new dimensions in Breathwork and living. Breath savoring can be sacred and honor breathing as an essential worker.

Conscious breath retention can increase our CCB capacity. Pausing a few seconds after inhaling increases lung pressure, giving lungs time to fully expand and increase their capacity. Blood traveling to the heart, brain, and muscles is more oxygenated. Pausing after exhaling (without anxiety) can connect us with deeper trust and inner peace about just being. CCB after conscious breath holding is powerful and integrative.

Box Breathing utilizes breath retention. Box Breathing is often taught as counting to four (usually seconds) for the inhale, four for breath retention, four for the exhale, and four for breath retention. It's a good baseline. Finding a count that works for us and adjusting it over months and years is better. We might start with two and eventually work up to 10, 15, or more.

Body positions, breathing rates, muscle movements, and attention can support or inhibit our breath retention capacity. CCB is wonderful for both Group 5 Breathwork and daily life, and conscious breath retention can serve specific purposes that enhance our overall capacity to be present.

Nose Breathing and Mouth Breathing

Our bodies have innate intelligence and are brilliantly designed. Breathing can happen through our nose or mouth, so there are good reasons for both.

NOSE BREATHING

Nasal breathing has manifold advantages over mouth breathing (Ruth, 2015):

- Filters out pollen, bacteria, viruses, and other pathogens because air passes through little fine hair nostrils called cilia and vibrissae.
- Humidifies inhaled air through nasal moisture, preventing lung and nasal passages from drying out.
- Increases oxygen uptake through extended exhalation.
- Creates additional resistance in the air stream (nostrils are smaller than mouths) strengthening lung elasticity.
- Produces nitric oxide—a powerful vasodilator—supporting oxygen absorption in the lungs.
- Optimizes memory consolidation and recall (Reynolds, 2018).
- Stimulates parasympathetic activation which calms us faster than mouth breathing.

In everyday moments, for healthy living, nasal breathing is optimal.

In *Breath*, James Nestor (2020) elucidates how various peoples, such as Indigenous North American and South American cultures, trained themselves and their children to nasal breathe for health, disease prevention, and beauty. Wearing soft, hypoallergenic, medical-grade tape over our mouth at night can train us to breathe nasally. First, we can practice closed mouth breathing during the day. Anders Olsson (2014) says the initial discomfort that can occur is usually a mental block that passes quickly. The Buteyko Clinic has uniquely well-designed tape (MyoTape) for nose breathing. Alternatively, James Nestor (2020) successfully used 3M Transpore Clear 1-inch Wide First Aid Tape to close his lips to avoid covering his mouth completely.

Alternate nostril breathing can increase comfort with nasal breathing. Alternate nostril breathing promotes temperature regulation; is believed to balance sympathetic and parasympathetic systems; increases left and right brain activity, and the integration between them; improves sleep quality; relieves stress; and lessens, inhibits, or halts anxiety and panic attacks. Our body naturally switches between right and left nostril breathing. (Kanorewala & Suryawanshi, 2022)

Some studies suggest, and numerous anecdotal reports say, that right nostril breathing is energizing, warming, and activates the sympathetic nervous system and left brain—and many yogic traditions teach this. James Nestor (2020) describes practicing 24 breaths of right-nostril breathing to "heat up [his] body and aid digestion" and breathing through the left nostril only "before meals and any other time [he] wanted to relax." The effects lasted about 30 minutes and were enough to prevent gastroesophageal reflux.

Many traditions also teach that left nostril breathing is cooling, calming, and activates the vagus nerve and right brain. In *Breath,* James Nestor cites a University of California–San Diego 3-year case study of a woman with schizophrenia who had "significantly greater left nostril dominance." The researchers hypothesized that this created hyperarousal of her right brain, amplifying her imagination. When taught to right-nostril breathe, "she experienced far fewer hallucinations" (Nestor, 2020).

Shirley Telles and her team do extensive studies of the ancient yogic texts. The texts refer to the natural shifting from left to right nostril, and suggest that when we breathe through the right nostril we should engage in energizing activities. When we breathe through the left we should be more contemplative. Notably, forced breathing through one nostril is not suggested. A May 2024 study by Shirley and her research team show that both right and left nostril breathing yield increased oxygenation. She pointed out to me that few studies compare uni nostril breathing to alternate nostril breathing through both nostrils, or simple breath awareness. She suggests there are immediate differentiated effects from breathing through each nostril; yet 15 minutes of breathing results in the same effects for each nostril—that the increased oxygenation of CB through either nostril elicits similar effects. What is clear is that alternate nostril breathing is oxygenating and increases nasal breathing capacity.

ALTERNATE NOSTRIL BREATH PRACTICE

Sitting or standing in a comfortable position with a relatively straight spine, slowly and deeply inhale and exhale. Close the right nostril with a thumb or finger, and inhale through the left nostril. Then close the left nostril and exhale through the right nostril. Now, inhale through the right nostril, then close the right nostril and exhale through the left nostril. This is one cycle of alternate nostril breathing. Practice at least three cycles up to 5 minutes. Advanced practitioners can practice longer.

We may have difficulty breathing nasally due to congestion, habit, or physiological challenges. Heath and emotional discoveries and regulation can be supported by comfortable, deep, nasal breathing, so it's worth the effort to remedy.

If nasal breathing is challenging due to conditioned breathing habits, we can practice methods that slowly increase air hunger tolerance, and we can practice alternate nostril breathing to cultivate ease with nasal breathing. When congestion hinders nasal breathing, various decongestion practices can help, such as the following Buteyko exercise.

ACUTE OR CHRONIC NASAL DECONGESTION EXERCISE

Refrain from this practice when pregnant or with serious medical conditions. With histories of anxiety and panic disorders, only hold the breath until light, moderate air hunger is experienced.

- Take a silent breath in and out nasally, as well as possible.
- Pinch the nose with the fingers to hold the breath.
- Walk as many paces as possible (or nod your head up and down if you're not mobile) with your breath held. Try building moderate to strong feelings of air shortage (air hunger).
- When resuming breathing, breathe only nasally and calm the breathing immediately. The first breath will likely be larger than usual. Calm the breathing by reducing the second and third breaths.

If breathing isn't calm within two to three breaths, we've held our breath too long.
- In a minute or so, repeat the exercise.
- Repeat this exercise five or six times until the nose is decongested.

Patrick McKeown (2020) describes the physiological effects of this exercise as "nitric oxide pooling inside the nose," which then moves into the lungs. Also, breath holding increases blood CO_2 stimulating inhalation. This practice opens the nose in about 4 to 5 minutes, even with a head cold.

MOUTH BREATHING

Breathing through our mouth comfortably and optimally is a vital ability!

However, mouth breathing bypasses the nasal breathing benefits described above; thus, mouth breathing in ordinary moments can dysregulate pH, induce hyperventilation, and in extreme cases cause fainting. Mouth breathing bypasses the nasal breathing benefits described above. Chronic long-term mouth breathing has been linked with reduced memory and learning capacity, sleep disorders, worsened asthma and other respiratory difficulties, reduced attention and academic performance, learning disabilities, abnormal jaw development in children, tooth decay, and more (Tsubamoto-Sano et al., 2019). Constant mouth breathing can stimulate perpetual physiological emergency reactions.

Yet mouth breathing can support physiological well-being in many ways. Additionally, evidence shows that mouth breathing can nourish emotional wellness by stimulating dopamine and other neurotransmitters that promote initiatory energy, focus, and abilities to act—all important to psychological well-being (McKeown, 2020).

Benefits of mouth breathing include:

- Breathing orally delivers oxygen to muscles quickly during strenuous activity and danger (LaComb et al., 2017). Whether running to catch someone who is falling or passionately running toward a

beloved, we often orally breathe spontaneously to initially receive greater volumes of air.
- Exhaling or sighing orally facilitates immediate relaxation. With relaxed jaws, we can completely relax the pelvic floor muscles as the lungs empty. This technique is found in abundance in yogic texts and medical sources alike. Toning and relaxing the pelvic floor significantly impacts urinary and bowel functioning, heals and prevents pelvic pain, and supports comfortable sexual intercourse.
- Deep, relaxed oral exhaling, or gently blowing through slightly pursed lips, induces deeper nasal inhalation, which increases lung capacity.
- Nasal inhalations followed by oral exhalations often deepens breathing and helps access physical and emotional energy during challenges.
- Efficient, healthy mouth breathing can support moderate to high-intensity exercise. University of Nevada researchers observed that during 4-minute periods of any exercise intensity, oxygen uptake was 8–10% higher during oral breathing than nasal breathing. They concluded that "oral breathing represents the more effective mode, particularly at higher exercise intensities" (LaComb et al., 2017).
- Especially when prone to anxiety, inhaling nasally and exhaling slowly through pursed lips can evince greater control and strength, reducing anxiety and panic attacks. While unconscious rapid oral breathing—depleting CO_2 and inducing hyperventilation—can cause anxiety, heightened CO_2 levels can instigate panic and anxiety too. The 4-7-8 breathing technique, championed by Dr. Andrew Weil, recommends a whoosh sound on the exhale, breathing a bit forcefully, yet slowly (Fletcher, 2019).
- The ability to sigh through the mouth may be critical to well-being and survival. We sigh nasally or orally about every five breaths to pop open our alveoli, preventing them from collapsing. For this reason, respirators include a super breath every five or so breaths. Neuroscientist Jack L. Feldman points out that when sighing is consistently suppressed, the lungs deteriorate fairly rapidly and life may be threatened. Jack notes that gasping through the mouth

physiologically rearouses the brain and awareness (Feldman & Huberman, 2022).
- Many Breathing Practices, including time-honored yogic traditions, involve deep inhalations followed by audible sighs. Mouth breathing is used in some yogic traditions to explore emotional depths and intrapsychic dimensions.

One ancient yogic technique, *Sitali Pranayama*, mirrors a dog's mouth breathing to cool body temperature:

1. We choose a comfortable seated position (as free of allergens and air pollution as possible).
2. We stick out our tongue and curl it to bring the outer edges together.
3. If our tongue doesn't do this, we can purse our lips.
4. We inhale orally, slowly.
5. We exhale nasally, slowly.
6. We continue breathing this way for up to 5 minutes.

When we breathe through our mouths consciously, we join our body's wisdom that, during joyful times, healthy exertion, danger-induced stress, or imminent needs for relaxation, the necessity for quick, larger volumes of oxygen can outweigh any dangers of mouth breathing. When we wish to explore our deep emotions and intrapsychic terrain, mouth breathing is extremely effective—it's used by some yogic practices and almost all Group 5 Breathwork. Mouth breathing can prepare our body with surpluses of oxygen to amplify energy and meet complex psychological issues, heighten life force, and perceive spiritual dimensions. Thus, many Group 5 Breathwork methods encourage mouth breathing, which also brings more immediate awareness to bodily sensations, helping us remain grounded during the magnitude of the journeys.

Many Breathers are rightly concerned that mouth breathing and rapid breathing often correlate with overbreathing and reduced carbon dioxide reserves, which can cause hypocapnia. We can compare three unhealthy breathing behaviors—involuntary fast breathing, chronic (not temporary or volitional) mouth breathing, and overbreathing. All three are usually motivated by air hunger, or worry about getting enough air, and are reinforced by whichever kind of breathing elicits anxiety reduction and feeling in control. In conversation, Peter Litchfield offered some salient guidance about this psychophysiological landscape:

> Avoid simple unidimensional mechanical explanations which are typically misconceptions about one physical action triggering another, such as mouth and fast breathing necessarily causing overbreathing, i.e., hypocapnia. Psychophysiological explanations include habit triggers, motivation, and outcomes based on a third factor that regulates all three behaviors. People who worry about getting enough air will likely be motivated to engage in all three behaviors. For a specific individual, learning to nasal breathe may result in reduction or elimination of fast breathing and overbreathing (normalizing CO_2 levels), thus confirming a practitioner's view that mouth breathing was the culprit. A breathing behavior analysis provides details about a person's relevant behavioral variables for mouth breathing. Some people have better respiration (CO_2 concentration) while mouth breathing than nasal breathing. In measuring CO_2 levels of countless people, we have observed numerous people mouth breathing who are not overbreathing. Indeed, switching from nasal to mouth improves CO_2 concentration in some people who overbreathe during nasal breathing. If overbreathing is triggered by trauma, learning one kind of mechanics vs. another becomes irrelevant.

Thus, conscious mouth breathing doesn't innately lead to overbreathing, rapid breathing, or hypocapnia. Patrick McKeown (2020) agrees that mouth breathing is beneficial for a short time when extreme physical capacity is needed to work on certain aspects of body mastery and for deep, soul-searching inner work.

Overall, nasal breathing is most healthy. However, it's essential to learn to utilize whatever breathing, including mouth breathing, is best suited for each step of the grace-filled, and sometimes arduous, trip through our past and present travails and future's promise. In Indigenous cultures where children had been guided from the beginning to breathe through their nose, perhaps they could process trauma and have personal growth breakthroughs solely through nasal breathing. In our modern culture, nasal breathing may be insufficient for the entire trek into becoming and integrating ourselves. Our need to unwind so much physical and psychological tension may require sighing more and drinking in deep gulps of air. Perhaps all the unconscious mouth breathing and overbreathing are cries for help being expressed through breathing—Breathwork sessions wanting to happen.

The Spectrum of Slow Deep Breathing to Powerful Fast Breathing

CONSCIOUS, SLOW, DEEP BREATHING

As we have seen conscious, slow, deep breathing has irrefutable benefits including:

- Reducing cortisol levels (Wehrwein et al., 2012)
- Resetting the autonomic nervous system into balance (Telles et al., 1994)
- Inducing calm
- Lowering blood pressure (Mourya et al., 2009)
- Stimulating the polyvagal response (Gerritsen & Band, 2018)

Positive emotional effects include:

- Slowing down, experiencing the present from larger perspectives—enabling more flow.
- Interrupting emotional reactivity, contextualizing and attending to challenging emotions.
- Transcending survival mode.
- Reminding us of life's goodness—that relaxation, peace, and joy are available.

- Supporting empathic listening to others, responding thoughtfully and creatively.

Many Breathers appreciate having specific techniques to learn how to consciously slow their breathing. Matrika Pranayama and Ujjayi Pranayama are two time-honored, recommended practices. Detailed instructions for Ujjayi Pranayama are in the section Tongue and Mouth Placement earlier in this chapter. Detailed guidelines for Matrika Pranayama are in the section Breathing Rates and Ratios in this chapter, and in Chapter 7.

CONSCIOUS, DEEP, RAPID BREATHING:

- Stimulates dopamine production
- Raises energy levels for activity
- Can build strength and endurance
- Raises blood pressure when needed
- Heightens alertness, focus, and attention
- Elicits greater response and activation of the caudal medial cortex for executive functioning (Herrero et al., 2018)

Behavioral and emotional effects of fast breathing include:

- Increasing confidence and capacity
- Heightening energy for expression and engagement with others
- Reducing fear
- Generating courage
- Strengthening rapid decision-making (Herrero et al., 2018)

Breathers new to Breathwork can safely benefit from fast breathing for up to a minute. With some training and expert guidance, 2 minutes can yield positive results. For sessions longer than 2 minutes, experience, knowledge about self-regulation, and guidance from well-trained Breathworkers are highly recommended.

Shirley Telles finds that all four of the most researched breathing techniques—*Bhastrika* (fast with equally active inhale and exhale),

Kapalabhati (fast, with active exhale only), *Bhramari* (bumblebee, humming sound while exhaling), and *Nadi Shodhana* (alternate nostril breathing)—reduce state anxiety. However, only Kapalabhati reliably improves attention without sympathetic arousal—making it ideal for calm, clear decision-making. The forceful exhale, longer than the inhale, stimulates attention while inducing parasympathetic activation and relaxation.

For Kapalabhati Breathing, also called Breath of Fire, we generate slow deep inhales, followed by nasal exhales with as many short and sharp segments as possible, up to 120 segments on one exhale. We use belly force to blow out nasally. Many Breathers move their belly forcefully toward the spine for each segment/blow. We can also make short sounds on each blow through an open mouth. The seed mantra *hoo* is often used.

Beginners should start with 20 segments per exhale. With experience, Shirley suggests either 120 segments per exhale for 1 minute of breathing, or 30 segments per exhale for 5 minutes, followed by 1 minute of slow deep breathing. Then repeat the cycle three times (Sharma et al., 2021). Kapalabhati is thought to aid in purification and detoxification due to active expulsion emphasizing the abdomen; whereas Bhastrika is usually taught for energizing, with most guidance emphasizing chest movement.

Although Bhastrika is often called Bellows Breath, Shirley says that equates blacksmith's bellows with deep breathing, whereas she found that a specific fifteenth century hatha yoga text doesn't suggest deep breaths, whereas 40% of modern published studies define Bhastrika as deep, fast breathing. The ancient text describes Bhastrika as mindful, specifically prescribing the depth as inhaling up to the heart lotus and exhaling between the chest, throat region, and cranium—never as diaphragmatic, or deep breathing. Shirley notes that by breathing fast, repetitively, and yet deeply, we would likely overbreathe, hyperventilate, and diminish the precious carbon dioxide in our blood (Telles, 2023).

- Begin Bhastrika Breathing by breathing nasally and deeply several times, expanding the belly during inhalation.
- Then start forceful nasal exhales and inhales, approximately one breath per second.

- Continue for 20 seconds to 2 minutes (only 1 minute if a beginner), followed by at least 1 minute of slow deep recovery breathing. Repeat the cycle up to several times.

The Art of Living Institute offers a version of bending our elbows by our sides and making a fist next to each shoulder. On each deep inhale, we raise the hands straight up with open fingers. With slightly forced exhales, we bring our arms and fists down to the original position. Twenty breaths are suggested, followed by placing the palms on the sides of the body and breathing normally for several breaths, then practicing two additional rounds (Singh, 2021).

Experienced Breathers, with expert guidance, can extend the time for rapid deep breathing, to exceptionally transformative effect. Jack Kornfield, renowned and beloved psychologist, author, and Buddhist teacher, spoke of the irreplaceable training and impact of intense quick breathing during an inspiring conversation:

> We are in the play of energy and our sense of self expands from separateness to vastness, from separateness to the great heart of loving awareness, which is what we really are. Along with practices of slowing and steadying the breath, there are also practices of deepening and intensifying the breath. In one Burmese monastery where I trained as a monk, we practiced the breathing techniques of Sun Lun Sayadaw. We would sit for an hour and a half to two hours several times a day in a great hall surrounded by mirrored glass and large gongs. The master instructed us to take 45 minutes to breathe as hard and deep as we possibly could over and over, riding that power of the breath as we breathed through every state of mind and body that arose. He explained that our distracted modern minds could not focus on breathing very easily anymore and so it was helpful, if not necessary, to intensify the breath. As we breathed hard and deep, riding the breath through restlessness and pain, through imagination and vision, through pleasure and pain, he would speak like [a] coach at a championship game. "If you want to really awaken, ride your breath—deepen it, breathe faster, breathe fuller," he would say.

"Keep it going. Steady. Let all things drop away. Become the breath itself. Breathe and breathe." And we did. After 45 minutes, he would ring the great gong. We were instructed to breathe in and rest in the stillness before our breath resumed itself. This would often be several minutes and in that vast stillness there was an openness alive with energy, radiant and luminous. He instructed us to sit in that luminous, alive presence that the breath had opened, the gateway that could encompass the heavens and hells of all experience. We sat without moving for another hour. The openness of that invitation, the power of the breath, and the ability to rest in vastness gave us an entry into remarkable states of mystery and healing and experiences of integration and understanding beyond the ordinary. . . . I use these practices to invite others to walk through these gateways.

BREATHWORK AND INTENSE RESPIRATORY EXPERIENCES

During Group 5 Breathwork, clients may briefly experience symptoms similar to hypocapnia or hyperventilation, such as tingling sensations or muscle contractions. Hyperventilation refers to a rapid rate of breathing that leads to overly expelling CO_2 which can lower levels of blood CO_2 (hypocapnia). However, these sensations often arise from blocked emotions, memories, or awareness rather than physiological imbalances. With proper guidance, Breathees can breathe through these experiences and achieve greater openness and emotional release. Indeed, researchers now look beyond hyperventilation as the sole cause of panic disorder symptoms, considering factors like autonomic nervous system states, slowly adapting stretch receptors, and polyvagal regulation (Eyerman, 2014). During apparent hyperventilation skilled Therapist-Breathworkers can offer various nose and mouth Breathing Practices that draw more attention to inhalation than exhalation, until hyperventilation symptoms have resolved.

Many Therapist-Breathworkers and Breathees have reported extraordinary experiences of transformation, memory retrieval, and expanded states of consciousness, after prolonged periods of voluntary hyperventilation in Breathwork. This is likely due to transient hypofrontality, a state in which neocortex activation is downregulated and limbic system activation is increased, like flow states experienced in creativity, sports, and performance. Group 5 Therapist-Breathworkers share the experiential wisdom that entering these expanded states of consciousness through deeper and/or faster breathing, while not engaging in exercise or activity, will heighten self-awareness and inner exploration. The extra effort required for fast breathing, and the intense physical and psychological phenomena experienced, can act as hormetic stressors (moderate-intensity, short-term stressors that build bodily resilience) potentially rejuvenating cells and tissues. This may contribute to the profound relaxation, power, and euphoria that Breathees report.

Hypoxia is a physiological state in which cells and tissues don't receive enough oxygen for normal, healthy functioning. Breathing to the rescue! Chronically hypoxic people are more prone to hyperventilation or hypocapnia during Breathing Practices. As previously stated, skilled Therapist-Breathworkers can offer practices that place attention on inhalation more than exhalation, using nose or mouth breathing as needed, until Breathees are breathing well. In fact, many Breathees report that important psychospiritual experiences arise from periods of apparent hypoxia or spontaneous breath retention during Breathwork. Indeed, consciously induced hypoxia, like all factors about breathing that are brought into conscious awareness, may have potential benefits, including that during hypoxia, oxygen is redirected to vital organs and extra red blood cells are released by the spleen (Alkan & Akis, 2013).

For example, free divers can hold their breath for up to 10 minutes and they enjoy reduced stress, increased lung function, improved fitness and flexibility, anxiety reduction, and lowered heart rate. To increase the amount of time they can stay submerged, prolonged hyperventilation using pure oxygen is part of the training. They sometimes hyperventilate for up to 20 minutes, which enables the body to expel CO_2.

Acute intermittent hypoxia (AIH) is the term for lowering oxygen levels to 10.5% (50% of normal) for varying amounts of time. When it's studied for spinal cord injury, two of the most desirable outcomes are respiratory integrity (including the hope for independent breathing) and motor capacity (e.g., arm and leg movement, walking). In a January 2022 review of 29 studies using AIH for various concerns such as ALS, sleep apnea, and vascular integrity, one study concluded that "daily AIH may ... preserve upper airway patency and/or swallowing ability in people with cervical spinal cord injuries and other clinical disorders that compromise breathing and airway defense" (Ciesla et al., 2022). The reparative and rejuvenating effects of short-term bursts of hypoxia make sense. There are correlations between aerobic exercise and longevity. Harvard Medical School Professor of Genetics David Andrew Sinclair (2020) says the hypoxic response "is great for inducing just enough stress to activate your body's defenses against aging without doing permanent harm." That's why people who run four to five miles per week reduce their risk of dying in general by 30% and their risk of dying by heart attack by 45% (Lee, 2014).

On the podcast *Breathing for Mental and Physical Health and Performance* with Stanford University neuroscientist Dr. Andrew Huberman, Jack Feldman spoke about episodic hypoxia (Feldman & Huberman, 2022). He described cyclical hyperventilation, in which Breathers hyperventilate for a minute followed by breath retention for as long as possible—either with lungs full of air or empty, which is considered one cycle. (Tummo Breathwork and Wim Hof Breathwork use cyclical hyperventilation.) Cyclical hyperventilation induces shifting from **hyper**ventilation to **hypo**ventilation, resulting in alternating low and high CO_2 levels. Jack says that after three or more cycles, "In humans all the time, it seems to have profound benefits on motor function and cognitive function." Jack noted that with episodic oxygen tank–induced hypoxia, CO_2 levels stay fairly stable and normal because the person is breathing the whole time. In contrast, during cyclical hyperventilation, oxygen stays relatively constant while CO_2 fluctuates "depending on emotional state and activity" (Feldman & Huberman, 2022).

Short periods of hypoxia during Group 5 Breathwork can be trusted as part of the Human Potential Breathwork journey *if* accompanied by well-trained and skilled facilitators. We will read more about these skills later in this chapter and in Chapter 9.

Breathers with chronic hypoxia can trust that Breathwork from all groups will aid in psychophysiological and behavioral healing of breathing. Indeed, a team at Mount Sinai Hospital in New York reported that Breathwork was the only treatment that made a difference for treating hypoxia related to long-term COVID-19. The team posited that the patients, "so many of whom suffered from dizziness and tachycardia, were also breathing shallowly, because of either lung inflammation even in mild cases or viral damage to the vagus nerve" (O'Rourke, 2021).

Hyperoxia (increased oxygen levels) likely stimulates the transcription factors (proteins that transcribe DNA into mRNA, affecting gene expression) that appear to stimulate stem cell proliferation and migration—as does hypoxia. Free diving (with long breath holds), intermittent breath retention in Breathwork, tissue saturation of oxygen during hyperbaric oxygen treatments, short amounts of hyperventilation, and even some hypocapnia during Group 5 Breathwork can all trigger positive physiological mechanisms that repair the body and support mental health. The fact that both intermittent hyperoxia and intermittent hypoxia can induce these factors is called the "hyperoxic hypoxic paradox" (Hachmo et al., 2020). Countless Breathees report positive psychological and spiritual benefits from both pathways. Hyperventilation, hypoxia, and hyperoxia should only be induced with presence, knowledge, and care—without these they can dysregulate the soma and psyche. With optimal coregulation—a well-trained Therapist-Breathworker, self-knowledge, and being an adventurous pulmonaut—fast breathing and transient hyperventilation can positively interrupt our normal physiology to adventure into our unconscious, expanded states of consciousness, and improved health. Peter Litchfield agrees that Breathees can be safely guided into and through these journeys like altered states of consciousness, without drugs.

Life Force, Tingling, Tetany, and Vibration

As Einstein, the ancient Tamil Yoga Siddhas, and quantum physics say in multifarious ways, everything is energy. Our body is energy . . . and when we relax and don't reject ourselves, our body's sensations become more effervescent, less foggy—a more vivid substance—yet less heavy. Consequently, quite spontaneously, without prompting or coaxing, beginning Breathees—including CEOs, professors, plumbers, politicians, parents, and children—frequently describe various sensations of vibration during Breathwork. Depending on what Breathing Practice is employed, and the individual's unique soma and psyche, the vibrational sensations or tingling are usually pleasurable or exhilarating, and often intriguing and energizing. Sometimes the tingling feels unpleasant—like pins and needles that occur when circulation returns after being diminished. In Breathwork, vital energy that has been blocked is being restored.

In extreme cases, we may develop tetany. Tetany is a state of involuntary muscle tension and contractions that often occur in the hands and feet and can surface in other body parts. The contracting muscles of the fingers and hands may cause tension and curling—most likely resulting from overbreathing or hyperventilation reducing calcium levels.

Psychologically, the overbreathing or hyperventilation that causes tetany is often instigated by specific unconscious or conscious emotions, memories, or thoughts that induce subliminal or overt fear. Fear makes it challenging to inhale deeply and exhale with relaxation. Instead, exhalations are forcefully blown out, siphoning off excessive CO_2. As we learned, without sufficient CO_2, we don't receive the proper signal that oxygen is needed. This can intensify fear and drive overbreathing. Conversely, we may unconsciously pause breathing until the CO_2 levels replenish and then feel breath urgency when we breathe. In either case, hyperventilation syndrome often ensues. It can be disconcerting and occasionally uncomfortable, but is not harmful.

Perhaps half of Breathees who practice faster, deeper breathing experience tetany. Although biochemical connections between rapid breathing, blood pH, and tetany exist, something more than physiology occurs. Breathing is psychophysiological—the body has an innate, often ignored, intelligence that Breathwork brings to light. Tetany, from this perspective, is body intelligence expressing energetic congestion to release, and then achieve and bolster wholeness.

Physiologically, tetany rapidly dissipates when Breathee CO_2 levels stabilize and acid-base balance is restored. We can stabilize our CO_2 levels simply by slowing the breath, inhaling deeply and fully, and consciously relaxing on the exhale rather than blowing.

Psychologically, tetany swiftly dissipates when the intrapsychic material that has surfaced the fear, difficult memory or emotion, or expansive life force has been met with awareness, processed, and integrated. Thus, some Breathwork schools perceive tetany as a healing doorway. James Nestor described it to me as "entering a very deep, alpha state, or having bursts of gamma. Whereas otherwise, if someone were running from a tiger it would be a full-on beta state. But when you're in control of it, your body relaxes."

Holotropic Breathworkers massage hands with tetany until Breathees work through whatever imagery, archetypal energy, unconscious material, birth memory, or trauma is surfacing. Some schools encourage breathing through the fear that triggered tetany. The deep transformational experiences and value of Breathees working through tetany cannot be discounted.

When tetany occurs, it is best ameliorated through slow, deep inhales and relaxed exhales, movement, emotional processing, and massage. If tetany continues escalating, we can gauge whether to slow, pause, or breathe through it. This assessment depends on willingness, stamina, and adventurousness. Many Breathees look forward to tingling and tetany because they experience important inner material. Some Breathees grieve when they've integrated the greater life force, and tetany stops happening!

Therapist-Breathworkers and Breathees can creatively address tetany by inquiring, as it's happening, "What wants to be experienced in life that I've been afraid to reach for... or do I desire to reach out and communicate with a person, yet fear is interfering?" It's amazing to identify someone or something, then physically stretch and reach our hands toward that. The energy contracting the hands opens and flows until the hands become like the sun's shining rays, frequently accompanied by enormous emotional releases. These experiences are impressive demonstrations of the somatic–emotional–cognitive continuum (SEC continuum).

The transformational effects that result from working through tetany are reframed by understanding that CB is never really hyperventilation, and is instead, as Dr. Eve Jones writes, "superventilation" (Ray, 1995). When we experience greater life force from breathing into lung space not ordinarily used, and breathe continuously, habits of fear, contraction, and depression transform. For Therapist-Breathworkers, accompanying Breathees into these experiences relies on the depth of our own inner work and comfort with expansive ranges of soma, psyche, and soul.

Breathing Ratios

Conscious inhalation has powerful effects. Conscious exhalation has powerful effects. Every aspect of the breathing cycle contributes to potent outcomes. These impacts can be magnified by giving more attention, time, or force to inhalation, exhalation or both. Learning about and practicing different breathing ratios yields some potent results.

I learned Matrika Pranayama through the 18 Tamil Yoga Siddha lineage, specifically Babaji's Kriya Yoga taught by Yogi S. A. A. Ramaiah, as a one-to-one ratio (1:1), meaning the inhale and exhale's duration are equivalent. This became a continual way of breathing. In contrast, 1:2 breathing ratios (exhalations twice as long as inhalations) relaxed me but did not induce the same level of alertness as Matrika. In Sanskrit, Matrika means Divine Mother or Matrix.

I kept hearing that the antidote for tension, stress, and many undesirable states was deep inhalations followed by longer, slow, deep exhalations, sometimes nasally, sometimes through pursed lips, and sometimes orally. Undoubtedly, this is initially relaxing and, especially with pursed lips, can mitigate respiratory ailments.

I came to believe that our imbalanced modern lifestyle so disposes us toward sympathetic arousal that exact, or close to exact, 1:2 ratios, induce an initial rush of relaxation, easing anxiety and other difficult emotions. That initial rush, relief from our usual sympathetic dominance, could be relaxing enough to induce parasympathetic dominance. Coherent Breathing founder Stephen Elliott, an avid seeker and researcher, described this phenomenon to me as a "prolonged exhalation relaxation response."

Yet Stephen's measurements have shown that our physiological systems are most responsive and resilient when balanced and regular. For everyday functioning, the body prefers equivalent inhales and exhales. Stephen found that breathing coherently for a few cycles, then extending either the exhalation or inhalation, then resuming Coherent Breathing, leads to vagal flow amplifying during exhalation and decreasing during inhalation. The heart rate increases and decreases respectively during inhale and exhale in a reciprocal and resonant relationship. However, when either exhalation or inhalation is prolonged for a while, that resonant action ceases and HRV falls to near zero, only returning to optimal frequency range when Coherent Breathing (a 1:1 ratio) resumes.

Stephen found that periods of prolonged extended exhalation induce relaxation responses of about 12 seconds. Then the heart accelerates, as if the autonomic nervous system is asking for more oxygen. This acceleration reflects a preference for rhythmic breathing patterns of equal periods because there is wave action in the circulatory system during equivalent time of inhales and exhales, regardless of the number of breaths per minute. When exhalation is prolonged, there's an initial corresponding brain wave and HRV relaxation response—yet it doesn't last. Eureka! It's the ratio that counts (pun intended). The 1:1 ratio—Matrika Pranayama—is ultimately the most life-enhancing and stabilizing.

Indeed, a remarkable, randomized, placebo-controlled, exceptionally large study of 400 Breathers shows no measurable benefits of 10 minutes daily for 28 days of Coherent Breathing at 5.5 breaths/minute compared to 10 minutes of 12 breaths per minute with equivalent inhale and exhale. Notably the researchers set out to prove a hypotheses of better outcomes from Coherent Breathing. Though HRV was not measured, both groups exhibited similar scores for significantly decreased stress, anxiety, and depression, and increased mental health and well-being (Fincham et al., 2023)! The study appears to indicate that as long as breathing rate is reasonably slow (12 or less breaths per minute), the 1:1 ratio is the primary factor for well-being and mental health.

I was enthralled with Stephen's impressive search and research. Wanting to understand why some teachers and researchers assert that five breaths per minute creates optimal coherence, and others say six, I discovered a fascinating history. A 1970s study of 20,000 to 30,000 people, and other studies from Luciano Bernardi, Paul Lehrer, Russian scientists, and the Heart Math Institute all found that the natural frequency of blood and fluid flow that optimizes circulation is 0.1 hertz, which translates to six breaths per minute (Russo et al., 2017), which became the gold standard.

Where did 5.1 breaths per minute come from? Stephen concurs that six breaths per minute supports enormous positive benefits for the average Breather. As we learned in Chapter 2, he was intrigued by what British biophysicist and psychobiologist Maxwell Cade called the *Awakened Mind*, when meditation and wakefulness come together in daily activity—what this book calls integrated embodied presence, awakened consciousness, or embodied consciousness. Feedback from therapists that employed Coherent Breathing with their clientele was immediate and consistent. Reports noted that Coherent Breathing elicited positive changes almost immediately, even in many cases that had long eluded treatment.

The Fincham study noted above wasn't measuring for the intriguing Awakened Mind. Indeed, Stephen is strongly interested in determining individual resonant frequencies. For example Stephen's (which he has measured), is 5.8 breaths per minute for everyday optimal autonomic balance, and 5.1 for the Awakened Mind. Most Breathers probably range from 4.5 to seven breaths per minute for optimal autonomic balance (Chaitanya et al., 2022), and three to seven or eight breaths per minute for the Awakened Mind. Consistently practicing for many months or years leads to significant variations.

Notably, Matrika Pranayama promotes a 1:1 ratio, and does not suggest a particular count or time, allowing for individualized resonance. Each breath, we can change the count.

SIMPLE MATRIKA PRANAYAMA PRACTICE

We choose a relaxed, potent, breathing position with relatively straight spine and conscious tongue placement. Now, we establish slow steady inhalations followed by slow steady exhalations. Once able to breathe more slowly, we count the inhale and then count the exhale. We gently adjust the inhale and/or exhale to arrive at the equivalent count for inhale and exhale, lengthening each breath as much as possible. The goal is to find an energizing pace that's not straining. If we've done enough Breathwork to experience significant physiological, emotional, and cognitive benefits, and expanded states of consciousness, we may be able to do Matrika quite slowly—down to one or two breaths per minute or less. It should be an organic arising, never forced, while the body adapts to the transformation.

Practice and Integration of Optimal Breathing

Ultimately, we we practice and master technique to be free from technique, and we learn to breathe from the breath itself. Optimal breathing is cultivated breath by breath. Through diverse techniques and practices, we can exercise the various aspects of optimal breathing we have explored, plus other dimensions in subsequent chapters. Ultimately, our automatic breathing can become the purveyor of our most actualized wholeness and flow.

I recommend a minimum of 7 minutes daily of practices from any Breathwork Group, or simply to do full-bodied optimal breathing. Five-minute sessions support substantive state changes, yet they don't seem to endure for a whole day. Ten minutes can seem daunting to beginners and busy Breathers, and many get sleepy or distracted when practicing that long, initially. Seven minutes seems to elicit a sweet spot for enduring state change and energetic engagement and commitment. Additionally, the number seven is a familiar application—including seven colors of the rainbow, seven days of the week, and seven notes in major and minor Western scales, a lot of African music, and some Indigenous music. Breathers who are inclined to work with the seven chakras can breathe 1 minute with each chakra. Every minute more than seven of daily Breathing Practice is a qualitative investment in well-being and conscious living.

Working effectively with the psyche transforms our breathing physiology. Applying the intricacies of breathing as transformative agents in personal growth and psychological treatment robustly supports healing and wholeness. The greatest power of Breathing Practices surfaces with the art of individual attunement. As we breathe towards that, in the next chapter, we will expand and strengthen our breathing fluency and capacity by exploring and practicing 11 potent Breathing Practices for wholeness and conscious living.

> *All I want is to breathe.... Won't you breathe with me?*
> —TALKING HEADS, "BORN UNDER PUNCHES
> (THE HEAT GOES ON)"

SEVEN

A Breathwork Kit for Whole Living

FIGURE 7.1: *Breath of God*
Lavinia Hardy / artist in mixed media, UK

For cultivating *wholeness* and embodying presence, wisdom, and love, Conscious Breathing (CB) is the most accessible, egalitarian health equity and force multiplier on the planet. To avail ourselves of this force, and foster *daily* growth, development, and integration (*wholeness*), this chapter offers 11 Breathwork Practices, each of which contributes vital nutrients for flourishing. The practices are easily learned and reflect three primary understandings we have been exploring:

- Breathing is our most immediate, accessible, and potent nutrient, medicine, friend, healer, and teacher.
- Whatever our personal history, worldview, or need, each Breather is endowed with potential to be nourished, to blossom, and to contribute to our loved ones, circles of influence, and the entire collective.
- The energy, wisdom, and creativity of CB can be integrated through Breathing Practices/Breathwork to optimize our physical, emotional, cognitive, spiritual, relational, and collective lives.

In a seven-week course I taught online, Breathwork for Human Potential, participants, ages 18–84, reported significant physical, emotional, cognitive, and spiritual benefits, including reduced anxiety and depression, clearing emotional blockages, heightened focus, and deepened intuition. As they enjoyed greater openness and resilience, their relationships with family and friends improved; they recognized the effects of past struggles, generating renewed hope and purpose; and they felt belonging to a larger *inter*connected and *intra*connected whole (per Dan Siegel, see Chapter 12). These changes significantly improved many participants' lives—before the course concluded! One participant, Lavinia Hardy, wrote, "The best consequence of the practices is the sense of being breathed and interconnected with nature, the folk I meet, and all creation."

Eleven Breathwork Practices for Wholeness

1. RECEIVING BREATHING

We are being breathed. We are being given breath. Yet most often we hear the instructions *take a deep breath*. And, indeed, at times we probably need to push against something that's internally or externally pushing against our breathing. Thus, without examination, we ourselves say, *take a deep breath.* Yet perhaps we might inquire, what is the pattern that is taking the deep breath, and who is the one taking the deep breath? Because, mostly, without our effort, we are being breathed. Thus, we might inquire, *are we fully receiving breathing* . . . are we deeply receiving the full riches each breath is offering physically, emotionally, cognitively, and spiritually?

When we receive breathing, we experience the felt sense that breathing is not generated by our efforts or ego. It's being gifted from reality. We can learn to surrender to breathing so our fear-based egoic behaviors don't *take over* breathing. Anything that arises while receiving breathing comes from breathing's intelligence and the body—the enteric brain, the cardiac brain, and the neural brain's intelligence about unwinding from the rejection or suppression of life force—opening pathways for abundant vibrancy. Indeed, it turns out, we can breathe most efficiently and robustly if we're receiving what is given.

Reports of Breathees feeling that they are *being breathed* during Group 5 Breathwork sessions abound. This may be partially due to enhanced gas exchange, oxygenation, and so on; however, most importantly, we have released, let go, and surrendered enough that we open to being breathed, by the powerful, rhythmic waves that comprise reality. When we are receiving breathing, we breathe softly and lightly when needed, and energetically and deeply when needed, for openings, releases, empowerment, and character building—all guided by integrated three-centered wisdom. It may seem we need to *take* a breath to breathe deeply or powerfully. Yet as we become more available and receptive, we breathe just as deeply and powerfully—or more so—by receiving breathing.

Initiating CB by *receiving*, rather than *taking*, generates radical shifts in perspectives, behavior, and relating. A sizable majority of participants in *Breathwork for Human Potential* described Receiving Breathing as the single most transformative practice.

Receiving Breathing contributes to wholeness by:

- Unwinding patterns of tension, overdoing, asserting control, mistrusting the present, and more.
- Learning to trust the safety and vibrancy of ease, receptivity, sensitivity, receiving, and connecting with energy and life.
- Reducing triggers and patterns of air hunger and overbreathing.
- Developing refined capacities for sensing energy and creation.
- Loosening the fear-based ego's need to assert an identity.
- Creating familiarity with authenticity.

RECEIVING BREATHING PRACTICE

- With open or closed eyes, we explore finding a position that feels effortless, inviting our spine to be relatively straight—wave-like, with mobility in the pelvic region around the spine. The spine will feel like it's rising from the pelvis, like a ribbon in the sky is holding us up from our head's crown.
- We bring attention to our breathing.
- Let us *receive* breathing. Differentiated from *taking* a breath, let us open and yield to each breath's vibrancy, intelligence, and depth. Let us receive breathing *as it is*, allowing it to deepen or lengthen organically.
- We allow our belly to expand during inhalation, bringing attention to our diaphragm to strengthen it and activate muscle memory. We allow the diaphragm room to move freely. The diaphragm's strengthening, flexibility, and power support breathing—the most powerful nutrient on the planet. The stronger our diaphragm, the more robust and resilient the physical aspects of our breathing.
- We allow our rib cage to expand laterally . . . also toward the front and back of our bodies . . . and vertically up and down.
- We breathe nasally and place our tongue on the mouth's roof, or make a conscious choice to mouth breathe.
- We bring breathing energy to the front, sides, and back of our body—filling the whole inner space with awareness of breathing, of being breathed.
- With each breath, we open to ways we can receive more . . . receive more . . . receive more.
- As we receive breathing, let us become aware of the power, energy, and intelligence of sensations throughout our body and invite the sensations to breathe. We allow any sensations, movements, emotions, thoughts, or images that arise.
- As we receive breathing, let us become aware of the power, energy, and intelligence of emotions, whatever emerges (joy, fear, love, grief,

anger, etc.), and invite the emotions to breathe. We allow any sensations, movements, emotions, thoughts, or images that arise.
- As we receive breathing, let us become aware of the power, energy, and intelligence of awareness and thoughts, and invite awareness and thought to breathe. We allow any sensations, movements, emotions, thoughts, or images that arise.
- As we receive breathing, let us invite sensations, emotions, thoughts, and awareness to breathe together... let us experience them breathing together.
- We release owning or controlling our breathing. Eight-plus billion people are breathing now, along with countless nonhuman animals—it's a collective experience. Breathing is our primary source of energy and nutrition. Let us become more intimate with breathing in its full capacity and splendor... to be loved by it... love it... be nourished by it... be guided by it... to open to the journey it invites. Let us welcome breathing's friendship and partnership... allow its care and love for us... fall in love with it... allow it to change however it will. Let us receive breathing.

Recommended minimum practice time: 3 to 7 minutes daily.

The transition to volitional Breathing Practices. Once we have learned to center Receiving Breathing we can initiate our journey into the power of volitional Breathing Practices by feeling the effortlessness of being breathed, and then directing our energy (that we get to decide what to do with at any given moment) to move with and contribute to that breathing. Where two or more are gathered, something is magnified. The partnership with Receiving Breathing is the most pure and authentic way to journey into volitional practice.

2. MATRIKA PRANAYAMA

Matrika Pranayama is the foundational volitional Breathing Practice of Breathwork! It's a controlled practice until we breathe this way automatically, which can take weeks to years.

Matrika Pranayama contributes to wholeness by:

- Calming and stabilizing the nervous system.
- Resetting energy and cortisol, renewing energy and vital force.
- Maintaining steady energy levels.
- Harmonizing with others, environments, and situations.
- Building steady, centered, and grounded states amid changing vicissitudes.
- Dissolving our distractedness and redirecting attention to what most matters and what we love.
- Regulating all our physiological functioning (see Chapter 6).
- Embodying awakened integrated presence into daily functioning.

We practiced a brief version of Matrika in Chapter 6 and learned that the most stabilizing, harmonizing, and regulating breathing rate is a (1:1 ratio)—equivalent duration of inhale and exhale. Here inhalation is our initial guide. We can also use exhalation—both doorways are fine. Some Breathers alternate in different sessions, to stretch beyond unconscious patterns.

MATRIKA PRANAYAMA PRACTICE

- We find a practice position with a relatively straight spine.
- Gently, we close our eyes and place our tongue on the roof of the mouth—either the tip behind the teeth, the tip at the top of the teeth, curling the tongue back so the bottom is against the mouth's roof, or placing the entire top of the tongue along the roof.
- We breathe nasally or consciously choose breathing through the mouth.
- We generate slow, deep inhales and exhales, extending them as long as comfortable without being forceful. We aren't concerned about the rate yet.
- We choose an inhale to begin counting—one, two, three, four....
- We invite the exhale to mirror that same rate. They may need to slow or quicken their pace. The aim is to equalize inhale and exhale in long, slow, deep breaths. We can do a version where we find a consis-

tent count. Sometimes the count can change slightly for each breath if there's no tension or discomfort.

Recommended minimum practice time: Daily for 5 to 10 minutes (longer is wonderful), then integrating Matrika's sensibilities into breathing throughout the day—particularly in challenging situations.

3. QUINTESSENCE BREATHING

We have explored many aspects of physical hardware for volitional breathing. *Quintessence Breathing* (QB) introduces software elements—building blocks of consciousness we can fertilize and harvest. These dimensions correspond with Carl Jung's four functions—sensation, feeling, thinking, and intuition. There's also correlation with George Gurdjieff's delineation of five centers—belly (three subcenters or instincts: self-preservation, sexual, and social), heart, and head. QB profoundly aligns with Alchemy's five elements—earth, air, water, fire, and quintessence. Quintessence is considered the space between, void, or ether. The ancient Greeks perceived it as nonsubstance or essence that Gods breathe—sympatico to people breathing air. Aristotle and Isaac Newton also both posited quintessence.

These elements are at play in any Breathing Practice; QB invokes them consciously and amplifies their transformative capacities. We may wonder why the quintessence element is designated as *action*. This deliberately recognizes our ultimate transformation as *embodied* essence (embodied presence), aligned with Greek philosopher Plotinus's teaching that ether is a nonphysical force penetrating creation in all manifestations.

Quintessence Breathing is a substantial lifelong practice like Receiving Breathing or Matrika Pranayama. QB is an ongoing adventure into dimensions of true self and aspects of being we have ignored or neglected—and their resonance in our body. QB also disrupts our imbalanced preferences, defensive behaviors, and overuse of temperament—thus opening our somatic, emotional, cognitive, intuitive, and creative capacities equivalently.

QB contributes to wholeness by:

- Cultivating felt senses of five elemental aspects of being.
- Developing sensing, feeling, thinking, and intuitive capacities.
- Softening rigid boundaries of false and projected identities.
- Engendering compassion for others' ways of being.
- Supporting flexibility in relatedness.
- Gently undoing unhealthy patterns and behaviors.
- Opening and deepening connections with self, life, and creation.

QUINTESSENCE BREATHING PRACTICE

We begin Receiving Breathing. Let us be with the breath as it is, allowing its own deepening or lengthening. We join the collective experience of eight-plus billion humans and quintillions of nonhuman animals being breathed. Let us welcome breathing's friendship and partnership . . . allow its care and love for us . . . fall in love with it . . . allow it to change however it will. Let us receive breathing.

Let us open to the aspect of breathing that reflects the physiological body, the abdomen and pelvis, somatic intelligence, sensation, and earth. Continuing to receive breathing, we relax our body . . . relax our belly . . . giving the diaphragm maximum room to move. . . . During each inhale, we allow our whole belly to expand in response, then allow our rib cage to

---

Quintessence Breathing

We receive breathing . . .

Then receive and deepen breathing into being with and exploring each of these aspects of being for 1 to 20 minutes each

1. Belly center—abdomen, somatic intelligence, *sensation*, and earth
2. Heart center—chest, emotional intelligence, *feeling*, and water
3. Head center—brain, cognitive intelligence, *thinking*, awareness, air
4. Soul, spirit, energy, *intuition*, fire
5. *Essence* in form, spirit in action, alchemical gold, creative human life, *conscious embodied action*, quintessence

FIGURE 7.2: Quintessence Breathing Practice Outline
Image created by Jessica Dibb, 2023

expand, and then let/encourage our chest to rise as the lungs fill. Breath infuses our lungs, then our trachea, up to our mouth, until we don't feel space for more air. When exhaling, we feel air flowing from our lungs and allow our chest to soften. Then the rib cage relaxes . . . then the belly relaxes or we pull it in strongly for cleansing or toning. Continuing, we become aware of sensations that breathing produces . . . millions of sensations throughout our body, all valuable. We invite each sensation to breathe. We inhabit the sensations . . . ultimately recognizing we're the sensation, connected to life force's immediacy and vibrancy. Even painful sensations are life force and somatic intelligence. We inhabit and give our whole attention to breathing's sensations. We likely experience physical energy building—maybe intensely because life force is infinite. We invite the increasing energy to breathe. We may wish to say internally or aloud *"every cell of this body"* to strengthen our awareness and love of our entire body. (Practice for 1 minute minimum, or up to an hour or more.)

Let us open to the aspect of breathing that reflects the heart center, emotional intelligence, feeling, and water. Continuing full-bodied CB, we release attention on breathing's sensations and bring attention to our chest, savoring its rise and expansion at each inhalation's height. Each exhalation, we allow increasing softening of our chest. Tenderly placing one or both hands on the center of our chest, we invite our heart to relax into being cherished . . . as if, if it softens, then melts, our hands will catch it with love . . . accepting and holding our heart's every need, wish, and yearning. Breathing slowly, deeply, with softening exhales, we envision what our hearts would feel if, from this moment forward, every newborn's first breath was surrounded by unconditional love, safety, and support for their authentic selves and potential. We allow our hearts to wish for all beings to be born and live this way. We can hope everyone lives life without unnecessary suffering—a life of fulfilled potential shared with the world. If we feel tears, we let them flow . . . if smiles or laughter, we let them arise. . . . Breathe. . . . Now, whatever we wish for others' first and every breath, we can wish for ourselves. Our breathing can open into unconditional love and support for ourselves, our lives, and our potential. If we feel tears, we let them flow . . . if smiles or laughter, we let them arise. We may wish to say internally or aloud *"every feeling [or every experience] of this heart,"* to welcome and embrace our vulnerability, caring, and every emotion. (Practice for 1 minute minimum, or up to an hour or more.)

Let us open to the aspect of breathing that reflects the head center, cognitive intelligence, thinking, and air. Continuing full-bodied CB, we release attention on our heart and bring attention to the center of our head, around the pineal gland, with awareness that choosing to consciously deepen our breathing nourishes and energizes our brain and neural pathways. Breathing builds awareness, dissolving dullness or cloudiness. We allow any visualizations of these phenomena, if they arise naturally. We can consider how wise it is to consciously partner breathing—to be receptive to learning from each breath's intelligence. Each breath brings new awareness.... Let us be changed by these insights. With each breath, we can focus more clearly on the present and what truly matters, letting distracting words and images dissolve. We can breathe into spaciousness, and its intelligence and guidance, allowing ourselves to be impacted and live from the wisdom, insight, intuition, vision, and creativity that arise. We may wish to say internally or aloud *"every awareness of this mind"* (or *"every recognition of this awareness"*) to invite the *knowing* within each thought. (Practice for 1 minute minimum, or up to an hour or more.)

Let us open to the aspect of breathing that reflects soul, energy, intuition, and fire. Continuing full-bodied CB, we release attention from the awareness and learning, and bring attention to the tips of our nostrils where they constantly meet air. Everything exists in a seamless flow of energy. Consciously breathing, we can be aware that the energy is our nostrils, the space within our nostrils, the air.... Rather than acquisition, breathing is a great intimacy. Energy is flowing and contacting more energy. Consider that breathing is energy flowing into energy, rather than giving us energy. We can tune in to our nostril's breathing sensations from this orientation and receive refined awareness of the energy and intimacy of breathing. This may feel joyful, light ... it may smell or taste of nectar. We allow ourselves to be energized, uplifted, inspired, or whatever comes. We may wish to say internally or aloud *"every atom of this spirit"*—"atom," to acknowledge that some substantive aspects of ourselves are invisible **and** real. (Practice for 1 minute minimum, or up to an hour or more.)

Let us open to the aspect of breathing that reflects spirit in form, essence in action, creative human life actualized, conscious embodied action, alchemical gold, and quintessence. Continuing full-bodied CB, we bring expanded attention to the previous four dimensions of breathing—sensation's power and life force; feelings when our hearts are open, contacting our needs, vulnerability, hopes, and love for ourselves and others; receptivity and curiosity about learning and envisioning; and the energy that *is* the breathing and everything else. Let us breathe all of this together. We now bring attention to the felt sense of our lived life . . . how we move; where we dwell; to whom we relate; our capacity to choose—any physical, emotional, cognitive, spiritual, and relational facets of our life. We can breathe with all dimensions of breathing while holding the sense of our lived lives. What happens if we are with the vitality, love, intelligence, and energy of breathing as we choose and act? How does it transform our body and movements? How does it evolve how we respond to ourselves and others? How does it metamorphose perceptions about ourselves, others, and life? We can say internally or aloud *"every action of this life"* to strengthen our commitment to breathing with presence during every action. We can also powerfully inhale and exhale through our mouths for three breaths or more to intensify vital force and commitment to embodied consciousness in action. (Practice for 1 minute minimum, or up to an hour or more.)

Recommended minimum practice time: 7 minutes daily—1 minute each of RB, sensation, emotion, awareness, essence, embodied action, and integration. Once a week, practice for 21 minutes to an hour or more to intensify development.

4. ACCELERATED BREATHING

Accelerated Breathing amplifies physical, emotional, cognitive, and spiritual energy and helps engage inner and outer challenges and emergencies, inner emergences of realization and growth, and outer positive emergences. The practice taught here is particularly effective.

Additionally many practices that are volitionally faster than normal (Kapalabhati, Bhastrika, cyclical hyperventilation, and so on) serve the same purpose.

Accelerated Breathing contributes to wholeness by:

- Generating muscle energy quickly.
- Strengthening attention and cognitive focus.
- Increasing capacity for intensity.
- Generating heat for warmth.
- Strengthening motivation and initiating energy.
- Supporting strength and empowerment.
- Loosening physical, emotional, cognitive, and spiritual rigidity.
- Helping us engage inner and outer emergencies and emergences.

ACCELERATED BREATHING PRACTICE

We generate a faster than normal breathing pattern, with inhale and exhale of equal duration (30 to 60 breaths per minute) for 30 seconds to 2 minutes. We then inhale deeply and retain the breath for 3 to 15 seconds, then exhale slowly, followed by 1 to 2 minutes of *slow* deep breathing. Repeat for three to 10 cycles. Beginners should start with 30 seconds of rapid breathing, followed by 2 minutes of slow breathing—then slowly increase the rapid breathing time.

Three variations: (1) energetic volitional inhale, relaxed exhale; (2) forceful exhale, automatic inhale (only 30 seconds at a time); (3) forceful inhale and exhale. Each variation can use nose or mouth breathing for rapid breathing, with nasal breathing for slow breathing portions.

Other variations: bringing our hands together in prayer position; stretching our arms straight up to the ceiling or sky; arms straight up during inhale, bending arms down by our shoulders during exhale; and moving our body in any way that facilitates faster breathing. If dizziness occurs, we should slow the breathing rate.

When a round of rapid breathing completes, and/or as the whole practice culminates, it's wonderful to place our hands in prayer position.

Stretching the prayer position toward the ceiling or sky, we generate several slow, deep breaths, then let our arms slowly float down, remaining present with the effects in our body as they integrate.

Recommended minimum practice time: 5 minutes daily to build capacity, and whenever we want to generate energy or concentrate.

5. CYCLICAL SIGHING

As we learned in Chapter 6, *Cyclical Sighing* is highly effective for reducing anxiety and increasing positive mood if practiced 5 minutes daily for at least 28 days.

Cyclical Sighing contributes to wholeness by:

- Lowering anxiety within a few breaths.
- Reducing respiratory rates, heart rate, and HRV.
- Improving mood over time.
- Relaxing emotional reactivity, bolstering presence in life situations.

CYCLICAL SIGHING PRACTICE

We inhale nasally, then inhale/sip a second segment to maximally expand our lungs. Exhale is a long slow deep sigh. Repeat for 5 minutes. Cyclical Sighing is beneficial whenever we are feeling anxious, depressed, out of sorts, or unfocused.

Recommended minimum practice time: 5 minutes daily and whenever needed.

6. ENHANCED FOCUS BREATHING

Accelerated Breathing generates general alertness, whereas *Enhanced Focus Breathing* elicits keen refined focus by combining the stabilizing force of Matrika Pranayama, the ability to notice and appreciate detail, and the capacity to sustain attention over long periods of time.

Enhanced Focus Breathing contributes to wholeness by:

- Strengthening our ability to focus deeply with ease and peacefulness.
- Dissolving patterns of distractedness and jumbled thoughts.
- Cultivating patience and capacity for presence.
- Training us to be alert and present when attending to details.
- Developing inner capacities for creativity.

ENHANCED FOCUS BREATHING PRACTICE

- We choose an object in our immediate space that is meaningful to us—a picture, sculpture, plant, our hand, an object associated with a loved one, a sacred object, a book cover, a tree, and so on.
- We pick one tiny section of it—a square inch or centimeter or even less. We look carefully to note small details we might not usually see. We stay focused and breathe deeply. If we have low vision or are visually impaired, we can touch a very small portion of the object and get to know the details of its texture while breathing deeply.
- After several minutes, we close our eyes and begin Matrika Pranayama. After counting for several breaths, we cease counting and continually breathe deeply and slowly.
- We begin generating the picture or sensation of the object's small portion within our awareness or internal vision, continually breathing deeply and slowly.
- We invite ourselves to generate smaller and smaller details—like a tiny speck of a wrinkle on our fingertip. We deepen and strengthen our breathing to cultivate focus, especially if feeling sleepy or bored.
- If extreme sleepiness or restlessness arises, we can open our eyes or hands and look at, or feel, the object again briefly, then return to generating the image or feeling inside.
- If our attention distractedly flips to a bigger portion or another object, we breathe extraordinarily deeply and keep internally generating our object's details. If our attention wanders, no blame or shame. We simply return attention to Enhanced Focus Breathing.
- After some time, we can gently open our eyes, or stretch our

hands, to look at, or sense, the object again. We may now be more curious to note details, shapes, patterns, textures, and colors. We may perceive levels beyond the Newtonian, like color or light emanating.
- We close our eyes again, breathing deeply and evenly, generating the object's image slowly and thoroughly.
- To culminate, we release the object's image or sense, breathe deeply, and look around our environment. What might we notice that usually we don't?
- An advanced version of this rigorous, rewarding practice is to use one small portion of the same object daily for weeks, months, or years, before moving to another portion.

Recommended minimum practice time: 5 minutes daily. This can be a challenging practice—an intense workout for cognitive capacities. Longer 15- to 20-minute practices twice a week can foster surprising levels of wakefulness and focus long term.

7. RESPIRATORY HEALING PRANAYAMA

This technique I learned from my Tamil Yoga Siddha training was called Asthma Pranayama. I call it *Respiratory Healing Pranayama* (RHP) now because I have observed, and found some supportive science, that it's helpful for most acute and chronic respiratory challenges. RHP induces lung muscle relaxation by transforming each inhale and/or exhale into several short segments interspersed with quick volitional stillings of the lungs. RHP provides the lungs ways to release unhealthy behaviors accrued during emotional distress or when they accommodate particular assaults such as viruses, bacteria, some fragrances, or air pollution.

RHP contributes to wholeness by:

- Repairing underbreathing and overbreathing habits.
- Interrupting chronic lung tension and spasms.
- Teaching our lungs how to unwind spasm and tension.
- Increasing lung strength, motility, and flexibility.

- When our respiration is challenged, because RHP has small breathing segments, we are empowered by breathing just a little, building confidence that we can breathe fully again.

RESPIRATORY HEALING PRANAYAMA PRACTICE

We breathe with pursed lips—inhaling like sipping through a straw and exhaling like blowing out a candle—both which help open breathing passages. As respiratory challenges ease, we can relax our mouth to normal position and continue practicing for a few minutes.

1. Receive as slow and deep inhalation as is comfortable. Exhale in 3 to 5 short segments. Repeat 3 to 10 times.
2. Inhale in 3 to 5 short segments. Exhale in one long, relaxed stream. Repeat 3 to 10 times.
3. Inhale in 3 to 5 short segments. Exhale in 3 to 5 short segments. Repeat 3 to 10 times.

Usually we practice all three variations each time. Yet sometimes Breathers in distress find that one or two variations is helpful, rather than all three, until breathing eases.

Recommended minimum practice time: All three variations once daily for lung resiliency and general respiratory health; whenever breathing is challenged due to illness or environmental stressors; three times daily for chronic respiratory challenges; and once per hour for acute conditions.

8. SLEEP PRANAYAMA

Through the ancient Tamil Yoga Siddha tradition, I was taught *Sleep Pranayama* with a ratio of 2:1 (inhale twice as long as exhale). It works! How can this be when the widespread consensus is prolonged exhalation for relaxation? As we learned in Chapter 6, Stephen Elliott and I surmised that when cyclic action in breathing is suspended, prolonged inhalation mimics breath holding, so our internal systems slow to conserve oxygen and energy. Stephen observes that during prolonged inhalation, heart rate goes high, then automatically goes low as if exhaling. However, it stays relatively low, indicating parasympathetic emphasis. Remember that prolonged exhalation initially induces lower heart rate, and then goes higher. Inhaling longer ultimately slows heart rate and slows all systems. Shorter exhales won't accelerate breathing. The combination of slowing the internal systems and lowering heart rate can lead to sleep reasonably rapidly.

Sleep Pranayama contributes to wholeness by:

- More quickly falling asleep.
- Reducing tension, anxiety, and so on, brought into sleeping time.
- Helping us return to sleep after awakening at night.
- Cultivating better sleep quality, gaining the numerous benefits of good rest.

SLEEP PRANAYAMA PRACTICE

- We relax into a rest/sleeping position and turn attention to receiving breathing, nasally if possible.
- When ready, we generate an extended inhale. After establishing long inhales, we count the duration of an inhale.
- We complete our next exhalation at half the duration of the preceding inhalation. There are two effective ways to explore:
    a. *Exhale softly and lightly, almost like not breathing out completely.*
    b. *Purposefully sigh so the breath is larger, yet still half the rate of the inhale.*

Most Breathers prefer one over the other.

- Note: Inhalation lengths will vary. Whatever the duration of each inhale, the following exhale should be half as long.

Recommended minimum practice time: any time we wish to sleep or access waking dream-like states.

9. SELF-HEALING BREATHING

This time-tested practice brings Conscious Breathing and Receiving Breathing to powerful next-level applications—to our ability to *intentionally* heal physically, emotionally, cognitively, and spiritually. We initiate Receiving Breathing. Then, instead of *breathing into* our pain, as is often the instruction, we invite what needs healing *to breathe*. We are shifting from the orientation that what needs healing is bad, wrong—a problem we are going to fix, or that it should be rejected. Rather, inviting what needs healing to share its full aliveness reveals its wisdom and contributes to wholeness. *Self-Healing Breathing* has the greatest impact when there's time and space to focus and freely express ourselves. Once the steps are learned, we can practice abbreviated adaptations amid daily life.

Self-Healing Breathing contributes to wholeness by:

- Contacting our inner healer and amplifying its potency.
- Learning more about our somatic–emotional–cognitive continuum.
- Providing immediate assistance for tension, emotional reactivity, troubling thoughts, unrequited yearnings, physical discomfort and pain, spiritual angst, and more.
- Quickly freeing stagnant or stuck energy.
- Supporting us to be more self-referential and authentic.
- Opening pathways for authentic expression.
- Experiencing being energetically held by essential wisdom and caring.

SELF-HEALING BREATHING PRACTICE

- Begin with Receiving Breathing (optional: add Quintessence Breathing).
- When there's increased energy and/or awareness, we specifically invite the following to join in the breathing, in this order: our phys-

ical vitality, any discomfort or physical pain, pleasurable emotions, any painful emotions, awareness, challenging thoughts.
- We scan our soma, psyche, and soul until attention is drawn to a physical, emotional, cognitive, or spiritual imbalance, discomfort, or distress (e.g., tension, pain, illness, jealousy, hurt, anger). The inner healer could surface this through breathing, or we can choose one.
- We invite the identified discomfort to breathe . . . really breathe! We invite it to join breathing *with* us.
- When the discomfort is fully breathing, we invite it to express itself—allowing our body, heart, and brain to express. There may be bodily movement, tears, laughter, words, sounds, shaking, and so on. The energy flow of emotions, thoughts, and images can sometimes be cathartic or expansive.
- We respect the expression's wisdom as part of us, not a problem, and give it time and space, which transmits caring to the discomfort.
- When it feels completely expressed, we breathe even deeper and invite the discomfort to share what it needs *from us* (not someone else) right now. For example, it might communicate, "I need you to move [in a particular way]. . . . I need you to be more aware of me. . . . I need you to hold me—put a hand here [on a particular place]. . . . I need to breathe more. . . . " Whatever it communicates, we listen.
- Breathing deeply, we respond and give what it wants right now, so there's embodied somatic–emotional–cognitive continuum shifts. We touch, move, talk, sing, assure, visualize, breathe, to respond as requested.
- Finally, we envision how our lives will feel differently when this need being met is integrated into the various facets of our daily life. With this need attended to, how will we now experience each moment? How will we show up anew?

Recommended minimum practice time: daily or weekly as desired, and whenever physical, emotional, cognitive, or spiritual discomfort needs attention. Weekly practice of 10 to 30 minutes is highly recommended for maintaining well-being.

10. FORM AND FORMLESSNESS COMMUNION BREATHING

The intrapsychic splits between spirit and matter, being and action, invisible and visible, formlessness and form, the Divine and humanity, are deep wounds that impair aptitude and facility for cultivating our full potential. The electrifying practice of *Form and Formlessness Communion Breathing* is deeply healing for bodily dissociation, aching hearts, feeling inauthentic, and feeling abandoned by, or disconnected from, the Source. FFCB can also help heal sexuality and support couples.

Our physical body is not only our visible body. Our body is comprised of constantly moving atoms, molecules, and cells which are, and are producing, energy that our normal eyesight cannot see. What we see or experience are the effects of energy processes, such as movements, temperature, and light. We see and feel our bodies as opposed to air because the atoms in our body are more condensed and moving slower than the air's atoms. We are energy in motion, and some of that energy is within us and around what we usually see—it is a part of the seamless fabric of energy that is everything.

Invisible to our normal eyesight, is a thin, energetic layer approximately half an inch to an inch beyond our skin. Beginning with one arm, we can caress this energetic layer with our hands or blow our breath through its space. At times we may touch our skin a bit, or our hand or breath may float up beyond the inch. We can learn to sense this energetic layer where the atoms of our body meet the energy field around us. FFCB emphasizes mending the rift between essence and embodiment, the tear between our soul and this life.

FFCB contributes to wholeness by:

- Invoking an embodied sense of sacredness about our body and life.
- Eliciting the felt sense of our invisible aspects—such as consciousness, presence, energy, awareness, and love.
- Helping heal trauma and dissociation from our bodies.
- Awakening awareness of our invisible gifts.
- Eliciting somatic experiences of interconnection with the rest of reality.

- Stimulating our intuitive capacities.
- Dissolving dislike, disdain, rejection, or hatred of our bodies.
- Bringing awareness to what Eastern traditions call our causal, astral, or etheric bodies.
- Experiencing our body as pure energy.

FORM AND FORMLESSNESS COMMUNION BREATHING PRACTICE

- We establish Matrika Pranayama until we are breathing consistently deeply; then we release the counting and breathe organically and deeply.
- Extremely slowly, we move our finger, hand, or breathing through the emanating energetic layer over our arm. At times we may briefly touch our skin, or our hand or breath may rise up beyond the inch. Continually breathing with awareness, we move our fingers, hands, or breath slowly over any body parts we wish.
- Where we feel strong emotions, or sense energetic stuckness, we pause and remain there, breathing until it clears or integrates.
- As the practice culminates, we sit or lie silently, breathing deeply for 1 minute minimum, or significantly longer if possible.
- As we move about, we breathe deeply and integrate what has been invoked in us.

We are healing any disconnection between our energy, bodily senses, and the visible and invisible aspects of reality.

Recommended minimum practice time: 5 minutes daily; even 1 minute can be therapeutic when feeling dissociated, depressed, or disconnected from ourselves or others; once a week longer solo practice, or with a partner, can help prevent anxiety, loneliness, and disconnection and engender worthiness and belonging.

11. EMBODIED NOVELTY BREATHING (ENB)

Embodied Novelty Breathing (ENB) is magnificently transformational; it opens and establishes the felt sense of awakened, integrated presence and flow. We can do this as focused practice; then eventually, as we become more adept, integrate ENB's orientation into our normal activities. ENB brings exquisite attention to where inhalation culminates and shifts to exhalation, and where exhalation culminates and shifts to inhalation. Conscious Connected Breathing also notes these junctures, ensuring that there is no pause or gap. However, in ENB, while we refrain from pauses, we extend those transitional points for a particular purpose.

Following inspiration, there's a postinspiration stage—a seeming pause in the breathing. Postinspiration doesn't always occur automatically (see Chapter 4). It can, however, occur volitionally almost anytime we choose.

Flow states tend to create experiences of embodied, awakened consciousness. One needed trigger for inducing flow is *novelty*—and the brain is a novelty-seeking organ (Bunzeck et al., 2011). Because inhalation and exhalation are reliably dependable, it's not easy to induce novelty through them alone. However, postinspiration is not a given; so that's the most salient aspect of breathing for inducing novelty with every breath.

In ENB we volitionally extend the postinspiration stage, which Dan Siegel and I decided to call *extended inspiration*. In extended inspiration, we continue breathing, however slightly, feeling into the subtlety and refinement, which varies in each breath. We're not *taking* this extra extended breath, nor are we *forcing* it; we're just allowing and *receiving inhalation* a bit longer. We are gently inviting our diaphragm, spine, belly, rib cage, chest, throat, and abdominal and thoracic cavities to soften any emotional and physical armoring we have created to avoid feeling pain or fear. We are savoring the life force more and more at the top of every inhale.

Because the duration and quality of each extended inspiration is unique, it stimulates the novelty-seeking aspects of our brain and increases capacity to bring presence to our usually unconscious feelings, thoughts, movements, motivations, and intuition, leading to the most extraordinary somatic intelligence I have ever personally experienced, or witnessed. It sparks unusual and beauteous movements that induce exceptionally wise healing. One hypothesis is that extended inspiration connects the voluntary capacity driven by the cortex deeply into the brain stem, so we learn we can influence our brain stem. So now, perhaps, the cortex is regulating the rhythmic processes that drive breathing—not just having awareness of breathing.

We're not retaining our breath at each exhalation's culmination either—we are savoring it. This is probably the easiest place to experience awakened, integrated presence and the Plane of Possibility (which we learn about in Chapter 12). And the whole breath is the Plane of Possibility—the *dynamism of awareness of awareness.* Savoring as exhalation culminates can amplify the relaxing of embedded fears, traumas, and narratives. Letting go during exhale's fruition is like letting go into sleep and dreams arising. Savoring exhalation is breathing's most resonant aspect with the *emptiness of awareness* of which Buddhism teaches. It reflects the unconditioned universal womb, available for new creation.

Three primary ways to generate novelty in breathing: (1) The most potent medium is *extended inhalation;* (2) the second best is *savoring exhalation;* (3) the third best is through *influencing the quantities and quality of our breathing.* ENB focuses on each inhalation's fruition to generate novelty because it's the nexus of the phenomenon.

ENB contributes to wholeness by:

- Opening new experiences and perspectives of reality.
- Generating flow states that can be embodied through breathing during daily activities.
- Generating significant unadulterated vital force—the life force of creation.
- Eliciting electric vibrancy and bliss.
- Teaching us that each experience within a particular breath—emotions, sleepiness, need, fulfillment, and more—can contribute to a flow state. Everything we experience can become part of flow.

EMBODIED NOVELTY BREATHING PRACTICE

- We engage in Receiving Breathing.
- As breathing deepens, we bring attention to the culminating point

of each exhale, savoring the experience of letting go, of being free from usual identities and binding compulsions.
- We now bring attention to the culminating point of each inhale. At those junctures, we relax some part of our bodies—a fingertip, our neck, an earlobe, our pelvis—enough that inhalation can extend, even imperceptibly. We may feel like breathing is ceasing. If, at that moment, we relax something, a little more breath may enter. We can keep relaxing various places until we cannot receive more breath. Whether we obtain another 2 seconds or 2 minutes of inhaling, we allow our body to move in whatever spontaneous way it's drawn to. Each extension is a new adventure. There's no right way—we're learning and developing.
- We begin paying attention to the culminating points of our exhalations. We relax our bodies enough to savor the exhalation until the last possible moment when it feels natural to breathe. We let go and allow ourselves to be emptied.
- We continue practicing as long as we wish. If we feel tears, we let them fall; we allow smiles or laughter. We allow however our body wants to stretch, move, and vibrate. Our body may enter flow states of very subtle or expansive flowing movements, many of which we would not know to do with our usual conscious awareness. Experience has proven them to be distinctly wise and healing. We keep centering on Receiving Breathing, meeting each extended inhale and exhale with awareness.
- If it feels like there's not enough breath, it's hard to breathe, or that we can barely inhale, we pause the extensions to breathe normally and regulate. Once regulated, we can begin extended inspirations.
- At the practice period's conclusion, with eyes closed, we savor all we are experiencing while breathing deeply; then open our eyes, breathing deeply, and continuing to savor what is opening within.
- As we move, we continue awareness of novelty and creation at inhalation's end, and the letting go, emptiness, and availability at exhalation's end.

We are being breathed within the atmosphere of breathing, our most essential function. We might say we are being baptized into a highly fluent stage of Receiving Breathing—of nonegoic breathing.

Recommended minimum practice time: Daily for at least 5 minutes, then allow the energy to permeate the whole day.

BREATHING KIT PROTOCOL

The combination of each practice's recommended minimum practice time totals 45 minutes per day (excluding Self-Healing Breathing and Sleep Pranayama). Every Breather deserves 45 minutes of CB daily to support well-being and optimal living. And, going beyond minimum times is superb!

Each Breathing Practice can be optimized by including Receiving Breathing. If dedicated practice isn't possible, due to challenges with family and work obligations, health conditions, socioeconomic circumstances, war-related disruptions, and degraded environments, we can practice RB throughout our day and utilize a minute or two between activities for other practices.

Together, these 11 Breathing Practices plus Group 5 Breathwork (especially *Conscious Responsive Breathing* that we will learn about in Chapter 11) are 12 pillars of Breathwork that, when diligently committed to over a year or more, can create breathing fluency, breathing aptitude, and breathing mastery in Breathers—and profoundly assist in optimizing physical, emotional, cognitive, spiritual, relational, and creative well-being and actualization. These Breathing Practice commitments may be our most important daily activity.

With gratitude to Lavinia . . . and every Breather.

EIGHT

Structural Supports for Breathwork Sessions

*Every change of mental state is reflected in
the breath and then in the body.*

—DEEPAK CHOPRA, *AGELESS BODY, TIMELESS MIND*

WE ALL breathe, so we are all candidates for some form of Breathwork. Curiosity arises: Which style? With myself, a friend, or a Professional Breathworker? Where? What can I expect? Will I be safe? Where can I find guidelines? What does my Therapist-Breathworker know? How skilled are they? What do I need to know to make good choices about Breathwork and have optimal experiences? The answers to these questions could be a whole book, and in some ways this whole book is some answers to those questions.

This chapter gives an overview of some practical and essential tools for Therapist-Breathworkers to offer excellent, safe, ethical, and potent Breathwork—and for those seeking Breathwork facilitators to have some guideposts for discovering and welcoming excellent, safe, ethical, and potent Breathwork facilitation into our personal growth and journey to wholeness.

Breathwork Readiness

Whether we are evaluating our own readiness for Breathwork, or we are a clinician evaluating another's readiness for facilitated Breathwork, considerations should include: degree of desire for personal growth, openness to using somatic–emotional–cognitive continuum (SEC continuum) techniques for healing, and willingness to be responsible for one's own health and wellness—with some guidance and support.

Ultimately, we each need to make informed decisions about whether a particular style, place, environment, facilitator is right for us. We should understand that Breathwork supports healing, self-exploration, and self-actualization; that it can contact deep emotions, memories, insights, and expanded states of consciousness; and that it can generate significant physical sensations. *And* that it can infuse our lives with regulation, energy, insights, and adventures in consciousness. Breathers wanting to experience change and learn more about themselves and their inner process is a prerequisite for fruitful Breathwork from Groups 2–5. We should also understand that Breathwork is not intended to replace any needed treatment or psychotherapy.

Again, we all breathe, so we are all candidates for some form of Breathwork.

Some special considerations include:

- Breathwork is potent during the special time of pregnancy for oxygenating mothers and babies, cultivating mothers' abilities to attune to babies in utero and after birth, and preparing for childbirth. Breathwork can help pregnant Breathers heal unconscious patterns or memories from earlier birthing experiences or their own birth, which can ease and enhance the birthing process significantly.
- Many Breathers utilize fast breathing during the first trimester. There are no reported deleterious effects, and, in fact, pregnant people often automatically breathe a little faster during weeks 1–14 due to more progesterone and increased oxygen needs. Out of an abundance of caution, Breathworkers have long recommended refraining

from faster than normal breathing during the first trimester because deep breathing can generate smooth muscle movement, potentially creating contractions. Instead we suggest slow deep breathing in the first trimester. Additionally, pregnant Breathers are generally in some kind of nonordinary state of consciousness, even subtly. Often just a short breathing period, even a few conscious breaths, can yield significant physical benefit and profound psycho-spiritual journeys.

- While everyone is a candidate for some Breathwork, adjustments may be required for some health conditions such as cardiovascular challenges, respiratory issues, epilepsy, psychosis, schizophrenia, bipolar disorder, recent surgeries, and neurological conditions. Breathwork participants should be informed about health conditions that might be impacted by Breathwork and be provided opportunities to disclose these to their Breathwork facilitator. Therapist-Breathworkers should be prepared to adjust Breathwork practices, including potentially referring to a more experienced practitioner.

- For Breathers with asthma, COPD, other lung diseases, hyperventilation syndrome, or breathing difficulty due to acute physical disease or its aftermath (e.g., Epstein-Barr, COVID-19), Breathwork is an appropriate, helpful, adjunctive therapy, and sometimes curative. Ideally, Therapist-Breathworkers should be knowledgeable about basic physiology of these conditions, and Breathing Practices that best address them, including the emotional processing that often accompanies or underlies respiratory challenges.

- Some Breathers with various types of acute, chronic, or complex trauma, PTSD, or complex PTSD understandably may fear the sensations and emotions that Breathwork may bring forth. They may not trust their body's wisdom because trauma often disrupts the body's sense of safety. Highly regulated Breathwork practices (mostly Group 3) can offer containment, agency, and trustworthiness. When employing Human Potential Breathwork, Therapist-Breathworkers must offer careful, attentive coregulation. Open eyes during Breathwork can foster safety and agency until Breathees feel safe excavating their protective system and allowing the unconditioned self to emerge (see Chapter 10 for Breathwork with trauma).

- When Breathers with past trauma can maintain contact with an inner adult, witness observer, or an aware ego that's friendly toward themselves, it's a positive indication that Breathwork can be beneficial to release trauma, regain sensations, contact emotions, enhance cognitive functioning, and build resilience.

- Easy self-regulating Breathing Practices should be used initially for Breathers with panic, dissociative states, and various psychopathologies (see Chapter 10). Matrika Pranayama (perhaps with open eyes initially) can be very effective. Because bipolar episodes can be triggered by excitation of the sympathetic nervous system, it's recommended that Breathers with bipolar commence with slow, deep, gentle breathing. Coherent Breathing (perhaps with open eyes initially) can be very effective—with the parasympathetic activation and regulated containment of timing helping with bipolar regulation. Breathers with bipolar who begin with practices from Groups 1, 2, and 3 can very gradually transition into Group 5 Breathwork, reporting substantial benefits (see Chapter 10).

- Breathwork is not generally contraindicated while using medications (see Chapter 14 concerning psychedelics). Yet since medications can affect us physically and emotionally, Breathees should be provided with opportunities to disclose medication usage with particular attention to those that cause central nervous stimulation or sedation, and those with increased risk of bleeding. Therapist-Breathworkers should work within their scope of training and not advise a Breathwork participant to change, stop or taper off a prescribed medication. Some Breathers have, with great caution and care, reduced or weaned from blood pressure medicine, cardiac medicine, antidepressants, and other psychotropic medications. This should always be done in conjunction with the prescribing health care practitioner. I highly recommend tapering that is significantly lengthened from typical protocols, and have seen notable success with Breathers doing Breathwork, and reducing antidepressants, arthritis, blood pressure, and cardiac medications over many months, partnering with the prescribing health care provider.

- Some schools don't recommend Group 5 Breathwork after major surgery—particularly cardiac surgery. I respect this sensibility, yet my experience is that slow deep breathing helps accelerate healing. Many anecdotal reports indicate that Breathwork can help release residual anesthesia and other drugs. Slow, gentle, deep breathing may be enough because surgery can induce nonordinary states of consciousness that linger.
- Slow nasal breathing, with moderate depth, can help reduce and prevent epileptic seizures. However, rapid breathing and mouth breathing are generally contraindicated for epilepsy and other seizure disorders. Overbreathing and hyperventilation can produce alkalosis—a known cause of seizures. Ideally, Therapist-Breathworkers should have basic skills for responding to seizures.
- Though Breathwork is a non-toxic, non-invasive, primary and/or complementary modality, standard professional health care and mental health care protocols should be utilized, including but not limited to: Therapist-Breathworkers obtaining contact information, history, and emergency contact information; any medical or medication information the Breathee wishes to share; the use of therapeutic consent forms; and screening for mental health conditions, thoughts of self-harm, and suicidal ideation. If such conditions are beyond the scope of our training, collaboration with an experienced clinician is warranted. Therapist-Breathworkers should also be prepared to handle potential emergencies such as seizure, loss of consciousness or panic attack (preferably having CPR and basic first aid training), and knowing how to contact emergency services in our current location.

Structural Supports for Breathwork Facilitators and Those Seeking Them

ETHICS

Therapist-Breathworkers facilitating Group 2 through Group 5 Breathwork should ensure they have obtained substantial ethical training specific to Breathwork, as some Breathwork trainings still may not explicitly cover best practices or ethics. The heightened energy field generated during guided Breathwork can magnify projections, transferences, and countertransferences more than traditional psychotherapy, so ethical boundaries and wisdom are vital. Additionally, Breathwork can easily access boundless states, which may override weaker boundaries in Breathees with trauma-related dysregulation, or inflate unhealthy boundaries in those with narcissistic wounding, increasing the risk of boundary transgressions. Understanding the ethics of working with expanded states of consciousness is essential.

The Global Professional Breathwork Alliance (GPBA) sets ethical standards, maintains a practitioner registry for Breathworkers agreeing to adhere to GPBA ethics, and also certifies Group 5 Breathwork practitioners and schools who meet the GPBA training standards. We will read about Breathwork training standards in Chapter 12. The GPBA Ethics Committee creates guidelines, updates ethics, and addresses concerns of potential ethical misconduct using a five-step Restorative Justice model.

The most important factor for Therapist-Breathworkers to embody safety, awareness, and therapeutic wisdom and creativity is commitment to self-care and personal healing and development. This builds capacity to be present when emotional expression, inner work, needs, trauma, deep potential, and expanded states of consciousness arise in Breathees without our own sensibilities or inner conflicts getting triggered.

This is why Inspiration Consciousness School, a GPBA Certified School, includes in our statement of ethics a commitment to self-care—somatically, emotionally, cognitively, spiritually, relationally, and ecologically. Each year, we reevaluate our personal commitment to the following:

- Managing our personal lives in a healthful fashion and seeking appropriate support for our personal problems, conflicts, and challenges.
- Caring for our bodies through healthy relationships with breathing, food, nourishment, movement, hygiene, and rest.
- Caring for our minds through reading, studying, meditation, learning from others, and conscious dialogues with our family, friends, peers, and teachers. We compassionately evaluate the quality of our thoughts.
- Caring for our emotional health by consciously cultivating a relationship with all our feelings. We can practice compassion for ourselves, all beings, and all life. We take actions that arise from loving-kindness, gratitude, and loving ourselves and others unconditionally.
- Caring for our spirits through conscious awareness of our relationship with the creative life force, through cherishing the essence in ourselves and all life, celebrating life, and maintaining awareness of the interconnection of everything.
- Creating healthy relationships through awareness of our Being and others'; our needs and the needs of others; our desires and the desires of others; and how our communication affects others. We support others in nourishing, empowering, and actualizing themselves. We strive to release projections, respect everyone's gifts, and honor their unique life journey.
- Caring for the Earth on which we live, through awareness of our relationship with nature, and maintaining respect for earth, air, metals, water, and fire. We make choices that promote the health of our environment and the earth.

When introducing Breathwork, Therapist-Breathworkers should consider what is meaningful for the Breather—not emphasize our favorite aspect of Breathwork or what we think is important. Breathwork should never have an element of pushing or force—only encouragement. The modality is most effective when guided by Breathee self-regulation and self-direction. Breathees should know that our presence is for support and offering our experience, guidance, and skills. We can encourage energized breathing—and Breathees can stop any time.

Some aspects of Breathwork to share about are: historical origins and lineages of Breathwork in various cultures or religions; inspiring science about Breathwork—and relevant to a Breathees' goals; anonymized stories of valuable Breathwork results; descriptions of the particular Breathwork process we facilitate; and explanations of the physical, emotional, cognitive, and spiritual, and expanded consciousness experiences that can arise in the Breathwork we offer. We should be willing to answer questions about our Breathwork training and experience.

VARIOUS METHODS FOR INTEGRATING BREATHWORK INTO TREATMENT SESSIONS

1. Begin each session with three deep breaths together for cortisol reset, parasympathetic activation, polyvagal response, and coregulation.
2. Begin each session with several minutes of deep, slow breathing. Invite Breathees to directly connect with their interior experiences—sensations, emotions, and thoughts.
3. Communicate the benefits of resetting or contemplating in silence at various moments during talk sessions, so Therapist-Breathworkers or Breathees may call for three deep breaths, or several minutes of breathing, to cultivate presence and awareness with a topic or emotions, or to embody a realization fully, any time during the session.
4. Give support by breathing deeply several times when Breathees have emotional or energetic shifts and life-enhancing insights. This can encourage Breathees to breathe deeply at those salient times, which then enhances memory consolidation of the experiences. Breathees then associate breathing with the new state and can use CB between sessions for further integration.
5. Suggest using Breathwork throughout the session whenever clients need to self-regulate.
6. Teach specific Group 4 Breathing Practices for personal development that serve a session's themes.
7. After a talking portion of the session, follow with longer prac-

tice from Groups 3, 4, or 5 to enhance realizations and facilitate continued transformation.

8. Begin the session with a longer, in-depth practice from Groups 3, 4, or 5, followed by talking to integrate the Breathee's insights. Breathwork right at the beginning, without sharing or explanation, can illuminate the vast intelligence of breathing itself, and *breathing itself* becomes the Therapist-Breathworker.

9. Because Group 5 practices can consistently give Breathees the experience of several psychotherapy sessions in one session, many psychotherapists have doubled session lengths when utilizing Breathwork, sometimes spacing sessions to every other week. We can discover the rhythm which is most effective with each individual.

INDIVIDUAL AND GROUP BREATHWORK

Historically and culturally, Breathing Practices have taken place in dyadic (one-on-one) sessions and group settings—each with advantages and potential missing elements. I encourage my students to participate in both.

In dyadic sessions, the practitioner's attention is maintained on the Breathee at all times, and that constancy and mirroring can support the Breathee in feeling supremely safe, held, and attuned to. Generally, private dyadic Breathwork is optimal for relational, corrective experiences, particularly for those who carry abandonment pain. The combined impact of personal attunement, focus on the Breathee, and having breathing mirrored by another can produce healing beyond words or imagination. In this privacy Breathees often more readily bring forth and share deeply personal experiences and disowned aspects of themselves. Breathers can also build agency and confidence because they are initiating and allowing the change, rather than a group driving the experience.

Many Breathers use Breathwork to reset, release, and energize, which certainly can provide increased resiliency and resources for inner transformation. For enduring change, we go deeper. Usually, individual Breathwork provides this deepening, yet sometimes group Breathwork can be more impactful.

In group Breathwork sessions, Breathees are often inspired to new heights by the effort, courage, and openness of others. The energetic field of multiple breathers consciously breathing together is palpable, leading to complementary experiences of well-being, emotional release, and mystical realities. Hearing others express can help Breathees identify their own stuck, unacknowledged experiences—some that felt too frightening or isolating to face.

In a group, allowing ourselves to feel the intensity of our interior landscape while supporting others' contact with their interior selves, elicits greater self-acceptance and curiosity. We gain a sense of belonging—no longer alone. Breathees often emerge from group Breathwork feeling more capable of being with others' diverse temperaments.

Some group Breathwork sessions have Therapist-Breathworkers guiding all participants in Breathwork simultaneously. In other formats, participants pair up for two rounds of Breathwork. In the first round, one Breathee does Breathwork, and the other is the designated sitter or companion. In the second round, roles are reversed. Sitters' wisdom and intuition can be astounding, as if they are being used as a vehicle by consciousness itself. However, all sitters need to be given explicit guidance about refraining from talking to, touching, or suggesting things to their breathing partner, unless the Breathee asks for something. Practicing with sitters gives Breathees the benefit of receiving full attention while in a group setting. And sitters can have profoundly enriching experiences, that can be equally or more transformative than their own Breathwork session.

Large groups doing Group 1 and 2 practices are frequently led by one facilitator. A yoga teacher might lead a class of up to 200 people. We strongly recommend increasing the ratio of facilitators to participants as we progress through group levels, with the highest ratio at Group 5 Breathwork. Holotropic Breathwork assigns one practitioner for every four participants—two dyads in which one person practices while the other sits, and the practitioner facilitates both dyads. At Inspiration Consciousness School, we place one practitioner for every two to three simultaneously breathing participants, and one for every one or two dyads. Richie Bostock, author of *Exhale: How to Use Breathwork to Find Your Calm, Supercharge Your Health, and Perform at Your Best*, places one Breathworker with every four participants for Group 5 Breathwork.

When Richie facilitates groups of 50 to 2000 using Breathwork Groups 1–4, he feels it's most ethical to employ fairly constant verbal guidance. A gathering of highly experienced Breathees could practice with fewer facilitators. Shirley Telles says that at Patanjali Yoga Research Center in Haridwar, India, they've had up to 10,000 practicing Pranayama—allowing emotional expression—typically with one facilitator for every 20 Breathees.

Breathworkers can circulate and guide during group Breathwork. Because the Breathees and sitters often develop empathic resonance, it's essential that circulating Breathworkers check in with sitters, and attune to Breathees, before intervening. They can also quietly coach Breathwork sitters about ways to support Breathees.

Breathees should be informed, and coached, about the potential intensity of Group 5 Breathwork. Breathing in groups can accelerate and amplify states from emotional to spiritual, so there's frequently more emotional affect and catharsis, memories surfacing, and spiritual experiences. Group verbal expression can become cacophonous. Introverts, Breathees with strong preferences for quiet, and some with trauma, may initially be bothered by group Breathwork. A quieter place to bring participants if needed or requested is beneficial. Yet if participants are willing to stay the course with the group—and good facilitation—discomfort usually subsides or transforms, and they may even derive more benefit from the group experience than others. Their tolerance for noise and unpredictability often increases in daily life too.

Ideally, there should be enough Therapist-Breathworkers in group sessions to provide sufficient individual attunement, mirroring, and coregulating for those with trauma. Group Breathwork can open significant opportunities to deactivate and desensitize trauma triggers and build and practice new resources and responses. Yet, because group Breathwork often amplifies all the quantitative and qualitative dynamics of Breathwork sessions, it's not a given that Breathees with trauma can experience optimal coregulation during group Breathwork. The sounds of others' breathing, vocalizations, or proximity may be triggers. This can be alleviated by Breathees understanding that learning to hear noise, feel physical closeness with others, and simultaneously feel their own potentiated life force can powerfully benefit their lives and ability to love.

BREATHWORK SPACES

The breathing spaces we create, whether in a psychotherapy office, healing room, conference hall, outdoors, or online can affect Breathwork journeys significantly. In indoor spaces, colors, lighting, wall hangings, objects, pictures, floors, and air quality can powerfully contribute to or detract from Breathwork's impact. Windows, air filters, negative ion generators, and UV lights can enhance air quality. Adjustable lighting and natural fragrances are beneficial, although we should check fragrances with Breathees first for sensitivities or allergies to certain scents, particularly mints and menthols. Plants improve air quality, add beauty, and produce natural scents. A University of Buffalo health study showed that air pollution is linked to poorer health and emergency room visits (Yoo & Roberts, 2024). Breathing spaces should have the utmost attention paid to air quality.

Nature environments are profoundly beneficial for connecting with our natural, authentic self. In the biophilia hypothesis biologist E. O. Wilson asserts that we have natural instincts to connect with nature emotionally (Wilson, 1984). Ecopsychology promotes doing therapy outside to activate this instinct and reconnect people with gifts that dwell within their relationship to the ecosystems of our planet. Before COVID-19, my students usually practiced indoors, with outdoor access immediately following sessions to walk, sit, and lie on the ground in a safe, private setting. Since COVID-19 I mostly teach and do Breathwork outdoors, and wish I always had. In outdoor Breathwork, we can experience the beauty of nature, our similarities with animals and plants, the nourishment of earth's electrons and the air's ions, feeling tangibly held by an enormously beautiful force larger than ourselves, having abundant space to move, being enchanted by natural sounds, communing with a particular creature or tree, releasing fears of darkness and the natural world, feeling the joy of enjoyment, and feeling one with the earth.

> *Take a breath offered by friendly winds. They travel the earth gathering essences of plants to clean. Give back with gratitude.*
> —JOY HARJO

ONLINE SPACES

A rich culture of sharing and developing innovative protocol and methodologies has grown in the online space. This is a boon for Breathers who lack access to in-person Breathwork settings due to distance, health and mental health situations, abuse histories, cultural mistrust, domestic violence, caregiving responsibilities, finances, and more.

Online Breathwork has obvious challenges—which can also be opportunities. In the absence of direct eye contact and touch, Breathees can experience more self-motivation, increased agency, empowerment, learning to touch themselves with kindness and wisdom, and trusting in their inner healer and depth. However, after Breathwork sessions, digital distractions can dissipate the intensity and integration of breakthroughs, so we encourage Breathees to immediately spend time with nature, journaling, creative expression, or silent reflection, rather than staying online.

Many Breathwork facilitators introduce first-time Breathees to Group 5 practices online, individually and in groups, with substantial reported benefits. Nevertheless, the International Breathwork Foundation and Global Professional Breathwork Alliance expressed concern early in the COVID-19 global pandemic that beginners could be at risk for insufficient support if their first Group 5 Breathwork medium is virtual. We could do simpler practices first, and then move to Group 5. At a minimum ample informed consent, preparation, integration, *and* follow-up are essential. Especially in large online groups, Breathworkers tend to think the Breathwork is doing good because enthusiastic Breathers return. However, Breathers who needed more support may never return or give feedback.

I advocate for offering beginners additional support from a facilitating team member after online breathwork sessions.

Beyond doubt, there isn't any equivalent substitute for in-person energy, eye contact, and touch. And virtual meetings carry dangers of internet addiction, depersonalization, and image making. Yet, online Breathwork can bestow gifts of ease, accessibility, affordability, forming community (some smaller groups love sharing the visual of their space and getting invited into other's spaces), greater authenticity, increased capacity for self-healing, and bringing the energy of healing and transformation into our personal space. Sometimes Breathwork online is lifesaving.

PROTOCOL FOR ONLINE BREATHWORK

Inspiration Consciousness School developed the following protocol for online Group 5 Breathwork using a team with a primary facilitator and other Breathworkers.

- Introduce Integrative Breathwork principles (or the designated Breathwork style being practiced).
- Each Breathee can share goals or hopes they have for the session. Groups of less than 20, remain in the main virtual room and complete the sharing in 20 to 60 minutes. Groups of 20 or more form small groups in breakout rooms with a facilitator.
- Five minutes for hydration, stretching, bio-break, set-up. Individual coaching is offered in breakout rooms if needed.
- During Breathwork sessions that include possibilities in breakout rooms, Breathees can request to go into a private breakout room with an individual Therapist-Breathworker by physically raising their hand or using the hand raise icon on their platform. Breathwork facilitators can also decide to bring someone into a breakout room if they ascertain that private coaching is needed. We suggest private meetings be limited to 3 to 10 minutes when possible—both so that the Breathee is mostly having the experience of breathing

within the group, and so that there are always practitioners free to work with others.
- Breathwork sessions are from 30 minutes to 1.5 hours, depending on the group's experience level.
- Breathees can share (optional) a few words to a few sentences about their most valuable or impactful healing or learning and/or they can ask questions after the Breathwork concludes.
- Suggestions for self-care and integration are shared.
- Participants are given email and phone contact info for additional guidance if needed.

BREATHWORK IN WATER

We begin life floating in amniotic fluid, with little pressure on joints, muscles, ligaments, tendons, and bones. Since memory begins in utero, we are born with water memories—floating and growing in water and transitioning from water to air. It is highly probable that our DNA contains knowledge of species that evolved from water life to land life in air.

In utero, even though our lungs are filled with fluid, we enact fetal breathing movements, similar to breathing activity after birth. In contrast, breathing outside the womb happens continuously, without requiring overt movement, although movement may enhance it. Hypoxia (lowered oxygen saturation) in utero inhibits fetal breathing movements, whereas in air, hypoxia induces lung activity—breathing. Thus, we have some kind of memory of lung movement and living in water, lung movement and living in air, and the transition from lung movement in water to lung movement in air. Understandably, being in water can be a relaxing, physically therapeutic, soulful and spiritual experience. And, since we begin our growth in fluid—conceivably with no perceived separation between physical, emotional, cognitive, or spiritual experience—it makes the utmost sense that growth work, learning, and self-development in water is profoundly impactful and regulating. For example, Aquatic therapy offers substantial therapeutic benefits for the body and many health conditions, and modalities such as aqua-psychotherapy and Watsu employ the medium of water for emotional well-being and spiritual growth.

Breathwork in water can bring forth astounding personal growth experiences—more than on land for some Breathees. Breathees can be held on their backs, face up with their mouth above the water by two facilitators; Breathees can use snorkels and nose plugs or masks to completely submerge (supported by facilitators); or Therapist-Breathworkers and Breathees who are very experienced scuba divers can use scuba gear, submerge (only shallowly) facing each other and holding hands. Although Breathees may close their eyes in water, the facilitator must always keep eyes open.

During underwater Breathwork, breathing combines *our ancient ancestors' experiences and wisdom of living and breathing in water* with *our experiences and wisdom of living and breathing in air*. Water Breathwork is a riveting intersection of consciousness, the present moment, and collective, species, ancestral, birth, and personal memory. In water, we can experience feeling supported and protected as our bodies let go into floating and being held.

Group 5 Breathwork in water often invokes birth and prebirth memories, transpersonal realms, and rebirth experiences wherein we emerge more fully ourselves into life. In water, many Breathees release the heaviness of trauma. We can also experience connection, belonging, and union with other species.

Breathwork in water often requires far less time than Breathwork on land, possibly because our mammalian diving reflex is triggered when facial nerves contact water (Godek & Freeman, 2022). We share this reflex with whales, seals, some birds, dolphins in particular, and all mammals. When activated, an immediate chain of physiological responses ensues, heart rate is reduced, and blood and oxygen are gathered from our body's periphery to sustain the brain (Panneton & Gan, 2020). Perhaps this heightened neural oxygenation triggers faster and deeper immersion into whatever state our inner healer wishes to surface.

Breathwork in warm water tends to support transcendent experiences and healing of physical symptoms and emotional traumas, particularly birth traumas. Breathwork in cold water tends to build resilience for traumatic memories and narratives, can improve immune functioning and physiological resilience (Epel, 2020), help develop body mastery, and surface transcendental experiences.

HYGIENE

Breathwork is about optimizing health, so for ethical reasons it's important for Therapist-Breathworkers to employ protocols that prevent illness and support vibrant health. Ideally, in-person sessions could include:

- Optimized air quality—consider using air filters, ionizers, and high-oxygen-emitting plants like ferns in a breathing room—and suggesting the same for Breathees working in their own space.
- Providing each Breathee with fresh clean sheets, bedding, and mats.
- Providing facial tissues or cloth handkerchiefs.
- Utilizing full-spectrum lighting with the ability to have varying degrees of light.
- Accessible restroom facilities supplied with natural (preferably organic) disinfectant and cleaning products.
- Hand sanitizer for in between each individual session, and each Breathee in group sessions.
- Consider using UV lights between Breathwork sessions, following manufacturer guidelines.

Most Breathwork involves deeper, prolonged breathing. So during times of high respiratory viral spread, masks can be considered for facilitators and/or Breathees who are educated about various aspects of wearing masks during Breathwork and make a conscious decision. An extensive exploration on mask research was inconclusive, as some studies show masks don't induce any breathing impairment (indeed, surgeons wear masks for hours and focus well), and some indicate that masks cause undesirable or unhealthy symptoms. Peter Litchfield pointed out in our conversations that, based on breathing physiology, most masks likely don't impair breathing, and people's symptoms while wearing masks may result from overbreathing. Also, masks may encourage dysfunctional breathing habits, and symptoms may also arise from personal, biological, or cultural factors.

Additional options include using an outdoor setting, or Therapist-Breathworkers wearing N95 masks while Breathees do Breathwork without masks. Some adventurous pulmonauts may actively engage in Breathwork with masks just to experience the psychological and physiological impacts, or to breathe into physical mastery states that transcend normal physiological reality.

INTEGRATING BREATHWORK INTO OTHER THERAPIES

Integrating Breathwork into psychotherapy and other modalities is usually remarkably simple and intuitive. For example, I invited Dr. Richard Schwartz, founder of Internal Family Systems (IFS), to dialogue during a course I taught on the Shift Network. To demonstrate bringing different Parts of self into greater communication, he asked me to attune to two very different aspects of my personality that I chose. Whenever I worked with the Part that I was less connected to, I volitionally breathed deeply to integrate this less familiar Part. Richard noted that the breathing was powerful and integral to the session.

A somatic model of IFS developed by Susan McConnell, in alignment with Richard and the original IFS model, uses CB as one of five pillars. The styles of breathing used seem to be primarily from Groups 2 and 3, and occasionally 1 and 4. Richard has had personal experiences of Group 5 Breathwork in a few advanced IFS trainings, and we noted many resonances between IFS and Breathwork, including: (1) IFS and Breathwork both dissolve shame using extraordinarily nonpathologizing orientations. Richard is so impressive in enacting this value that it is inspiring. (2) A pivotal motto in IFS is that *all parts are welcome*. Breathwork also welcomes every aspect of self and reality into the present moment—into the breathing moment. (3) IFS shepherds the client into self-leadership. Breathwork requires constant self-initiating energy.

When verbal analysis or repatterning is needed, the values of cognitive and talk therapy should not be overlooked. They can be easily integrated into Breathwork sessions. Integrating Breathwork skills can bring more artistry and depth to any form of therapy.

The Light of Service: Burnout to Burning Bright

What is to give light must endure burning.
—VIKTOR FRANKL

CB is a life practice for psychotherapists, Breathworkers, and other healing professionals for sustaining their work and preventing burnout. The rate that dedicated mental health and healthcare professionals experience emotional exhaustion, moral distress, or burnout has precipitously risen. Yet whether Therapist-Breathworkers have spacious schedules with lots of self-care time and boundaries, or are compelled to serve 25/8, lung-deep in trauma work, I've never heard anyone whose employer is Breathing use the word burnout. (Of course, we do describe fatigue or exhaustion for periods of time, and we do need work-free periods!) The low to no rate of Breathworker "burnout" is likely because of autonomic nervous system regulation through daily CB, breathing deeply with Breathees, and being inspired by the immense transformation we are privileged to accompany.

Therapist-Breathworkers are essential workers for alleviating suffering, and preventing or addressing mental health challenges, violence, medical conditions, and personal and collective trauma. The known value of Breathwork is proliferating, and like other mental health professionals, Professional Breathworkers may be called to the front lines, and as first responders, in future collective crises and tragedies.

It would be wise and fun for Therapist-Breathworkers to support themselves and other healthcare professionals in implementing breathing support groups or breathing buddies as an integral structure during work—perhaps scheduling 7 minutes of CB every 4 hours with breathing buddies virtually or in person! Quick self-care practices, such as washing hands after sessions, scanning the horizon, using natural fragrances, and engaging in daily CB, are also essential for well-being.

Dr. John Haworth was a personal mentor and great exemplar for self-care. A highly respected general physician who inspired countless doctors, medical students, nursing staff, and patients, he was on call for 23 hours and 40 minutes every day, inclusive of his regular 12-to-14-hour work days. Any hospital staff could call him in the middle of the night if we were concerned about a patient. However, from 7:00 to 7:20 a.m. every morning, 7 days per week, Dr. Haworth was unreachable. In those 20 minutes, we knew he couldn't be contacted because he was doing self-care. He practiced this way for 37 years, tending to and saving an incalculable number of people. We can create 20 minutes daily for the self-care of Conscious Breathing—no matter what!

PRACTITIONER SELF-CARE: BEST PRACTICES

The most important factor for Therapist-Breathworkers to provide safety and creativity in facilitating powerful Breathwork is commitment to self-care, and personal healing and development as follows:

1. Committing to CB practices daily for 7 minutes or more.
2. Deepening our inner work to strengthen connection with our authentic self.
3. Committing to holistic self-care: hydration, healthy food, movement, exercise, and more.
4. Practicing deep conscious breaths, directly prior to each session.
5. Continually contacting our interior during sessions and intentionally breathing more deeply every minute or two.
6. Utilizing CB to support sustained eye contact with Breathees.

7. Being present with breathing throughout sessions, especially when Breathees are speaking about, expressing, or reacting to, trauma.
8. Exchanging ideas and experiences with colleagues about Breathwork skills and facilitation, including regularly participating in clinical supervision.

We can support clients with relaxation, regulation, alertness, and presence, without recreating trauma or taking on secondary effects. If we have difficulty breathing fully, feel stressed, or exhibit signs of secondary trauma from working with others' trauma, we can engage in longer personal breathing sessions and Human Potential Breathwork sessions with another well-trained Therapist-Breathworker.

CB connects us somatically with wholeness, contributing to the healing and well-being of ourselves and others simultaneously, and strengthening interconnection with those we serve.

> *If I had to limit my advice on healthier living to just one tip, it would be simply to learn how to breathe correctly. There is no single more powerful—or more simple—daily practice to further your health and well-being than breathwork.*
>
> —ANDREW WEIL, MD

NINE

Components and Processes of Human Potential Breathwork Sessions

I often plagiarize breath, who does most of the work.
—CHELAN HARKIN, SUSCEPTIBLE TO LIGHT

THE WORD *psychotherapy* originates from the ancient Greek *psyche*, which translates as "breath, spirit, and soul," and *therapeia*, which translates as "healing or medical treatment." Psychotherapy's original orientation could thus be said to be: breath healing, breath medical treatment, or spirit or soul healing or medical treatment. Integrating Breathwork and psychotherapy may support psychotherapy's original intent—using one's own biological, emotional, cognitive, and spiritual resources to become whole—to be one's integrated and authentic self.

Our life's ultimate purpose is not to heal the wounds of our childhood, be free of pain, and be happy, though those are worthy and important experiences. Our most fulfilling life purpose is contacting the wells of love and creative life force within and creating pathways for their expression and contribution to our personal and collective lives. Within that journey, defenses, patterns, and repressions that block creative life force flow may be revealed; we can then attend to these parts of our psyche—including childhood and adult neglect, harm, and trauma—as an aspect of supporting the flowering of our fully potentiated self.

Innovative concepts and reenvisioning the field have been intrinsic to the evolution of psychotherapy since its inception and often result in paradigm shifts. Freud envisioned and introduced the ego, id, and superego; Jung revisioned psychotherapy's central role as searching for individuation and integrating the personal and collective unconscious with the conscious mind; Carl Rogers offered client-centered therapy and *unconditional positive regard* (Rogers & Kramer, 1995); Abraham Maslow developed humanistic psychology; Murray Bowen and Virginia Satir surfaced dynamic healing potential through family systems theory (Bowen, 1986; Satir, 1988); Eugene Gendlin (1982) brought forth the importance of nonverbal, somatic, intuitive body feelings—the felt sense; Alice Miller (1997) invited holding childhood formative experiences tenderly and understanding catastrophic consequences of parental child abuse and neglect.

Today psychotherapy has been reimagined through growing understanding of attachment, trauma, and neuroscience. John Bowlby's and Mary Ainsworth's attachment theory transformed negative views about children's parental dependency, validating children's innate drive to seek "proximity to another individual" (Bowlby, 1969). We now understand that healthy attachment fosters good neural functioning (Siegel, 2012), development of our potential, and ability to form healthy romantic relationships. Psychotherapy is also integrating mindfulness, sparked by Jon Kabat-Zinn's (2013) research and programs. Dan Siegel (1999) and interpersonal neurobiology are refining our comprehension of the mind and integration. Internal Family Systems has de-pathologized our "dysfunctional" parts or subpersonalities with faith in their positive intent (Schwartz, 2001, 2021). Revisioning and "re-enchanting" psychiatry, psychology, and psychotherapy was coined by Stanislav Grof (2012) to include the need for Holotropic experience—moving toward wholeness and integrating our entire human experience. Indeed, the psychotherapeutic field is increasingly dedicated to healing soma, psyche, and soul.

Breathwork's transformational power and capacity can be integrated into all methodologies of therapy—including psychoanalysis, founded in 1896—to enhance breadth, depth, efficacy, integration, and self-actualization. We are at a seminal time for reenvisioning psychotherapy through Conscious Breathing (CB) and Breathwork, creating best practices for Breathwork, and centering breathing in the arts and sciences of healing and well-being.

> *Without full awareness of breathing, there can be no development of meditative stability and understanding.*
> —ĀNĀPĀNASATI SUTTA,
> TRANSLATED BY THICH NHAT HANH

There's hardly anything more direct and robust than Breathwork with an experienced and wise guide to support healing, self-actualization, and the discrete components and building blocks of psyche and self. This chapter offers some orientations, tools, and processes to assist. Let us notice, and set aside, any assumptions that Breathwork is simply an auxiliary tool. Let us open to the deep paradigm shifts that Breathwork can create in therapeutic processes and healing.

Therapist-Breathworker Presence and Orientations

These following ethical orientations help Therapist-Breathworkers to be present, effective, and in service during Breathwork. They also help prevent Breathees from becoming disempowered, dissociated, or fearful of expansive experiences. Additionally, they strengthen attunement between Breathees and facilitators, so sessions remain guided by a Breathee's authentic needs and journey.

- *Always* maintain continual breathing awareness to cultivate presence in our SEC continuum. This is foundational.
- *Always* maintain awareness that simply a few breaths can open new, special, or sensitive states of being in Breathees.
- *Never* offer a suggestion, however wise, during Breathwork about what Breathees ought to do with their life, body, and relationships. Because CB can access deep parts of being, and surface hurt,

trauma, and potential, Breathees may open to suggestions during Breathwork without engaging their own discernment. Life decisions that Breathees wish to explore should be initiated and directed from within themselves during Breathwork. If they say, "I don't know what to do about _____," we can invite the feeling of "not knowing" to breathe. What does that feel like in their body? What did their body feel when they definitively knew and made a good choice? We can invite the sensations to breathe.

- *Always* ask Breathees what they are *experiencing* first. The word *experiencing* ensures they notice what is central for them, whether sensation, feeling, awareness, imagery, or energy. If warranted, we can specifically explore emotions by asking what they feel; for thoughts, what they think; and for bodily sensations and information, what they sense.
- *Never* ask or infer *who* is causing a sensation, feeling, or awareness. It is suggestive and can harm. Instead, we can inquire, "What does the pressure/hatred/attack feel like? . . . Does it have a shape? . . . Does it have a color? . . . Does it have an emotion? . . . Where is it most strong in your body? . . . If the pressure could talk, what would it be saying? . . . What do you want to say to the pressure?"
- *Always* remember and trust that both automatic and volitional breathing are vastly intelligent and will guide the session with immeasurable resources.

ENHANCED CO-EMPOWERMENT AND RELATIONAL MODELING

- Breathwork fosters significant self-responsibility and self-reliance, inviting an enhanced model of co-empowerment between Breathees and Therapist-Breathworkers. Breathing is the authority; Therapist-Breathworkers are like skilled midwives, medicine people, Sherpas or guides; and Breathees are the participant and explorer.
- Healthy coregulation is easily established in sessions by affirming the Breathee's individual breathing and physical regulation, and through Therapist-Breathworkers and Breathees breathing synchronously or with awareness of each other's breathing.

- Breathwork can increase attunement and resonance between Breathees and Therapist-Breathworkers. Breathing in sync and connecting beyond language can repair preverbal ruptures and elicit experiences of connection that model healthy relationships.
- When Therapist-Breathworkers and Breathees breathe together, and the Breathee's experience is respected and valued, they learn about generating equality in their relationships with authority, as well as those they guide, such as children, clients, and employees.

THREE TRANSFORMATIONAL BREATHWORK PATHWAYS

Healing: Conscious Breathing helps restore and revitalize the somatic–emotional–cognitive continuum (SEC continuum) for optimal functioning. Through release and relaxation, the SEC continuum expresses its natural vibrancy and inherent wisdom, generating energy and readiness for further growth and wholeness.

Development: From conception onward, our early experiences shape our fundamental physical, emotional, and cognitive building blocks and neural pathways. When these function optimally, we can utilize our temperament, physiology, and genetic propensities for thriving. Early experiences of neglect, lack of attunement, abandonment, harm, social injustice, and trauma, impact our psychophysical structures and activate unconscious defenses that limit our capacity to develop and self-actualize. Breathwork can help us recognize and release stagnant or blocked energy, optimize our adaptations, reframe our personal narrative, positively impact our gene expressions and biological functioning, and reveal dormant life force in our soma and psyche. We become more aware of healthy capacities we have protectively hidden—allowing them to breathe, grow, and respond to the present with more love, wisdom, and well-being.

Essence: We are made of the same Essence and Source that constitutes everything. We are emanations of that creative life force. Recognizing and embodying this enables us to be more constant, emergent expressions of love, wisdom, and presence. Every conscious breath can engender immediate contact with this truth, enabling us to meet our personal manifestations and journey with greater compassion and wisdom. It makes it possible to discover and develop our gifts and potential without shame or hiding our light.

Human Potential Breathwork (Group 5) Processes

The following processes range from physiological to spiritual. There's never one formula or *one-size-fits-all* Breathing Practice because each Breather and their breathing is unique.

INTENTION

Beginning something consciously benefits from intention, and we can embed intentions, aspirations, and affirmations into breathing. Enhanced breathing can amplify those thoughts and intentions. These partnerships can potentially drive enhanced attention and somatic support for building new neural pathways. The seemingly binary system of inhaling and exhaling provides metaphorical frameworks for activating healing and transformation, and opening universes of creativity. Seeding an intention into an inhalation occasions a potent structure that can complement or contrast with another distinct intention during exhalation. Through breathing we create a more flowing process between the two, dissolve any favoring of inhale or exhale, and embody more whole integration.

The number, type, and quality of designs coming forth from this tool are legion. Consider some examples:

- Inhaling life force . . . exhaling tension or numbness
- Inhaling the sweetness of life . . . exhaling fear of living
- Inhaling self-compassion . . . exhaling compassion for all
- Inhaling confidence in our wisdom . . . exhaling into surrendering to life's wisdom

- Inhaling life force into a physical discomfort or pain... exhaling the pain
- Inhaling to accept this moment as it is... exhaling to allow change and flow
- Inhaling spirit or essence... exhaling to let it be shared with others
- Inhaling our ability for self-reliance... exhaling into life and others supporting us
- Inhaling our visions for our life... exhaling to let go of what does not serve those visions
- Inhaling into our value and gifts... exhaling to let them flow through us, into the world

BREATH CYCLES

Surges of physical energy, emotional energy, and awareness are fairly universal for all Group 5 Breathing Practices. Breathees will experience these physically (sensations of warmth, cold, tingling, solidity, fluidity, lightness), emotionally (appreciation, gratitude, grief, rage), and cognitively (awareness that something different from our normal default is happening). Therapist-Breathworkers will usually notice the intensification of energy. The energy initiates the movement toward emergence. The building of energy and process that ushers Breathees into emergence can be described as a breath cycle that has four stages.

1. **Building energy** through Breathwork, creating a change or charge in physical and/or emotional state that feels more energized or heightened than when the session started. Generally, this takes anywhere from one breath to a few minutes, though sometimes much longer.
2. **Opening or clearing** as evidenced by feeling significant changes in the energy. Opening is an emergence of potential, essential qualities, or enhanced well-being. A clearing occurs when blocked emotions, memories, or physical tension arise and are expressed or processed somatically, emotionally, or cognitively.
3. **Releasing or relaxing** (letting go) of physical tension, emotion, or dysregulated energy, effecting a physiological or transformational

change in our body that unburdens or opens life-giving energy. Releasing may be physically signified by a *breath release*, deep sighs, smiling, crying, trembling, vibrating, stretching, and so forth. A breath release is: (1) feeling that we can breathe significantly more deeper than before with a feeling of being freed from constriction, (2) feeling as if we are being breathed fantastically deeply. Many Breathers describe feeling that they are on a cosmic respirator.

4. **Integrating**—feeling regulated with any or all of the following: a *new or increased* sense of physical energy or well-being; a *new or increased* degree of openness to emotion and/or our heart; cognitive comprehension of something we've experienced during the Breathwork and its effect on us in the past, present, or future; a spiritual insight or experience. Most often we will feel an amplification of one or all of these: grounding, harmony, peace, life force, power, energy, connection, awareness, love. We may be drawn to touch places on our body—feeling this new state. We may share insights with our Therapist-Breathworker. We may experience gratitude. Or we may simply have more clarity about the inner work we need to do. Most often integration will entail long, slow, deep breathing, sometimes quite energetically and powerfully, sometimes more quietly and contemplatively. Integration usually has little to no pain, fear, or tension; instead, a sense of lightness ensues—while feeling more substantial.

A breath cycle's normal duration is anywhere from 5 minutes to an hour; can range from a minute to 2 hours or more; and, on rare occasions, is one breath. In Group 5 Breathwork sessions, Breathees frequently have more than one breath cycle—two or three is common, and five or six is not rare.

UNCONDITIONAL POSITIVE REGARD, MIRRORING, AND EYE CONTACT

Breathwork amplifies unconditional positive regard in two remarkable ways.

1. Breathing itself becomes an unconditional, unbroken, powerful, and steady matrix. This phenomenon is amplified the more we receive the increasing vitality and intelligence of the breathing, and whatever emerges from vibration and aliveness.
2. Breathwork can readily and simultaneously contact our pure authentic presence and enhanced mirroring with our facilitator, so we learn to feel safer about presence as our fundamental matrix in ordinary moments.

CB magnifies mirroring dynamics. We feel mirrored by our breathing, which alone can surface our vulnerability and precious capacities. A second layer of mirroring can ensue when Breathees and facilitators breathe in tandem, harmoniously and/or synchronously. Adding embodied eye contact can amplify mirroring further. The combined mirroring of CB, coregulation, and eye contact is profound.

Empathic eye contact can powerfully stimulate mirror neurons. In Breathwork this supports us in experiencing our authentic selves while simultaneously being present with the life force in others. Sight is not imperative. Mirroring can occur through voice, writing, music, art, touch, and breathing together.

Prolonged gazing into one another's eyes while consciously breathing requires Therapist-Breathworkers to self-reference while holding space for Breathees' emotional expressions, needs, revealed memories, enactments, and transpersonal experiences. Subtle to substantive projections of unresolved relational tensions from early childhood by Therapist-Breathworkers and Breathees can be appreciably heightened combining the intensity of prolonged gazing and Breathwork. Therapist-Breathworkers should inhabit the sensations of their own breathing (especially when synchronously breathing), maintain interoceptive awareness, and readily support Breathees' internal or external movements toward stopping, avoiding, pausing, and how inner guidance, individuation, or integration affect eye position—including breaking eye contact.

Eye gazing can be mesmerizing for both parties. Thus, Integration may be inhibited or thwarted for fear of displeasing the other by breaking eye contact. Eye gazing can also induce trancelike states that one or both may have longed for. They may attribute the longed-for state to eye gazing and/or the relationship with the Therapist-Breathworker, rather than an always available capacity. Therapist-Breathworkers are responsible for guiding Breathees to internalize experiences of relational gazing, to know it as a capacity they can bring to their personal relationships.

Positive change is often accompanied by eyes looking directly upward. We would not want to impede this process by becoming attached to eye gazing with each other. There are remarkable correlations between Integrative Breathings principles and the theoretical foundations of Accelerated Experiential Dyadic Therapy (AEDP) founded by psychologist Diana Fosha—including about eyes looking upwards during transformation. Fosha observes:

> A specific biomarker of transformational processing is the gaze-up (head straight, eyes gazing straight up neither to the right nor the left) phenomenon. Over the years, I have found this type of gaze to accompany the healing effects and herald the emergence of resilience. (Fosha, 2017)

Breathees can be given hand mirrors to *see* themselves in the new states—in silence and/or speaking aloud self-encouraging and affirming. When speaking to themselves, they can observe how their breathing and face are affected. Tilke Platteel-Deur, with almost 50 years of experience as an Integrative Breath Therapist, beautifully describes this process in her book *The Art of Integrative Therapy*, and notes, "The person we see, when looking in a mirror, is the only human being we will ever have the opportunity to absolutely, completely, and deeply know, the only one who will always accompany us through every moment in life" (2009, p. 172).

BREATHING TOUCH

After breathing, touch has incomparable power to heal, imprint, transform, elevate, induce contraction, harm, destroy, and actualize embodied wholeness. The body releases endorphins, serotonin, and oxytocin when pleasingly touched, strengthening our immune systems and reducing stress (Intermountain Health, 2023).

Our own touch. Touching ourselves with attunement, kindness, and wisdom is profoundly healing, transformative, empowering, and integrating. No one else can attune to the exact place, pressure, and way our shoulder, for instance, wants to be touched. Touching our body with love is invaluable. During Breathwork it can feel surprisingly natural to place our hands on our chests and abdomens. The magic begins—touching when breathing reduces tension, softens us, amplifies senses, increases receptivity, surfaces emotions—and activates a superhighway between interoceptive and exteroceptive experience.

Therapist-Breathworkers partnering to utilize touch. Traditionally, in psychotherapeutic training, touch is avoided. Reasons to refrain from touching a client during psychotherapy are irrefutable for preventing clinicians from acting out sexually with clients; clients developing dependency on receiving nurturing or special attention from clinicians; and clients excessively desiring, or inappropriately seeking, sexual interactions with clinicians. As stated in Chapter 8, as in psychotherapeutic training, Breathwork facilitators should receive ethics training and be certified as ethically compliant through the GPBA.

Touch is not inherently unethical. While ethical codes of psychotherapy professional associations in the United States—including the American Association for Marriage and Family Therapy, American Psychological Association, and American Counseling Association—view violence and sexual (with current or recent clients) touch as unethical, they don't disallow nonviolent and nonsexual touch in therapy.

To prevent overriding the authentic self, amplifying defenses, or retraumatization, therapeutic consent to touch is essential and should occur *before Breathwork* because Breathwork can be sensitive and intense, and we shouldn't interrupt the flow with requests. Also, Breathwork can involve childhood memories, regression, and trauma; asking for consent midsession might mean we are asking younger parts who can't say no. Consent agreements should include particular words or movement which communicate that touching should stop. Even with agreements, Therapist-Breathworkers should usually check in again right before touching. We can't assume that silence means okay, or that quick responses are the whole truth.

Long-term experience has demonstrated that touch can be exceedingly beneficial in Breathwork. Indeed, withholding touch can be harmful or retraumatizing in some instances. Not touching when needed and beneficial can be experienced as insensitive, unsupportive, violent, and traumatic—recapitulating early relationships that were detached, disinterested, avoidant, cold, or abandoning. The complexity of this is prodigious. Simply put, each touch can evoke reams of terror, hope, or love.

Touch can add significant healing and therapeutic benefit to Breathwork by supporting body awareness for optimal breathing; generating sensations of realness, belonging, and grounding; releasing tension and loosening restrictive muscular patterns; and relaxing depersonalization or dissociation tendencies when caring touch is safe. In many cultures, reaching out to touch someone's hand or hug in times of celebration, pain, grief, or fear is an extremely natural response. Similar moments will surface in Breathwork. Yet some cultures experience any touch as intrusive. The sensitivity and precision of touch's impact is an art and constant learning process.

Conversely, Breathees can experience inappropriate, unattuned, or rough touch, as intrusive, traumatic, or overriding the authentic self. Harm is compounded when Breathees hesitate voicing discomfort and risking disruption or separation from Therapist-Breathworkers.

Cultivating fluency and artistry in touching with Breathwork can reliably elicit profoundly corrective experiences for the authentic self and relational interactions. It would be impossible to count the number of times Breathees report Therapist-Breathworkers touching them in the perfect way at the perfect time. Alignment and partnership of Breathees' inner healers with Therapist-Breathworkers elicits somatic and intuitive communication. The Breathee and the Therapist-Breathworker both experience embodied, integrated possibilities and examples of actualized relationships.

It is a privilege to touch someone opening themselves to growth, so Therapist-Breathworkers should practice with other facilitators, as well as touching ourselves with tenderness and confidence in the same places we could touch Breathees.

MOVEMENT AND TOUCH

In order to move, breathing is a necessity, and where there is breathing there is movement. Movement is a universal medicine. We learned about Breathwork positions in Chapter 6, all of which can be foundations for movement. Here are some additional particularly powerful movements that support transformation in Breathwork.

The heart pump. When Breathees initially practice deeper continuous breathing, they may experience abdominal and chest constrictions and breathing weakness. Unwinding these patterns produces greater relaxation, energy, emotional releases, and well-being. The heart pump's effectiveness may be because our heart contains the *little brain*, with 40,000 neurons that are similar to brain neurons. Cardiac neurons generate massive connections to key regions in the neural brain that affect emotional and cognitive factors in pain (Alshami, 2019). Inducing relaxation and coherence in these pathways through the heart pump may significantly reduce emotional and cognitive dysregulation, pain, and trauma signaling.

This technique can require practice to implement well. Having skilled facilitators apply the heart pump to trainees is invaluable. Trainees practice with one another, willing friends, and family. The heart pump induces psychophysiological change, activates body responsiveness, and rapidly supports optimal breathing.

We should only use the heart pump on Breathees with prior cardiac histories if we are extremely skilled and experienced, they are in agreement, and we use extraordinarily light touch. With those conditions met, Breathers with significant cardiac conditions have felt that the heart pump was healing and restorative for them, as if their heart felt whole again. (Please note that the heart pump is contraindicated for Breathees with pacemakers.)

To begin the heart pump, Breathees inhale deeply and relax on the exhale. Locating the center of the Breathee's chest—the breastbone and slightly above—facilitators place one hand upon the other, palms facing down, with the wrists aligned comfortably. During exhales we pump our hands with gentle pressure (about one-eighth to one inch deep, depending on Breathee physique, strength, and breathing volume) in a frequency that feels resonant with the Breathee's exhalation vibration. The frequency can range from two pumps per second to one pump every three seconds and is unique each session.

We can apply the heart pump for one breath or up to 10 at a time. Alternatively, we can heart pump four or five times, pause for a few breaths, then continue the heart pump. Breathees describe this experience as significantly relaxing and pleasurable and will sometimes cry or laugh as somatic and emotional fear dissolve. Breathees can become euphoric, experiencing openness and freedom.

FIGURE 9.1: The Heart Pump
Jessica Dibb. Image created by Liz Slaterbeck.

I was in a very dark place inside and feeling the worst atrocities committed by humankind, seeing into the souls of the people who committed these acts. My Breathworker did the heart pump technique and I felt incredible emergences of love. Little pieces of armor protecting my heart broke off and dispersed. No longer identifying with the darkness inside these people, I saw the goodness and love inside them and myself.

Touching two places simultaneously. This can forge awareness and connection between disengaged or disconnected places. Someone may feel rage toward their mother in their abdomen yet feel love for them in their chest. Facilitators or Breathees can place hands on the two places. Simply breathing with awareness of both areas can open their communication and flow. Breathees might describe that anger has turned into power for setting boundaries while offering positive change to the mother they

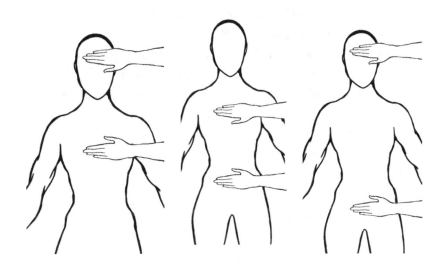

FIGURE 9.2: Heart and Forehead
Jessica Dibb. Image created by Liz Slaterbeck.

FIGURE 9.3: Heart and Abdomen
Jessica Dibb. Image created by Liz Slaterbeck.

FIGURE 9.4: Forehead and Abdomen
Jessica Dibb. Image created by Liz Slaterbeck.

love. Creating connections between our psyche's isolated functions and components builds capacity for multidimensional knowing, experiencing, and integration.

Shaking, tremoring, and vibrating. These movements can accelerate healing and transformation rapidly. We experience involuntary tremors or shaking when frightened, agitated, or excited to automatically discharge stress or regulate energy. We can intentionally invoke this capacity for therapeutic benefit. If Breathees don't have structural challenges or medical conditions that are easily exacerbated by shaking, they can vibrate or shake to interrupt habits, defenses, and patterns; enhance right brain functioning; discover new aspects of self; release tension; increase energy and alertness; reduce or dissolve fear; move blocked emotions; feel more freedom; and rewire physical, emotional, and cognitive patterns.

We stand, feet shoulder-width apart, knees slightly bent, inhabiting our feet contacting the ground. From the feet, through the legs, into the pelvis, the whole body moves freely with our natural pelvic energy and strength. Vibrating can be initiated by moving the body rapidly up and down, moving like a dog shaking off water, or imagining standing on a vibrating machine. Full breathing is continuous throughout, with bent knees, relaxed jaw and face, freely flowing arms, and allowing the head and neck to flow with the movement. We can also visualize or sense electromagnetic energy coming through the earth into the feet, or electromagnetic pulses moving in from the air. Therapist-Breathworkers can inspire Breathees by vibrating too, while watching them for safety.

The body wave. During Group 5 Breathwork, the body wave can amplify healing, releasing, awareness, and integration by inviting the body to experience coherence that's imbued with fluidity and spontaneity. Inspiration trainees practice the body wave with each other prior to working with Breathees to feel how amplitudes and oscillation rates are unique for everyone.

With permission, we place our hands on either side of the Breathee's waist, about one or two inches away from the body. We gently pass the body back and forth between our two hands, creating a wave by ensuring only one hand touches their body at a time, so they feel free motion on the other side. The amplitude distance can vary widely, with some an inch or two, and others three to six. We establish oscillations at the waist, then slowly move our hands up and down the torso from armpits to hips. The oscillation rates seem to reflect each Breathee's emotions and life force.

Optimally the wave will reflect an *S wave*, like a rope held at one end, with motion sent through it. The chest, torso, and hips don't move to the same side simultaneously, yet they move harmoniously as one wave. Facilitators' hands move in a fluid, nonstop motion up and down from chest to hips as slowly or quickly as we sense blocked energy needing attention or new energy opening and joining *the wave*. When a Breathee's torso moves less readily, we can pause there and continue to work with that one area until it moves in sync with the whole wave. If it's not loosening easily, we can migrate to another area and then return. The body wave can be done for a few seconds up to several minutes.

Movement that arises spontaneously. Spontaneous movement during Breathwork unlocks somatic wisdom. These movements contain emotions, and potentials, that haven't been authentically expressed. When enacted in the present, the corresponding emotions or visions, may arise. Breathers with unresolved trauma may move in ways they wanted to but were prevented from. Spontaneous movement can free mechanical and emotional energy; restore embodiment and physical authenticity; build trust in our body; and strengthen new pathways for aliveness, empowerment, and joy.

Facilitators may have the perception that there's very little energy, and believe suggesting a specific movement would help. Sometimes that helps. Other times there are reams of subtle movement occurring in the fascia, fostering significant awareness. We can learn to listen, watch, and discern. Heightened life force in Breathwork can move our bodies in ways not possible in ordinary waking or defensive states. It's extraordinary to see someone who says they could never bend backward, bending back with exceptional flexibility.

> *The True Man breathes with his heels; the mass of men breathe with their throats.*
>
> —CHUANG TZU, THE COMPLETE WORKS OF CHUANG TZU, TRANSLATED BY BURTON WATSON

Spontaneous body movements in flow states. These flow states are akin to Kundalini experiences. Yet, unlike Kundalini experiences that can come unbidden, Breathwork opens spontaneous movement from presence and we *intentionally* surrender to it.

Spontaneous movement in Breathwork can be a convergence of extraordinary and transcendent states with embodied presence that transcend, yet include, ego and boundary awareness. Breathees' bodies can move in astonishing ways, including arching, twirling, skipping, somersaulting, and rolling—sometimes several of these woven together fluidly and gracefully. Many Breathees say they could never do these things, including people 80 and over, and yet it can happen.

Embodied CB during spontaneous movement flows provides a continual grounding mechanism for experiencing all the benefits without concern about boundary dissolution. In Integrative Breathwork groups Breathees remain aware of others. When the flow concludes, they are more awake and grounded—without dissociation—and describe exceptional healing experiences and expanded awareness.

Mark Walsh, a leader in the embodiment field, shared in conversation, "If a therapist asked me which is more important for clients, Tai chi or Breathwork, I would say Breathwork. **I can't imagine embodiment as a field without Breathwork—Breath is its center."**

SOUND IN BREATHWORK

Similar to touching, sound can be unifying and integrating. Sounds used during Breathwork should harmonize with the Breathee's authentic experience, rather than overriding it.

The sound of Breathees breathing. **The most powerfully integrating sound for a human being is the sound of their own breathing.**

Studies have shown that the human brain is affected by sound, even to the last moments of life (University of British Columbia, 2020), and Sufi Sheikhs tell us that the sound of breathing in a newborn baby's ear is essential for the development of consciousness. The oceanic sounds produced through Breathing Practices, such as Ujjayi, are extremely regulating and can elicit bliss. Our breathing accompanies us through every internal and external experience we had, have, or ever will. The sound of our own breathing can heal us, dissolve self-rejection, and unify fragmentations of self.

When breathing automatically, we may not overtly hear sound in our breathing, yet all vibration has sound whether we hear it or not. The more intimate we become with our breathing, the more we can sense the vibrations—and *hear our breathing*. And certainly, when we breathe more deeply, or are breathed more deeply, the sound becomes audible to the human ear. These principles have proven so powerful that I almost always culminate individual and group Breathwork sessions with Breathees listening to their own breathing. It becomes a tuning fork for their daily life that can recall them again and again to presence.

There is no need to generate a sound in our breathing; it's enough to sense the breathing and listen for whatever vibrational frequency and/or sound we can hear. During Breathwork, after beneficial impacts, we can volitionally generate Ujjayi sounds to associate with the benefits, then use the sound during daily activities to recall the beneficial experience.

Vocal sounds from breathees. All five groups of Breathwork contain techniques that utilize breath sounds such as mantras, sighing aloud, breathing in deeply to sing, and so on. During Group 5 Breathwork that encourages expression, we may speak, cry, laugh, yell, sing, drone, or tone, always following the pulse of breathing's emergent energy.

If Breathees talk to unconsciously dissipate heightened energy, awareness, or a powerful emotion, Therapist-Breathworkers can guide them to focus on an important aspect of what they are saying—then suggest they breathe deeply with it. If Breathees talk without presence, they can be guided to notice the greatest bodily sensation related to what they are saying and invite the sensation to breathe.

Long, *droning* vocalizations sound like or resonate with bodily pain, tension, and uncomfortable emotions. Most often, droning is not melodious and has an anguished, raw, deep-throated quality. Therapist-Breathworkers can encourage Breathees to drone for several minutes. Sometimes we can sound with them to mirror and normalize their expression and reduce discomfort. We should use their exact sound as closely as possible and never overpower it. Droning helps move stuck energy by bypassing normal defense mechanisms so new life force and awareness can enter. Breathees feel like something "really cleared" or they "let it go."

Long *toning* sounds reflect life-enhancing qualities. When newly aware of qualities like joy, confidence, radiance, self-love, love, or power, Breathees can embody it by sounding it in a tone during exhalation. Toning is usually a melodic sound, ranging from low to high pitched. Therapist-Breathworkers can generate the same sound to support safety and expression. When Breathees emit extremely quiet sounds and feel unsafe, we can match their tone and gradually crescendo, inviting them to sound with us. We should use their exact tone without overpowering. With discernment, we can occasionally initiate the toning to invite a healthy or essential quality into their awareness.

Droning and toning can be combined. We can drone for a few breaths to express a hurting part, then tone to express self-love and Essence. We can alternate drones and tones until they inform each other, harmonize, and eventually become one note, so the wisdom of both are unified and enhanced. Breathees should be reminded to inhale deeply during droning and toning.

Vocal sounds from Therapist-Breathworkers. An authentic and empowered voice that expresses intimacy with life is a great instrument to convey safety, inspiration, nurturing, empathy, and guidance. Yet Therapist-Breathworkers' vocalizations can support or detract from Breathees' experiences, so awareness and discernment are important.

As the sound of our own breathing is the most integrating sound, the sound of another human mirroring or complementing our breathing is the most coregulating sound we can experience. Most Breathees **LOVE** hearing a trusted facilitator breathing deeply while attending to them. Yet some Breathees associate another's breathing sounds with trauma. Others have powerful inner critics who feel pushed to breathe certain ways when they hear facilitators breathing, and others find it distracting. Additionally, sometimes Breathees are experiencing subtle inner guidance and want quiet. Attunement about our breath sounds is essential.

Chanting. Practicing Hindus, Muslims, Buddhists, Christians, and Jews, may chant in Group 5 Breathwork sessions. If childhood included chanting, Breathwork may provide a profound connection with it. In expanded states of consciousness, Breathers may chant spontaneously from a tradition other than their own, or even if they don't have one.

Chanting can be an alternative to toning or stand on its own. Encouraging deep breathing between each phrase can intensify the power. Breathees can inhale deeply, then chant, inhale deeply, then chant. Or chant, breathe deeply several times, chant, and continue alternating. Many chants are phrases based on reverence for breathing; some chanting traditions were developed specifically to support Breathing Practices.

Music. Music during Breathwork can accelerate imagery and magnify contact with emotions and memories. It can relax, regulate, mirror, and inspire willingness to grow and access transcendent states. Music can also overpower a Breathee's genuine experience by invoking inauthentic emotions and interfering with the natural direction of their authentic emergence; so it should be applied with consideration and attunement to what supports a particular Breathee or group. Though numerous Breathers value Breathwork accompanied by music, *ultimately it's most empowering and useful to learn to do Breathwork, even Group 5, without music—just with the sound of breathing,* that is there in all life situations.

EMOTIONS

Emotions and feelings are highly experiential states that contribute to consciousness. Breathwork excels as a medium for presence with these states. Breathwork magnifies contact with emotions, feeling, and affect, which can resolve somatic and intrapsychic tension, with efficacy in discerning between emotions (raw reaction) and feelings (interpretation).

As people become stressed, rigid, disorganized, depressed, dissociative, or traumatized, contact with authentic emotions and genuine emotional expression progressively or abruptly disappears. Accessing and recovering truthful feeling brings forth dimensionality, beauty, and meaning that is indispensable for loving and caring for ourselves and others. As babies we move instinctively toward pleasure, delight, and growth, and naturally recoil from pain, sadness, and limitation. Our feeling function evaluates what supports wholeness. When authentic feelings are denied, punished, or attacked, we override our feelings to survive. We lose natural mechanisms for optimizing choices about self-care, relationships, and vocation. The more we contact our authentic feelings, the more we optimize growth, pleasure, power, and self-expression.

During Breathwork, habitually constructed mechanisms that deny, dissociate, or pretend, have reduced functioning because those mechanisms generally require distancing from our feelings. CB facilitates inhabiting our sensations and body, so we experience our actual emotions and feelings.

Breathwork is almost unparalleled for channeling emotions and feelings into positive pathways. We can have a visceral experience of sadness, honor what it shows and informs us, and celebrate how it increases our capacity to feel and love amid a complex, unsettling world. We can learn to feel sadness, yet not create an identity or narrative about the future from it. We transform from feeling "I am a sad (or depressed) person" to "I feel sadness, and I am a good and whole human being who values living and wants a meaningful life."

In Breathwork the following emotional processes can be considerably amplified.

Emotional expression. Most Breathers are surprised with the intensity of feelings and their growing ability to express them after doing Breathwork sessions. Awareness about the impact of our emotional expressions on ourselves and others is part of emotional intelligence. Breathwork is a mighty medium for accepting, regulating, and developing our emotions.

Emotional externalization. This term denotes a gradation from emotional expression of *what is immediately felt*, to the wise, *conscious expression* of unconscious, blocked or held-back emotion. This releases somatic tension and numbness, freeing unconscious information and energy about self and reality. Particularly during Group 5 Breathwork, Breathees can be encouraged to externalize emotions.

Emotional release. When a wild animal feels in danger of attack by another animal, their genetic, epigenetic, or learned behavior of fight, flight, freeze, faint, or fawn will ensue. If they survive, they will shudder and shake their bodies—then stretch, readjust, and continue with life. It's important to allow the full flow of emotions through our SEC continuum, otherwise vital life force is used for managing emotions, and we risk becoming devitalized, depersonalized, or depressed. Breathwork helps emotion flow, creating access to emotional intelligence about ourselves and life.

Catharsis. Emotional and physical catharsis is used in bioenergetics, primal therapy, and other expressive therapies for Breathers to open feelings, resolve trauma, reunite with power, and welcome self-expression. Many describe how relieved, discharged, and relaxed they feel when feeling authentic feelings and sensations. It can be emotionally and physically lifesaving.

Yet when Breathees dissociate or don't maintain adult awareness while expressing childhood events, retraumatization can occur either during, or directly following, catharsis. (Skilled facilitators can prevent this from happening.) Additionally, Breathees may appreciate the cathartic release during sessions, yet without embodiment or integration, become dissociated later and/or resist continuing the healing journey.

Catharsis is eminently useful in the right situation at the right time. Skilled Therapist-Breathworkers can support healing shifts by facilitating the integration and embodiment of catharsis to help Breathees gain more information and freedom through these experiences. It's important to track what the Breathee's system needs to discharge in catharsis and ensure that the process is never so intense or unconscious that it replaces internal experiences of authenticity, empowerment, and actualization.

Psychologist, researcher, and breathworker Alicja Heyda suggests that during embodied Breathwork, memories, sensations, and emotions in cells are moved from muscles, viscera, and so forth (see also Squire & Kandel, 2009). This information then moves from dorsal ganglia around the spine to the spinal cord. Alicja explains that when Breathwork induces transient hypofrontality and the neocortex is less activated, radiography shows that alpha and theta waves get more prominent, slowing brain waves down. The sensations of trauma in the muscles associated with repressed traumatic memories stored in the amygdala and hippocampus now have a chance to present themselves through crying, shaking, trembling, yelling, and so forth. Alicja reminds us that the empathic, attuned, and healing presence of a Therapist-Breathworker is critical for new pathways of healthy attachment to be formed.

With full consent, and empathic containers, catharsis can help Breathees access and fully express buried feelings and memories so that the stored information moves from the body's periphery to the central nervous system and neocortex, where we bring awareness to the experience and make sense of it. When catharsis is immediately followed by CB that is focused toward learning and building new pathways, powerful progress can occur through discharging tension and blockage and freeing defensive energy. When catharsis is only discharge, it can still be useful for healthy and regulated Breathers long term. It's less likely to help Breathers with unregulated intrapsychic structures because it can instigate emotional flooding, causing further dysregulation. However in both cases the feeling of release, even if it's just temporary, can give Breathees an experiential knowing that release is possible, and can be worked towards more enduringly.

Skilled Therapist-Breathworkers will track what the Breathee's system is discharging in catharsis and ensure that Breathees are not engaging in the practice only from desire for discharge without developing pathways for deeper healing and transformation. It's an honor for Therapist-Breathworkers to accompany Breathees through the various painful and suffering levels that were never met with love and wisdom earlier in life and move with them through the treacherous memories they were intelligently hiding with the deftness and stealth of a master thief. We are present as lost fractals are recovered and new vistas of soul are born.

RECOMMENDATIONS FOR THERAPIST-BREATHWORKERS TO USE CATHARSIS

- Do our own inner work with emotional expression, externalization, release, and catharsis.
- Work with our own voices and body movements.
- Develop somatic, expressive, and trauma-informed skills to address flooding and overwhelm in Breathees.
- Obtain training for unwinding layers of trauma and unmet needs in clients through movement, dialogue, mirroring, somatic expressions, and touch.

- Ensure the practice space can accommodate emotional release, loud sound, and appropriate physical safety to punch pillows, shake, jump, use a foam or padded bat on pillows, roll, and so forth.
- Follow the catharsis of Breathees and use our breathing, voice, eyes, and touch (with consent) to accompany and mirror tears, laughter, pain, grief, anger, excitement, passion, and joy. What comes up in catharsis was likely never held and mirrored. We have opportunities to midwife that healing.
- Ensure that Breathees integrate by verbally processing their experience, with guidance about how it may affect their sense of self, joy, agency, and value moving forward.
- Ensure that Breathees integrate by being somatically oriented in the present through CB, movement, dialogue, drawing, and so on.

WORKING WITH ANGER AND RAGE

Anger is a powerful life force that can create safety, balance, and empowerment, and generate energy for change in the face of harm, violence, injustice, or forging new life-supporting pathways. Almost all expressive healing modalities, including many Breathwork Practices, see value in transforming suppressed anger and harnessing its energy for autonomy, agency, and empowerment.

Dr. Pat Ogden, creator of the Sensorimotor Psychotherapy method, advises caution about expressing anger too quickly or without awareness because it could easily activate the fight/flight defense and fixed ideas, causing clients to become more dysregulated as subcortical defenses are activated. Yet, in Pat's experience, expressive interactions with anger are not only possible but highly therapeutic for moving from hostility to anger to power and strength (Journey's Dream, 2021).

Anger, when fueled by trauma, anxiety, depression, or a temperament inclined toward irritability, is a cry for wholeness, belonging, and developing and contributing our capacities. When we feel unsafe to be ourselves, others don't value us, connections with important others are severed, or we lose agency to advocate or choose for ourselves, we may react with aggression or even rage. At core, anger signals that there is activated life force.

Pathways for anger in Breathwork:

1. Breathwork oriented toward CB with whatever comes up and integrating the energy and awareness without emotional expression, will encourage *breathing with and through the anger* until we are present with its energy, contain it, and direct it toward life-giving choices and behaviors. There may be some trembling, vibrating, intensified breathing, tears, laughter, and some slight movement; however, Breathees are encouraged to experience and integrate the anger without expressing it overtly. When needed, slowing and lengthening the exhales can quickly increase parasympathetic and polyvagal activation, reducing the anger. The aim is to increase capacity for presence with all emotions and accept and channel destructive energy into positive pathways.
2. Breathwork that encourages movement and expressing emotion creates ways Breathees can express, release, and transform anger to open to power, confidence, motivation, sexual energy, agency, and more. *While expressing anger, CB and somatic grounding should be employed throughout* as it maintains neocortex and executive adult functioning and circumvents fight, flight, freeze, fawn, or faint reactions. Fear, shame, and sadness may arise, which can also be expressed and integrated. Breathing may intensify, and expression or catharsis may follow. Facilitators can ensure that Breathees are consciously aware during anger expression by noting if they can pause deep breathing for responding to questions. If they cannot talk easily, body language may still indicate they are aware and tracking.

We are relational creatures, and anger is often fueled in relation to others. In the overall arc of being whole, the metamorphosis of anger into power and action might be best served by not directing hostility toward someone from the past because it may reactivate old wounds instead of integrating embodied strength and agency. We can direct anger from our childhood attachment and object relational wounds, somatically (methods given below), toward the cultural or intergenerational conditions that allowed and perpetuated behaviors and conditions which hurt us. This may be particularly crucial if we felt anger toward our parents and caregivers during our childhood as it may preserve the possibilities for connection in the present.

Everyone's somatic pathway for anger is unique. Our bodies are intelligent about what physical expression accurately reflects our sensations and feelings. Through this intelligence, lifelong tension and anger can melt away in one, or a few, sessions. Pounding, pushing, throwing pillows, stomping, kicking, or hitting pillows on the floor or ground with a firm foam bat can work. Martial arts and boxing training blocks are effective tools. Some facilitators provide tennis rackets for pounding pillows. For safety and respect, and because it can hurt our psyches and souls to direct physical, emotional, or energetic hostility to life of any kind, I strongly discourage hitting humans and nonhuman animals, plants, and trees.

Two additional interesting anger pathways:

- *Tearing cloth or newspaper:* Some Breathers have somatic urges to rip something apart—as if ripping the confusion, delusion, or lie that has kept a traumatic secret. Ripping yard-long pieces of cloth that easily tear (with the tearing sounds quite audible) has been astonishingly impactful, and has shattered trances of denial and dissociation. I sat with a timid female survivor of incest who ripped cloth diligently for about 20 minutes while consciously, deeply breathing. She was enduringly a more vibrant and engaging person moving forward.
- *Breaking glass:* This may sound controversial and destructive; however, many Breathers describe dissociation or disconnection as being *behind a glass wall*. One effective and ecological way to break glass is at local recycling centers! For several years, I worked with a highly functioning survivor of sexual abuse. She felt that her constriction and introjected rage caused overeating and would stop through hearing glass break. We both saved glass bottles for recycling between sessions and went to the recycling center for sessions. She would position herself at huge, steel trash containers, and throw

the bottles in, one by one—hearing the glass shatter. We went four times over two months. By the third time we went, staff at the recycling center were cheering her on. By the end of the fourth session, the need to hear glass breaking dissolved, never to return.

Somatic intelligence is brilliant. The body knows what it needs. One process that developed in my work invites Breathees to speak from immediacy and presence about their body needs in the moment to experience healing and wholeness. Breathees begin with CB to increase contact with somatic sensation. The facilitator then inquires gently, "What do you need *right now*? Trust your body. Whatever it wants to experience right now, trust it. Does it need to hear certain words? Does it need to move or be moved in a particular way? Does it want to be touched [nonsexually], and if so, how and where? Does it need to have me [and other Breathees if a group] embody a specific quality or express exact sentiments?"

Trusting the body's intelligence while breathing consciously induces transformation swiftly and phenomenally. Requests might include help relaxing our shoulders; feet being held and grounded; a special song being sung; being rocked; being lifted; dancing alone or with someone; key phrases to be spoken loudly or in whispers; dialogues and inquiries into particular themes; others breathing synchronously with us; or the Therapist-Breathworker and/or group contacting psychological or spiritual states such as joy, faith, autonomy, self-love, forgiveness, and power. A *stream of embodied requests* is the most transformative—as one need is met, facilitators continue inviting the next need. The process becomes a flow state of contacting somatic wisdom. Each need emerges and cascades from the prior need—and we know when we feel complete and whole.

Three-Centered Process Exploration

INQUIRIES THAT SUPPORT BREATHEES' SOMATIC AWARENESS

- What are you experiencing in this moment?
- In what part of your body is sensation strongest in this moment?
- Is there anywhere in your body that feels particularly hot or warm in this moment?
- Is there anywhere in your body that feels particularly cool or cold in this moment?
- Is there anywhere in your body that feels numb or like you can't feel on the inside?
- Is there any part of your body that feels a wish or a need to be touched? (They can then touch or bring attention to that part.)
- If this sensation of _____ had a voice, what would it be saying? (After they identify that and invite it to breathe more, we can ask, "Tell me about the sensation in your _____ now.")
- If this sensation of _____ had a color, what would it be? (After they identify that and invite it to breathe more, we can ask, "Tell me about the sensation in your _____ now.")
- What is a way you are experiencing the power, intelligence, and life force of your body and sensations in this moment.

INQUIRIES THAT SUPPORT BREATHEES' EMOTIONAL AWARENESS

- What are you experiencing in this moment?
- What are you feeling in this moment?
- What emotions are you in touch with in this moment?
- If the sensation of _____ was a feeling or emotion, what would it be? (If they say they don't know, we ask them to invite the sensation to breathe while we name a few emotions. We name *sadness, grief,*

fear, anger, rage, happiness, joy, love—pausing a few seconds between each. We ask them to choose one that resonates. We may need to repeat the list a few times, always ensuring they're breathing deeply.)
- How do you feel toward yourself in this moment?
- What is your heart wanting for you in this moment?
- What is a way your heart is being affected in this moment.
- What is a way your heart is affecting others or life right at this moment. (Only use this question if we are certain of positive mood. The question will then expand a sense of relatedness or impact.)
- What is a way that you are experiencing the sensitivity, receptivity, intelligence, and love of your heart in this moment.

INQUIRIES THAT SUPPORT BREATHEES' KNOWING

- What are you experiencing in this moment?
- What are you aware of internally and externally in this moment?
- What thoughts are you having in this moment?
- Are you having any thoughts about you, others, or life in this moment?
- What is a way you are experiencing awareness in this moment.
- What is a way you are experiencing curiosity in this moment.
- What are some ways you experience spaciousness, stillness, insight, intelligence, and awareness in your head/mind.
- What are some ways you are experiencing the spaciousness, stillness, insight, and intelligence of your awareness in this moment.

For embodied integration, it's best if any emergent experience during Breathwork includes a kinesthetic or somatic cue, emotional congruence and appreciation of what is being experienced, and awareness of how the emergence can transform perception and orientation toward ourselves and others. Until we learn to bring all three of these into embodiment and awareness, we usually describe our experience most vividly in only one or two centers of energy flow. Thus, we might say, "My heart is [or I am] filled with gratitude for everything that has made it possible for me to be experiencing this.... There's a sensation of heat in my upper chest." In this case, we feel the opened life force in our body, as well as a nourishing gratitude. While it likely will impact our day (maybe several), to ensure it impacts our whole life moving forward, we would also optimally gain cognitive understanding of the transformation. So, in this case, Therapist-Breathworkers could ask Breathees something like, "If you contacted this gratitude and opening in your chest in your daily life, how would it transform the way you are with yourself, others, or life? What would be new?"

In another example, if they say, "I'm now aware that it's not good for me to hold back my ideas for how to support other members of my team." In this case, cognitive awareness is prominent, so we facilitate an emotional component and somatic cue. Thus, we might ask, "When you breathe with the knowing that your contribution will matter to others, how does that make you feel? What happens to your heart?" They might say, "I feel worthy and joyful, and feel a greater desire to contribute." We then suggest they breathe with the knowing and feeling together. Then we could ask, "When you know that these contributions matter, where in your body do you most feel the sense of value and mattering?" And they might say, "It feels like warmth in my stomach." And we might say, "Let's invite that warmth to breathe deeply." Now they are aware of the warmth, the feeling of worthiness and joy, and the knowing that offering their ideas is beneficial. We then suggest they breathe with all three together. We can also use touch on the three centers to foster belly/heart/head coherence.

JOURNEYING WITH SLEEPINESS, DISSOCIATION, AND EXPANDED STATES OF CONSCIOUSNESS

Breathees may fall asleep; drift in and out of a dreamy state; be breathing, yet unable to hear or answer our questions; or cease breathing yet not seem asleep. This is a very important area for Group 5 Breathwork facilitators to learn about and develop experience with.

Breathees may fall asleep because:

- Breathing, rather than ego, is keeping watch, so defenses lower, relaxation increases, and sleepiness ensues.

- Breathwork is significantly more physically or emotionally intense than usual, and sleep is an instinctive way to lessen the energy.
- Embedded painful memories or trauma feel too challenging to explore or current inner resources are not adequate.
- Dormant life-enhancing qualities may emerge that are ego dystonic—for example, serenity may be ego dystonic to temperaments that are cathected to fun and excitement. Breathees can be invited to breathe deeply and notice the quality, such as relaxation, peace, spaciousness, or open-heartedness that is arising.
- Mystical and boundless states can induce bliss, and younger and/or traumatized parts may relax and sleep, feeling safely held by a loving, pleasurable, and all-encompassing force.
- Meeting points between form and formlessness may initially feel dreamlike, buzzy, or like utter peace we cannot embody while awake.
- We can be genuinely tired and in need of sleep!

Occasionally, Breathees fall fully asleep. More often, they drift in and out and may say that an image or word is floating around while stirring into wakefulness (a hypnopompic state), which they may remember or not. These images can either be important or fairly random. If the image is not salient to what they are working on that moment or long term, I generally recommend moving attention to breathing again. My experience is that over 75% of the time, the hypnopompic images are way stations on the path to a more important truth—and the breathing will move them toward that revelation. Sleepiness can open exploration. We cycle through various versions of this process until enough life force has engaged for an emergence of awareness and transformation, and the cycle completes.

Alternatively, we can trust the wisdom of fatigue. If people are exhausted for legitimate reasons, I will sit peacefully, breathe with presence and love, and let them sleep for 2 to 20 minutes. They usually feel remarkably relaxed and grateful upon awakening.

Sometimes Breathees need to cultivate will and physical capacity to breathe into inner and outer wakefulness. In that case, we can:

Components and Processes of Human Potential Breathwork Sessions | 223

- Breathe with them audibly and synchronously.
- Guide them to change positions (sitting, standing, on hands and knees, etc.) or stretch.
- Use touch or movement methods.
- Coach them to breathe with open eyes.
- Open windows or doors.
- Offer warm or cold washcloths for their face, hands, or feet.
- Give water or juice.
- Do Breathwork while walking or dancing.
- Move outdoors.
- With permission, waft essential oils that they like under their nose or place some drops between their upper lip and nose.

In addition to sleepiness, Breathees in expanded states may appear breathless, because they:

- Have blown off too much carbon dioxide and aren't feeling the breath urge (they will breathe shortly).
- Are unconsciously encountering pain, trauma, or buried potentials they can't yet bring into conscious awareness.
- Are not present somatically, emotionally, and/or cognitively.
- Are disembodied and captivated by memories, images, thoughts, feelings, and so on.
- Have dissociative defenses that include breath-holding and/or trancing out.
- Are immersed in an internal experience and are making a nonreactive choice to refrain from speaking, perceiving (sometimes inaccurately) that speaking aloud will disperse the experience.
- Don't yet have concordant language for the expanded or mystical states they are experiencing.

Over time, Therapist-Breathworkers will learn to distinguish between these possible causes. Ultimately, Breathwork is in service of supporting conscious living with embodied relational awareness of self, other, the collective, and life. Ideally, we cultivate the ability to consciously breathe while talking, thinking, moving, and making decisions. On the journey toward that, when Breathees' states are dissociative, disembodied, or without presence, we can apply touch, movement, sound, and so on to create neural connections between experience and awareness, and left and right brain. If we perceive that Breathees are in mystical states, it may be best to refrain from asking them to speak right away; yet even then we can encourage embodiment. If Breathees get upset or angry that we have "disturbed" or "taken them out of" a particular state, we can apologize for any lack of skill, yet, with confidence, remind them that the goal is integration with reality, however it is unfolding.

Importantly, there is a special case in Group 5 Breathwork Practices where active breathing ceases for an exceptionally long period for biochemical reasons and/or because of immersion in deep intrapsychic material or mystical states. In this case, when the body needs to breathe again, we may experience one of the following:

- Concern and/or bemusement about where we have been.
- An eruption of intense emotions or memories (causing some Breathees to cry out).
- A sudden classic tetany with muscle contractions, sweating, and physiological panic. (All the suggestions for tetany in Breathwork can be used, especially deeper inhales and relaxed exhales.)
- Strong internal fright upon returning to normal waking consciousness after being in expanded states of consciousness.
- Emergence in a blissful and high-vibrational state. We may experience luminous wisdom, guidance and vibrational oneness with creation or love.

Expanded States of Consciousness and Breathlessness

The vibrational frequency of expanded states of consciousness can engender seemingly breathless states into which Breathees can be inducted. In the East enlightenment is often referred to as Samadhi, and sometimes as the breathless state of Samadhi. This is because during what people describe as complete absorption into the Absolute/The Source/The Divine, they sometimes appear to stop breathing as if there is no need for breath, we are directly connected to the source. There are varying descriptions of what happens during this breathless time, and how long it can continue, with reports of minutes to years, however one cannot remain there and move around on this planet. And we are interested in embodying consciousness in our lives for ourselves and for others. Based on my own experiences, studies and observations, I gently question the conventional wisdom that Samadhi is completely breathless. Might the breathless state of Samadhi, whatever the duration, actually be one elongated, slow, deep breath—so slow that it's imperceptible to normal observation or measurements? Or, could Breathers with enough consciousness development generate energy through electron transport in additional ways to breathing, and breathe extremely lightly, not generally observable, yet enough to sustain the physical body, similar to the Buddhist teaching that in the 4th Jhana meditation state we only breathe through the skin.

A breathless state of Samadhi could, in some ways, reflect the intrapsychic split of body and spirit, or matter and energy. While fascinating that a body could be here without needing to breathe, we can ultimately learn to breathe *with* expanded or mystical states which supports their integration into our lives and actions, and into the collective—an evolutionary step.

Thus, during Breathwork there may be times that Breathees are so absorbed in the infinite that they appear to not be breathing. Perhaps they are breathing very lightly, almost imperceptibly. We explore this threshold in Chapter 7 with Embodied Novelty Breathing. We can support these Light Breathing spaces for several minutes, and if they are genuine the experiences can be life altering. We just need to be aware that if they are not truly in those expanded states of consciousness they could arouse from the state with physical and/or psychological distress as described above.

With all of these states—sleepiness, dissociation, and expanded states of consciousness—whatever we experience or describe as we become aware may also reflect a somatic birth memory. Generally, adventurous

Breathers, truth seekers, and consciousness seekers value all of these experiences, while others are less comfortable when they arise.

It is essential for Therapist-Breathworkers to be familiar with this territory and watch for it to avoid unnecessarily abrupt transitions. We can then guide Breathees to integrate any deep intrapsychic and/or mystical material more fluidly and consciously. We can be alert, notice when breathing has essentially ceased, and gently coach Breathees to breathe before such eruptive states arise. Yet, for Breathees who process this way and find it meaningful, including the eruptive emotions or tetany, we need to learn to be present with that as well. For most Therapist-Breathworkers who facilitate Human Potential Breathwork, discerning between sleep, dissociation, and expanded states of consciousness, and attaining the experiential knowledge for accompanying them, is a steep and rewarding learning curve.

Transference and Countertransference

Relativity and quantum theory inspire us to recognize the fundamental and ever-present relationality of life. The potential within that relationality is harnessed and magnified in the therapeutic relationship by intentionality in relationship and the vulnerability and transparency offered by Breathees and Therapist-Breathworkers. There is a mutual commitment between them for healing and personal transformation to occur.

Our inner experiences and our current significant relationships are affected by both positive and negative aspects of our early life experiences and relationships with caregivers and others. Because Breathwork so powerfully aligns the SEC continuum, contacts the unconscious and conscious mind, and opens us to more expansive possibilities for ourselves—all within an embodied experience—transference energy can be greatly intensified, particularly with Group 5 Breathwork. This means countertransference can be heightened as well.

Conscious Breathing expedites and heightens transference and countertransference. However, it also dissolves the tendency for them.

For Breathees: When breathing with presence, Breathees are less identified with their defenses and more in contact with the integrated presence as a matrix. Emotional reactivity is reduced, and what arises can be **reparented by breathing itself.** Only the most troublesome and entrenched attachment behaviors and object-relational patterns will be transferred.

For Therapist-Breathworkers: When breathing with presence, Therapist-Breathworkers are continually aware of a larger energetic field that holds the relational field with Breathees. This enables referencing our relative and object-relational conditions from the integrated presence, dissolving tendencies to project onto others.

Here is a poignant sharing from Maria, illustrating entrenched transference issues being transformed through Integrative Breathing:

> *My relationships with previous psychotherapists and my Breathworker are similar in that the transference relationship has been front and center. The yearning for unconditional mother love is the deepest wounding of my life and was projected onto my therapists with ferocity. Psychotherapy felt limited and could only take me so far. No amount of talking could budge these intransigent mother projections. Although my psychotherapists were loving and insightful and provided me with corrective emotional experiences, it wasn't enough to make significant changes in me or my life.*
>
> *Breathwork offered me two alternative means of healing and transforming my pain: Essence and breath. Breathwork showed me that the core of my being is love and goodness. The most mysterious aspect of my healing has been through the breath. When I lay down to breathe on the mat, I am instantly taken to another realm. I get caught in early somatic memories of trauma, crisis, disconnection, and mistrust. My body tenses, and tears are falling. Despite this anguish, the breath keeps moving; some part of me knows that breath is benevolent and trustworthy. Alongside breathing, my Breathworker lovingly and intuitively touches certain parts of my body, and soon enough something inside softens. I return to love.*

> *In one sweet session I found my little-girl self stationed in a deep, dark well, talking to God with her Breathworker right there. This little girl looked up to her Breathworker and for the first time saw her as a trusted guide, not the idealized mother or wounded mother of her childhood.*
>
> *Seeing reality in pure form was the greatest feeling of freedom I have felt. The breath becomes a container to hold, love, heal, and transform my deepest wounds and an invitation to live from freedom and love. The difference with psychotherapy is that the dissolving of the transference had no place to land. Doors would open, I would be on the cusp of change, but there was nothing to fall back on other than self or ego—no understanding of something larger and more reliable than self. For me, conscious breath is a physical manifestation of Essence, God, life force, and love. It's pure and reliable. It's holding me and infusing me as I do internal work to free myself from what holds me in being fully alive and living into my potential.*

Maria's Breathworker, Alice Wells, an Inspiration trained, GPBA certified Breathworker, and a senior supervisor of Breathwork at Inspiration Consciousness School, shares how she cultivates herself during the work with Maria.

> *Breath offers the space in which we can transcend history, the particular formative circumstances of a life that may still be in force in our lives as adults. It is precisely in the moments of touching this history in the space of a loving and responsive relationship with the Breathworker, and ultimately, within the space of the breath itself, that these moments captured in the amber of memory can be seen, related to, and integrated. Conscious breath offers and forges a living, visceral, somatic, energetic experience of unconditionality that has the power to infuse our entire being.*
>
> *I carry the awareness that Maria has never left the ground of being that is her birthright and matrix; her place in the circle of love and belonging, as disruptive as her early experiences had been. As a Breathworker, I offer entwined facets of being at different moments—the ener-*

gies of friend, mother, teacher, fiercely calling out distortion, mirroring goodness, space for the bell of truth to ring and resonate through every fiber of Maria's body, mind, heart, and soul in the room, and into the world.

Over the years of working together with Maria, I have watched the depth of the transference gradually give way to a depth of rich authentic relationship between us as she roots with increasing discipline and devotion in the breath, and her own essential nature. In doing so, Maria becomes my fellow traveler on the path of awakening. Like the Buddha challenged by the demon Mara in the final hours of his labor under the bodhi tree, we begin to see that healing, growth, and awakening serves not only ourselves, but everyone. This essential truth was in the room with us on the day of Maria's first session, although she may not have been aware of it: that she and I are one. And out of the one, we may become many in service to love and life.

The relational field between Maria and Alice is clearly imbued with many complex dimensions of relating. It's critical to understand that what Maria and Alice are describing is a depth of contact that touched these various places within them, without ever transgressing the time-honored, ethical boundaries of psychotherapy and healing. There have been many disruptive enactments between them throughout the years, all of which have been utilized to open and nourish Maria and Alice's individual and relational capacities. No power plays on either side have been unexamined, no movements into personal relationships have been enacted, and so forth.

Maria and Alice navigated both their "collision of subjectivities" (Ogden, 1994) and uncertainties produced by enactments with mutual respect and caring, so they each could find meaning and growth. Breathwork was, as Maria articulated, indispensable. It would be virtually impossible to count the number of times that taking several deep breaths interrupted an unconscious abreaction or enactment; the number of times that breathing quietly together, looking into each other's eyes, reestablished the core values of their relationship; and the number of ways Integrative Breathing invited them both to relate to the presenting material with open creative possibilities, instead of formulaic therapeutic responses or unconscious reactions to transference or countertransference.

Psychological and Consciousness Development

Because Human Potential Breathwork cultivates contact with places where boundaries, boundlessness, and the Plane of Possibility (Chapter 12) meet, it is essential for Therapist-Breathworkers to become familiar with, and oriented toward, personal experiences of these states. We can then skillfully guide Breathees to integrate healthy boundaries and nuanced aspects of boundless consciousness.

Breathwork enhances self-valuing and attention to boundaries through awareness of the SEC continuum and recognizing the reciprocal resonance of our emotions and sensations—helping us feel real and grounded rather than unreal and free-floating. This wellness is a springboard for healthy boundaries. As we realize our fabrications of self-identity, we often yearn to free ourselves from fear, defensiveness, and promotional behaviors. Many Breathers have picked up the nomenclature of "letting go of" or "killing" the ego. Therapist-Breathworkers need to explore this territory in ourselves to relate to concepts and language used to describe the spectrum of ego to egolessness, and avoid minimizing Breathees' perspectives.

The boundless energies and qualities are inherent in reality, whether we view the universe as originating with cosmic inflation, the singularity of the big bang, an origin story, operating as a no-boundary wave function, or the big breath (Currivan, 2022). These intrinsic qualities of existence include power, harmony, energy, depth, functioning, immediacy, and generativity, and are not the fear-based ego's version of them.

Various fields describe them as something we contact or create through cultivation; something larger than ourselves and all-encompassing from which we are created; something we can relax into and become a transparent expression of in the world; and as Plato viewed them, Essences. Essences are almost always perceived as ineffable . . . newborn, yet everborn, always here, without end. From this perspective, apparent paradoxes are resolved and seen as a unified whole, yielding something unprecedented, highly creative, and wise. We experience the fundamental unity of even seemingly contrasting values, energies, and situations.

Unlike traditional psychotherapy, this is a never-ending process because in referencing our experiences from pure awareness, we open more to an infinite fountain of emergent potential. And CB births embodied emergence. It is the dynamism of emergent consciousness.

There are artful and sound ways to reconcile the seemingly opposing orientations of developing an ego and being egoless, without succumbing to the "having to have an ego to let go of an ego" linear, left-brain point of view. A larger vantage point—a reconciling and emergent third pathway—can open if we neither argue for or against, but instead gather the gold and intelligence from each and from all stations along the journey.

Russ Hudson, coauthor of *Wisdom of the Enneagram*, and I have cocreated a didactic and experiential model for contacting the qualities of Essence that arise from creation. The model shows how we can relax egoic patterns that limit freedom and creativity, while retaining the attributes and skills that support embodied awakening. Fear-driven ego and unhealthy breathing habits co-opt the unconditioned transmission of Essence and reject many capacities and expressions of Essence—primarily the ones that don't align with our idealized self-image.

Resonant with our model, I created the following Group 4 Breathwork practices and movements that can be done on their own for powerful shorter aspects to therapeutic sessions, or easily integrated into Group 5 Breathwork. Therapist-Breathworkers and all of us can utilize these practices for experiencing the boundless qualities while simultaneously developing healthy boundaries and highly functional human behaviors.

> *Can you gather your vital breath*
> *And yet be tender like a newborn baby?*
>
> —LAO TZU, *TAO TE CHING*

ALIVENESS/POWER/CONFIDENCE/IMMEDIACY

Breathing Practices that activate a profusion of energy in our muscles and sensations of the pelvis, abdomen, thighs, and feet will support embodiment of these qualities.

Positions and movements with continual Conscious Breathing:

- Legs shoulder-width or wider apart, knees slightly bent with hands on hips. Maintain the position for 3 breaths to 5 minutes or more.
- Legs shoulder-width apart with one foot about a foot in front of the other, knees bent, pressing the pubic bone and tailbone (first chakra in yogic philosophy) as far forward as possible, hands on the hips. Maintain for 3 breaths to 5 minutes or more.
- Legs shoulder-width or wider apart, knees bent as low as possible while feeling balanced, hands on the thighs. Maintain for 3 breaths to 5 minutes or more.
- Legs shoulder-width or wider apart, knees bent as low as possible, hands and arms out to the sides and bent at the elbows, fingers pointing straight up. Maintain for 3 breaths to 5 minutes or more.
- The Vitruvian Man—slowly and quickly moving our arms through all the positions from pointing to the sky, to stretched out to the sides, to straight down to the ground.
- Inhaling, we jump up with our hands straight up to the ceiling or sky. Exhaling, we thrust our arms completely downward and land with deeply bent knees to the best of our ability. Practice for three breaths to 1 minute or more. As a variation, we can call out the word *yes* from deep within our belly on the exhale.

Group 4 Breathwork Practice. Standing or sitting, enter Matrika Pranayama (Chapter 7) with eyes closed. After a few minutes, we continue Matrika with open eyes, looking around our external environment. (Being outside or looking out a window is ideal.) We acknowledge the life force and power of the various things we see. Using any of the above standing positions, eyes open or closed, we breathe deeply and rapidly in and out through the mouth or nose (or alternating) five breaths or more—followed by slow, deep breaths while bringing awareness to the tailbone and pubic bone as if breathing originates there. It's very effective to do several rounds of five fast deep breaths, interspersed with several slow, deep breaths; maintain awareness of sensations of the diaphragm and pubic bone; and think about, imagine, feel, sense, or invoke the color red. After several rounds, we inhale deeply, and on the exhale loudly project the word *ha* from the belly, then clap our hands together quickly and intensely for about five seconds, then return them to the thighs or hips. We allow ourselves to feel the immediacy, vibrancy, strength, and power moving through us physically, and likely now emotionally. Repeat the clapping several times. We then walk about with this awareness, sensing our feet, legs, pelvis, and belly each step—simultaneously feeling the life force and power in ourselves, the ground, our breathing, and everything around us.

PEACE/UNITY/BEING/HARMONY

Breathing Practices that invite reset and relaxation of the nervous system, and harmony between, and engagement with, both our inner and outer experience, will support embodiment of these qualities.

Positions and movements with continual Conscious Breathing:

- Hands in prayer position in front of the center of our chest (fourth chakra in yogic philosophy), breathing deeply and slowly.
- Hands softly over the center of the chest, breathing deeply and slowly, relaxing and softening the chest into our hands with each exhale.

Group 4 Breathwork Practice. We place our hands softly over the center of our chest, breathing deeply and slowly, relaxing and softening our chest into our hands during exhalations, feeling any well-being that arises. Then, while inhaling, we stretch our arms out to the side like the sun's rays, envisioning our hands contacting whatever comes into our awareness that moment, such as a friend, brother, dog, the air, dust, black holes, the sun, an elephant, our sadness, someone's anger, bodily pain, someone's suffering, violence, an inspiring person, the love between people, and so forth . . . just one thing. Exhaling, we bring our hands together, upon each other over the center of our chest, gathering what we have just touched into our heart center. Immediately, we inhale, stretching our arms to the sides, also expanding the center of our chest as we *touch* whatever is now in our awareness this moment . . . then exhaling and gathering it into our heart. For several minutes we continue this same breathing—stretching the arms during inhalation, gathering them over the heart during exhalation. When we reach out, we cultivate the sense of touching anything and everything in creation—whatever appears in our awareness—without rejection or aversion (we can touch any aversion and gather it in)—sensations, emotions of any kind, events, objects, beings, ideas, pain, joy, and so on, with nothing left out. When we breathe out, we gather it into the center of our chest.

ALIGNMENT/WILLINGNESS/INTEGRITY/SACREDNESS

Breathing Practices that invite focused activation of our physical energy, caring, and attention being directed toward something important, sacred, or beneficial will support embodiment of these qualities.

Positions and movements with continual Conscious Breathing:

- Hands in prayer position, stretched straight above our head. We fold all the fingers down except the pointer finger for greater sense of focus and alignment with the truth.
- Hands straight out in front with soft, slightly bent elbows and palms up, head slightly bowed, in a gesture of giving or receiving.
- Lying on the floor face down, with hands in prayer position stretched above the head on the floor.
- Kneeling, bending over and placing our head on the ground, allowing greater blood flow toward our head.
- Standing with one foot slightly in front of the other, about shoulder-width apart, knees slightly bent, with arms either straight or bent at the elbow by our sides with the palms facing straight out. We raise our chin about an inch, looking toward the horizon.
- Creating a flow between several of the above postures.

Group 4 Breathwork Practice. We direct awareness to both the diaphragm and throat. We inhale through pursed lips, slowly sucking in air as if through a straw, paying attention to air sensations contacting the back of our throat (fifth chakra in yogic philosophy). We exhale through the nose and lift our chin about an inch as if looking into and past the horizon, and feeling the lift in our spine. We place our hands in prayer position or prayer position with pointer fingers straight up, and the other fingers folded down. Keeping hands in prayer pose, we raise our arms straight into the air, inviting five, slow, deep, diaphragmatic breaths. We invoke our aspirations and willingness to bring some goodness into the world, to be a vehicle of blessings to life. Then we slowly, gently let our arms float down and savor the opening and elevation of our spine, the lifting of our chin, and the awareness of breathing on the back of our throat.

RESPONSIVENESS/NURTURING/KINDNESS/ATTUNEMENT

Breathing Practices that invite a softened and open chest, relaxed and engaged eyes, energized relaxed responsiveness to whatever is being experienced within and without, and harmonious and cohesive flow with any two seemingly opposite dynamics will support embodiment of these qualities.

Positions and movements with continual Conscious Breathing:

- Soft, energized hands over our chest's center with each exhale softening our chest as if melting into our hands.
- Simultaneously placing each hand on the opposite shoulder, touching ourselves with tenderness and sensitivity, with the backs of our hands touching the air with tenderness and sensitivity.
- Smiling with eyes closed while breathing slowly and as fully as possible for as long as we wish, then continuing with eyes open for as long as we wish. We can do Embodied Novelty Breathing (Chapter 7) for a heightened experience.

Group 4 Breathwork Practice. We establish slow, easeful, deep breaths, bringing awareness to our navel where our umbilical cord was attached (third chakra in yogic philosophy). Breathing as slowly and fully as possible, we potentially contact the cellular memory of receiving constant nourishment without any effort when we were in utero. We envision the umbilical cord energetically connected to everything and everyone, and everyone's umbilical cord connected to ours and each other's. We breathe and envision constant flow of giving and receiving for ourselves and everyone, alternating open eyes for some breaths and closed for others. We allow a slight to enormous smile if possible. Standing, with open eyes, we allow our body to move in response to the breathing humans, animals, plants, air, sun, water, earth that is in our space, feeling the joy of being an attuned partner. This kind of attunement is coming from the heart and from somatic intelligence—especially the navel where, in utero, we were so intimate with our mother.

VALUE/PERSONAL ESSENCE/RADIANCE/MANIFESTATION

Breathing Practices that open, stretch, and expand the chest as wide as possible as if we are energized and celebrating the capacities and gifts of ourselves and others will support embodiment of these qualities.

Positions and movements with continual Conscious Breathing:

- Standing, arms outstretched to the sides like the sun's rays, focusing on expanding our chest while smiling with open, shiny eyes.
- Arms outstretched to the sides, turning to face as far as possible to one side and then the other several times in unbroken fluidity.

Group 4 Breathwork Practice. We place our hands on our chest's center (fourth chakra in yogic philosophy), softening the chest into our hands with each exhale and valuing the preciousness of our heart and its unique vulnerabilities and gifts. Contacting the gifts of the softened chamber of our heart, we stretch our arms out in all directions, inviting the energy and gifts of our hearts to flow into our shoulders through our arms, and then through our hands, out into the world—radiantly, as if the energy flowing could raise our arms indefinitely. With fast or slow breathing, we can begin vibrating and wiggling the fingers as if they are sharing the preciousness, as if they are showering everything with stardust.

DEPTH/MYSTERY/INTIMACY/BEAUTY

Breathing Practices that invite full intimacy with the depth of our pelvis, belly, and back of our body; the depth of our being—its sorrow, joy, yearning, potential, and mystery; and creation's risings, fallings, beauty, and origin—will support embodiment of these qualities.

Positions and movements with continual Conscious Breathing:

- Lying on our back, knees bent up toward the ceiling with feet flat on the ground, we allow the bent knees to fall gently toward the ground (placing pillows under the outside of our legs if needed). We place our hands tenderly on our lower abdomen—the area of our body that houses the ovaries in female physiology and the seminal vesicle in male physiology (the second chakra in yogic philosophy). We alternate eyes open for several breaths, then closed for several breaths.
- Standing with feet shoulder-width apart, one foot about 6 to 12 inches ahead of the other (whichever is most stable), knees slightly bent with soft arms and hands slightly out in front or to the sides, like they are feeling and listening for a sensitive voice or air moving. Inhaling, our pelvis stretches far to the left, then rotates as forward as possible, circling clockwise far to the right. Exhaling, from far right we circle as far back as possible, then arriving far left. Inhaling, we begin the same cycle again. Rotations are full, mindful, and fluid, as we inhale and exhale as slowly as possible for several breaths to several minutes.
- Now we reverse the process, beginning with the pelvis far to the right, rotating forward, circling counterclockwise for several breaths to several minutes.
- Now we use clockwise circling, inhaling while rotating back and exhaling while rotating forward for several breaths to several minutes.

- Now we use counterclockwise circling, with inhalation accompanying the rotation to the back and exhalation accompanying the forward arc for several breaths to several minutes.
- Standing with feet about shoulder-width apart, one foot about 6 to 12 inches ahead of the other (whichever is most stable), knees slightly bent. Inhaling as deeply and slowly as possible, we place gentle hands on the soft under part of our belly (about two to four inches above our pubic bone), closing our eyes and gently lowering our head just slightly. Exhaling slowly and deeply (perhaps with increased audible breathing sounds), we open our eyes and stretch our arms and hands to the front and up, halfway between straight out and straight up, with eyes looking beyond our hands. We can do the same sequence several times or remain in open-arm stance (the *yearning* position) for several breaths, then initiate another sequence.)

Group 4 Breathwork Practice. We stand with feet about shoulder-width apart, one foot 6 to 12 inches ahead of the other (whichever creates most stability), knees slightly bent. We generate soft arms and hands slightly out front or to the sides, as if feeling and listening for a sensitive voice or air movement. We gently press our pelvis forward with the emphasis halfway between our pubic bone and navel in the soft underpart of the belly at the level of the ovaries and seminal vesicles. Gently pressing the pelvis forward, we breathe into the space between that point on the front and where it corresponds to on the spine. We breathe slowly and deeply, holding awareness of this part of our body's needs, vulnerability, pain, pleasure, strength, beauty and all it experiences. We breathe into this contact and intimacy with ourselves and life's vicissitudes. We breathe as deeply as possible to hold this position, to relax into it. (If we are physically unable, we can place one hand on walls or chairs in front of us.) At some point we move into the yearning position with outstretched arms and eyes open and contact the yearning for deeper intimacy with creation—the Beloved, the Origin, the Divine, the Mystery, the All—the beauty, the mess, the chaos, the hope.... We breathe in this position as much as we want. Then, bringing our hands back down to the soft underpart of our belly, we breathe and breathe into the pelvis gently pressing forward. Perhaps we can envision this intimacy deepening forever because there is always more to discover. If we feel heightened reverence for the beauty of self, life, and creation, we can allow ourselves to feel besotted and intoxicated by breathing.

> *Flow down and down into always widening rings of being.*
> —RUMI

CLARITY/AWARENESS/CURIOSITY/LEARNING

Breathing Practices that heighten contact with the sensations in the interior of our heads, all the way up to the crown (seventh chakra in yogic philosophy), the back of our neck and our eyes, such that we experience relaxed alertness and awareness of the expanse of inner space, will support embodiment of these qualities.

Positions and movements with continual Conscious Breathing:

- Eyes closed, we focus within our head to the top where the fontanels were (2 soft spots on our infant skulls where the bony plates are not yet completely connected). Breathing deeply, we explore interior sensations of that area, allowing any images, colors, memories, feelings, and awarenesses to arise.
- Focusing on exhalation: With gently cupped hands over both eyes we relax our eyes, especially while exhaling. We notice whatever images, colors, thoughts, memories, insights, sensations, and emotions flow into awareness. After a few minutes, with hands still cupped, we open our eyes and investigate the darkness, noticing what arises from inside. (Loose blindfolds can be used, yet I suggest our hands for ultimate integration.)
- Focusing on inhalation: We strongly inhale as if purposely smelling something of great beauty, bringing awareness to the head's interior up to the crown. Gently exhaling, we cultivate awareness that oxygen is moving through the blood-brain barrier into the center of the

brain, activated and illuminated by breathing, supporting good brain functioning. We practice for several breaths to several minutes, while maintaining awareness of both the center and top of our head.

Group 4 Breathwork Practice. We establish Matrika Breathing (Chapter 7). Aware of breathing activating and nourishing our brain, during inhalation we bring attention to our head/brain's center and envision our brain lighting up. Exhaling, we send this light and energy out through our skull to join light and energy in the surrounding air and in everything. We cultivate awareness that because everything is light (energy), there's no break in it—only frequency fluctuations. Thus, the light, energy, and space in our head is seamlessly connected to—one with—the light, energy, and space of infinity. We continue Matrika with awareness of the light, energy, and space within and outside our skull . . . then we invoke the frequency of light that is absolutely clear, like a transparent diamond . . . We envision that everything can be seen and known within this transparency—this uncluttered and unobstructed transparency. While breathing with this we may, at times contact a clear black diamond-like light—visually or as sensation—within the clear light . . . like the black of space with extensive spaciousness, like the formless substrate of everything where nothing false can exist. This practice can lead to significant clearing of chaos and arising of spaciousness, clarity and stillness so we may tend to still our breathing. Though there are advanced practices like that, it is of inestimable benefit to continue Matrika with the stillness and light for forging pathways to embody clarity in daily life.

AWAKENESS/GUIDANCE/CONNECTIVITY/WISDOM

Breathing Practices that heighten contact with our heart center and the center of our head, while recognizing both the particularity and connectedness of every particle of self and existence—and feeling awakened by that awareness—will support embodiment of these qualities.

Positions and movements with continual Conscious Breathing:

- Placing one hand upon the other over the center of our forehead (sixth chakra in yogic philosophy), we cultivate awareness of the sensations, images, feelings, and thoughts that arise. We inhale strongly, then sighing on the exhale we place one hand on the center of our chest (fourth chakra in yogic philosophy). We establish Matrika pranayama. Then each inhale we invite attention to move from our heart to our forehead; each exhale we invite attention to travel from our forehead to heart, for at least 10 breaths, up to 10 minutes.

- We place one hand over the center of the forehead and stretch the other arm and hand out to the sky. We maintain this position for several breaths to a minute and then alternate our hands so that our brain's left and right lobes practice both positions. (This helps unconscious and shadow material to participate in cultivating our Inner Guidance.)

Group 4 Breathwork Practices.

1. Breathing slowly and deeply, we write or draw, stream of consciousness, with our dominant hand for 3 to 7 minutes. Continuing deep diaphragmatic breathing, we write or draw, stream of consciousness, with our nondominant hand for 3 to 7 minutes. We can do more cycles as desired.
2. Breathing slowly and deeply, we place our hands over the center of our chest and feel for any pulsing we can—our hearts, blood flow, life force, acupuncture pulses, and so forth. We welcome the pulsations into the palms of our hands for 10 breaths. With slow breathing, we stretch our arms forward into the air, elbows bent, with open palms facing forward. We bring the sense of breathing to the palm of our hands, feeling the contact between to our pulses and pulsations of the air. We can also practice this with any aspect of reality such as our friend, brother, dog, dust, black holes, sun, an elephant, our sadness, someone's anger, bodily pain, suffering, violence, an inspiring person, and so forth. We begin pulsing our hands forward a few inches and back. Pulsing forward we exhale, meeting someone, someplace, something, some situation, some quality. Inhaling,

we pulse back to our heart and check in with ourselves. Now we play with breathing and pulsing slowly to rapidly!

JOY/GRATITUDE/GENERATIVITY/POSSIBILITY/ALCHEMY/VISION

Breathing Practices that invite us to contact the sensations on and behind the center of our forehead (the *third eye* or sixth chakra in yogic philosophy), as well as the sensations of our hands—front, back, and within—while experiencing gratitude for the abundant possibilities in each moment, will support embodiment of these qualities.

Positions and movements with continual Conscious Breathing:

- Spreading the arms to the sides, waving them up and down as if experiencing a natural resilience, ebullience, and readiness to embark. We inhale deeply through the nose like we are purposely smelling something pleasurable. We exhale through the mouth, letting the breathing flow out slowly.
- With gently pursed lips, we draw the sense of breathing into our forehead, as if sparking something. We blow out slowly, gently, yet purposefully, as delicately and playfully blowing on a baby's skin. With this breathing pattern, we invite our arms to move like wings flying, and then begin creating shapes and patterns in the air, allowing our body to turn, bend, stretch, squat, skip, and twirl as it wants.

Group 4 Breathwork Practices.

- Breathing deeply while in any position that feels like an expression of gratitude for any fulfillment we feel in that moment and have felt throughout our lives. We practice Receiving Breathing for as long as needed until we feel like we are breathing optimally. This would be enough. Optional: Move into the universal position of gratitude and connection with the Divine, called *Orans*. Both arms are raised from the side and slightly to the front, with slightly bent elbows, forming a semicircle with our arms, hands outstretched—

welcoming blessings and offering gratitude and/or prayers for blessings. If possible we practice Embodied Novelty Breathing (Chapter 7), meeting the air and every aspect of existence with reverence and gratitude.

- Feet shoulder-width apart, one foot ahead of the other, we bend both knees for easy movement. We breathe the *awakeness* of the previous quality (awakeness and inner guidance) into our palms. With deep audible savoring oceanic breaths (Ujjayi), we brush our palms through the air creatively and playfully as if meeting each atom of air/reality, being affected and changed by each atom of air/reality, and changing each atom of air/reality. We open to seeing possibilities we didn't see before. It may feel like alchemical qualities flowing through us.

Burning Brightly in Service

One of the most reported endangerments for Therapists is the introjection of clients' intrapsychic material or affect cascading into burnout, depersonalization, dissociation, or secondary trauma. However, although Breathwork tends to bring up even more energetic phenomena, emotional affect and expression, and trauma material, as shared in Chapter 6, I've never heard a well-trained Breathworker use terms like *burnout*—or describe losing their sense of self. In fact, Breathworker stamina for being present with a person's process can be remarkable.

At a Breath Immersion Conference at Kripalu Center for Yoga and Health, I had assembled a team of highly experienced certified Breathworkers as faculty. Shirley Telles and I constructed a group Breathwork process for about 75 Breathees where every pod of four Breathees had at least one senior Therapist-Breathworker with them. The pod was formulated as two dyads, and in each 90-minute session, one person in each dyad was the Breathee and the other was the sitter. The senior teacher was supervising and interacting with both dyads for each 90-minute segment.

One of the pods had the great fortune of being attended by Dr. Stanislav Grof as their Breathworker. During one session, a Breathee entered somatic and emotional expression of ongoing childhood sexual trauma. Stan, who was 85 at the time, committed himself to seeing this session through to a true resolution of symptoms that had been plaguing the Breathee for a lifetime. Stan stayed with the dyad for over four hours, guiding the Breathee and the sitter verbally, kinesthetically, energetically, with skilled touch and absolute attention. My role was as overall group facilitator and a free-floating Breathworker who could accompany any pod for additional assistance when requested. It was profoundly inspiring to witness the devotion and stamina of Stan's love and attention to the Breathee and to participate with him for over two hours after the rest of the room completed and left. I consider it one of the honors of my life to have been in this experience. And I have known myself to commit to this same kind of attention and time with Breathees, as well as witnessing this capacity in many other Breathworkers.

What makes this, and similar experiences, possible, including preventing burnout and not taking on the Breathee's material? A quaternity of factors makes it possible: experience, faith in the inner healer of the Breathee, Conscious Breathing, and training in maintaining an embodied experience of ourselves and the other simultaneously.

With Human Potential Breathwork applications, it may seem Therapist-Breathworkers should consider what is happening, and then choose one application. That can work; however, it's more transformative to utilize a flow of applications. Here is an example with continual Group 5 Breathwork throughout the entire process.

- A Breathee is breathing deeply but seems myopically focused on their thoughts. We can see their eyes moving in REM patterns underneath closed lids. We inquire about their experience, and they say they're seeing images.
- We ask them to choose an image that has meaning for them. Or we might suggest an image they shared with us from a dream that elicited great emotion or was notably significant. We guide them to invite the chosen image to breathe.
- We ask where in their body resonates most with the image. We invite them to touch that area of their body or we touch it (excluding sex-

Components and Processes of Human Potential Breathwork Sessions | 245

ual parts) with their permission, and/or both of us touch it, resulting in hand upon hand—often a potent and meaningful experience.
- We ask if there is an associated emotion with this sensation and they say that can't feel one. We ask, if there were an emotion what would it be? They say they aren't sure and they seem shy about sharing. We coach them to breathe even more deeply while we say a list of simple emotions slowly. We inquire about which one feels most resonant. When they choose one, we suggest inviting the emotion, sensation, and image to breathe together.
- Perhaps they are holding their lower abdomen, and the emotion is fear. With permission, we begin the *body wave*. Initially, the pelvis is very tight, the wave amplitude is small, and the oscillations seem stagnant; eventually, the wave begins to increase.
- More energy appears to be flowing, and we ask what they are experiencing. Perhaps they say anger or flashes of red. Their breathing intensifies and it seems like they are becoming quite alert and energized, yet also unsettled. We say, "If the red had a voice, what would it be saying?" They say, "I want out. I want to get out of here." Inquiring into the voice, perhaps they find that it's the joy that they buried as a child . . . or the feeling of being trapped by childhood abuse . . . or the power to do what they want to do. Let us say it is the power to do what they want to do.
- We affirm the value of their power, We ask them to move their body into a position where the power can be fully felt while they are breathing deeply. They squat and are breathing so intensely now that they are shuddering. We get behind them so they can lean against us and let go. Then they might say, with teary eyes "I know this seems ridiculous, but I feel like growling."
- And we might say, "Growling can be a powerful way of experiencing your instinctual energy both to protect yourself and to move forward with strength. You can growl! [Or 'Let's growl']" Maybe we growl with them, and they're trying, yet not much is coming out, so we say, "Let's breathe even deeper into your belly for that growl."
- With permission, we put a hand on their belly, press in a little. As the growling intensifies, either they ask us to press very deeply on their

belly, or we have the sense to do it slowly and surely. Suddenly, a big growl bursts forth.
- We hear them say, in a very soft voice, "I want," and we say to them, "Be and say what you want." They voice one thing that they want and begin talking about something else, and we say, "Let's breathe deeply some more before you speak." They breathe deeply for a minute or two.
- "Okay, now say something else you want." They do, and we immediately say, "Okay, breathe deeply [they do].... Okay, now say what you want." They say, "I want myself," and we hold their back and their arms because in the squatting position they begin to move and make noises like they are giving birth. Tears fall.
- At some point, their whole body begins to relax, and we hold them and guide them to lie back down so they can't fall suddenly. They are breathing extraordinarily deep inhales and spontaneously toning while they exhale. The toning fades away, and long, slow, deep breaths emerge, about 30 seconds each.
- We inquire if this power and new sense of self wants to experience anything more, and they immediately, without pause (notice that evolution) say, "I want to feel welcome."
- We coach them in saying aloud, "I welcome myself [deep breath], I appreciate myself [deep breath], I honor myself [deep breath], I love myself [deep breath]." Or we ask them to speak about how the quality of their life and relationships may evolve as they continue contacting the power within, and we guide them to breathe deeply several times between each insight they voice.
- We coach them to breathe with simultaneous awareness of their belly (somatic cue), their wanting and welcoming themselves (emotion), their insight about empowerment (cognitive), and the energy of the power (Essence) ... while listening to the sound of their breathing.
- When they open their eyes, or want to sit up or move, we ensure that we are present for whatever degree of eye contact, gentle touch on the hand, affirmation, warm hug, supportive information, reminder to feel their feet, walking (or dancing) inside or outdoors, and so forth, is needed or not for them to feel mirrored, interconnected **and** self-reliant and inwardly resourced.

- As they move towards their next actions and experiences, we coach them to inhabit their movements and choices from within the atmosphere of breathing.

This chapter contains a small sampling of the healing and transformational experiences that can arise in Human Potential Breathwork and how they unfold instinctually, somatically, emotionally, cognitively, and energetically. Remarkably, almost always, after a therapeutically energetic flow, when Breathees speak about painful incidents, patterns, or limiting beliefs about themselves, these topics do not induce pain. The pain has already been processed, and the transformation has already occurred. Now they are integrating further cognitive understanding of it. They may cry softly or tremble as residues of stagnation, pain, or trauma release. As is common in personal growth processes they may cry with realizations of what could have been if earlier they had known these things, forgiven themselves and others, loved themselves and others more deeply, known what was possible, been closer to the Divine, and so forth. What is distinctive, and perhaps unparalleled—except in genuine mystical experiences—is the remarkable frequency and degree to which Breathees cry jubilantly ... simultaneously crying profusely (sometimes quietly) and laughing ecstatically (sometime internally, in which case their cheeks and face are filled/flushed with rosy color) with embodied awareness that they are intrinsically worthy, interconnected, loved, and loving ... and that others are intrinsically worthy, interconnected, loved, and loving ... that life is intrinsically worthy, interconnected, loved, and loving ... that every breath is sacred, and an opportunity for healing, transformation, polishing the jewel that we all are, and loving who we truly are into full flowering,

> *... if you can allow yourself to breathe into the depth, wonder, beauty, craziness, and strife—everything that represents the fullness of your life—you can live fearlessly. Because you come to realize that if you just keep breathing, you cannot be conquered.*
>
> —OPRAH WINFREY

TEN

Inviting Psychological Distress To Breathe: Repairing, Restoring, Re-forming

"Memory, suffering, trauma, joy, and possibility, and all that has been recorded in our life is stored in our body. The wisdom of breath invites the body to open to a mode to tell its stories not from our head but from a deeper place."

—JACK KORNFIELD

ALL PHYSICAL, emotional, and cognitive distress is a plea for help. Each distress symptom provides information about underlying issues in the somatic–emotional–cognitive continuum (SEC continuum), as well as potential remedies for restoring homeostasis and fostering well-being. Breathwork can be used to explore, ameliorate, or resolve psychological distress symptoms and possible underlying causes of biochemistry, situation, temperament, and trauma. Various Breathwork practices can support the following processes in addressing psychological distress.

- Relaxation—releasing (or relaxing out of) tension and reactivity.
- Presence—recognizing what we are experiencing; befriending and/or releasing denial, fear and reactivity; and dissolving dissociation.

- Regulation—creating physical, emotional, and cognitive equilibrium that supports understanding ourselves and our history; recognizing and integrating our strengths and capacities; generating life force; and functioning well in the present moment.
- Expression—understanding and releasing embedded patterns, emotions, beliefs, and trauma; experiencing somatic and emotional strength; opening life force and flow; and experiencing new possibilities and ways of being.
- Resiliency—by contacting our unconditioned self (pre-verbal, closer to Essence) and / or experientially contacting somatic memory pre-trauma, we are more readily able to sense our potential and gifts, supporting posttraumatic resiliency. Also, experiencing the ability to breathe fully during distressful emotions empowers us.

Therapist-Breathworkers can begin by facilitating small samples of each of these five processes for Breathees experiencing psychological distress—both to assess what is most impactful, and to support Breathees in understanding how they can utilize various Breathing Practices for immediate, short-term, and long-term healing.

Breathwork for Depression and Anxiety

The stresses of living in the twenty-first century may account for the skyrocketing rates of depression and anxiety, yet depression and anxiety have been with us throughout history.

When we feel something of great value has been taken from us or harmed—when there is grief—there is an enormous void and changes we must traverse physically, emotionally, cognitively, and spiritually (depression). When something happens that is challenging, potentially dangerous, or harmful—when there is fear—it makes sense that our body would maintain a state of alert until the situation could be resolved, accepted, or integrated (anxiety). We know depression and anxiety can have diverse causes and are often not only a biochemical phenomenon (neurotransmitters that are insufficient or misfiring).

Sometimes, depression is situational and can benefit from altering life choices, and better resources and support from families, communities, nutrition, and social infrastructure. Other times, depression is more spiritual than psychological—a time of necessary liminality to relinquish how we have been and birth something new. Sometimes it is a true dark night of the soul. Inside ourselves we may find, at first, only emptiness and darkness; yet, these are time-honored elements of inner change that spiritual pilgrims have used for awakening. This darkness can be where scaffolds that maintain our fixations and false certainties are revealed. We may then find grace, strength, and unshakable love for rebuilding our lives on the foundation of our authentic selves—replacing personality constructs that no longer serve.

Many Breathers have discovered that journeying through the experience of depression is a crucial first step to clearing illusory and inert aspects of self. In addition to personal grief, depression may arise from sensitivity to the grief and anxiety of our species, other species, and the planet. It is natural for our heart to grieve about assaults to life's beauty, majesty, and love that may be happening through collective sociological, virtual, political and environmental mediums.

New life germinating within us can sometimes be signaled by feelings of depression, anxiety, or both. Conscious Breathing (CB) can generate energy and space to honor this life force and intelligence. Andrew Solomon, author of *The Noonday Demon: An Atlas of Depression*, offers that depression's opposite is not happiness; it's *vitality* (Kierkegaard agrees). Johann Hari, author of *Lost Connections: Uncover the Real Causes of Depression*, suggests that regardless of chemical, sociological, genetic, or circumstantial triggers that cascade into depression, the primary remedy is *connection*. CB answers both. CB circulates lifeforce throughout our being, generating vitality along the SEC continuum. CB can also create profound connection—to our disconnected selves and to each other. CB can generate hope and possibility.

Coregulation between Therapist-Breathworkers and Breathees through attunement coupled with CB is particularly effective in facilitating relational connection and resonance that makes deep and enduring healing possible. For example, when someone is experiencing anxiety, and even trauma, in the immediate aftermath of a car accident, a good Therapist-Breathworker can facilitate breathing with those manifestations until the wisdom inherent in the shaking, racing thoughts, and fear has been revealed. This breathing coregulation can be essential for creating profound changes when there is complex long-term depression and/or anxiety, as we see in this story from Inspiration trained and GPBA Certified Breathworker Heather Davis.

> *A young man in his mid-20s came to Breathwork as part of a healing plan that he created with his doctor to find the root causes of anxiety, clinical depression, and anger that were affecting his ability to work, study, and live happily. I gently guided his awareness to his breathing with one hand on his belly and one on his chest so he could feel his breathing and body together. As he learned to flow between consciously connected breaths and a free natural rhythm of breathing, the intense tension and sensation in his body decreased and access to his emotions opened. Feeling his emotions had not been easy. As he learned to stay with his breath, he realized he had pressured himself with expectations to perform and be certain ways. Growing breath awareness, consistent Breathwork sessions, and a committed daily breathing practice (using Coherent Breathing) strengthened his ability to stay present with his feelings. His mood, sleep pattern, and sense of self-direction improved. He now feels peace inside as he discovers how to care for himself and lives the ups and downs of daily life. Regular Breathwork sessions promote acceptance and a growing love for himself and life. He is back to work and structures his life in ways that best support his needs. Conscious Breathing is now a permanent lifestyle addition.*

BREATHING THROUGH DEPRESSION

My treasured approach for supporting Breathers with depression is to use Integrative Breathing (Group 5), movement and dialogue to awaken the breathing (life force) within the felt sense and emotions of depression. In addition to these longer sessions (or when long sessions are not practical), here are three Breathwork practices for depression:

1. Balancing and regulating Groups 2 and 3 Breathing Practices—such as Alternate Nostril Breathing, Coherent Breathing, or Matrika Breathing—at least once (preferably two or three times) daily for 7 minutes, or up to 30 minutes.
2. Rapid Breathing Practice, such as Bhastrika, Kapalabhati, or Accelerated Breathing—breathing 20 to 30 times quickly, transitioning with a deep inhale retained for a few seconds and a slow exhale, then breathing slowly for 2 minutes, for several cycles—at least once daily for 8 minutes (up to 15 with experience). This practice can be combined with bodily shaking.
3. Moderately paced breathing, deeper than normal, with hands touching the body and connecting with sensation (for instance palms together, top of thighs, bottom of feet, cheeks, forehead, massaging or stroking the arms)—at least once daily for 5 minutes or more.

This is a total of 20 minutes daily (more if desired).

I was having bad, destructive images. My entire body felt toxic. My Breathworker asked me to find a place of goodness in my body. I couldn't, so she suggested a neutral place. I fought her because I wanted to stay with the "bad" images, but she insisted. The only part of my body that didn't feel anything was my feet. I breathed into my feet, and little by little a tingling sensation emerged with images of me as a little girl. I felt the goodness of my little-girl self, watching her play, dance, skip, and jump down a winding path, appearing carefree. I concentrated on my feet and my little girl playing. Breathing deeper, I felt her goodness spread up my legs, my thighs, my torso, and into my entire Being. It erased all the badness I felt completely! How amazing! I was healing myself. Everything I needed was right here in my breath. I even had a thought that I didn't need to latch onto my beloved Breathworker. The power of the goodness in that little girl was all I needed, with my Breath-

worker as a witness and loving presence ... The most potent piece of learning: I can heal myself. I'm able to take the illusion of badness that I feel and erase it from my body with breath and the innate goodness that's always been there. (from K. P.)

BREATHING THROUGH ANXIETY

Interestingly, many of the physiological circuits that produce fear and anxiety also generate excitement and joy. This was evident when a caregiver for my father was diagnosed with Ehlers-Danlos syndrome, and it triggered significant anxiety in her over a two- to -three-month period. She said, "I'm desperate. What about Integrative Breathing?" and I said, "Let's see." It produced her first sense of relief. She continued Breathwork with so much resultant joy that she changed her education track from physical therapy to psychotherapy. She was accepted into Rutgers School for Social Work and decided to incorporate Breathwork into her dissertation and future work.

In addition to Group 5 Breathwork, two Breathing Practices that are effective in regulating anxiety are (1) Cyclical Sighing and (2) body movement combined with CB.

We learned about Cyclical Sighing in Chapter 7, and how it reduces physiological arousal (anxiety) and enhances mood (Balban et al., 2023). The instructions are simple: Breathe in through your nose. When you've comfortably filled your lungs, breathe a second, deeper sip of air to expand your lungs as much as possible. Then, very slowly, exhale through your mouth until all the air is gone (Leggett, 2023).

Additionally, walking while doing CB (moving the arms when sitting) for 7 minutes or more daily can help depathologize anxiety states and integrate the intelligence and energy anxiety generates. Breathing rates can change during the 7 minutes, ranging from extremely slow to very fast, as long as walking continues. Moving the arms while walking and breathing is especially effective—stretching them up, sideways, down, straight ahead, making circles and playful, flowing gestures. This practice harmonizes with anxiety's excitable energy, creating mirroring from an empowered intentional consciousness. Afterward we can stand or sit quietly, feeling the effortlessness of automatic breathing.

Another reason movement during CB works for anxiety is that anxiety often causes overbreathing (even if we don't notice it), and that means we have too much oxygen and not enough carbon dioxide. This is why Buteyko recommends breathing lighter for anxiety and not breathing deeply. Alternatively, if we move in energetic ways while doing CB, our muscles create CO_2 which helps rebalance the oxygen/carbon dioxide ratio.

Laura, a mother and Therapist-Breathworker shares about Breathwork with her son, age nine:

> *Abraham continues to do breathing at certain times, often when he's anxious, feeling his emotions escalate, or feels an allergic episode starting. In hopes of regulating himself and calming down, he tries your breathing technique of 10 breaths in and out quickly, jumping 10 times, then clapping three times and repeating. He also uses the technique of three breaths in through the nose and out through the mouth (repeating around 7 to 10 times). After these breathing techniques, even if done briefly, he is physically calmer and less agitated overall, and there's a notable change in his energy. He's a strong-willed, sensitive, and emotional child who prefers for an adult—often me (his mom)—to join him in breathing. When we breathe together, he prefers synchronizing our breaths which creates a therapeutic quality unto itself. At times he has resistance; however, as daily healthy breathing habits are instilled in his routine, he's experiencing the benefits, and resistance is lessening. I'm deeply grateful for the breathing tools for my children and myself when I need to reconnect with myself, body, and spirit. I'm thankful to have techniques for real-time frustrations. Breathing is always available, waiting to carry us deeper into our more centered, peaceful selves. For this mother, psychotherapist, and human being, it's a true gift.*

Breathwork With Antidepressants and Anti-anxiety Medications

Generally, Breathwork is not contraindicated when using antidepressants and anti-anxiety medications, and some Breathers experience greater improvement in emotional regulation, mood, and energy when both Breathwork and medication are used. As referred to in Chapter 6, after experiencing beneficial results from Breathwork some Breathers wish to discontinue medication. Breathers can sometimes access expanded states of consciousness that allow them to cease medications suddenly, however, Therapist-Breathworkers should never recommend or encourage this. Sudden withdrawals from psychotropic medications, even with the potency of Breathwork, could be problematic—if not immediately, after a few days, weeks, or months. I've had considerable success partnering with the prescribing physician and creating a much longer weaning schedule than standard protocol—taking as long as needed, even four to six months or more, to stabilize incremental medication drops while using Breathwork and other support before reducing further.

Trauma: Breathing Regulation Into Dysregulation

Please note: This section may contain triggers related to sexual violence, war, and genocide. If you choose to read it, please be mindful of optimal breathing and self-care.

It is not an overstatement to say that Breathwork is evolutionary in working with trauma. Breathwork with a compassionate, trauma-informed, and attuned Therapist-Breathworker is a superlative relational regulation model and healing experience. When we experience trauma, our soma and psyche are *immediately* challenged, and often adversely affected. Conscious Breathing also has an *immediate* impact, one that, with expert facilitation, is almost always beneficial to soma and psyche. The ramifications of this *twinned immediacy* are profound.

Given the pervasiveness of various collective traumas such as marginalization, the COVID-19 pandemic, wars erupting, and the global ecological crisis; as well as personal trauma that may have been incurred by childhood neglect, rejection, abandonment, or abuse; or personal grief, shock or harm we have experienced as adults—virtually all Breathers carry some degree of trauma.

Studies show that the firing of the vagus nerve elicits enhanced well-being and relaxes the limbic brain. CB activates the vagus nerve and polyvagal response and seems to have beneficial effects in mediating reactions to trauma in the present, or embedded reactive patterns generated from past unhealed trauma. Slow deep breathing can also reduce depression by stimulating the vagus nerve which in turn increases thalamic GABA levels. The three things that we know help to stimulate polyvagal response are singing/humming/chanting, Conscious Breathing, and social engagement mirror neuron contact. Stephen Porges told me that breathing is the most powerful of the three. Breathwork can accelerate trauma healing, so withholding or using it improperly due to lack of training would be tragic. Therapists should seek Breathwork training, and Breathworkers should seek trauma training.

All five groups of Breathwork can help prevent, respond to, and resolve the immediate effects of trauma on the soma and psyche. Integration is accelerated when Breathers:

- Want to work through reactive feelings or paralysis when triggered by past trauma.
- Want to recall and hold suppressed memories with less fear and greater presence.
- Seek to solidify fragmented memories and prevent future fragmentation.
- Want to feel empowered and make sound decisions in challenging situations.

CB, vocalizing, and safe eye contact can activate the vagus nerve and polyvagal response, elicit well-being, and help regulate reactions to trauma. Breathwork can reconnect awareness and sensation, building neural pathways that contextualize trauma within the present moment.

The repetition syndrome frequently stems from a desire to regain control of situations where we were helpless and were harmed. Acknowledging and telling the story of trauma is an important step, yet usually does not free the embedded trauma in our muscles and nervous systems. Breathwork can free the repetition syndrome associated with trauma and buried or frozen memories by creating an unbroken, seamless matrix of organization that is larger than disorganized trauma memories. Also, the intensity of positive experiences during Breathwork can supersede the intensity of prior trauma, expanding a sense of possibility when integrated well.

CB provides a way to triumph over the perception of helplessness or imprisonment caused by trauma. It offers the possibility of remaining with the safety of immobility, dissociation, or folding while intentionally breathing—opening pathways beyond the limitations of those strategies.

BEFORE AND AFTER BREATHWORK: CREATING A CONTAINER

When using Breathwork to address and heal trauma, it is crucial for Therapist-Breathworkers and Breathees to collaborate on identifying and strengthening inner resources. Breathwork can activate somatic memory and increase energy, so skillful titration is necessary to ensure that Breathees can consciously utilize this energy for building resilience and growth, not simply reliving the trauma.

To ensure informed consent and support, Breathees should understand the potential for enhanced emotional release, and receive guidance on titration, pendulation, and stabilizing practices such as slow, deep breathing with open eyes. Before the Breathwork, the Breathee can locate a place in their body that feels safe or relatively at ease. Pendulation (alternating attention between this pre-established place of safety and the trauma-impacted area) can support integration and prevent overwhelm. Therapist-Breathworkers should trust breathing's capacity to guide Breathees while also watching for signs of dysregulation and emotional flooding. (The possibility that the Breather will experience one or more of these symptoms should be covered in any informed consent form.) Proper trauma training and postsession follow-up are essential, as

Breathees may consciously or unconsciously downplay their distress, or experience decompensation after sessions.

After sessions involving trauma work, Therapist-Breathworkers should assess the Breathee's embodiment and emotional regulation; offer additional support if needed; provide suggestions for integrative activities between sessions, such as self-care, journaling, exercise, and art; and refer them to another appropriate professional clinician if needed. Follow-up calls or email exchange should always be available to Breathees.

BEST PRACTICES FOR BREATHING WITH TRAUMA: CAUTIONS AND METHODS

> *There is a pain so utter*
> *It swallows substance up*
> *Then covers the Abyss with Trance*
> *So Memory can step*
> *Around—across—upon it*
> *As One within a Swoon*
> *Goes safely—where an open eye*
> *Would drop Him*
> *Bone by Bone*
>
> —EMILY DICKINSON

Breathwork can take months and sometimes years off the healing journey for Breathers with trauma. Yet Breathees heal at different paces. Common missteps among healers are either moving too quickly from eagerness to see Breathees' suffering relieved, or too slowly from an abundance of caution. With too much eagerness, something essential invariably gets overlooked, while overcaution can lengthen suffering unnecessarily. Training and experience help us identify the appropriate pace of healing for each Breathee.

Dr. Pat Ogden, founder of Sensorimotor Psychotherapy and author of *Trauma and the Body* teaches that inviting a person with trauma to "take a deep breath" can be counterproductive if the client's diaphragm is so tightly wound that they cannot breathe deeply, or if deep breathing arouses unpleasant emotions or memories without a healthy context for holding them (a good reason for Receiving Breathing). In our conversation Pat talked about clinicians needing to be aware of two common issues:

- Trauma survivors often have tight diaphragms. We can explore ways for them to loosen the diaphragm (see Chapter 6) such as bending over to stretch it out or lengthening the spine so there's more space for the diaphragm to contract and extend.
- Many people with trauma overbreathe because it has helped them cope. Deep breathing can bring up survival fears and instigate a dorsal vagal shutdown that may create freeze or faint reactions, exhaustion, weakened muscles, and dizziness.

Thus, facilitators having good skills about breathing paces, styles, pathways, and ratios (see Chapter 6) is critically important for supporting Breathers with trauma.

For Breathees who have experienced trauma, several mediums can support healing and regulation: movement, voice, fragrance, and sound.

- Adding movement to Breathwork can help release and empower the life force that was suppressed during the traumatic event. Guided movements such as stretching, twisting, pushing, kicking, or stomping—while consciously breathing—can reclaim power from the past (see Chapter 9).
- Singing, humming, toning, or droning can be a gentler entry point to deeper breathing if breathing is uncovering buried shame, fear, or feeling damaged. Singing familiar songs may evoke positive memories, calming the nervous system and enhancing polyvagal response. Therapist-Breathworkers can use a soothing, soft voice and gradually introduce silence and eye contact—then transition to Coherent Breathing or Matrika, and then Group 4 and Group 5 practices.
- Olfactory stimulation supports deeper breathing and state changes. Calming scents like lavender, rose, and grapefruit can slow breathing and reduce hyperarousal, while invigorating scents like lemon, lime, clove, and cinnamon can increase wakefulness and deepen inhala-

tions for hypoaroused Breathees. (Remember to check for preferences, sensitivities, and allergies, especially mint and menthol.)
- Rhythmic sounds, such as vocal instructions, Tibetan bells, ocean waves, or metronomes, can guide the breath to the regulating 1:1 Matrika Pranayama ratio and also stimulate polyvagal response, promoting neural and emotional regulation. This coherence rhythm can be particularly helpful for Breathees with psychotic breaks, bipolar disorder, or emotional instability.

Therapist-Breathworkers should be sensitive to potential triggers, such as the sound or sensation of heavy breathing, as we see with Kailana who attended an Integrative Breathing workshop hoping to alleviate her depression, stemming from childhood sexual abuse.

Kailana was initially triggered by the deep, strong breathing of the male facilitator assigned to her pod. Despite his caring demeanor, she became agitated and asked him to move away. With the support of a female facilitator, Kailana processed her trauma through deep breathing and verbalization, expressing her right to bodily autonomy. As she continued to breathe, staying present with her somatic experience, she found strength, life force, and ultimately, bodily joy. She realized she could feel fully alive and safe in the presence of others. By the end of the session, Kailana felt comfortable enough to hug the male facilitator, expressing a sense of empowerment and integration that she likened to "six months of therapy in one session."

On some occasions during Breathwork, flashbacks can be triggered and then integrated with embodied present moment awareness. Dr. van der Kolk observes the importance of this dynamic. He writes, "If the problem with PTSD is dissociation, the goal of treatment would be association: integrating the cutoff elements of the trauma into the ongoing narrative of life, so that the brain can recognize that 'that was then and this is now'" (van der Kolk, 2014).

A woman had been doing Integrative Breathing with me for about a year when, during a session, she abruptly began to relive what turned out to be a five-hour rape in the woods between her school and home when she was 10. The first minute or two, she was that 10-year-old running to the windows and trying to escape. Holding her hands, looking into her eyes, using a soft and steadying voice, and breathing at her rate, however erratically fast or slow each breath was, provided companionship for the present and the past; she became aware that we were working through the vivid intensity of this memory together.

Ordinarily, the entire time of an event would not be played out; however, here it had a life of its own, and we were in resonance, so we kept going. She consciously breathed through the whole enactment with short breaks for the little girl to say what was happening, interspersed with her adult self speaking as choices were made together about how to attend to this. Embodied Breathwork and attunement enabled her to live in two worlds while meeting every moment of the assault memory. We were together for nearly 6 hours—15 minutes of speaking and entering Breathwork, 5 hours of reliving the rape while continuing Breathwork, and 40 minutes of integrating until she felt strong, ready, and wanting to go home. She was eager to experience feeling safe going outside for the first time in decades. We went outside together and it was glorious—the light in her eyes and smile was luminous. She then wanted to walk by herself.

In a session the following week, she expressed feeling like a completely different person—empowered, less afraid, and more able to connect with people. She processed other trauma in later Breathwork sessions, but remarkably needed minimal processing about the rape. Ordinarily, this exceptional healing might have taken years. The key was present-day mirroring with breathing during the flashback so that younger parts of herself could feel the somatic presence of two caring adults, herself and the Breathworker.

Consciously breathing with flashbacks helps make the transition from explicit memory to implicit consolidation. Especially with preverbal trauma, or trauma that has caused immobilization or a freeze/faint response (and the corresponding inability for verbal expression), merely talking during a flashback will not interrupt the core of the flashback nor enable a person to consolidate or respond to the memory. Breathing, however, is preverbal and a substrate of all experience, so CB creates explicit pathways for relating to core trauma material. In every kind of deep CB, there is likely polyvagal or parasympathetic activation or enhancement, so there's an aspect of relaxation even with hyperarousal and flashbacks. Cortisol levels are decreased, allowing the brain to have a present-day relationship with past material. The key is supporting breathing and body awareness.

BREATHWORK AND TRAUMA TRAINING CONSIDERATIONS

Therapist-Breathworkers should cultivate sensitivity and skill in utilizing Breathwork for trauma healing. Breathwork provides extraordinary opportunities to unpack layers of introjected trauma and witness the strength of adaptive resilience once energy is freed up. Therapist-Breathworkers working with trauma ideally should develop proficiency in: Breathing Practices from each of the five groups; trauma-informed training; modalities that support regulated expression of somatically embedded trauma, such as Somatic Experiencing created by Peter Levine; ethical, skillful, and trauma-sensitive touch, such as NeuroAffective Touch created by Dr. Aline LaPierre; understanding the specific sensitivities required for various types of trauma (e.g., sexual assault, domestic violence, addiction, racial and ethnic marginalization, child abuse, military service, medical service, homelessness).

A CONSCIOUS BREATHING AND TRAUMA HEALING NARRATIVE: CONCENTRATION CAMP TO COMMUNICATION

Alice Kraus was a survivor of Auschwitz who lived with intense anxiety and fear. Her son Ron had found wholeness through Breathwork and deeply desired healing for his mother. She had never shared her story of Auschwitz with anyone and refused to talk about it. After 2 years of Ron gently encouraging her to come "talk with me," she finally came "for him." The first 20 to 30 minutes were a polite detente with occasional flashes of connection around our shared caring for Ron. She steadfastly maintained that she never had talked to anyone about Auschwitz, and it was not going to happen with me. I simply breathed deeply and acknowledged her right to refuse to share. I assured her I knew that anyone who had not been there could never truly understand her experience. When I sensed she felt heard, I would say something like, "That is so meaningful. Let's just pause so *I* can breathe deeply and really feel this," and she would breathe deeply with me for that one breath. We kept politely inquiring of each other, occasionally with intense flashes of eye gazing, speaking caringly about Ron, as I was acknowledging her capacities, and, upon her request, sharing about suffering in my life. And through it, every 2 to 5 minutes we would breathe a deep breath together.

Something began to happen. She started breathing more than one deep breath at a time. At some point I instinctively lay down on the mat while she sat in a rocking chair (it was usually the other way around!), and Alice told me her story of surviving Auschwitz. We spent almost three hours together. It's one of the most sacrosanct memories of my life. She even smiled afterward and told me she was glad she came.

A few years later when movie producer Steven Spielberg's team was interviewing Holocaust survivors, Alice Kraus contributed her story. She never talked about her experience other than during the Breathwork session and in the Shoah interview, which is still up on their website.

COLLECTIVE TRAUMA

Breathwork can aid in healing collective trauma by enabling embodied contact with internalized collective trauma, intergenerational memories, and archetypal energies. Healing can be accelerated in group Breathwork with others who either share similar, or different, collective trauma.

For instance, in 1995, a Caucasian woman raised in Christianity became aware of her oneness with all life upon receiving the Maori Hongi (sharing of breath). Subsequently she was "staggered" and "so completely overwhelmed with ancestral pain" during a ceremony with a Plains Indian tribe that she felt unable to breathe. She "hid from the pain and sense of responsibility, avoiding Conscious Breathing for 13 years." Finally, during some Breathwork sessions, she said she felt, "the joy of my traditional birth into an Indigenous family hundreds of years ago. I slowly came to understand that my work is learning to balance joy and pain." She has since created a well-funded organization that partners with hundreds of tribes to protect and preserve their sacred places, cultural traditions, and languages. Shared Breath and Integrative Breathwork became the mediums and medicines for revealing collective trauma and dissolving barriers, and Love became the guide for restoration and evolution.

SOCIAL AND DISASTER TRAUMA

When students and clients experience shock, whether from a fender bender or the sudden death of a loved one, I mobilize to get them Breathwork support as expeditiously as possible. Society works to address the physical needs of the victims and survivors when there are disasters or public violence. The immediate needs of victims and survivors to process trauma emotionally, somatically, and cognitively are too often neglected. If everyone had basic Breathwork education, CB could be initiated before the wounds of trauma are deeply embedded. In the wake of natural disasters, wide-spread public violence, war, genocide, and other crimes against humanity, supplies of food, water, and shelter may be cut off for days to months. Pharmaceuticals may not be available. CB may be one of the only resources we have for energy, health, releasing shock and trauma, and emotional and neural regulation. Immediate and abundant, CB is free and never runs out.

BREATHWORK GUIDELINES FOR TRAUMA TREATMENT

- Breathwork can create a powerful *felt sense and intensity* of life force in our present day body, voice, movement, and coping strengths. This can dissolve the supremacy of the intensity of traumatic memories, as well as build agency, and foster resilience for dealing with past and future trauma.
- CB can provide stability and control, offering a template for experiencing and organizing disorganized traumatic memories.
- Fast, shallow breathing may initially surface trauma, yet can also reinforce embedded trauma. So it can be effective for dislodging tension and emotions if used with awareness, however, slower, deeper, breathing generally supports authentic affect, creating new

life-giving pathways. Guiding Breathees back to slower breathing after stirring memories is optimal.
- Therapist-Breathworkers can deepen their own breathing and use a soothing voice to support polyvagal response in Breathees.
- Therapist-Breathworkers can change Breathwork techniques fluidly to avoid emotional flooding or fatigue in Breathees.
- Breathees may understandably want to retrieve exact memories to validate and make sense of their internal experience. However, because memory is malleable, a more critical part of trauma recovery is freeing unexpressed physical sensation and emotion—restoring pathways for authenticity and presence. Recovering memories can occur readily with Breathwork, yet, its most salient use is for experiencing authentic emotions, thoughts, and sensations from the past (even without clear cognitive memories) while breathing in the present moment for empowerment and integration.
- Trauma often happens in darkness, so low lighting can induce dissociation or trigger trauma responses. Yet some Breathees feel safer in darkness. Breathees should be consulted about lighting prior to each Breathwork session.
- Adjust pace and volume of breathing to downregulate or upregulate as needed.
- Acknowledge, honor, and work with hesitance or resistance—rather than using Breathwork to override or ignore them.
- Encourage Breathees to open eyes, orient to the present, change positions, and engage in movement, as needed, while continuing CB.
- Use calming fragrances for hyperarousal and energizing fragrances for hypoarousal, after checking for appeal and medical safety for Breathees.
- Create contact with warm, cool, safe, or pleasurable objects, in addition to breathing, to remedy disembodiment or dissociation.
- Gradually slow breathing to normal automatic breathing and use conversation, eye contact, and touch (with consent) to stabilize the experience. It is essential when working with trauma to culminate every session this way to ensure that Breathees have integrated the

realizations into ordinary awareness and functioning and are not in a trance state.

Nuanced sensitivity in verbal and physical interventions with Breathees with trauma is essential because unresolved trauma often hinders development of capacities and skills essential for self-coherence while in contact with others. When the body and brain fire in protective patterns, Breathees may be unable to feel or say what feels helpful, harmful, or neutral, and emotional flooding and retraumatization may occur. This repetition of an abusive situation stored as a wound in the subconscious can reaffirm inner split, while the facilitator, unaware of underlying dynamics, may mistakenly believe the session has been productive. Austrian Therapist-Breathworker Wilfried Ehrmann cautions that any intervention not adjusted to the client's real needs can cause re-traumatization. He shares that "Relief and relaxation prevailing at the end of the process is no guarantee that deeper issues have been resolved. It can also be an adaptation phenomenon: A repetition of the original form of dysfunctional trauma integration, combined with a strengthening of the inner resistance" (Ehrmann, 2019).

When working with trauma, Therapist-Breathworkers should never assume that a particular breathing practice is needed. It's critical to partner Breathees' authentic breathing, slowly inviting movement toward more optimal breathing. Frequently, trauma may have caused breathing impairment, and externally directed breathing may recapitulate the trauma. If so, activities that naturally relax, slow, or deepen breathing, such as humming, toning, singing, or listening to soothing music can be helpful. As breathing deepens, facilitators can acknowledge it supportively. Developing proficiency in Breathwork refinements is a lifelong practice and art that requires humility, regular practice, ongoing study, and consciously breathing while facilitating.

THE FIVE BREATHWORK GROUPS FOR TRAUMA HEALING

Group 1 Breathwork can support swift release of physical and emotional tension and rapid resolution of feeling disembodied. Group 2 can help with feeling more present thereby contacting a sense of self that is not primarily identified with trauma. Most Group 3 Breathwork promotes physical and emotional regulation and engender empowerment and agency. Occasionally, Breathers who meditate regularly may become triggered or dissociative, not due to Breathwork itself but because their approach to meditation has reinforced avoiding challenging emotions and memories. Embodied Breathwork with attuned facilitation rarely leads to dissociation. Group 4 Breathwork helps develop the strength, clarity, and self-confidence, as well as self-compassion and kindness, that are pivotal for healing trauma.

Group 5 Breathwork offers enhanced depth processing and accelerated change, making it promising for therapeutic trauma healing and transformation. Intense abreaction and memory recall can arise which, with expert facilitation, can be highly transformative. (However, remember that intense emotion should not be automatically equated with progress.) With proper Breathwork and trauma-informed training, the right access, holding, catharsis, expression, insight, and integration can happen.

Some people have deep concerns about Group 5 Breathwork activating sympathetic arousal by triggering, and thereby retraumatizing, rather than regulating. Sadly, this can, and has, happened with unskilled practitioners, group settings without enough individual support, and undesirable environments. Yet anecdotally, we know countless people who feel that their trauma was finally addressed by Group 5 Breathwork with great results. And in one example, eight sessions of CCB were used with a Breather with PTSD in a case study in Brazil, who experienced full resolution of PTSD symptoms, as well as significant improvements in HRV (de Wit & Cruz, 2021).

Group 5 Breathwork can also aid in discerning between personal and intergenerational trauma. Breathwork's amplification of the felt sense of our bodies makes it quite easy to recognize when energy patterns belong to others such as our father, mother, sibling, grandparents, family lineage, or cultural heritage. Witnessing Breathees clearly knowing "*this* is my pain and *this* pain is yours," and allowing the energy of the other to be breathed out through the nose, mouth, skin, and energy field, is often rapid and astounding.

A single Group 5 Breathwork session was powerfully transformative for an Indigenous American woman who had both personal and intergenerational trauma. During Breathwork the woman initially felt skeptical and self-conscious. However, as she lay on her back with knees up, her body position and breathing brought up the memory of giving birth. Simultaneously she saw herself as a young child, she said, "hiding underneath a table, knees pulled up to my chest, hiding from the environment and world around me that felt like danger and chaos." This juxtaposition between the scared, lonely child and the woman giving birth became "an opening to [her] own integral realm, to [her] heart center," confirming both the impact of the anxiety and trauma she experienced and the inner strength she accessed that supports her in being herself. The experience was a moment of "immense overwhelm" but also "an opening into an experience of great healing" that she "will hold on to . . . forever" (Curtice, 2023).

Psychopathology: Breathing Order From Disorder

Breathwork offers promise for physical illnesses (and some psychiatric conditions) that involve insufficient tissue oxygenation as a cause. People who have been correctly diagnosed, or labeled, with neurodiversity, personality disorders, psychosis, and dissociative disorders may benefit. Breathwork practices from all five groups may be extraordinarily effective as noninvasive, nontoxic, adjunctive modalities. Since Group 5 Breathwork's orientation is that all manifestations of affect and behavior have life force and intelligence, we can view dysregulated mental states as *psychological distress* which exists on a continuum with psychological well-being. Breathwork can augment healing for dysregulated Breathers when combined with psychodynamic therapeutic support focused on building internal structures and references. Entering Breathwork with simple, slow, brief periods of breathing is advised at first.

Some notes: (1) Breathers with trauma or histories of mental health diagnoses should always work with a well-trained and trauma-informed Therapist-Breathworker, (2) Breathworkers who are not psychodynamically trained or trauma-informed should refer Breathees to more experienced Therapist-Breathworkers or work in partnership with a Licensed Clinical Therapist, (3) In cases where Breathee's have suicidal ideation, Breathworkers who are not clinically licensed should only proceed with Breathwork in partnership with a Breathee's licensed clinician.

Psychiatrists such as Thomas Szasz, Peter Breggin, and R. D. Laing did not view extreme mental distress as illnesses (Farber, 2012; Laing, 1983). R. D. Laing worked from the strong belief that all mental imbalances were truths being communicated that needed to be integrated—into the individual, but also into the collective. To many this sounds radical, however, these perspectives are predecessors to Positive Psychology and Internal Family Systems (IFS), which teaches that there are *no bad parts*—be they seemingly bipolar, dissociated, schizophrenic, and so on.

According to Dr. Shirley Telles, Breathwork can be an effective complementary treatment for schizophrenia and other personality disorders. Dr. Telles spent a month at Athma Shakthi Vidyalaya, a nongovernmental organization in Bangalore, where she taught yoga and yogic breathing to 24 residents with mental health issues, mostly schizophrenia, who also received various therapies including Transactional Analysis, Cognitive Behavioral Therapy, art therapy, drama, exercise, and counseling. She reported that "therapists and residents noted that the yoga and breathing... [offered] greater cognitive flexibility, calmness, reduced fear and paranoia, and less outbursts of aggression when yoga and breathing were included" Further studies have shown the benefits of yoga (including yogic breathing) for schizophrenia (Cramer et al., 2013).

Breathworkers have observed for years that particular attention is needed for Breathers with bipolar disorder, especially concerning Groups 4 and 5. It appears that the stimulation and excitation of an enhanced sympathetic nervous system (though usually in tandem with enhanced parasympathetic activity) can trigger chemical shifts in bipolar brains that may initially feel life-giving but ultimately trigger a manic episode. Having done Breathwork with bipolar clients for several decades, I have also noted that, conversely, depressive phases may be mitigated by Breathwork.

When Breathers with bipolar tendencies come to Inspiration for Integrative Breathing, we most often use Breathwork from Groups 1, 2, and

3, especially Coherent Breathing or Matrika Breathing, slowly ensuring they can engage expanded consciousness without triggering mania. We recommend they begin with individual sessions because group energy can be very stimulating. In conjunction with attending psychiatrists, we can often support someone with bipolar disorder in reducing medication over extended periods. This process always originates with the Breathee—we do not offer, advocate, or push for it.

For example, an 18-year-old man came to work with me 15 years ago, prompted by intense spiritual realizations and heightened energy. Several members of his family had been diagnosed with bipolar disorder and wanted to support him holistically. As I assisted him with somatic grounding through Breathwork, I consistently acknowledged his truly poignant and inspiring insights. It was an extraordinary, rich time—one he still refers to as a tuning fork for embodied, higher states of consciousness in daily life. Yet during that initial period, it was clear that bipolar pathways had been activated, and their intensity kept increasing. After about 5 or 6 days I suggested we go to an excellent hospital for a medical evaluation to stabilize his brain chemistry while we continued acknowledging his personal growth.

He was in the hospital for 6 days and medication was prescribed. Upon discharge, he worked with me using CB, meditation, and verbal exploration. His goal was to wean himself off the medicine and experience the same heightened spiritual awareness without triggering a bipolar episode. Over a 2-year period, we used very slow deep breathing, always monitoring his level of excitability. By the time he was 20, he could enter heightened states of awareness without triggering bipolar symptoms. Eventually, he was also able to do Group 5 Breathwork practices without activating any triggers and he weaned off his medications. He got married, had a beautiful daughter, and became a respected business owner and structural integration bodyworker. Twenty years later he still uses breathing, mindfulness, and somatic presence to continue his very fruitful life journey. These kinds of healings are possible with Breathwork when Therapist-Breathworkers are well trained, trauma informed, and have enough clinical understanding to support such a process.

Breathwork for dissociative strategies and identities can be beneficial.

For about 20 years I worked with a number of Breathees with 3 to 67 distinct personalities or identities. Most were professionally diagnosed. I found that *each personality, when related to with unconditional positive regard could be taught to breathe consciously.* The personalities would talk to each other and then breathe together, expediting integration. Personalities usually had different types and rates of CB, yet because they could recognize others' breathing as *breathing*, they could merge through breathing. This allowed them to feel co-conscious body sensations, develop empathy for one another, become willing to work together, and eventually join the core self's breathing. One Breathee integrated 67 people/parts into her core self over three years.

This same technique can work for most dissociative disorders. First, we acknowledge and have empathy for any disowned emotional states or personalities. Through unconditional positive regard and validating the strengths of each being (also called people, alters, identities, Parts, personalities) we can teach each identity to breathe consciously and more optimally. Eventually their breathing can connect to the breathing of the core self on which every other identity's breathing depends.

Accurately discerning the differences between a spiritual state and a chaotic or delusionary state is imperative. With major depressive episodes, bipolar symptoms, or schizoid-affective sequelae, containment and redirection through traditional models such as hospitalization and medication may be necessary. Even then, we should not eschew the power of Breathwork.

In the process of contacting one's authentic self and cultivating self-actualization, there can be periods wherein our normal psychic structure no longer functions, but the new operating system is not yet installed. Somatic, emotional and perceptual symptoms may be extreme. Stanislav Grof and his late wife, Christina, named this kind of episode a *spiritual emergency* (Grof & Grof, 1989). Competent Therapist-Breathworkers will want to learn how to discern between psychological distress, and spiritual emergency, and when a genuine spiritual or mystical emergence is occurring. Sadly, I have met and worked with Breathers who, when younger, had genuine spiritual experiences that were deemed pathological and who received medication, treatment, or hospitalization that was misaligned with their true needs. I have also worked with people who didn't receive helpful treatment, medication, or hospitalization because someone around them without therapeutic and consciousness knowledge assured them they were having a spiritual experience.

In addition to therapeutic and consciousness training for Therapist-Breathworkers, conscious community may be an enormous contribution as it was for the young man with bipolar. If Breathees open significantly without availability of follow up guidance and community they may become scared of Breathwork and tragically never want to use this vital medicine again. This is why this population should always work with well-trained Therapist-Breathworkers with clinical knowledge. Each moment a Breather is uncovering the pain of dissociation or a disorganized internal landscape through CB, it reveals the authentic self's resilience. Still, in this territory Breathwork is most effective when combined with wisdom that has been honed through psychotherapeutic and clinical knowledge about symptoms and intrapsychic structures.

Therapist-Breathworkers who are well trained in psychodynamic understanding, skilled in attunement, and committed to working with their own intrapsychic material can generally utilize Breathwork for any psychopathology, psychological distress—or perhaps we might call it *resilience adaptation,* to good effect. CB is never bad for anyone, and it is essential. Just like water and food, the amount, type, and quality make a difference.

> *As long as you are breathing, there is more right with you than there is wrong, no matter how ill or how hopeless you may feel.*
>
> —JON KABAT-ZINN, *FULL CATASTROPHE LIVING*

ELEVEN

Full-Spectrum Healing and the Evolution of Breathwork

*I will learn to see with my heart again /
I will learn to breathe and start again.*

—ALEX SIEGEL, "LONELY DAYS"

Conscious Breathing and the Somatic–Emotional–Cognitive Continuum

VIBRANT PHYSICAL health can support our psychological well-being and spiritual journey, just as psychological well-being and spiritual growth can foster excellent physical health. Some people passionately advocate for all illnesses being created by thoughts; however, a unitive consciousness perspective recognizes each aspect of reality as reflecting the source. Thus, the *wholeness* of body, feelings, thoughts, and spirit is supported by embracing the power and intelligence of all aspects of reality—recognizing that there's no split between psyche and body. The body is a vital source of information, intelligence, and resources, as is the mind. Let us align our vision to see that the body's influence on the mind is equivalent to the mind's impact on the body.

Going a step further, we can work with the entire somatic–emotional–

cognitive continuum (SEC continuum) to activate our full potential for physical, emotional, cognitive, and spiritual well-being. Thus, consciously caring for the body *is* caring for the mind *and* our relationships. Developing our capacity for awareness *is* caring for our bodies and relationships. Opening to loving and being loved *is* caring for our bodies and enlightening our minds. These are all intelligent activities for optimal physical wellness, psychological well-being, harmonious and fulfilling relationships, an actualized life, the development of consciousness, and our planetary stewardship.

We can address physical dis-ease by working with it emotionally or cognitively. We can also address it by working with physical sensations.

We can address emotional or cognitive dis-ease by working with it emotionally or cognitively. We can also address it by working with physical sensations.

Suppose a person experiences unresolved grief for so long that they become afraid to open to new experiences and the possibility of more loss. With constant stress, tension, and anxiety, the body becomes habitually contracted and armored. These defensive postures trigger even more substantial stress hormones, generating a vicious cycle. Stress hormones suppress the immune system, making illnesses more likely—from colds to cancers.

Dr. Peter Litchfield described to me how every physiological function is behavior that consists of psychological elements, since our physiology is imbued with consciousness. A physiological process is triggered, there is an outcome, and the organism intelligently regulates itself based on that outcome. Each physiological function's root has a stimulus or motivation. This is critical to understanding the biological substrates of somatic intelligence.

Peter uses the example of breath and air hunger. Many people immediately experience air hunger when they feel confined, for example, when a blanket covers their head. Since this air hunger is triggered instantly, it cannot be due to increased carbon dioxide or oxygen deficiency; it's psychophysiological—a learned emotional reaction. Similarly, eating because we feel hungry can be radically out of sync with our actual blood sugar needs and whether the body needs energy physiologically.

It is realistic to say that for cultivating somatic–emotional–cognitive wholeness, breathing is our single most powerful nutrient and medicine.

Countless times, Breathworkers have witnessed Breathers breathing with and into physical symptoms, and discovering reflective, frequently unconscious, emotional challenges. We can invite physical symptoms to breathe so their inherent wisdom and life force have paths for transformation and belonging, which supports greater integration and life force. When emotions are invited to breathe and integrate, physical symptoms either lessen, dissolve completely, or are met with less emotional angst—tending to ease physical pain and promote healing. Breathing Practices for emotional regulation may also prevent pain and disease from developing because the body is under less chronic and repetitive stress. Basically, Breathwork activates the SEC pathways, supporting health immediately and enhancing our ability to attend to and transform our psyche and soul. Simultaneously, Breathwork connects rapidly with the psyche, affecting our biological states and capacities.

Researcher Therapist-Breathworker Alicja Heyda, who we met in Chapter 9, has many case studies that illustrate how the potency and expanded consciousness of Group 5 Breathwork practices can powerfully and beneficially impact serious and life-threatening illness. Two of her case studies follow:

> *A patient who was treated for infiltrating Ewing sarcoma reported high-intensity pain not explained by disease progression, great fear of walking, and panic disorder. During 42 psychotherapy sessions, I used Conscious Connected Breathing [Group 5], symbolic guided imagery, and dream analysis, with improvement after a few sessions—much less pain, walking freely, and panic attacks ceasing. Breathwork sessions brought bliss, trauma release, and joy. Several symbolically meaningful dreams showed healing and winning with the disease. In 2024, the patient is healthy, despite a very poor initial prognosis in 2003.*
>
> *For 2 years after stopping cancer treatment, a patient had frequent panic attacks when alone and agoraphobic abreactions when outside. She reported taking antidepressants and anxiolytics without improvement. She medicated herself with alcohol to ease grief, anxiety, and depression, and couldn't leave home alone. During the first Conscious Connected Breathing [Group 5], her body spontaneously breathed deeply.*

The next four sessions had trauma abreactions with strong catharsis and whole-body vibrating, leaving her relaxed and calm, without panic attacks or agoraphobia. After 10 CCB sessions, depressive symptoms disappeared... and she had a dream with a feeling of total victory. In 2024 she is happy and healthy despite a poor prognosis in 2001.

The SEC continuum's potency in physical and mental healing during Breathwork is exhilarating to witness. Here are two stories where I used Integrative Breathing (Group 5):

Jonathan had a reputation among other hard-core addicts for swallowing handfuls of amphetamines and continuing to function relatively normally. After several bottles of alcohol, he could still ski—doing slaloms! His first Integrative Breathwork session was so seismically powerful that it superseded the intensity and impact of his drug experiences. He got and stayed mostly sober over the next decade—with three relapses, each lasting several days to several weeks. During the second relapse he almost died.

During his third relapse, he was so intoxicated that he entered fullblown drug- and alcohol-induced psychosis from which the doctors were afraid he might not completely recover. Alcohol-induced psychosis can permanently convert to schizophrenia, especially in men (Niemi-Pynttäri et al., 2013).

When he was admitted to the hospital, we encouraged deep conscious breaths when it was possible to penetrate his dissociation, as well as using psychodynamic communication and body awareness to corral his wild ramblings. Deep breathing optimizes physiology, providing beneficial conditions for detox; it can also accelerate delirium tremens (DTs), which is why somatic grounding with good therapeutic communication is essential when utilizing Breathwork in addition to medical support. Basic Group 1 relaxing breaths were used to assist the detox as quickly as possible for the best chance of recovering total brain coherence. As a veteran of Integrative Breathwork (Group 5), each breath's impact on his psyche was likely magnified. After 10 harrowing hours of CB for 2 to 3 minutes, every 10 minutes or so, he came through.

That was only a precursor to a more fantastic experience of CB's power with the SEC continuum. Three years later, this consistently sober client was happily living life as a devoted husband, father, and AA sponsor for over 20 people. Loved ones were alarmed when he began muttering to himself, including in public, and appeared to have conversations with angels or entities, listening to their advice and following their dictates—undeniable symptoms of psychosis. One "guide" told him to swallow a small plastic toy, which he did, necessitating an ER visit.

Around this time, his wife told him she wanted a divorce and would take their young child to live with her. Jonathan begged her to attend Awakening, a Consciousness and Breathwork course at Inspiration. His impulse control was now quite poor. He talked loudly to his wife during class and sometimes followed me around the room as I taught. Several times, the assistants had to lovingly walk him to the room's edge and help him regulate. He was barely sleeping, hardly eating, and he was delusional. His psychiatrist was unclear what to do because Jonathan was not imminently harmful to anyone, and he would not agree to hospitalization.

Everyone was convinced he was using drugs and alcohol again because his symptoms were similar to his relapses, though he insisted he was clean. He submitted to three surprise tests for alcohol and drugs, at least two when he couldn't possibly prepare and deceive us. Over a five-day period, every blood and urine test was negative for drugs or alcohol.

I had known Jonathan for 15 years, and this bizarre, erratic behavior and incoherence were alarming. He was exhausted beyond description, described having zero energy, and he could barely stand up straight.

Jonathan came to an individual Integrative Breathwork session. He told me about his life, including his wife possibly leaving, and never feeling he could get his mother's approval. I asked him, "Have you ever felt truly unconditionally loved?" He immediately said, "Yes, I have felt loved like that," and seemed quite clear about it upon further inquiry.

With nothing to lose, he lay down and gently entered Integrative Breathing. It was hard for him to focus—it took guiding him one breath at a time. Twelve minutes in, he opened his eyes and said with incredible clarity, "You know what? I don't think I ever have felt unconditionally loved." Almost instantly his eyes cleared from their distant psychotic state—and I saw Jonathan again.

His psychosis completely stopped at that moment. He continued breathing and processed his feelings about never having felt unconditionally loved. In a new state of tender self-love, he could feel the love of others more deeply than ever.

A psychodynamic explanation could be that disorganized attachment, perhaps caused by severe neglect or abuse, led to dissociation. Severe dissociation can lead to Schneiderian symptoms that look like psychosis (Longden et al., 2020). Jung, Grof, and others say that resolving deep symptoms often requires entering the deep unconscious, which can be very dark, and will likely amplify symptoms temporarily.

Before this psychotic incident, Jonathan may have had a relatively organized, yet limited, self, and then something stressed his system to bypass the compensating defensive abilities of his relatively organized self. Perhaps, amid this distress, trust with a Breathworker supported his breathing to move below his defenses, into that dark place. That may have thrust his implicit memory into contact with his unconditioned self and integrated presence, giving him access to more resourceful states, which may have helped reorganize him. During this kind of transformation, a Breathworker needs to have the skills to hold the spectrum of physical and emotional chaos to potential and essential goodness, without becoming afraid and overly containing the process. Additionally, the psychotic symptoms had disrupted his social engagement functioning, and CB, especially with a coregulating facilitator, restored full social engagement.

We may never know what triggered Jonathan's defense system to break apart. Was it some emotional distress prior to or subsequent to his wife telling him she wanted a divorce, or was it physiological?

All along, I had been concerned that he had a severe vitamin B_{12} deficiency, which several studies have correlated with schizophrenia, dementia, catatonia, delirium, hallucination, and prominent Schneiderian first-rank symptoms, which include the "thought alienation phenomenon, commenting and third person auditory hallucinations, delusions of persecution and reference, and passivity phenomenon"—even in patients without physical symptoms commonly associated with vitamin B_{12} deficiency (Jayaram et al., 2013). Consequently, I had urged Jonathan to test his vitamin B_{12} and D levels, which he did a day *before* that breakthrough Breathwork session. The results were due three days after the session.

While Jonathan still complained of extreme fatigue after the Breathwork session, he now remained coherent, lucid, and nondelusional with normal behavior. The blood test subsequently revealed that his vitamin D was 7, with low-normal being 20 or 30 (which many doctors consider insufficient for optimal health). His B_{12} was 115, with low-normal being 200 (which many doctors consider inadequate for optimal health). So, it is possible the entire episode was triggered by substantially deficient vitamin B_{12} and D levels. Upon receiving B_{12} injections and high-potency vitamin D, his energy was restored.

The interesting phenomenon is that the psychosis suddenly and completely ceased during his Integrative Breathwork session when he realized that he had never felt unconditionally loved. This insight and resolution of the psychotic symptoms occurred *before* he got treated chemically—and it lasted for four more days before he received a B_{12} injection, after a several-weeks-long psychotic episode.

Whatever the trigger, Breathwork facilitated contact with extraordinary resources that allowed Jonathan's emotional symptoms to resolve and life quality to be restored, when he was at risk for a therapeutic containment that could have pushed the symptoms' origins further into the psyche and/or required chemical intervention for functioning.

Daniella came to do Breathwork with me when she was 30. She was wondrously bright and sensitive, and had great passion for life. She had always delighted in contact with the natural world, great ideas, the arts, politics, and loved ones, yet as a teenager had suffered dramatically—feeling unmet, disregarded, and exiled in her home. She described writhing on her bedroom floor in silent screams for hours at a time, feeling isolated from her father, mother, and three brothers.

At age 19, she experienced an acute asthma attack and was rushed to the hospital, where for several days she lived inside an oxygen tent. She remembered crying, wailing, and begging for someone to put their hands in and touch her. The sense of isolation she felt during childhood had manifested outwardly. No one touched her in the hospital, except for medical procedures. Daniella was discharged with prescriptions for daily and emergency rescue asthma medications.

During her first Integrative Breathwork session, the memory of her hospitalization emerged, and she began shaking and writhing. The whole set of sensations from that time arose; the trauma that she wouldn't live because her breathing was so compromised, and that she would die untouched—truly a metaphor for her life to that point. Because of her asthma, she could not breathe deeply during the Breathwork session without coughing. Her breathing was becoming more and more shallow and constricted. I knew she might be at severe risk.

As discussed in Chapter 9, it is always an art to decide when touch is corrective and produces evolution for a Breathee, and when touching is soothing but not ultimately transformative. In this case, it seemed that being touched would be a new experience leading to significant insight and a felt sense of the realness and value of her body. Gently and slowly, I began softly touching her arms, torso, belly, legs, feet, face, hands, and spine. Just as her breathing was becoming almost frozen, with a violent spasm that would not allow breathing, she suddenly felt "the goodness and warmth of her lungs." Against all odds in her perception, her lungs relaxed, opened, and breathed with life force.

She went on to do scores of other Breathwork sessions and her asthma symptoms resolved permanently within the first year. Thirty years later, she still does not own or use inhalers or medication.

> *Of all ebriosity, who does not prefer to be intoxicated by the air he breathes?*
>
> —HENRY DAVID THOREAU, *WALDEN*

Other healing and therapeutic modalities can play a significant role in stimulating, accelerating, and integrating deep SEC continuum transformation for Breathers. In the wake of imbalance, distress, or disease (Figure 11.1), is a simple chart with rudimentary suggestions to help orient toward options for therapeutic interventions. A primary principle is to discern the most optimal interventions for well-being and resilience according to a Breather's natural cellular state and daily life. A second primary principle is that choosing the intervention that supports our body's capacity for self-healing with the least toxicity, yet sustains the body, will support the most long-term well-being. CB will produce the most robust long-term health, yet may act more, or too, slowly during acute health challenges. Allopathic medicine will often elicit the quickest response (certainly needed in urgent situations) but sometimes adversely impacts the body's natural resiliency. When facing a physical, emotional, cognitive, or spiritual challenge, the ideal would be to choose the interventions that accomplish the following: (1) sustain the body; (2) incur no greater harm than needed to sustain the body (minimize invasiveness and introduction of toxins); (3) ignite or fuel the body's healing capacity; (4) support the most enduring foundational health.

Breathers who want to utilize Breathwork for physical health issues are encouraged to consult with their primary care physician or other certi-

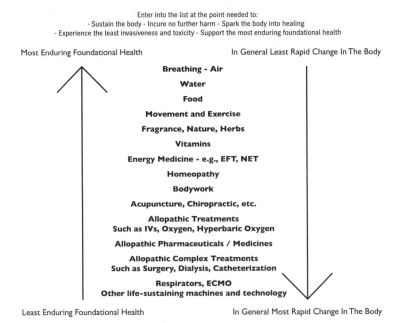

FIGURE 11.1: Spectrum of Wellness: Nutrients and Medicine
Jessica Dibb. Image created by Altruce Poage and Sharon Elsberry.

fied professionals, if they wish, before engaging in Breathwork or seeking advice from Breathworkers.

The Future of Breathwork for Full-Spectrum Healing and Awakening

> *Breathe, breathe in the air.*
> *Don't be afraid to care.*
> —PINK FLOYD, "BREATHE"

Through the joy and honor of teaching Integrative Breathing, training Breathworkers, and facilitating over 20,000 Breathwork sessions, I have observed the profound benefits Breathing Practices offer—from simple relaxation to deep soul-accessing experiences. The combined learning and experience leads me to envision that the future of Breathwork lies in helping individuals find their optimal breath rate, depth, and focus *in each breath* to support well-being and coherence in each moment. The multidimensional effects of breathing can be immense when titrated to the needs of each situation and Breather's personal development.

We can call this specific approach *Conscious Responsive Breathing* (CRB)—with *Breathing* interchangeable with *Breathwork*. CRB is a Group 5 Human Potential Breathwork practice that includes all groups, and indeed may utilize all five groups in a single session. Let's explore some salient factors that contribute to the potential power of this practice before we describe what it may look like.

Many factors affect our breathing. Obvious differentials are height, weight, muscularity, and genetics. Strong evidence exists that other powerful influences on development include life stressors, attachment history, adverse childhood experiences, dysregulation from trauma incurred at any time from the womb to the present, and environmental factors during formative years (e.g., exposure to chemical toxins, heavy metals, and excessive noise). Inherent temperament, correlated to neurotransmitter levels (Bond, 2001), can play a role, as can the unique ways Breathers condense memories to create personal narratives. Indeed, variability and differentiation in embedded cortical patterns arise from each person's bio-individuality (Davidson, 2014).

Epigenetic factors affecting breathing, optimal well-being, and self-actualization are therefore highly individualized and not universally measurable. Other salient effects may arise from the fact that 80% of brain cells are glia—free agents not predetermined as part of our DNA and therefore extraordinarily flexible.

As discussed previously, numerous studies show that emotions control breathing, and breathing affects emotions (Sarkar, 2017; Ashhad et al., 2022). A study at the University of California San Diego Center for Mindfulness, directed by Dr. Fadel Zeidan, showed that breath awareness practices reduce Breathers' perceptions of chronic pain (Wells et al., 2020). The study suggests that consistent Breathing Practices may change default settings of neurotransmitters, brain frequencies, and heart rate variability. Thus, long-time Breathwork practitioners might generate brain changes that would change the rate or type of breathing that produces optimal coherence over time.

There is significant evidence that attention directed to breath sensations can build capacity for interoceptive attention (Farb et al., 2023). Additionally, the more precise focused attention is brought to these sensations, the more what occurs in the current moment is given priority in the brain over neocortical awareness. A groundbreaking paper published in June 2021 called "Keeping the Breath in Mind: Respiration, Neural Oscillations, and the Free Energy Principle" describes how our systems prioritize paying attention to situations where what actually happens differs from our expectations. The body and brain keep adjusting (Boyadzhieva & Kayhan, 2021).

Therefore, we can posit that the more conscious change occurs in Breathwork, the more awareness develops, the more interoceptive attention is built, and the more conscious awareness of our interoceptive landscape ensues. CRB, attuned to our psychophysiological state each moment, and therefore supporting subtle and sizable changes, would yield the most information for well-being and self-actualization. The effects might not be felt as immediately as fireworks. However, when the fireworks, arise they might be amplified—and most importantly, be more enduring.

When we're inspired to actualize deeper potential, transform our thinking and behavior, or achieve a goal or vision, our system switches from seeking dependability to seeking autonomy. We like to feel our capacity to stretch, to reach a goal, to become. Researchers Edward Deci and Richard Ryan established self-determination theory and the dynamics involved in motivation. They discovered that when people's basic needs (food, shelter, etc.) are met, they become significantly more motivated when given a choice to reach a goal, in contrast to *controlled motivation*, which is generated by external sources. Instinctively, people do not like to be pressured, coerced, or seduced to achieve a goal. Thus, theoretically, having set breathing rhythms and practices (manipulating our breathing according to an outer directive) could be *less sustainable over time* than consistent CRB, which would motivate us over the long run. CRB might engage us much longer in life by continually stimulating our autonomous motivation, which engages our natural self-initiating energy and is emanating from existence's self-initiating energy.

Rebecca Alban Hoffberger, the polymath founder of the American Visionary Art Museum (AVAM) in Baltimore, Maryland, shares my passion to understand all things related to the energy of breath and breathing. She mused about her love affair with exploring life's "primary and most powerful influential forces," explaining to me about the choice of AVAM's second original thematic exhibition, *Wind in My Hair*:

> Think about our primate/primal feeling of swinging through the trees, or as kids swinging for hours pumping our legs to go higher and higher, or as adults driving with the top down, on the back of motorcycles, or fast downhill skiing. There's a powerful human drive to kindle some sense of gleeful aliveness that reminds us that our spirit, our consciousness, is not limited to our body—an active interplay between the rush of wind on our flesh that speaks to our unbridled joy in pure spirit.

With CRB, Breathers move toward optimal levels of physiological and emotional well-being—gleeful aliveness! And we become more attuned to the variance and nuances of each breath that best supports us. This attunement increases trust in our full life force and its intelligence; amplifies conscious awareness and the *felt sense* of our interoceptive states and intelligence; and cultivates willingness and capacity to be breathed more deeply so that we can ride the waves of our primary impulses.

Thus, CRB is not a passive process, nor controlled breathing. It's akin to what many Breathers experience toward the end of Breathwork sessions—being breathed like we're on a cosmic respirator, yet participating by consciously inhabiting whatever depth, rate, and cadence are occurring.

Let's consider the significance of the primary impulse in breathing and respiration. CRB is resonant with our primary impulses to play, work, create, and participate. Breathing is the life pump, the purveyor of messages between us and everything else. Respiration is the chemical pathway for getting needed elements or nutrients to our body, soma, and psyche and exchanging those elements with life around us.

Breath manipulation practices, while extremely therapeutic, can subtly reinforce separation from our primordial life impulses. As Peter Litchfield said when I explained CRB to him, "Yes, when you take over the breathing and get ego involved in trying to breathe a particular way, rather than following it naturally, you will often get a disconnection between breathing and respiration." Therefore, it's ideal to practice voluntarily adjusting each breath in ways responsive to our psychophysiological state in that moment, as well as mindfulness practices that simply follow the breath—watching life force and intelligence unfold and flow. This way we learn to both *act* in what is, and *be* who we are.

Optimally, during CRB we can do both simultaneously—consciously adjusting breathing in response to our authentic psychophysiological state and urge to grow, and letting breathing guide us.

Practicing CRB

Action and participation that arise from full interpenetration and integration of the self with all aspects of reality, including the Source, requires a fully present organism and potential that contains many mature attributes. CRB attunes to a Breather's optimal, authentic, bio-individual coherence, whereas, at times, breathing per instructions may cause slight dissociation from this coherence. Nevertheless, developing our will and capacity for engaging in controlled Breathing Practices can help open us up to receive the full potential of CRB by encouraging our willingness to listen and surrender to the natural intelligence in each breath.

Thus, learning and practicing controlled Breathing Practices with particular manipulations can serve our journey towards CRB by (1) increasing lung capacity; (2) undoing physiological constrictions and patterns that inhibit full breathing; (3) strengthening diaphragmatic full-bodied breathing; (4) learning to quickly access amplified life force; (5) cultivating three-centered presence to ourselves and life; and (6) experiencing emotions, memories, awareness, transcendent states and more. Supported by the beneficial ways these practices stretch us, the natural rhythm, volume, entry, exit, and so forth in each of our breaths will be more robust. So too, the cognitive and experiential intelligence with which meet each breath will generate precious impactful refinements.

During CRB breathing may shift from long to short, mouth to nose, forceful to passive, shallow to deep, sighing to exultant, continuous to retained, with vocalization or silence, and so forth—these changes will elicit alignment with free-flowing life force. This becomes practice for everyday breathing that is deep, vibrant, emergent, and in *flow*. Indeed, since novelty is a primary trigger for *flow states*, and CRB engages novelty, *CRB will induce flow more readily than patterned breathing.*

We can only allow these results; we cannot force them. We know that Accelerated Breathing, for example, can open intrapsychic material, from trauma to mystical states. As long as Breathers *join these induced breathing rates volitionally*, and with presence, beneficial results seem to ensue. However, when Breathers take breathing research results and frameworks out of context, practice in ways that may not align with optimal health, and disseminate this information to others, the expected results may not materialize. This harms perceptions about Breathwork's efficacy. In CRB, all these factors participate in each breath: knowledge, experience, wisdom, life force, responsiveness, integrated presence, effort, effortlessness, surrender, love, unconscious and conscious awareness, invisible and timeless collective wisdom, and contact with primary drives of existence. As first stated in Chapter 6, ultimately, we master technique to be free from technique, and we learn to breathe from the breath itself.

> *When ego gets a hold of breathing it can become a catastrophe.*
>
> —RUSS HUDSON

FIVE MODELS FOR UTILIZING CRB IN SESSIONS

1. Breathwork practice from any group, then CRB for 7 minutes or more.
2. Breathwork practice from any group, then an equivalent time in CRB.
3. Training Breathees in a variety of Breathwork practices for increased breathing capacity, awareness, physical and emotional responsiveness and regulation, healing, and expanding consciousness. After significant experience of those CRB is introduced.
4. CRB for 7 minutes to enter Group 5 Breathwork session.
5. CRB for entire Group 5 Breathwork sessions.

Envision the possibilities of breathing our personal resonance in each breath!

Certified Therapist-Breathworker Training of the Future

We have learned about Breathwork's potential to facilitate full-spectrum healing, transformation, and growth—somatic, emotional, cognitive, and spiritual wholeness. Therapist-Breathworkers need to be able to facilitate bio-individualized Breathwork, CRB, full-spectrum healing, and expanded states of consciousness—and be essential workers that can support Breathers in times of trauma, medical situations, mental health crises, or collective disasters. Indeed, communities and cultures throughout the world are expressing interest in Breathwork. Over time, they are likely to see the immense value of including Therapist-Breathworkers in all of our social structures and processes for humanity's well-being and quality of life. By staffing well-trained, certified, experienced Breathworkers into health care settings, schools, workplaces, community centers, fire departments, police departments, gyms, art and theater venues, birthing rooms, end of life rooms, and more—we will enhance physical, emotional, cognitive, and spiritual well-being; prevent many physical and mental health challenges; support relational well-being and cooperation; inspire and foster creativity; nourish spiritual growth; create new pathways for Breathers to contribute to our collective well-being; and engender respect and care for all life and our planet. Therefore, I would love to see an expanded standard curriculum and training period that includes:

- Commitment to daily Breathing Practice, ongoing self-care, and self-development.
- All GPBA training modules content, and commitment to GPBA ethical standards.
- Significant practice in all five Breathwork groups, and mastery in one or more.
- Basic breathing science and human anatomy proficiency.
- Understanding physiological, emotional, cognitive, and spiritual impacts of Breathwork.
- Ability to facilitate focus, full emotional expression, and integration.
- Ability to do our own inner work including work with boundaries and boundlessness.
- Ability to facilitate inner work including work with boundaries and boundlessness.
- Ability to do CRB for long practice periods.
- Ability to facilitate individualized authentic breath and being.
- Training and/or licensure in: temperament, attachment, trauma, interpersonal neurobiology (IPNB), object relations, othering (marginalization, colonization, diversity, equity, and inclusion, and belonging), birth, death, neurodiversity, sexual awareness and wellness, some knowledge about mental health and medical conditions (especially lung, heart, neurologic, and medications), basic emergency medical response (e.g., CPR, first aid, seizure training)), and disaster response training.

Full-Spectrum Breathwork and Psychotherapy in the Twenty-First Century

In a 2019 paper called "Trauma and Breath: A Clinical Approach to Trauma Resolution Utilizing Breathwork," Kyle Buller noted that "the general practice of Breathwork is split between the clinical and the spiritual and very few programs, if any, bridge that gap."

Since that time, there has been significant movement toward integrating clinical theory and understanding with psychospiritual training. The single most powerful nutrient, healer, and medicine is within each person's body and awareness—Conscious Breathing. We need to develop Breathwork—empower pathways to study, fund, and research it, and train Therapist-Breathworkers in excellent applications to foster well-being and potential in every Breather.

Breathwork wisdom is bursting into our collective awareness, its extraordinary power ushering in an evolution that will not be deterred. Simultaneously, psychotherapy is more enriched than ever, and continually surfacing new understanding and methodologies for treatment. These fields' advances are responding to soaring stress levels from the ever-increasing pressures of 21st-century life; the burgeoning awareness of trauma's impact on our personal and collective well-being and functioning; and resounding calls for personal, relational, and collective healing.

There are also internalized and explicit pressures of breathlessness from disease, racial and gender oppression, socioeconomic injustice, and ecological upheaval and degradation. To the shock and dismay of our collective psyche, wars continue to erupt—a reminder that our species still considers violence an option to resolve disagreements and fears. At any time, up to three dozen armed conflicts are occurring on five continents.

More people than ever seek guidance, tools, and sustenance for personal and collective well-being. We yearn for peak and breakthrough experiences. Breathwork and psychotherapy are answering the call. Integrating Breathwork and psychotherapy, or employing Breathwork as the sole therapeutic method itself, we may discover the need to reimagine the parameters of time-honored paradigms of psychotherapy and healing methodologies. This is an exciting endeavor, as we access the deep roots of psychodynamic wisdom to interface with Breathwork, supporting a comprehensive framework for healing. Integrating Breathwork and psychotherapy can stabilize the transpersonal states that Breathwork reliably engenders.

New processes are emerging with the potential to be accelerated and metamorphosed by Breathwork. Like the outer internet, the potential of the *innernet* communication of breathing within us, and the *intranet* of the planet's one breath cycle among us, can move at the speed of light—in the Plane of Possibility.

> *Breathe with unconditional breath /*
> *the unconditioned air.*
>
> —WENDELL BERRY, "HOW TO BE A POET"

PART III

Expanding

TWELVE

The Plane of Possibility and Breathwork

> *I place on the altar of dawn:*
> *The quiet loyalty of breath*
>
> —JOHN O'DONOHUE, "A MORNING OFFERING,"
> *A BOOK OF BLESSINGS*

All of reality is energy. Some years ago, Dr. Dan Siegel wondered how energy becomes life. Quantum physicists explained that energy is possibility moving to actuality. The possibilities for us to experience integrated, whole, and embodied individual and relational presence emanate from what Dan now calls the *Plane of Possibility*, which he describes as the source of presence and awareness, the dimension of reality where all possibility exists.

Furthermore, what affects the movement of *energy as potential* to *energy as actuality* is the *degree of probability* created by a synergy of particularities (from within a field of diverse possibilities) meeting particular points or durations of time. Both diversity and time are infinite, so potential is infinite.

The Plane of Possibility exists throughout time, gives birth to, and contains all time.... It's the infinite source of energetic components for all that ever has been, is, or will be.... Its nature is infinitely dynamic—infinite mathematical space from which anything can occur. On a diagram, time or change is represented along the horizontal or *x axis*, with the infinitely diverse things that can occur placed along the *z axis* that jumps toward us from the page. The vertical *y axis* represents the *probability* that a particular thing, event, idea, and so on will occur at a discrete moment or duration of time (Figure 12.1).

The higher the probability position, the more cosmological properties and objects materialize. The higher the probability position, the more various life forms appear. The higher the probability position, the more we—our thoughts, feelings, intentions, and actions—actualize. For example, as the probability distribution factor increases, the more specific a mood would become, and the more visible forms would emerge on the graph—which Dan calls *plateaus*. As the probability curve intensifies, these moods, ideas, and emotions would inform specific thoughts, words, choices, or actions—which Dan calls *peaks* (Figure 12.2).

Another good example is the formation (actuality) of a word choice. In the Plane of Possibility, everything needed for language to exist is present as momentum and potential. When the probability increases to the point where the infinite number of words on the plane has narrowed to the number of words a Breather knows in a specific language, a plateau is created. Over time, as the Breather amasses more experiences, probability increases toward a particular word—a higher plateau. This plateau can include our emotional needs, the languages we know, the relational field between us and who we're communicating with—there's a panoply of factors. As the need and momentum for action increases, the probability distribution curve rises, eventually producing an ultimate activation, an actuality—a particular word (peak).

The diagram shows infinity continually creating and interacting with itself as time, change, and infinite diversity—producing actuality, including life. Thus, the Plane of Possibility is like a state of continual, seamless verbs—momentum and dynamism (no nouns)—that are intrinsically *inter*connected. Indeed, a term Dan has created—***intra****connected*—is more apt. ***Inter****connected* denotes internal and/or external connections between two differentiated elements, processes, Breathers, and so on. *Intra*connected describes the infinite potential and manifestation of everything arising from the intrinsic wholeness of the Plane of Possibil-

The Plane of Possibility and Breathwork | 295

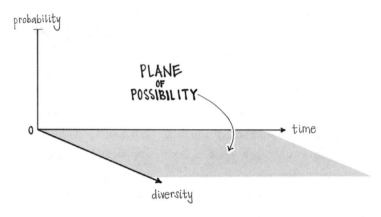

FIGURE 12.1: Plane of Possibility, 1
Illustration by Madeleine W. Siegel as depicted in Siegel, D. J. (2018). Aware: The Science and Practice of Presence. New York: TarcherPerigee. © Mind Your Brain. Inc.

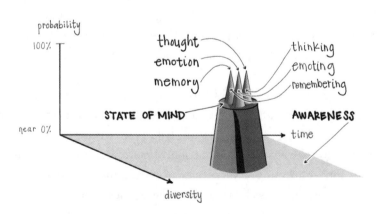

FIGURE 12.2: Plane of Possibility, 2
Illustration by Madeleine W. Siegel as depicted in Siegel, D. J. (2018). Aware: The Science and Practice of Presence. New York: TarcherPerigee. © Mind Your Brain. Inc.

ity. This innate intraconnection infuses and supports us, each particle of existence—everything visible and invisible.

*Inter*connection is an important and powerful dynamic, bolstering integration, creativity, and relatedness. Interconnection elicits greater valuing of connectedness between people, places, and things. We should aspire to extend interconnectedness toward others and all life.

Within *intra*connection, the differentiated aspects of ourselves and life *don't* lose individual integrity; they exist in a field of wholeness with everything else. One of the most salient properties of *intra*connection is its invocation and contact with immediate wholeness for us. Indeed, from here, *feeling broken breaks us open* to more complex and flowing creativity and connection. The following story from Sandy Wiggins offers a compelling glimpse of how Breathwork facilitates such a breakthrough.

> *I opened my eyes and felt both empty and complete, connected both internally and externally to everything. I was present in a way I have seldom felt. And whole. My Breathworker welcomed me. She suggested I invite my mother in and to speak to her. I closed my eyes and breathed, then summoned her. I told her that I didn't want to feel guilty because I was awake, and she was not. We put a large pillow on my chest—my mother's burden that I carried. I gave it back. "This is yours. I won't carry it anymore. Take it back. You have everything within you to awaken and be whole. I love you. How can I help you?" I was filled with powerful compassion for her and felt compassion extending to everyone, everywhere.*

When we contact the Plane of Possibility—pure awareness—through practices, peak states, flow states, and being present with the three centers of energy flow, we experience being held by something beneficent and larger than ourselves—creation, the source, pure awareness—the wholeness of intraconnection. Experiences of intraconnection tend to elicit essential acceptance, lovability, and the sense that we and all life belong. Within intraconnectedness, we know ourselves and everything else as intrinsically whole and connected to potential, *and* we are compassionate toward everything in ourselves and others that isn't currently experiencing or manifesting wholeness and well-being. When we acknowledge our intraconnectedness, we are invoking our ultimate identity as *verb-ing*, as being infinitely dynamic possibilities. Intraconnection underpins the perennial wisdom teaching throughout time and cultures that we and everything are *one with all of creation.*

Breathing is *the* human physiological process that unceasingly makes contact with the Plane of Possibility. And virtually everything on earth is participating in various oxygen cycles—like one breath. Conscious Breathing (CB) can readily elicit the felt sense of intraconnection. Breathing is an emergent dynamic that is the embodiment of *inter*connection and *intra*connection, manifested in actuality—on the physical plane. CB is a somatic experience of intraconnection of virtually the whole planet and all we experience. With enough intimacy, expansion, and Breathing Practice, we could bring the consciousness of what sees beyond in-group/out-group—intraconnection—into actuality.

Every breath contains a dynamic invitation and physiological portal to being, awareness, awareness of awareness, the Plane of Possibility, and intraconnectedness. **CB and Breathwork increase the probability** that we will notice this invitation, strengthen attention to it, and breathe into contact with the Plane. To avail ourselves fully of this potency, we will benefit by learning about the *Wheel of Awareness* practice.

One day, as Dan looked at a circular table with a clear glass center surrounded by an outer wooden rim, he perceived a visual metaphor of the mind. The central clear glass represented awareness—knowing; and the wooden rim represented thoughts, sensations, feelings, associations, memories, images, and ideas that we can be aware of—the knowns. Wanting people to experience their pain and hardships, as well as joys, with expanded consciousness, Dan developed the Wheel of Awareness practice for cultivating knowing—awareness (Siegel, 2018).

We visualize a wheel where the central clear glass of awareness/knowing is the *hub* of the wheel; our human experiences/the known is the wooden *rim*; and pointing our attention to any wheel part creates a *spoke* of the wheel (Figure 12.3). Attention—the spoke—connects the knowing of the hub to the knowns of the rim. Essentially, the hub is a visual metaphor for the Plane of Possibility, and the rim is a visual metaphor for the variety of our experiences.

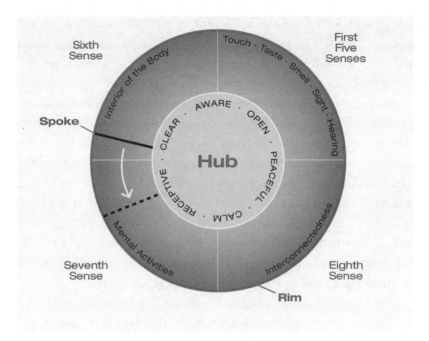

FIGURE 12.3: Wheel of Awareness Visual
Illustration by Madeleine W. Siegel as depicted in Siegel, D. J. (2018). Aware: The Science and Practice of Presence. New York: TarcherPerigee. © Mind Your Brain. Inc.

We envision the rim divided into four segments/categories of knowns: our *five senses*, our *body's interior signals* (sensations), our *mental activities* (feelings, thoughts, memories), and our *connection* with others and nature—our *relational sense*. We slowly, systematically move our spoke of attention into each segment's content and experience. Then we bend the spoke of attention back toward the hub so that we are experiencing attention on awareness. This elicits the experience of *awareness of awareness*, or *awareness itself*.

Dan has led over 50,000 people in person, from almost every continent, through the Wheel of Awareness. Consistently, across cultures, spiritual orientations, gender, race, education, and so on, people describe their experience of the awareness at the hub as a deep sense of interconnectedness with everyone and everything, feeling empty but full, timelessness, expansiveness, spaciousness, total peace, and like God. The one word used far more frequently than any other is **love.**

The Wheel of Awareness practice gives rise to experiences of unity, spaciousness, and love by creating embodied harmonious linking and integration of differentiated aspects of consciousness, which optimizes our physical, emotional, and cognitive health and functioning. The Wheel practice integrates expanded consciousness—the Plane of Possibility.

If we could continuously contact the Plane of Possibility (love) in our actuality...

This is where breathing, Conscious Breathing, and Breathwork deliver abundantly.

1. Breathing predates our self-concepts, words, skills, and most memories. So in our automatic breathing, to the extent it even creates plateaus (breathing is psychophysiological and therefore affects and is continually affected by emotions and physical conditions), biological mechanisms for breathing would be relatively small plateaus, not far from the Plane of Possibility.
2. A single conscious breath is the most accelerated, immediate, embodied pathway for creating integrated presence (all three centers of energy flow).
3. Breathing is the verb at the substrate of all other verbs of human experience. The more fully present we are with breathing, the more we approach the infinity of presence itself and the Plane of Possibility and its verb-like nature. CB supports presence with the dynamism of creation/actuality.
4. Conscious, relaxed exhalations engender coherence, awareness, and pure being. The founder of Polyvagal Theory, Stephen Porges, posits that when the vagal ventral branch is activated, the *social engagement system* is turned on, and that a moment of breath awareness induces the coherence that is likely turning on the ventral vagus nerve (Porges, 2011). The lungs themselves are innervated by this vagal ventral branch, so breath awareness robustly promotes social engagement system activation. An exhale that is extended without force—not breath holding, not pausing at the end, but savoring the emptying—experientially invites significant letting go of worry and

supports *just being* with its pure peace. Conscious, relaxed, extended exhalations give us living, embodied experiences of pure being.

5. Breathing is the salient dynamic of mindfulness (awareness), as Jack Feldman and his slowly, deeply breathing mindful mice demonstrated.

6. Awareness of awareness—the Plane is in the quantum realm and timeless, whereas what emerges from it and our actions are in the Newtonian realm, which includes time. *Each aware breath connects us to the timeless source of reality and its possibilities—yet the function of breathing takes place in time.* Thus, each conscious breath contacts the horizon, bridging timelessness and time, bridging pure awareness, love, and our actions.

7. Dan Siegel points out that ongoing coupling of in-breath and out-breath arises from, and interacts with, the brain's anticipatory nature in trying to be ready for whatever happens next, especially potential threats. It uses SIMA—the *sensory implications of motor action* (Siegel, 2007). Our brain figures out what's going to happen through a parallel distributing process where our prior experiences provide information for assessing the present moment. From this vantage point we survey the past and speculate about the future—not the future we're planning, but the future emerging from probability.

    When we inhale, the SIMA process searches for the next event, and lots of experience says—exhale! SIMA predicts an inhale when we exhale, and vice versa. For our entire life, breathing is a matrix of coherence and steadfastness in the face of inner and outer vicissitudes, because the brain always anticipates the next inhale or exhale, and almost always that is what occurs. This accuracy builds a cache of certainty, increasing as we log more automatic breaths over time. This cache of certainty is strengthened the more we breathe with awareness.

8. We can influence our breathing, and it can become a powerful influencer for enhancing health, emotional regulation, cognition, intuition, and vision. The implications for integration in Breathwork's ability to both accentuate relaxation into coherence and stimulate novelty (which can engender flow), are stunning.

9. Breathing is most often invisible—like the Plane. Indeed, breathing is relatively unobservable with our classic senses. Only smell, engaged by nasal breathing, consistently perceives it—which we saw in Chapter 1 may be the sensorial vector for God Consciousness ... the Plane of Possibility. Thus, breathing itself is an immersion into the Plane of Possibility. When we embody it with awareness, we can experience its formlessness readily. Yet we're breathing in a human body, and the apparatus and structure that supports breathing is in form. CB is the bridge between form and formlessness.

10. *Conscious Breathing and specific Breathwork practices are the royal practices of all practices.* Why? Because in every other practice we can contemplate—such as Tai Chi, meditation, Sufi whirling—we practice, then need to stop to transition into ordinary activity. With most practices, we can drop into the Plane, and over time the fruits of the practice integrate into ordinary activity. Yet we need to cease the practice of dance, meditation, Tai Chi, and so on to wash dishes, converse with friends, and travel. Exceptionally, breathing awareness and many Breathing Practices can continue seamlessly as we engage in ordinary activity. The profound implications are still vastly, almost incomprehensibly, unrealized.

Breathing is a direct bridge between the Plane of Possibility and actuality—the actuality of us existing, being human, and taking actions in our lives. And the bridge—breathing—is itself an *embodied* actuality, not just conceptual. *The system is pervasively integrating.* When we breathe consciously, we are bringing *awareness itself* to this extensive integration, creating a kind of ultimate integration or *expanded consciousness in our bodies with each breath*. CB is the central engine of our awareness of awareness—the Plane. It is the central engine of our experience of interconnectedness (relatedness and relationships) and intraconnectedness (oneness). *And* CB can be maintained during our ordinary actions and relationships, both as an abiding engine for embodied awareness and as a tuning fork and conduit for the expression of the Plane. For all these reasons and more, I offer that ...

*Conscious Breathing is the **dynamism** of awareness.*

Practicing Breathwork bestows dazzling gifts of probability on this phenomenon. Consider—the experiences of our day are various differentiated actualities and actions. Experiences are energy flow, and physicists tell us that energy is the movement from possibility to actuality (Siegel, 2016). We have the capacity to move energy by increasing the probability position (Figure 12.1). Breathwork builds greater conscious somatic, emotional, and cognitive awareness to breathing—to the physiological mechanism that bridges formlessness and form. Indeed, the more we use Breathwork to regulate, to clear imbalances (contractions, distractions, compensations for embedded trauma, etc.), to create pathways for integrated three-centered embodied presence, and then to practice awareness and optimal breathing in daily action—the more energy is freed and new energy is generated.

Rumi luminously describes this oneness of breathing and the Plane of Possibility in his poem "Only Breath."

> ... My place is placeless, a trace
> of the traceless. Neither body or soul.
>
> I belong to the beloved, have seen the two
> worlds as one and that one call to and know,
>
> first, last, outer, inner, only that
> breath-breathing human being.
>
> —RUMI, "ONLY BREATH,"
> TRANSLATED BY COLEMAN BARKS

Thus, the more we practice Breathwork, the greater the probability that our plateaus (feeling, believing, remembering, self-concepts, and mental models about the world that filter our processing) will be closer to, informed by, and directly reflective of awareness itself, the Plane of Possibility—love and loving. In turn, the cultivated quality and nature of those plateaus increase the probability that our peaks/actualities (words, choices, actions, etc.) will at a minimum reflect, and at a maximum be, the embodiment of pure awareness, the Plane of Possibility—love. Through regular Breathwork, we can develop the felt sense of consciously breathing and contacting the Plane of Possibility—greatly increasing the probability of embodying presence and the Plane of Possibility in our choices and actions. This generates a *continual living practice,* and a life of expanded capacity, meaning, consciousness, and love.

> *By our breathing we are attuned to our atmosphere. If we inhibit our breathing we isolate ourselves from the medium in which we exist.*
>
> —ALEXANDER LOWEN, *THE VOICE OF THE BODY*

THIRTEEN

Authentic Breathing, Authentic Life Urge, Authentic Self

> *And as I looked a quickening gust*
> *Of wind blew up to me and thrust*
> *Into my face a miracle*
> *Of orchard-breath, and with the smell,—*
> *I know not how such things can be!—*
> *I breathed my soul back into me.*
>
> —EDNA ST. VINCENT MILLAY, "RENASCENCE"

Authentic Life Urge

WHEN EXTERNAL and internal sensations feel good, we often instinctively desire to freely flow with our life force and feel fully alive. Ideally, we would experience the free flow of our life force in our first breath and then each breath thereafter. Each inhalation would express *yes*, wanting to embrace aliveness and become a unique differentiation birthed from the infinite womb of existence. The exhalation would be *letting go* as if saying "I trust this," allowing the flow of life to support us—a willingness to relax into infinite life force and be transformed by it.

When interior or exterior sensations do not feel good, our bodies instinctively contract. We conserve energy to cope and try to alleviate the hurt. Our breathing begins to reflect these contractions. We construct defensive patterns that become habitual coping strategies to deflect pain. We live with a mostly unconscious tension derived from the constant gauging of how much aliveness we believe is allowed before we are seen as bad or dangerous—or something painful happens to us.

I once brought a burning question to a group of nine accomplished Breathworkers with 290 years of collective Breathwork experience:

> Is there ever a Breathwork session where we don't have to overcome an initial minute, even just a moment, of resistance to breathing fully? It's like we have to overcome something to get into the flow or stream of effortless Conscious Breathing. What is that? When we know so well it's going to be so positive, why do we have inertia and resistance?

A poignant silence ensued as people considered the question and its ramifications. Profuse deep breaths were audible. Then a highly skilled Breathworker of several decades, Binnie Dansby, said, "Ashley Montagu [anthropologist, infant and child advocate] called it the phobic stir." In Ashley Montagu's (1986) actual words, "every breath we take, even as adults, is preceded by a faint phobic stir."

We explored its meaning—that perhaps, because life usually has pain, every time we breathe we would experience a slight phobic response because the first breath and/or subsequent ones were accompanied by pain. Maybe this resistance mechanism can be explained by what neuroscientist Matthieu Boisgontier describes as our brain's innate attraction to sedentary behaviors. He states that moving away from sedentary behaviors requires increased energy output from the brain and that "anything that happens automatically is difficult to inhibit. But knowing it is happening is an important first step" (Lee, 2018). Yes! So, Conscious Breathing (CB) interrupts the sedentary behavior, fear, or refusal. It could be the first step to the conscious effort of transforming the inertia.

Intrigued and "stirred," I researched and discovered that the original creator of the term *phobic stir* was psychiatrist Lawrence S. Kubie, who clearly understood that breathing is a psychophysiological process:

> There is a warning mechanism for every instinct, it is a mechanism of anxiety.... We breathe for psychological reasons before we have to breathe out of physiologic necessity. There is a faint phobic stir underlying every breath we take, as the breath-holding Yogis well know. (1948)

So, when our 290 collective years of seasoned Breathworker experience postulated the term *phobic stir* to describe resistance to initiating a Breathwork session as a phobic response because breathing brought us into some embodied memories of pain, it was also related to Kubie's meaning. While there's a *physiological* warning system that drives us to breathe, we are *psychologically* driven. The phobic stir is our anticipation that something bad may happen.

THE PHOBIC STIR IN BREATHWORK

We fear both future deprivation and pain we've experienced in the past. Thus, each time we begin consciously breathing, we enter awareness and intimacy with the phobic stir. And, as Boisgontier inferred, we need to *choose* to become aware of it to begin to change it—so there would be a lag time (Lee, 2018). Parts of our brain are drawn to sedentary behaviors and states. Particularly in Group 5 Breathing Practices, at a minimum we're unconsciously amplifying the phobic stir and, at a maximum, consciously experiencing the fear associated with it.

We might then ask what would compel so many Breathers to engage in Breathing Practices over years, decades, or a lifetime. It turns out that our beautiful brains *also* have an almost irresistible craving for new, unpredictable, and complex experiences. The moment we give our full attention to inner space, the depths of our psyche with all of its angels and demons, traumas and blessings, ordinariness and radiance, opens more. Thus, the more willingly we move through the phobic stir and turn our attention inward toward each breath, the more likely we are to be propelled into extraordinary and altered states of awareness, accelerated healing, and transformation.

Working with our life force can be spectacularly shepherded by CB.

Each inhale can be experienced as formlessness becoming form, yet also as receiving substance from life. Each exhale can be experienced as releasing form, yet also a medium for giving to others and the world. Ultimately, CB nourishes and integrates all experience and the totality of the unique, complete self.

Our protective instinct can take hold with the tiniest slip of unconscious behavior during these odysseys into life force, manifesting in any number of ways. Some believe that life force resistance is akin to Freud's death or destructive instinct; however, that theory is largely discredited because biological instincts move toward well-being, pleasure, and love. What earlier thinkers saw as death instincts, John Mills (2006), professor of psychology and psychoanalysis at Adler Graduate Professional School in Toronto, teaches as "restoring or reinstating a previous state of undifferentiated internal being." At core, any death or destructive instinct is a desire to experience our undifferentiated life force. Thus, any manifestations or symptoms of resistance to breathing emanate from the desire to thrive.

We are born from and are the sum total of what is, was, and can be. We contain Walt Whitman's multitudes. We contain becoming and letting go, creating and dissolving, and so much more. The mechanism that can consciously contain all these experiences and unite their functioning in service to our life is breathing.

Breathwork creates a thoroughfare for conscious functioning by requiring moment- by-moment, breath-by-breath choice. We volitionally gather our life force with every breath and invest it in care and development.

Now we can emerge into the next evolutionary opening—let us consider Receiving Breathing and then partnering it before volitional Breathwork as we did in Chapter 7.... If we are receiving breathing... if we are being breathed... we would not trigger the phobic stir as when we choose to "take" a deep breath (even if we love taking a deep breath!). Thus, we would not have to overcome the inertia of attraction to sedentary behavior by "taking charge" of the breathing. *Breathing would get deeper by being breathed.* Then we can initiate our choosing (effort) energy to join the effortlessness breathing—we partner Receiving Breathing. Now our unconditioned self is breathing. This is authentic breathing that will accompany us to wholeness.

By maintaining their own daily breathing practice, Therapist-Breathworkers can transmit energetic fields of willingness to embrace the life urge. This strongly supports Breathees when they have fear or hesitance. Therapist-Breathworkers can invite the fear to breathe while expanding their field of attention. One way is to open their eyes if closed and close their eyes if open. Breathees who are reticent or inert can be encouraged to physically move. Conscious breaths between any verbalizing can tip the scales in favor of the life instinct.

It's paramount for Therapist-Breathworkers to regard all manifestations of Breathees as containing inherent and valuable wisdom about what they need for thriving. It is incumbent upon Therapist-Breathworkers to mirror an environment of unconditional love and possibility. Our goal in Breathwork, therapy, and life should always be to nourish life force. There's a delicate balance between not trespassing on that precious domain and "tilling the Soul" (Paine, 1984)—gardening organically and working *with* the *prima materia*, not against nor trying to tame it. CB is an excellent matrix and architect for this metamorphosis. We should engage in rigorous self-practice and training to become worthy caretakers of the life urge in ourselves and those with whom we breathe.

When I was 17, I had an experience that imprinted my soma and psyche with the powerful alignment when life force's intelligence meets an optimal and attuned environment. To this day I am taught by the priceless memory. I was in a group traveling towards Badrinath temple, 10,170 feet into the Himalayas. The winding, exhilarating and terrifying one-and-a-half lane dirt road dropped straight down the mountain on one side, and straight into the fortress-like mountain contours on the other. We paused halfway up the mountain to practice Pranayama while immersed in near-frozen glacial water, and arrived at Badrinath's summit close to sundown.

Almost everyone shed joyous tears upon discovering we each had a wooden platform bed with three outrageously thick wool blankets. We wanted to burrow ourselves under those blankets without emerging. Yet, our teacher urged us to move toward the temple and central hot spring that steamed like Yellowstone's "Old Faithful." It gave one marked pause to consider getting close.

I watched one of our companion's life force revealed in all its splendor as she moved with uncharacteristic speed and grace toward the hot springs, shedding the heavy shawls atop her sari like a romantic slow-motion scene from a movie. Without hesitation—without testing the water—she slipped her entire body into the steaming hot waters, as if dropping onto the most comfortable cloud-like mattress on the planet. The rest of us took anywhere from five to 20 minutes to work our bodies into this extremely hot pool. This land was novel terrain for all of us, yet the life force within her body knew that those particular waters were a safe, healing sanctuary that would relieve her arthritis. When her needs were met by the environment, it was safe to let her life force lead.

I have never forgotten this testimony of our life instinct's brilliance and beauty. Often viewed by others as plain-looking and clumsy, she became radiantly beautiful and nimble instantaneously. We might never have seen who and what she could reveal, who she truly was at her core. I am forever inspired to become an attuned environment for each Breathee's life force, to honor the wisdom of the authentic life urge within their ways of being.

Authentic Self

Something is experiencing the life force in our unique human bodies each moment. What, or who, is it? Traditionally we call it the self—usually *my*self. This is a dubious nomenclature, as it implies ownership of the self, when we have seen that the self is *inter*connected and *intra*connected with all. Still, it does seem to be the piece of the universal garden that each of us is given to cultivate. Whatever *it* is, it is drawn to experience love, value, and meaning, and comes into life wired to do so. And whatever *it* is, it has been in motion since its inception—growing, developing, emerging.

Eastern views tell us that if inner and outer conditions remained optimal throughout our lives, we would retain awareness of our original authentic being—the *true self*. As this is rarely the case, most of us lose that awareness. We have a path to finding *it* again through practice and orienting toward the origin of all things, going into a center that is incorruptible. When the true self contacts the suffering and trauma of our lives, our pain is held by a wiser awareness that can transcend and transmute those conditions. Western views tell us we can build a *self* that is whole and creative out of the raw material we are given to work with, or we can heal and grow from suboptimal or traumatic conditions and build our authentic self anew. Both views have a perception of an *ego*, and both recognize self-development and self-actualization as good.

In the increasing thirst for personal healing and growth, these orientations are merging, yet still collide, subtly to directly. West is absorbing the East, and East is being penetrated by the West, and more than ever people easily obtain exposure to varying views, such as self-determinism, surrender, ego as a bridge between spirit and human life, and ego as a fear-based defense that is maladaptive. We will benefit immensely if we orient toward this phenomenon from *a fundamental unity of even seemingly contrasting views and values*, and if we breathe with all of it.

Therapist-Breathworkers should become fluent in as many of these orientations as possible—not through a particular framework, but rather through presence itself. Through the lens of three-centered presence, we are much less likely to polarize, trigger, shame, marginalize, or perpetuate microaggressions. Nor will we circumvent the intelligence and creativity in Breathers in daily life or those who enter our Breathing rooms, bringing in fusions of ideas and experiences about themselves, ego, possibility, and the like.

The journey toward authentic self can support beneficence, community, cooperation, and cocreativity in the world, and solve some of the collective predicaments we face due to narcissism, inaction, and despair. Social change can transpire without psychological transformation of all involved. Yet to sustain and support future iterations of well-being, psychological transformation must either precede social revisioning or follow in its wake quickly enough to avoid backlash or regressive reactions. It is imperative that we forge a level of consciousness that can solve the problems we have created for each other and the planet since, as Einstein famously said, "We cannot solve our problems with the same thinking we used when we created them."

The authentic self and its capacities are much more nuanced than the paradigms of relaxation, relief, letting go, blissing out, and peak states that much of the Breathwork field lusts after or has settled for. While those results are improvements over the anxious, traumatized, disembodied, production-driven models of much of consensus reality, they obstruct full wholeness and consciousness.

The authentic self is a radiant emanation of essential life force, imbuing every conscious breath. It is an unadulterated expression of our core being, beneath the layers of conditioned concepts, trauma-driven defenses, and ego-driven behaviors. Through CB's potency, we can relax into the truth of our authentic self, discovering a wellspring of liberation, self-acceptance, and peace. The journey to the authentic self is a path of courage, compassion, and presence, guided by breathing wisdom, leading us to boundless dimensions of our being and the interconnectedness of all life.

In service to that work, I offer a brief guide to what we will likely meet along the journey to the authentic self through Breathwork—a journey with stages moving from fear-based, defended, and conditioned ego to authentic self. Breathers may enter at any point—from states of fear, pain, or ego defenses to a greater sense of possibilities for our authentic and awakened self.

Progress can be particularly accelerated through Group 5 Breathwork. We can expect a certain amount of unbidden back-and-forth movement between steps, stages, and stations on the journey to the true self. This seeming bouncing around is helpful. The more contracted states bring awareness about obscurations in our soma, psyche, and soul to our more expanded states—helping to potentiate nuanced and refined development of self and consciousness. The more expansive states provide enriched environments for the contracted places to explore new ways of being. Breathing becomes the reference rather than the state of contraction or expansion.

> *You don't know where you're goin'*
> *But you know you won't be back.*
> —BRUCE SPRINGSTEEN, "LAND OF HOPES AND DREAMS"

Authentic Breathing: Inauthentic Self to Authentic Self

The arc of breathing from inauthentic to authentic self, transforming inauthentic breathing to authentic breathing, takes us to the core and depths of our being and manifestations—from gnarly to luminous, and everything in between. Accompanying the whole journey with breathing awareness and Breathwork gives steady companionship, grounding, and guidance. We simultaneously hold the full spectrum of learning and perturbations of our human journey—healing, regulation, trauma, yearning, what is unexpressed, Essence and its boundless expressions—and the Plane of Possibility.

Ego first develops by utilizing our natural temperament and gifts to navigate our pain and fears in life—and to protect our gifts. Thus, ego is a creative attempt to support the authentic self. Yet, unexamined and unmet by awareness, this position begins to repress, obscure, divert, and squander our authentic life force and gifts.

Through self-exploration and CB, we can understand we are not the position which we have been taking ourselves to be. We can understand that when ego operates without our conscious awareness or presence, it functions as an image-making process that contains compensating behaviors to mitigate fear, loss, and suffering. We can then hold our ego's manifestations with insight and compassion for our fear, hopes, needs, and the mysteriousness of our existence. We can cultivate caring and curiosity about what the ego is trying to experience.

These tectonic adjustments of our psyche and sense of self free colossal amounts of energy within our somatic–emotional–cognitive continuum (SEC continuum) which can now tend to a more real self and its endowment of gifts. The journey toward the real self is propelled forward, and we may begin to have a felt sense, cellular memory, or vision of the Plane of Possibility. This realization accelerates our growth from fear-based boundaries to authentic boundaries and embodied boundlessness during the Breathwork journey and in life.

To give an example of the development that can occur, let's take the desirable qualities of joy and fulfillment. Initially we might—because of depression, repression during childhood, or personal or collective trauma, for instance—be unable to sense or feel real sensations and facets of joy. Therapeutic processes could aid us in recognizing some moments of pleasure or satisfaction—and learning how to make choices that align with these new feelings. We discover more joyful moments—eventually connecting those moments together for longer durations of joy. As therapy continues, we can develop a healthier ego that can sense and discern what does and doesn't make us happy. We learn to advocate for our well-being and happiness in nontoxic, life-enhancing ways. Relationally, we become more interested in whether our contact with others supports their contact with joy. We may breathe deeply to relax when tense, feel when numb, and let go when consternated. We can open to joy through breathing. This is great progress, yet joy is still conditional, dependent upon internal and external conditions being arranged such that dopamine is released.

The next level toward wholeness engages archetypal joy. We more readily recognize symbols and stories that represent the potential and presence of joy. Curiosity deepens about how joyousness contributes to the overall fabric of our life and collective life. We begin sensing the inherent joy in breathing—like we can feel breathing's joy.

When we open to boundless states, which includes contact with infinite depth, we begin recognizing that joy is an inherent quality of existence. That we exist is joyful. Joy is present whatever the conditions, so our experience of joy is not dependent on particular conditions. Joy is causeless. Symbols of joy are no longer needed, though they are enjoyed. We experience joy as intrinsic, with each moment infused with generativity and possibilities. This pervasive joy liberates us from limiting stories of who we are or what life is. Joy is an ever-present stream of unconditional buoyancy and positivity in us and in others. Breathing is a constant conduit for the presence of joy.

Experiences of pure consciousness may emerge, in which we no longer feel need or desire for joy, even as a universal quality. We experience the okayness, and even beauty, of a life and universe if joy didn't exist. We become porous and available to emergent potentials in reality, without fixity or adherence. This is an ultimate freedom of our life force and the life force of creation. We do not fear entrapment or lack, nor do we compensate with an effortful drive toward spontaneity and expression. Our very being is a transmission of freedom, creativity, and vision which we feel joy and gratitude for experiencing.

> look at me
> i am not a separate woman
> i am a continuance
> of blue sky
> i am the throat
> of the mountains
> a night wind
> who burns
> with every breath
> she takes
>
> —JOY HARJO

The Partnership of Boundaries and Boundlessness

The wedding between healthy boundaries and boundlessness is a wondrously exciting, at times arduous, of personal and collective human potential. The boundary/boundlessness communion is profoundly integrating. Because perceptual orientations about boundaries and boundlessness often collide, it's worth intensifying our examination of this crucial, seeming conundrum. Together, the three transformational pathways—healing, development, and essence (Chapter 9)—and the spectrum of boundaries to boundlessness is a comprehensive matrix for authenticity. Therapist-Breathworkers can be guides for this landscape if they do their own exploration first and continuously.

I developed the Plane of Possibility Practitioners Presence Process (the 5P Process) to enable Therapist-Breathworkers to be present to the physical-emotional-cognitive content in themselves and Breathees without reactivity, and with compassion and heightened ability to engage all their resources. It invokes a medium for presence with boundaries and boundlessness in every moment. The process incorporates many elements of transformative psychotherapy and Breathwork sessions that we explore in this book. It provides support for the life urge, enhanced unconditional positive regard, eye contact and mirroring, the boundless qualities, spiritual experiences, and transference and countertransference, while building and ensuring healthy boundaries and integrating expanded states into grounded living and connectedness. This practice can also be used by all Breathers in their interactions with others. It is presented here in the way it is learned at Inspiration Consciousness School. We are invited to practice it together right now.

Plane of Possibility Practitioners Presence Process (the 5P Process)

> *To Love you deeply and well is to choose the vision of my soul that can never fail to see your deepest longings.*
> —HUGH PRATHER

1. **Receive Breathing.** We soften and open to its sensations ... the great vitality it makes possible in each moment ... its emotional invitation, the way it touches us ... the awareness it opens ... the widening vision it gives rise to.
2. **Inhabit our bodily sensations as completely as we can.** Be here. There is nowhere else to be. Here is where life and love are possible. With each breath, we inhabit the sensations of our body, and do not leave them.
3. **We embrace our unconditional nature without hesitation or argument. We see ourself as Presence or the Divine sees us, and we do not waver. We are that.** To the best of our ability, we immediately contact and say yes to the most whole sense of ourselves we have ever experienced. This step is about not arguing, wavering, or doubting that experience and truth. With determination and steadfastness, we remain present with the potential our essential wholeness.

4. ***Within that experience, we cultivate a willingness to become aware of any relative conditions that may still exist within us, without aversion, judgment, attachment, or fear.*** Understanding this step is pivotal for the Therapist-Breathworker's mastery in creating an enhanced field of unconditional positive regard that can meet the temperaments, challenging narratives, contractions, defenses, compensations, object relations, hurts, Parts, attachment styles, traumas, psychological distress, addictions, and unhealthy habits of ourselves with awareness, compassion, and dynamic creativity. We practice this step with the following awareness:

   a. *This step arises out of the first three steps. Otherwise, we reinforce our normal response to our emotional states and behaviors. We can return to the first three steps to ensure we are firmly inhabiting them while engaged with this step.*

   b. *Relative conditions meaning: Our unconditional nature is like the nature component of us, our natural temperament, who we are and our potential. Our relative conditions are a product of the quality of nurturance from within ourselves, caregivers, and life, and the way that our temperament meets that nurturance and forms personality. Relative conditions could include things like feeling insufficient, unlovable, unworthy, defective, undeserving, angry, resentful, and so on. They also encompass situational challenges such as grieving loss, feeling disappointed, being affected by criticism, having health issues, trauma, and so on.*

   c. *We are cultivating a state of being where we are willing to be aware of these relative conditions without needing to identify a particular one. We are developing a heart and capacities strong and aware enough to hold both our wholeness and our limiting manifestations, and we are able to choose whether or not to engage with a particular relative condition.*

   d. *The four orientations of aversion, judgment, attachment, or fear can be said in any order silently or aloud. It's beneficial to consciously change the order each time to bring fresh recognition to each orientation. Buddhism describes these states as specific obstacles to our natural state of being and development of the* true self. Aversion is a reaction of strong dislike, hatred, or hostility that causes us to retreat from being present with a particular person, place, or situation. Judgment is the comparison of something or someone to something or someone we deem preferable, which generates distance and lessens contact. The term attachment here is different from the positive attachment that we want to form with our caregivers early in life and our loved ones later in life. Here, attachment is the tendency to overidentify with, or depend on, our connection with a person, place, or thing as crucial to our well-being—to the point where we feel we will be crippled or in too much pain without it. This can lead to possessiveness and codependency. Fear is contraction and mistrust that our authentic life force can meet each situation and person. It engenders anxiety that can be specific, such as "I am not up to this," or it can be free-floating and attach to any internal or external symbol consciously or unconsciously. All four of these orientations result in putting ourselves out of our hearts and disconnecting from the potency of love and awareness.

e. Using the word *may* is intentional and critical. Science increasingly provides evidence that our unspoken feelings and thoughts affect others. Thus, a great gift we can give to ourselves and others is not to assume that we are functioning within distortions, defenses, and behavior patterns from the past, even if we were 10 minutes ago. If we or someone is functioning from a highly integrated state in that moment, assumptive thoughts about how they were are not supportive. Our inner critic tells us to collapse, withdraw, or berate ourselves about our sensitivities and foibles, and that if we look at them from a beginner's mind we will stop being vigilant and hurt someone. However, if we are present and contacting the Plane of Possibility in our orientations toward ourselves and others, our hippocampal circuits will remember past behaviors, yet will be open to the possibility of change having occurred.

5. **We become aware of the other.** We might have thought that we were meeting others with awareness. This step invites us to be aware of

others from our wholeness, less predicated on what others think of us, or who we think we might need to be for them. We can be present with someone with innocence, authenticity, and curiosity—able to meet them without previous stories about them or who we are in relationship to them. We are not ignoring useful information. From integrated presence we are able to utilize embedded information about another in ways less subject to our judgments, emotional reactions, and countertransference. We are able to be more contactful, compassionate, objective, discerning, and highly creative in responding.

6. **We embrace the other's unconditional nature, without hesitation or argument. We see them as Presence or the Divine sees them, and we do not waver. They are that.** This step is the mirror of what we have established with ourselves in Step 3—being offered to the other—to begin a relational field that is more connected to the Plane of Possibility, the place where breathing becomes the dynamism of awareness of awareness.

7. **Within that experience, we cultivate a willingness to become aware of any relative conditions that may still exist within them without judgment, fear, attachment, or aversion.** This is the mirror of Step 4 with ourselves, now applied to the relational field. It enhances our capacity to be compassionate, objective, and creatively responsive to the relative conditions of others. The possibility of unconscious or highly reactive countertransference is now greatly reduced. Any countertransference we experience would be infused with a wellspring of tolerance, understanding, and insight... and an ability to hold ourselves with loving-kindness and boundaries until we can work with it. This step is very helpful for Therapist-Breathworker's creating an enhanced field of unconditional positive regard that is able to meet the temperaments, challenging narratives, contractions, defenses, compensations, object relations, hurts, Parts, attachment styles, traumas, psychological distress, addictions, and unhealthy habits of Breathees with compassion, awareness, and dynamic creativity. This generative, creative, and sometimes miraculous state brings novel possibilities for therapeutic processes.

8. **We generate and offer an exquisite energetic contact to the other, so**

intimate that they cannot help but feel a benevolent presence and support from us ... so without pressure they are not in any way tempted to alter, hide, or protect their authentic self and essential nature. Authentic healthy intimacy is precious and challenging to actualize in any relationship due to unmet childhood needs, trauma, codependency patterns, and the like. Therapist-Breathworkers can provide an extraordinary field of enhanced positive regard and responsive emergent creativity, and model healthy corrective relational experiences with Breathees so they can move outside of the healing room with more relational skills. To learn to be absolutely present with another human being in a way that does not trigger their defensiveness, to open a field of undefended love, is an art that requires patience, perseverance, authenticity, participation, and a willingness to live in the unknown. I developed this step from studying in the school of Tai Chi Chuan founded by Cheng Man-Ch'ing. After several years of studying the central form, we were trained in *push hands*—meeting force with chi. One of the first lessons is learning to hold a rose petal between our hands and the hands of a friend or enemy with whom we are engaging and moving, without in any way crushing the rose petal. And, Tai Chi emphasizes breathing! It was a remarkable awakening for me of what could be possible between human beings. It allows for both power and relaxed receptivity. It allows for firmness and maximal flexibility. It invites life force and wisdom in relationship. In that tradition they call the holding of the rose petal *four ounces of pressure* (Gorman, 1995). In the 5P Process, I call it *exquisite energetic contact* and conceive of it as *contact without pressure*. Our practitioners are trained numerous times to hold rose petals with many different people, and it transforms their life and practitionership. During training, we generate exquisite contact with others numerous times in silence, while dialoguing, sometimes without touch, sometimes with touch. During formal Breathwork, energetic exquisite contact is offered silently and energetically as there is already an explicit agreement to work together. And in any case, we are *offering* it, not assuming it is wanted. If we wish, we can ask permission to do this before the session. Exquisite contact is continually recalibrated throughout a Breathwork session.

9. *We allow ourselves to become aware of a relative condition within this person that, if it were responded to, would support enhanced healing and wholeness.* Some facilitators are so intuitive that much of their facilitation training happens experientially while working with Breathees, and innovative applications and interventions can arise. Yet Step 9 also presupposes substantive psychodynamic and Breathwork skills training. Awareness of what relative condition could be addressed can emerge from what is being shared through words, body language, emotions, dreams, images, and so forth. It can also emerge through awareness about Breathees' breathing mechanics and energetic transmission.
10. *We allow ourselves to perceive of a skill that could be applied to this relative condition to support healing and transformation.* In addition to skills and innovative applications arising intuitively during sessions, Step 10 also presupposes substantive psychodynamic and Breathwork skills training, Awareness of what skill could be useful will be guided by the content of what is being shared through words, body language, emotions, dreams, images, and so on; awareness of the breathing's physical mechanics and energetic transmission.
11. *We apply this skill or process.* This is a self-evident instruction, and this is a good time to revisit all the steps and reaffirm them, so that we are exquisitely attuned to the Breathee during the process.
12. *Throughout the session, we remain aware of how the skills and processes impact Breathees. We keep calibrating all prior steps, and add or change skills as guided (Chapter 9).* We use any of the skills we have learned about in Chapters 3 and 6 through 11.
13. *As the session concludes, we ensure Breathees have consciously experienced the transformational sensations from the session, contact with how their hearts are affected, and awareness of changing perceptions about self or life. We invite them to breathe deeply with this awareness while moving from the session to what's next.* We can use the questions in Chapter 9 for contacting the three centers of energy flow.
14. *We see them as whole; see ourselves as whole; see both of us as Presence or the Divine sees us.* We are combining Steps 3 and 6 here,

which we were already practicing by step 6, and this is an excellent culminating step.
15. *After they've departed, we breathe deeply for one or more minutes. We remind ourselves that life force and awareness was the healer; we do not own the session or the results of the session. We offer gratitude for being able to participate and contribute.*

Each stage can be practiced from 5 seconds to 5 or 10 minutes, or longer before and during sessions. Initially, we practice 3 to 5 minutes per step, lengthening particular stages as needed. It can be both exhilarating—as we practice experiencing our most present self in a field of relatedness and service, and extremely challenging—as it prompts and challenges us to relinquish habits of distraction, sense of separation, and our most cherished defense mechanisms rather immediately.

What follows is a prayer I have offered after each session or class over the last 25 years. I have never taught it, and rarely share it. In sharing it now, I pray it will be of use.

Creation, whatever I have or have not done inadvertently that may have caused harm to [Breathee's name] or diverted them in any way from their awakening, please let it be lifted and fall away from them now. Whatever they have experienced that has benefited them and contributed to their awakening, may they now receive all the inner and outer guidance needed to know it is real and to embody it in every breath.

In the end, it all comes down to the art of breathing.
—MARTHA GRAHAM

FOURTEEN

Breathing Expanded States of Consciousness

Why want to eat the forbidden fruit to gain knowledge, instead of cultivating one's own breath? Breathing itself invites to an awakening, and the divine knowledge is within me.

—LUCE IRIGARAY, *KEY WRITINGS*

How exciting and crucial to know that Breathwork can elicit expanded states of consciousness easily and readily. Moreover, the genre of expanded consciousness states that we often describe as intuitive, transpersonal, spiritual, or mystical are prevalent in all forms of Breathwork, with particularly profound experiences of these states arising during Human Potential Breathwork. Here we explore some key components of these journeys. It is essential for Therapist-Breathworkers to cultivate understanding of these trajectories and how to steward them skillfully and respectfully. *Indeed, in Breathwork sessions, spiritual and intuitive experiences may become cofacilitators.*

Breathing Expanded Intuition

Conscious Breathing (CB) engenders greater interoceptive awareness, which supports the amplification of intuition or inner guidance. Intuition figures prominently in Group 5 Breathwork. Additionally, many Breathees appreciate and want to cultivating their intuition. Therefore, it is incumbent upon Therapist-Breathworkers to support Breathees in utilizing intuition phenomena for their growth.

Intuition is commonly understood as a form of direct, instinctive knowing. Science points to various regions of the brain involved in intuition, the complex interplay between the neural and enteric brains in *gut feelings* and *conscious insight*, as well as the role of *heart coherence* in accessing intuitive information.

Dr. Terry Marks-Tarlow, a clinical psychologist, observes, "no matter what their modality, all clinicians tend to use clinical intuition as a non-specific mode of perception and response during the actual practice of psychotherapy" (2012). Skillfully navigating intuition is critical in the therapeutic space. Clinical intuition bridges theory and practice, attunes therapists to relational dynamics, and facilitates deep change.

Because Breathwork can open floodgates of intuitive and transpersonal experiences, Therapist-Breathworkers must be versed in discerning genuine intuitive wisdom from fantasy, projection, delusion, or unintegrated material. Grounding intuitive work within a rational framework and relational containment is essential and a part of real intuition, which takes into account all aspects of reality.

COMPONENTS OF WHOLE INTUITION

Science and technology are beginning to demonstrate the reality of mind-to-mind communication and the *innernet* of connected consciousness, which may underlie intuitive processes. Empirical evidence suggests that thoughts can be transmitted between individuals across great distances with surprising accuracy, indicating that global energy fields facilitate neural coherence. Intuition may operate through these subtle fields of shared awareness.

Global neural coherence, which involves engaging both right- and left-brain hemispheres, is critical for integrating intuitive and rational ways of knowing. Examples from the work of psychologist Milton Erickson illustrate how this whole-brain approach operates in therapeutic and professional contexts, yielding practical wisdom and creative breakthroughs. The common emphasis on right-brain dominance in intuition may be overcompensating for the cultural marginalization of emotional and intuitive intelligence. True intuitive wisdom arises not from one hemisphere but from a dynamic synthesis of both.

Radical self-honesty prevents intuition from being hijacked by unconscious fears, desires, and agendas. We must be willing to continually examine our motivations and blind spots if we are to be clear vessels for authentic knowing. Fearlessness enables us to open to challenging intuitive guidance and also sit with the discomfort of not-knowing.

Intuition is not a rare talent or special power, but a natural capacity that can be developed through committed practice. By cultivating presence, self-honesty, courage, flexibility, and the integration of somatic, emotional, and cognitive intelligence, we can tap into the wisdom of the *innernet* and become skillful agents of personal and collective intuition. We access a profound source of creativity, insight, and compassionate action in service to the wholeness of all.

Three-centered intuition opens and integrates information delivered through somatic, emotional, and cognitive pathways. Missing any of the three pathways will direct us into cul-de-sacs of meaning or keep us confined to a limited reality. Let's open understanding for each of the three pathways. Then we'll engage in Breathing Practices to contact these pathways.

SOMATIC INTUITION

Fundamental to all bodily functions is the ability to receive sensations, impressions, sounds, and nutrients. We can love, work, and create because of what we take in—receive. One way we receive information is through the gut—the enteric brain.

The more willingly present we are to our interoceptive and exteroceptive sensations, the more we can be guided by these sensations to receive invisible information to guide us, and to heal ourselves and others. When we experience *gut feelings*, it is usually in the form of *yes* or *no*, moving toward something or away from something, from what we feel is good or bad for us, right or wrong. Nonhuman animals are known for feeling in their bodies when earthquakes and tsunamis are about to happen, and many human animals have these capacities without knowing it. Some Breathers with strong somatic intuition can even mirror precise mannerisms of people they focus on, without ever having met them.

CB and Breathwork are direct routes to somatic intelligence, creating space within which we develop trust in the body's receptive wisdom. We may be very still in the transmission process, as if listening for the drop of a pin. Or we may open into wild, uninhibited movement as the information is received. We can also allow voice, imagery, song, chanting, toning, and language to be expressed directly from the sensations and breathing.

HEART INTUITION

Heart center intelligence is more encompassing than attraction, feeling personal love or connection, being drawn to or repelled by something or someone, and even empathy and compassion. It is most frequently facilitated through unconditional love or empathic caring and attunement. Broadly, it comprises precognitive feelings of what can or will be occurring emotionally in human and nonhuman animals and events, and also *tuning in* to what is unsaid, desired, or invisible. The more we have developed the ability to meet the vicissitudes of life with equanimity, the more objective heart intelligence will emerge. As psychologist John Welwood said, this "intimate, grounded kind of inner attunement with ourselves ... can help us more easily relate to others where they are stuck as well" (Fossella & Welwood, 2011).

The primary conduit to heart intuition is love—a deep desire for beings to be relieved of suffering and experience the goodness of life. Awakened heart intuition lands us in the plane of unconditional love, therefore the Plane of Possibility. In an energetic field of unconditional compassion, coupled with a stable heart of equanimity, we can perceive what actions can lead to well-being and joy. One poignant route into heart intuition is through intimate connection with a loved one from our past, present, or future, including relatives and ancestors who have died.

Rollin McCraty and the HeartMath institute have demonstrated that

CB, when focused on the heart with a positive feeling of appreciation, can induce physiological coherence that resonates with a frequency shared by others around the world, and the planet itself. It can open us to unseen emotional information (McCraty et al., 2009). Further, they found that heart rate often decelerates five seconds before a significant event. The stronger the emotional response the event will elicit, the more dramatically the heart rate slows down (McCraty et al., 2004).

When Therapist-Breathworkers are emotionally honest and refrain from merging with Breathees or their journey, when we relax into loving connection and kindness, we will be surprised at the wisdom and words that may flow from empathic accuracy and support others to heal, find their way, and feel empowered in their purpose.

INSIGHT INTUITION

Curiosity, intention, focus, and quiet, expanded, receptive awareness are each fertile ground for experiences of insight and direct knowing. Objective truth, insight, guidance, or *higher wisdom* most frequently arises as images, symbols, dreams, and words or numbers that are heard or seen. It may also emerge as a direct energetic knowing without words or images from the vastness of an inner space that reflects the infinite nature of outer space. Direct knowing can open a portal of knowledge or creativity that is instantaneous. Steven Edwards points out that Roberto Assagioli and Carl Jung described intuitive insight as "the immediate total sense of the object as a whole" (Edwards, 2014).

Consciously cultivated stamina and the ability to breathe with awareness the moment insights emerge are both needed to stabilize intuitive insights in a way that is useful to others and not harmful to our life force. Even when we cannot influence outcomes, our knowing, feeling, and speaking what we know may have some effect. Though the insight may not directly lead to change, expressing it aloud may have a positive impact on the situation as well as contribute to the growth of our intuitive capacities. Remaining true to a vision that seems impossible may stretch our capacity and can lead to initiations into higher-order thinking and perception.

INTEGRATED (THREE-CENTERED) INTUITION

Cultivating integrated intuition involves consciously receiving and breathing with information from all three centers of energy flow and intelligence—the SEC continuum. Checking our intuitive hunches with all three centers before acting on them may initially feel cumbersome, yet developing a refined sensitivity to integrated truth is worth the effort. Consulting all three centers, along with rational discernment and community input, allows our intuitive knowing to metamorphose into enduring wisdom.

The holistic veracity of intuition for all Breathers will be more robustly enhanced and vetted when ethics, moral conscience, and examination of what is being accessed and its implications are being held with a Therapist-Breathworker and, hopefully, a peer group of *intuinauts*. *Breathees who want to use intuition in a consistent way should be encouraged to regularly practice consciously breathing with their intuition.* Rigorous training in intuition development and ethics is available to prevent harm to self or others. Becoming inflated or derailed by intuitive experiences or using intuition to bypass the hard work of development are pitfalls to avoid. Therapist-Breathworkers who are in the early years of offering Breathwork for healing and transformation may experience strong, and sometimes mesmerizing intuitive hunches about Breathees. In these cases, it's wise for Therapist-Breathworkers to seek supervision, and also work ongoingly with a peer group of *intuinauts*.

BREATHING PRACTICES FOR INTEGRATED INTUITION

Any practice that amplifies physical, emotional, and cognitive receptivity, fosters imaginal development, or awakens ability to sense energy, aids intuition. Breathing Practices that steer us toward inner quiet, spaciousness, and awareness help, as do practices supporting internal visualizing. CB is a critical component of these practices. Form and Formless Communion Breathing, Enhanced Focus Breathing, and Embodied Novelty Breathing (all in Chapter 7) are excellent practices for opening, developing, and strengthening intuition. For up-to-date intuition about each situation, we must enter a flow of emergence and dynamism, which may also feel uncomfortably still and spacious until we become familiar with it.

SOMATIC INTUITION BREATHING PRACTICE

1. We establish a breathing pattern, if possible through the nose, that feels resonant with our state of being.
2. We direct attention to sensations (anywhere in the body) produced by breathing.
3. The sensations are not just static, they are part of the dynamism of breathing. We begin to tune into the momentum within the sensations. The more we tune into the momentum, the more intensity we are likely to experience. Each inhalation can be utilized to meet the full impact of the momentum. With each relaxed exhalation, we can integrate the increased energy. At some points we may feel guided to breathe through our mouths when contacting somatic energy and intelligence.
4. When awareness of the energy has reached a peak, matching, if not exceeding, our prior experience of practice, we direct our attention to our feet and where they contact the ground, chair, mat, and so on. We experience our capacity to be grounded while contacting this level of energy.
5. Advanced: Once we firmly establish Step 4, we allow the momentum to move our bodies. The movements should be slow, deliberate, and constantly connected to our breathing and feet. If we continue, it is likely that our movements will enter a flow state. When we are done practicing, we sit quietly doing Matrika Pranayama for 2 minutes or longer.
6. Somatic Inquiry Practice: Using the sensations of wholeness with which we have become more familiar, we breathe a choice we need to make into those sensations. Breathing deeply, we spend time discerning if the first option relaxes into us and can merge resonantly with the wholeness. We can then breathe alternative decisions in, doing the same, and then comparing the two, three, or more.

HEART-CENTERED INTUITION BREATHING PRACTICE

1. We receive breathing and invite it to breathe as slowly and deeply as possible, while we release hesitance to being breathed.
2. With each inhale, we bring attention to the center of our chest. With each exhale, we soften our chest, releasing tension and armoring—as if our chest is melting. We can cup one or both hands over the center of our chest with respect for our heart—our emotional center—and invite a feeling of our chest melting into our hands to be held. We can also inhale our experiences of loving, being loved, and being love, cherish them in our chest, and exhale the sweetness of love and cherishing to flow into the world.
3. We invite ourselves to recall somatic, emotional, cognitive, and spiritual experiences of the most love we've ever felt or feel for someone—breathing deeply and fully. Eventually, we let go of the person as the source of love, and simply breathe the quality of love.
4. We can also call up the most love we've ever felt or feel for ourselves, then let go of any story or memory and just connect with the quality of love.
5. This is great preparation for the following inquiry practice.

HEART-CENTERED BREATHING INQUIRY

1. We receive breathing into our capacity for well-being. We note the somatic signatures of our well-being and any images or cognitive orientations that arise. We continue breathing deeply and cultivating a sense of wholeness that does not require anything from a particular person or situation.
2. Having established unconditional love in our preparation practice, and wholeness in ourselves, we allow our hearts to feel the intrinsic value of anyone involved in the inquiry. We see them so resourced and supported that the radiance and gifts that dwell within them could flow into our world—whether or not we personally receive their gifts.

3. While breathing extraordinarily softly, deeply, and slowly, we allow our hearts to open to any impressions about what could support this Breather's well-being in general or in a particular situation.

INTUITIVE INSIGHT BREATHING PRACTICE

1. We receive breathing through our whole body and then bring attention to our heads, aware of how each breath is energizing our brain. We can imagine or visualize energy from our breathing moving right to the center of our head like a laser beam, and then expanding as a light that illuminates our entire head space.
2. Since we know that the mind and awareness are embodied relational flows of energy and information, and through CB we can sense the relational field between ourselves, others, and life, we can extrapolate that knowing is bigger than what we are consciously aware of. As breathing illuminates the brain and awareness, it also illuminates our relatedness. And we are in relationship with everything. We are in relationship with infinity! And things that are illuminated can be seen. Thus, theoretically, everything in infinity can be seen and known. We can breathe with this awareness for a while. This is the building and preparation phase.
3. If we wish to access information and guidance, we formulate a question in words or an image and place it in the space of infinite awareness where all is held and all is known.
4. We continue receiving breathing, sitting in silence and receiving whatever response arises. Responses may come in images, words, sounds, music, geometric shapes, numbers, scents, or direct knowing.
5. Wisdom, guidance, and intuition, like all dynamic phenomena, are emergent, so it is recommended that we breathe for some time with whatever is arising, as it may morph and reveal more nuanced layers.
6. Deep embodied breathing becomes a medium for carrying this information into our day, working with whatever fears may arise, and generating somatic alignment for any needed actions.

It is beneficial to keep a journal of the experiences from our intuition practices, any guidance and in what form—and, if we follow the guidance, what the result is, what we learn, and how the quality of our decisions and life is enhanced.

As African Indigenous healers practice *breathing is the unifying initiator, healer, teacher, and guide when it comes to intuition* (Edwards, 2014). We simply cannot become imbalanced with gut, heart, or cognitive intuition if we consciously breathe to access the information from all three centers and combine it with rational understanding and community support and challenge. With integrated intuition through breathing, partial or fixated views dissolve, a 360-degree view opens, and we relax into the unknowing that leads to all knowing. We will know what we need to know, when we need to know it, about past, present, and future, choices, relationships, and the collective.

> *Breath, you invisible poem —*
> *pure exchange, sister to silence,*
> *being and its counterbalance,*
> *rhythm wherein I become.*
>
> —DON PATERSON, "BREATH, AFTER RILKE"

Psychedelics and Breathwork

With the robust resurgence, in the twenty-first century, of psychedelic research and use for therapeutic benefit and experiencing expanded consciousness, explorations of the comparisons and potential relatedness of Breathwork and psychedelics are rapidly accelerating. Let's survey a bit of what we can learn about the similarities and differences.

Countless people have used religious rituals, spiritual practices, fasting, meditation, sexuality, sound, and natural and synthetic chemicals to experience altered states of consciousness. Many have reported spiritual awakenings through psychoactive substances. Recent studies with psilocybin, LSD, and other psychoactive substances have demonstrated improvement or cures for a wide range of mental and physical conditions, relief of suffering, and the emergence of positive states of mind.

I have reverence and gratitude for the gifts of plants and mushrooms—their nutrients, medicine, and expansive capacities. Plants can heal and shift consciousness in brethren plants, humans, and other animals. Indeed, the communication I feel from psychoactive plants is that they are consciously trying to help us to remember our true nature, that we can heal and be more than we think.

Similar to what I heard healer–botanist Stephen Buhner say, I feel that plants live in a field of unconditional love, that their root system is almost identical to the neurotransmitters of our nervous system, that they communicate to us energetically, and that they give selflessly to humanity. If it is correct that the plants, mushrooms, and mycelium are committed to supporting this planet and humanity, then we can acknowledge and be utterly grateful for the field of unconditional holding and love they bring to us. Plant medicines and all plants deserve for humanity to relate to them with care, consciousness, and stewardship. Additionally, with respect to humanity's potential to embody awakened consciousness, we should carefully consider the scope of possibilities and the limitations of what psychedelic journeys can yield for ourselves and for the plants.

And then there is Conscious Breathing (CB). Remembering our true nature can also occur within the ecosystem of our breathing and its connection with everything on earth. Expanded states of consciousness arise within our neural circuitry, biological processes, and relational field. These can be altered through CB, so theoretically we can stimulate any expanded state simply through CB. And unlike many other methods, CB has no adverse psychological side effects. Breathwork is also unique in that it may engender more enduring positive psychological changes because we continue to breathe every moment, as compared to other sources of altered states that may be ephemeral or that we cannot continue indefinitely.

SOME PSYCHEDELIC EXPLORERS AND CONSCIOUSNESS RESEARCHERS

Dr. Rick Strassman, a clinical associate professor of psychiatry at the University of New Mexico School of Medicine, studies the drug DMT (the psychoactive substance in ayahuasca), consciousness, and altered states. His groundbreaking research revealed to him that exogenous DMT amplifies our own personal material within our psyche.

When John Chavez, founder of DMT Quest, discovered that a few simple breaths through the nose could transport him to the same altered state as reports of exogenous DMT, he began studying endogenous DMT production through various methods including Breathwork. He shared with me that he believes that Breathwork can upregulate endogenous DMT to alleviate depression and promote overall health.

To compare the benefits and risks of psychedelics and Breathwork, we could hardly do better than the wisdom of the late Dr. Roland Griffiths, a leading expert in psilocybin research for depression, addiction, and occasioning mystical states—and a longtime Integrative Breathing student. His research showed that psilocybin can reliably induce mystical-type experiences. From his research experiences, Roland maintained that psychedelics should always be administered in clinically controlled settings, with careful medical and psychiatric screening and multidimensionally trained tradition-informed therapists, or with highly respected and experienced shamans, due to the potential dangers of precipitating psychotic disorders such as schizophrenia. He also strongly believed in the importance of integration methods that stabilized valuable insights that can emerge during psychedelic journeys, including therapeutic follow-up and Breathwork.

Because Group 5 Breathwork regularly elicits breakthrough and expanded consciousness experiences, comparing and contrasting it with the breakthrough and expanded consciousness experiences produced by psychedelics can yield useful findings. We hear about the similar breakthrough experiences. We hear less about experiences some longtime practitioners of Breathwork have reported, such as:

1. The consciousness shifts psychedelics induce aren't as enduring as the shifts from dedicated Breathwork practice, even though Breathwork may be slower.
2. Hallucinogens can *subtly bring down* the ongoing level and quality of awareness and consciousness and the refinement of mystical experiences.

3. Psychedelics create glimpses, visions, and changes, yet they often *scatter some of the subtle energetic substance* that accumulates through Breathing.

The broadened consciousness that psychedelics facilitate is characterized by greater spontaneity and less integration compared to everyday awareness (Schartner et al., 2017). Cultivating neural pathways to access these states through breath awareness and Breathwork could provide a means to tap into expanded consciousness in ordinary moments.

Leading researchers in psychedelics have developed ethical guidelines for entheogen use in clinical settings and protocols for psychedelic-assisted therapy. Some have expressed concern that claims about the efficacy of these treatments are possibly overblown. In 2022, 5 years after her revolutionary TEDx Oxford talk on the power of psychedelics, Dr. Rosalind Watts wrote, "If I could go back in time, I would not now be so foolish as to suggest that a synthesized capsule, by itself, can unlock depression. It takes a village, it takes community, it takes time." Perhaps when it comes to lasting therapeutic benefits, the most important aspect of a treatment is that it is delivered as part of a holistic therapy model.

MAPPING THE BENEFITS OF BREATHWORK AND PSYCHEDELIC EXPERIENCES

Many in psychedelic circles are exploring Breathwork as a modality that can produce extraordinary benefits without dangerous side effects or recovery time. Breathwork can meet and match the altered states of positive psychedelic experiences and regulate the nervous system so the experience may be better integrated (Bahi et al., 2024). Breathwork can be done much more frequently than psychedelics (in fact daily, in fact minute by minute!) without a toll on the body or brain. Finally, it is a powerful integration tool for all expanded states of consciousness, whatever other means have opened them.

While Breathers' life perspectives are often radically transformed by using psychedelics, we rarely maintain peak consciousness states because our body has not learned *how*. With Breathwork, our body is experiencing the awakened states of consciousness while we are breathing, and "neurons that fire together wire together" (Shatz, 1992). Also, during Breathwork, Breathers can consciously build healthy boundaries within boundless states. That is not always the case with entheogen experiences, especially when experimenting without the guidance of a skilled shaman, healer, teacher, or researcher. Even some Breathers with experience in Breathwork and spiritual practices have had previously unconscious material burst forth when taking psychedelics in a personal or recreational setting, causing harm to themselves or others.

Dr. Shirley Telles and I designed a "Breathing Room" protocol and applied it on two occasions, each time with a group of 60 people doing 15 minutes of yoga asanas and pranayama (Group 3), followed by 60 to 75 minutes of Integrative Breathing (Group 5). Over 90% of participants who had prior altered states of consciousness induced by psychedelics reported that Breathwork was as or more effective, particularly noting that, as one participant put it, "I'm able to integrate the experience into ordinary living right away."

BREATHWORK AND PSYCHEDELICS PARTNERSHIPS

The use of psychedelics pathway will continue to draw people, as many have found relief from the suffering of depression, addiction, and PTSD. Can Breathwork and plant medicine partner in healthy ways? Roland and I hoped so and envisioned many possibilities. Consider that breathing is an essential part of any psychedelic experience already and is more foundational to us. Here are accounts of a few practitioners who have partnered psychedelics and Breathwork with some success who spoke with me for this book.

Mark Huslage, a brain injury rehabilitation social worker, found that both psychedelics and Breathwork provided him with healing and profound wisdom. In a psilocybin study at Johns Hopkins University, he experienced mystical and healing journeys. Breathwork sessions at Inspiration Consciousness School, six months after his final psilocybin journey, brought Mark to the same places as his psychedelic experiences. Over years of Breathwork practice, he accessed similar healing, deep self-exploration, and mystical experiences. Breathwork allowed him to reenter and integrate the insights from his psychedelic experiences in a grounded and elevating way.

Kappy Laning, Inspiration trained, GPBA certified Breathworker never thought her practice would involve psychedelics until learning that 30–40% of her clients had tried them. She observed that her clients' psychedelic experiences often did not integrate well without Breathwork, as they left people ungrounded or with inaccessible insights. Breathwork helps them find their inner resources and process them in a conscious, embodied way.

Lauren Going is a psychotherapist who saw that talk therapy could help people who had experienced multiple traumas, yet she kept hitting a limit with them, which inspired her search for other modalities to complement traditional therapy. Of these, Breathwork felt the most personally powerful for her. She told me that it moved her "into accessing body and emotions where trauma and adverse experiences are stored and beyond the thinking analytical mind." Lauren has seen that while most people can use Breathwork to achieve nonordinary-state experiences, some with complex trauma and dissociation may initially benefit from a psychedelic experience to learn that such states are possible.

RECOMMENDATIONS FOR BREATHWORK AND PSYCHEDELICS

1. Precede psychedelic sessions with education, screening, counseling, and training in daily regulating breathing practices and at least one Group 5 Breathwork session, a few weeks prior to psychedelic sessions.
2. If Breathwork proves insufficient, make psychedelic interventions available in certified professional clinical settings that are also tradition-informed, or with highly respected, indigenously recognized shamans.
3. Follow up psychedelic sessions with counseling, integration techniques, daily regulating Breathing Practices, and one or more Group 5 Breathwork sessions.
4. Invest in research to discern the factors in Breathwork that reliably elicit expanded states of consciousness.

5. Create more multidisciplinary psychedelic trainings for healing professionals, with a strong emphasis on ethics.
6. Develop an Indigenous-led coalition to create guidelines for the ethical growth, distribution, and use of psychedelic plants, honoring their spiritual context and the wisdom of Indigenous caretakers.

CONSIDERATIONS AND DISCERNMENTS

In conversation with me, Rick Strassman noted, "I feel like what's lacking in the psychedelic community . . . is the desire or interest to work on one's intellect. To know. Because if you don't have the discernment, you could have a white light experience and then just open up to your own meaning of it."

In a class Roland Griffiths and I taught to Breathworkers he suggested that Therapists and/or Breathworkers in training not use entheogens:

> If you're beginning a meditation practice, and you really want to gain its fruits, then psychedelics are going to be a distraction—and worse, a kind of a temptation, because everyday meditation experiences may pale in comparison to acute and powerful psychedelic experiences. Meditation, and to a lesser extent Breathwork, often require repeated practice to understand and stabilize the nuances of awareness and practice. . . . I personally think there is wisdom in not mixing psychedelics and Breathwork, especially when in training.

Roland also warned that Breathers with high or borderline blood pressure should exercise caution as both psychedelics and Group 5 Breathwork can elevate blood pressure. For this reason, and many others, doing psychedelics and Group 5 Breathwork simultaneously is not advised. Dr. Pippa Wheble, UK physician, GPBA certified Breathworker, and representative of the International Breathwork Foundation's science and research group states, "Conscious Breathing cannot be practiced while under the influence of mind-altering substances, when it is not possible to be fully conscious. Where Breathwork is used in combination with plant medicine or other psychedelics, it is no longer conscious breathwork."

(R)EVOLUTIONARY VISIONS FOR HUMAN–PLANT RELATEDNESS

Perhaps, as we teeter on the brink of catalyzing unparalleled destruction, the mycelium, mushrooms, and psychoactive plants are making themselves more known, becoming even more available, to help us awaken in time to save the planet and all other species. What if they are revealing the power of their network to inspire us and nudge us toward mastering our own network of breathing, rather than having dominion over theirs? What if one purpose of these psychoactive plants and mushrooms, with their consciousness evolved within their own bodies, is as essential workers—to aid us in realizing that we can also do that within our bodies? What if, at core, they are inviting us, and hoping we will follow their guidance, to awaken to our full consciousness—self-sufficiently—through the breathing that we are given and the breathing that we share and exchange with plants, fungi, and the planet?

> *Plants have transformed the world into the reality of Breath*
> —EMANUELE COCCIA

Breathing Transpersonal, Spiritual, and Mystical Experiences

> *Breathwork, for me, is often a mystical experience. Each session is different but one common element might be called transcendence... an awareness of being in divine presence, the irrefutable knowledge of our interconnectedness, or an artistic expression of a spiritual reality.*
> —KAREN MILLER

Breathwork draws us to our origins and the mysteries of life. Whether we are atheists, agnostics, in a particular religion, on a spiritual path, or mystically inclined in general, the more we engage in Breathwork, the more likely we will encounter transpersonal, spiritual, and mystical dimensions. Spontaneous visions are not uncommon. Even those who thought they had life figured out may wonder anew about the nature of existence.

As we integrate these expanded awarenesses through Conscious Breathing, we often feel a visceral contact with a benevolence that can permeate every aspect of our lives. We may experience a sense of greater wisdom about our lives, and we may divine possibilities that seemed previously unimaginable. Many describe these experiences as *Essence, God, Goddess, the Divine, Creation,* or any name we use to convey something consciously generating, informing, and holding the fabric of existence.

There are many doorways to these realms for humans, probably as many as there are humans. Generally, the source and meaning of life can be experienced secularly through service and kindness, through unitive experiences, through accepting impermanence, through mystical experiences, and through science. Dan Siegel brilliantly ushers us into an infinite level of depth through science without using traditional *spiritual* language or concepts. Yet people from every spiritual tradition tell him that he is speaking the precise truth underlying everything they aspire to. In lectures, Dan has shared the term "G.O.D., the generator of diversity."

Whatever door we enter, there is a long history of invitations into the invisible dimensions of existence. Most prominently, those invitations come from faith traditions and mystical schools. Other examples are the inscription on the Temple of Apollo at Delphi, "know thyself"; Carl Jung's advocacy for the power of the imaginal; Rainer Maria Rilke's call for the undefended real; and Stan Grof's explication of Holotropic consciousness. Each has pointed out losses incurred by ignoring our inner, invisible dimensions. When our life choices and trajectories are based solely on external experiences, and we dismiss imagery, dreams, visions, and subtle dimensions, we are in great peril of never being fully expressed, awake, or fulfilled—let alone having access to the most replete wisdom. If we are fortunate, we may receive a level of sophisticated transpersonal, spiritual, and mystical guidance from early in our lives, even as early as birth.

As quoted in the book *The Teachers of Gurdjieff* by Raphael Lefort, a Sufi sheikh said:

> Do you know why a Sheikh breathes into the ear of a newly born child? Of course you do not! You put it down to magic, primitive symbols representing life, but the practical reasons, the deadly serious business of nourishing the inner consciousness, passes you by. (Matthiessen, 2008)

This level of complex and intricate understanding is, at least, an aspect of our potential—and our birthright. As we did in Chapter 5, let us pause, breathe deeply, and imagine how the quality of our personal and collective lives would be impacted if breathing was the first significant sound in our receptive newborn ears—and that our life was regularly interwoven with these kinds of initiations.

Mystical experiences are not an end unto themselves, nor are they something with which we should become fascinated or try to replicate. From the perspective of integration and self-actualization, mystical experiences can beget transformation of our sense of self, our capacity to love, and an ability to navigate life—all the while anchored in a larger view of reality in which everything is unified yet differentiated.

> *I had a profound Rebirthing Breathwork session, that's still with me 40 years later. I started taking conscious connected breaths. I could feel my old friend "resistance" in my consciousness but kept relaxing and breathing through it.*
>
> *My breath deepened, along with my consciousness. I wasn't actually breathing—I was being breathed. I was no longer "I" but was the breath. Then I was not the physical body, not the breath—I was everything, the blanket covering me, the mat I lay upon. There was no longer my Breathworker sitting there, no longer the room, only the connectedness and feeling I was part of everything and was everything.*
>
> *This became an overwhelming sense of love that permeated every part of my being and the experience. I was simply love—all the love in existence! The consciousness that was me now seemed to know, feel, and be everything. Just by thinking of something, I knew all about it, I knew the*

answer to everything was love, and no separation.

I experienced years, eons, going by. Stars were born and burned out and new stars born. After whatever time transpired, I felt I was returning to a self, but strangely didn't regret that—I understood I would always be a part of everything! (From Tom Rigler)

Rilke's words stand the test of time in his penetrating call to remember our most valuable treasure when he writes:

The experiences that are called "visions," the whole so-called "spirit-world," death, all those things that are so closely akin to us, have by daily parrying been so crowded out of life that the senses with which we could have grasped them are atrophied. To say nothing of God. (1954)

What Rilke calls "the most inexplicable . . . the whole so-called 'spirit world,'" frequently blossoms forth in Breathwork sessions. As we accept humanity's great thirst and need for contact with the transpersonal, and broaden the scope of our healing rooms, Therapist-Breathworkers may reconstellate ourselves as attendants to the mystery within each Breather.

Kabir says: Student, tell me, what is God?
He is the breath inside the breath.

—KABIR, *ECSTATIC POEMS*, TRANSLATED BY
ROBERT BLY

Is it possible for psychotherapeutic principles and methods to enhance and stabilize spiritual awakening without limiting it, without pathologizing transcendence, without pulling Breathers back from the plenum of heaven's and hell's initiations?

Psychotherapist Debra Flics talks about the interface between psychological well-being and the opening of spiritual experience in psychotherapy sessions:

For example, what a meditation teacher may call aversion, a Psychotherapist may see as self-hatred. What a meditation teacher may see as sloth, a Psychotherapist may recognize as depression. What a meditation teacher may see as restlessness, a Psychotherapist may see as anxiety or PTSD.... In optimal circumstances, the difficult emotions and experiences that have previously been unconscious emerge slowly and safely so the client can integrate them without becoming overwhelmed.... Having opened and healed many of our wounds in psychotherapy, we no longer use our defenses to shield us from our pain; without this armor against suffering, we become more responsive to the world around us. Now when we meditate, we see more clearly. We go deeper. (2021)

CAUTIONS

It is critical that Therapist-Breathworkers learn to discern between genuine spiritual development and mental health challenges and decompensation when helping Breathees navigate transcendent experiences. We must first be aware of spiritual bypassing, a dynamic identified by East-West psychologist John Welwood. Spiritual bypass induces inattention to, or avoidance of, psychological vulnerabilities, leading to inflation, abuse of power, ungrounded living, harm, or victimization. Spiritual bypass can also cause us to create or reinforce codependent relationships and suppress our autonomy, needs, views, and creativity.

Additionally, embedded unworthiness, deprivation, or abandonment stand a great chance of being softened, massaged, ameliorated, and healed in the presence of the ineffable. A cardinal caution for Therapist-Breathworkers and Breathees is to take note when either of us, through thought, word, or deed, begins to believe that we are the source of these experiences. This can lead to an intoxicatingly inflated identity. We can begin to chase after this experience as relentlessly as if it was an addictive substance.

Cultivating three-centered presence through CB can keep expansive emotions and visions from ensnaring us. When we emerge from transpersonal and mystical experiences, the next step should always be cultivating gratitude, humility, surrender, and an earnest endeavor to integrate the transformation for the alleviation of suffering in ourselves and others, and the support of our Awakening. We can generate slow deep breathing—Matrika or Conscious Responsive Breathing are ideal—coupled with simple physical gestures and expressions of gratitude or prayer, walking outside or doing a household chore.

The transcendental energies we encounter during CB often connect us to the Plane of Possibility and therefore quantum reality. This terrain can give rise to capabilities that defy Newtonian or consensus reality sensibilities. We may experience laying on of hands, sending heat, energy, or visions to others, and more, as superpowers we crave to possess. These abilities (or an attraction to them), can be potent and miraculous, transformative contributions to our life and the world, yet can easily mesmerize and pull us off the journey to real love. Discerning when capabilities that come through us are only bestowed for particular purposes at particular times is paramount. Three-centered breathing, gratitude, prayer, emptying, and body movements of humility, surrender, and willingness can make all the difference, as can peers who keep us humble and real, and mentors and teachers who have walked before us.

So too, opening to the field of interconnectedness with all things without embodiment can easily induce unintegrated trance states or dissociation. To promote somatic awareness during Breathwork with mystical states, we can consciously generate physical sensations by vocalizing, body awareness, and conscious movement.

Additionally, Therapist-Breathworkers can misjudge our own breakthrough experiences as permanent attainments and can believe that we're modeling spiritual development, especially if Breathees have strong idealized projections towards us. It is essential to remember that—reflective of healthy breathing, which is always desirable—even when one is already in states of wholeness, the spiritual journey is ongoing.

Breathwork can open transpersonal and boundless states quickly while simultaneously engendering rapid contact with sensations, emotions, thoughts, and trauma that have been ignored or hidden from awareness. There are risks of dissociation, spiritual bypass, retraumatization, breaching of boundaries internally or within the therapeutic relationship, and developing grandiosity. When we honor and maintain healthy personal and interpersonal boundaries while experiencing mystical states, we can experience luminous qualities of unconditional love, moral intuition, and preternatural wisdom about how we can contribute to the collective.

The *DSM-5* characterizes mystical states as depersonalization disorders (American Psychiatric Association, 2013). However, philosophers, researchers, and theorists—William James and Andrew Newberg among others—point out that mystical experiences, unlike psychotic states, generally engender a loss of pride, quiet the mind, and empty us of false perceptions of ourselves (D'Aquili & Newberg, 1999; James, 1958). Psychotic experiences usually create fear or distress leading to social disconnection or states of inflation that can induce perceptions that one is especially chosen to deliver messages, healing, or transformation.

Gary Weber offers these discernments:

> Mystical experiences have rich, deeply featured, coherent sensory experiences with the complexity of daily life, and feel real, even more real than everyday life. TLEs [temporal lobe epilepsy] and most psychotic hallucinations feel real while you're having them, but returning to "normal life" you perceive them as a fragmented, unreal dream created by the mind.

He shares that Saint Teresa of Avila said:

> God visits the soul in a way that prevents it doubting when it comes, but it has been in God and God in it, and so firmly is it convinced of this truth that, though years may pass before this state recurs, the soul can never forget it, to doubt its reality. (Weber, 2015)

In general, a true spiritual or mystical experience will lead to greater engagement with love, service, caring, honesty, peace, and benevolence. Many who have mystical encounters during near-death experiences become more centered, peaceful, and committed to bringing love to everyone.

RIGOR AND RESPLENDENCE OF SPIRITUAL AWAKENING

Mystical experiences, spiritual awakening, and spiritual practices can lead to radical encounters with our previously held notions of self, others, and life. Thus, we may feel deeply challenged, as if our sense of self is crumbling. Sometimes the mystical aspects of growth can lead to such intense awareness and introspection that we can experience a dark night of the soul. It can also induce complete letting go of ourselves as we knew ourselves to be—*no self*, as was described by Bernadette Roberts (1993) in her book *The Experience of No Self*. While these experiences can feel dangerous, they are time-honored stations of Awakening, and Breathwork can help us ground in the present, with self-care and connection to others.

> *If every breath is sacred*
> *God I want to breathe*
> *Deep enough to feel something*
> *Deep enough to believe*
> *That every breath is sacred*
>
> —SLEEPING AT LAST, "BREATHE DEEP"

Examples of genuine spiritual development, reflecting intensity and rigor, may encourage us and help allay our fears as we tread this unfathomable territory.

Hakuin Ekaku, later a renowned Zen patriarch, embarked on a relentless quest for truth at age 15. His journey was marked by periods of intense doubt, asceticism, and psychological and physical challenges. Despite hardships, Hakuin persevered in his meditation practice, which aimed to build the capacity to face any situation without attachment to a particular outcome.

Through his practice, Hakuin experienced a profound transformation. He described facing great doubt as standing in a vast, empty plain, free from fears and thoughts. By advancing single-mindedly, he experienced a sudden awakening, likening it to a sheet of ice breaking or a jade tower falling. This awakening brought immense joy and a sense of transcendence beyond birth, death, and nirvana.

Hakuin emphasized that realizing this profound truth involves a certain amount of suffering. However, the fruits of his practice were evident in his later life. Even in his 70s, his vitality surpassed that of his younger years. He could go without sleep for days without any decline in mental clarity. Hakuin attributed his remarkable endurance and mental strength to the power gained from his introspective practice.

While Hakuin's experiences might be viewed as masochistic or dissociative from a traditional psychotherapeutic perspective, his journey exemplifies the transformative potential of deep spiritual practice and the cultivation of a resilient heart, body, and mind. There is no doubt that if we are to awake to Essence, we must prepare to undergo some discomfort of inner, and sometimes outer, structures being dismantled and metamorphosed.

> *And God's light came shining on through*
> *I woke up in the darkness, scared and breathing,*
> *born anew*
>
> —BRUCE SPRINGSTEEN, VALENTINE'S DAY

Experiences can be so resplendent and transcendent that, whether we identify secularly, religiously, or spiritually, we may call them *sacred*. These moments can be so remarkably sublime and fulfilling that we are transported into some degree of profound gratitude and reverence. Through these sacred moments, we often realize we are much more than we knew ourselves to be, or no-self—certainly uplifted and transformed. We may also experience this when a child is born or in heightened lovemaking. There is nothing that elevates, fills, and thrills like the sacred. Whatever the tenor of the mystical experience, it is the place where separation, the veil between formlessness and form, everything and everything, dissolves into the Plane of Possibility.

It is that which I have called Beloved;
Now I see my original face.
It is the jewel beyond all price;
Now I enter the cave of jewels.
It is the luminous inner light;
Our sun is the moon of this.
It is the flame that never dies,
Fed by the breath of the infinite.
—JENNIFER WELWOOD, "THE SECRET, INDWELLING HEART,"
POEMS FOR THE PATH

Together Breathwork and Psychotherapeutic wisdom can support these luminous, joyous, and sometimes harrowing, transpersonal and spiritual sojourns. By integrating psychotherapy's evolving understanding of structures and processes that facilitate well-being with Breathwork's ability to move into the boundless and transcendent, we can cocreate safe, healing processes for personal and collective wholeness—and sacredness.

Practicing Conscious Breathing throughout the day will build our capacity to receive Essence in every moment, in every place, with every person, in every situation. Breathing is union, continuously, in every moment. Each breath is a discovery of how to enter that union from a new place, and how to enhance that union so that our temple expands. We open and respond to the call of the source of life, respond to the vibration of creation itself as our North Star, simultaneously releasing our grasp on anything needing to be a certain way, knowing there is possibility in every moment—living and breathing in the experience that all are held, all are cherished, all are beloved.

Instead of you breathing, it's God breathing you.
—ADYASHANTI

FIFTEEN

Toward a Breathing-Centered World

There is a furnace in our cells, and when we breathe we pass the world through our bodies, brew it lightly, and turn it loose again, gently altered for having known us.
—DIANE ACKERMAN,
A NATURAL HISTORY OF THE SENSES

Wage peace with your breath.
—JUDYTH HILL, "WAGE PEACE"

BREATHING IS our most fundamental, accessible, potent, and comprehensive nutrient, medicine, healer, friend, teacher, and beloved. Breathing is the primary, unifying language of the human species—our most intelligent and direct communication with each other and all life.

In a breathing-centered world, we might transform our speaking to more closely align with our personal authenticity and our Self as *interconnected* and *intraconnected* with all. Rather than saying "How are you?" we might connect through supporting each other's breathing. We could gently begin initiating this change right now, as psychotherapist and writer Gabes Torres does with her friends.

We ask: How is your belly? Your breath?... It is both a check-in and an invitation to pay attention to our bodies and see how we're coming together as we connect... like "my breathing feels a bit shallow today." There are less expectations tied to the response, which can allow for a more authentic one. (Torres, 2023)

We could greet each other by breathing deeply together a few times before speaking.

Evolution toward a breathing-centered world could give rise to a throughline of solidarity, cooperation, and creativity that could elevate our world. The Universal Breathing Declaration is dedicated to this potential.

The Universal Breathing Declaration

Breathing is life. Being grateful for our own breathing, we support the essential right of all people to breathe safely and well. We believe in cocreating a world in which all people (Breathers) have the freedom to breathe and share healthy air. We commit to collectively explore and support healthy breathing for all, so that individuals, families, communities, and our collective life can thrive, and we can share our gifts with one another.

The world itself breathes as everything participates in the oxygen cycle. Being conscious and reverent about our shared breathing we move from separateness to community, to interconnection, wholeness, and love. We acknowledge the responsibility to care for the sustainability, health, and beauty of our planet; we honor and support all people's breathing—including their first and last breaths; we support clean, healthy air in every space on earth; we support beneficial treatment and compassionate care for respiratory challenges, and all illnesses; we dedicate ourselves to removing barriers to safe optimal breathing and ending the suffering due to ecological imbalance, violence, war, marginalization, economic deprivation, or injustice. We dedicate ourselves to the wellbeing of our ecosystems and to all that breathe within them—the humans, other animals, plant life, and all beings.

Remembering this we will take time to consciously breathe every day with gratitude, and recall our commitment to respect and support the right of all to breathe safely and well. May we benefit from the power of our individual and collective breathing and care for this breathing earth.

We can breathe the world. All stewards of health, culture, learning, and love, all Therapist-Breathworkers, and *all Breathers*—we have the opportunity to become breath activists, breath lovers, and love activists. This is our charge. It's on our watch. We can breathe the world.

Let us receive Breathing...

Appendix: Index of Breathing Practices

Anger

Integrative Breathing (Chapters 3, 9)
Matrika Pranayama (Chapters 3, 6, 7)
Release of Tension Breath (Chapter 3)
Self-Healing Breathing (Chapter 7)

Anxiety

Breathing Through Anxiety (Chapter 10)
Buteyko Breathing Recovery Sitting Practice (Chapter 3)
Coherent Breathing (Chapter 3)
Cyclical Sighing (Chapters 6, 7, 10)
Matrika Pranayama (Chapters 3, 6, 7)
Receiving Breathing (Chapters 7, 13)
Self-Healing Breathing (Chapter 7)

Depression

Cyclical Sighing (Chapters 6, 7)
Breathing Through Depression (Chapter 10)
Integrative Breathing (Chapters 3, 9)
Quintessence Breathing (Chapter 7)
Self-Healing Breathing (Chapter 7)
Sudarshan Kriya Yoga (SKY) (Chapter 2)

Emotional Regulation

Coherent Breathing (Chapter 3)
Equanimity Breath (Chapter 2)
Integrative Breathing (Chapter 3, 9)
Matrika Pranayama (Chapters 3, 6, 7)
Quintessence Breathing (Chapter 7)
Receiving Breathing (Chapters 7)
Self-Healing Breathing (Chapter 7)
Sudarshan Kriya Yoga (SKY) (Chapter 2)

Energy

Bhastrika Breathing (Chapter 6)
Embodied Novelty Breathing (Chapters 7, 9)
Integrative Breathing (Chapters 3, 9)
Kapalabhati (Chapter 6)

Equilibrium

Equanimity Breath (Chapter 3)
Coherent Breathing (Chapter 3)
Matrika Pranayama (Chapters 3, 6, 7)
Receiving Breathing (Chapters 7, 13)

Fatigue

Accelerated Breathing (Chapter 7)
Bhastrika Breathing (Chapters 6, 7)
Enhanced Focus Breathing (Chapter 7)
Integrative Breathing (Chapters 3, 9)
Kapalabhati (Breath of Fire) (Chapters 6, 7)

Focus

Enhanced Focus Breathing (Chapter 7)
Matrika Pranayama (Chapters 3, 6, 7)
Mindfulness Breathing (Chapter 3)
Zen Breathing (Chapter 3)

Mystical Experiences

Conscious Responsive Breathing (Chapter 11)
Embodied Novelty Breathing (Chapters 7, 9)
Integrative Breathing (Chapters 3, 9)

Personal and Spiritual Development

Conscious Responsive Breathing (Chapter 11)
Embodied Novelty Breathing (Chapters 7, 9)
Form and Formlessness Communion Breathing (Chapter 7)
Group 4 Human Development Breathing Practices (Chapters 3, 7, 9)
Group 5 Human Potential Breathing Practices (Chapters 3, 9, 11)
Heart-Centered Intuition Breathing Practice (Chapter 14)
Intuitive Insight Breathing Practice (Chapter 14)
Mirroring Breath (Chapter 3)
Plane of Possibility Practitioners Presence Process (Chapter 13)
Quintessence Breathing (Chapter 7)
Receiving Breathing (Chapters 7, 13)
Somatic Intuition Breathing Practice (Chapter 14)
Tonglen (Chapter 3)

Respiratory Health

Buteyko Breathing (Chapter 3, 6)
Coherent Breathing (Chapter 3)
Respiratory Healing Pranayama (Chapter 7)

Sleep

Coherent Breathing (Chapter 3)
Receiving Breathing (Chapters 7, 14)
Sleep Pranayama (Chapter 7)

Stress

Bumblebee Breath (Chapters 3, 6)
Coherent Breathing (Chapter 3)
Equanimity Breath (Chapter 3)
Integrative Breathing (Chapters 3, 9)

Matrika Pranayama (Chapters 3, 6, 7)
Receiving Breathing (Chapter 7)
Release of Tension Breath (Chapter 3)
Self-Healing Breathing (Chapter 7)
Sudarshan Kriya Yoga (SKY) (Chapter 2)

Trauma

Relaxation

Coherent Breathing (Chapter 3)
Matrika (Chapter 3, 6, 7)
Receiving Breathing (Chapter 7)
Presence
Form and Formlessness Communion (Chapter 7)
Receiving Breathing (Chapter 7)

Regulation

Coherent Breathing (Chapter 3)
Matrika (Chapter 3, 6, 7)
Receiving Breathing (Chapter 7)

Expression

Integrative Breathing (Chapter 3, 9)
Self-Healing Breathing (Chapter 7)

Resiliency

Accelerated Breathing (Chapter 7)
Coherent Breathing (Chapter 3)
Embodied Novelty Breathing (Chapter 7)
Integrative Breathing (Chapter 3, 9)
Quintessence Breathing (Chapter 7)
Matrika (Chapter 3, 6, 7)

Acknowledgments

Dear Companion Breathers,

Like you, I have been breathing my whole life. The yearning to breathe fully and wholly is intrinsic to our nature, yet we need nurturing, illuminating experiences to consciously sense, understand, and appreciate the primacy and potential of *breathing*—our physical, emotional, cognitive, and spiritual activator, progenitor, and guide. We can then experience, as Rumi said, "there is a breath of love that takes you all the way to infinity." With crystal clarity I know that my wondrous discovery, understanding, and embodiment of the mechanics, mystery, and miracles of breathing has been impacted and informed by everyone I have ever breathed near—countless family members, friends, partners, teachers, students, colleagues, acquaintances, and cocreatives. Only breathing and love could carry the multitude of words, pages, and poems I would wish to write to convey the incalculable enormity of what you (and regretfully, I may forget to write some names and ask your forgiveness) have breathed into this Breathing book. I breathe with you now and offer a sprinkling of words of gratitude.

Breathing gratitude and respect with the Norton Professional Books team: Andrea Dawson, who initiated the book's concept and purpose. You reside within my awareness as a magical being who found me amidst the Breathwork field, explaining "I looked around and sensed you were the person." My lifetime gratitude for being inducted into a lifetime adventure. Ben Yarling, you serenely guided me through the initial outline and contract signing; words may never fully honor my depth of appreciation for Deborah Malmud, vice president and publishing director. From the day we met and discovered we both wanted to transform the book's architecture, to your understanding when life events forced a writing pause, to time and space you created for the book's vision—which emerged enough material for three books—to astute and catalyzing feedback for extracting and crafting this one, I am forever endeared; Mariah Eppes, managing editor, you are a wonderful gift and blessing, offering steady, supportive, insightful guidance for the various stations of editing and polishing with delightful ease and alacrity—I can't imagine doing this without you; Sincere appreciation to the cheerful associate editor Jamie Vincent, behind-the-scenes assistant project editor Olivia Guarnieri, the marketing team—Kevin Olsen, Joy Mizan, and Talya Kaltman-Kron; designer Lauren Graessle; and Jessica Friedman—attorney extraordinaire. If all attorneys were as knowledgeable, sagacious, and personable, our legal system would be elevated. Together, the Norton team provided yeoman service for the fields of Breathwork and psychotherapy.

Breathing gratitude and blessedness with the emergent book team, enacting perfect tasks at perfect times: Rachael Pitts, you midwifed my writing more words of this book than anyone—yet words can scarcely describe my appreciation for your devotion, ingenuity, organization, computer skills, weeping and laughing, holding the mystery, and accompanying the grounding; Mary Rawlinson, you are an astounding, surprising, blessing of always peacefully, intelligently, kindly, and creatively listening, reflecting, and suggesting—with luminous encouragement and prayerful visions for the book and *all* Breathers; Laura Fox, your selfless, objective editing counsel taught me the elegant art of deep pruning, and your sublime goat pictures were revitalizing; Trevor Sprecht for peaceful computer wizardry; Jenna Witman for making me drink water before you typed; Sarah Van Sciver for beauty, care, and quote precision research; Jaime Kauffman for critical references; Jeannette Cooper for expert standardization coaching; Altruce Poage and Sharon Elsberry for prime graphics; Liz Slaterback for expressive drawings; Mary Blue for breathing science graphics; Martha Matt, Kristin Pauly, Emily McCay, Amy Vernon, Tara Molina (my 2 a.m. cocreative), and Mary Blue for generous first draft editing.

Breathing gratitude and honor with the Global Professional Breathwork Alliance (GPBA) Board and Advisory Board—for inspiration, collaboration, and friendship. Your leadership in aligning Breathwork, ethics, and training standards accelerates best practices worldwide: Jim Morningstar, Ann Harrison, Viola Edward, Binnie Dansby, Judith Kravitz, Alice Wells, Dr. Ela Manga, Peter Litchfield, Richie Bostock, Anthony Abbagnano, Dana Dharma Davi, Ashanna Solaris, Tilke Platteel-Deur, and Judy Gee (in memoriam).

Breathing gratitude and profound love with the Inspiration Consciousness School Certified Breathworkers who endeavor to transmit love, wisdom, and presence in every breath. I am honored by your requests for training and moved by your commitment to depth. In many ways this book was made possible by you relentlessly asking, "explain what you are doing and how you know to do it." Patricia Waddell for myriad consultations, and the legacy of organization, ethics, and innovation; Barbara Morris, the "mother of Inspiration" who infuses our work and rooms with beauty, positivity, and light; Rochelle Savetman for real unconditional love; Tom Rigler, healer extraordinaire and fearless explorer of invisible dimensions; Alice Wells for passionately integrating energy, intelligence, love, and probing questions; Kathy Sirota, the most humble, utterly wise Therapist-Breathworker I know; Mike Barocca for exuberantly assisting the Awakening course; Paul Phillips for expanding beyond conventions and boxes in wholly practical ways; Carol Seddon, for awakened harmony transmitting diamond-like light into our Breathwork and circle; Kappy Laning, for dedicated service to embodying and facilitating Breathees' discoveries into everyday moments; Michael Breslin for laying out stepping stones as portals to the luminous; Heather Davis for epitomizing never-ending love, harmony, and faith; Mary Blue for weaving science, love, and God; Sandy Wiggins for visions of Conscious Breathing for every ecosystem and every being; Curtis Nielsen for ecstatic recognition of the 5-P Process and embodying its proof, and supreme faith in this book; Julie Harris for exemplary dedication to the reciprocal integrity of practitioner and client wholeness; Kate Pappas for faith beyond faith and stimulating intellectual queries; Lauren Celec Cafritz for joy and creative uplifting love messages; Erin Bishop for ongoingly responding to

Breathwork's continual transformation; Ilaria Luckovich for devotion to grounded wildness; Laura Tomacari for exquisite purity of intention and attention; Rory Turner for coemerging the words "the fundamental unity of even seemingly contrasting values"; Gretchen Steidle for contributing to and living the Universal Breathing Declaration; the late, beloved Eileen Katz for modeling what never giving up and surrender look like together; enduring contributions from Breathworkers Anne Frances Martin, Barbara Johnson, Janet Calico, Ron Orem, and Sindee Ernst; and all 2023–2025 Breathworker Apprentices for your support, flexibility, and love for this book.

Breathing gratitude and inspiration with other Breathworkers who have elevated this journey: Shirley Telles for endearing, enduring friendship and collaboration, and excellence and discernment in yogic Breathing research and practice; Sondra Ray for lovingly, firmly drawing me from the inner laboratory into the global Breathwork scene, and likely facilitating more Breathwork sessions than anyone on earth. Dr. Richard Brown and Dr. Patricia Gerbarg for modeling and calling for excellence, efficacy, and beneficial results in Breathwork; Patrick McKeown, I deeply value our shared understanding that the various lenses of breathing we each articulate lead to wholeness; Stan Grof, for your courage, wisdom, and expansive heart, your mighty contribution to Breathwork's therapeutic validity, and your powerful teaching and example at "Breathing: From Science to Samadhi" conferences; James Nestor for opening a gargantuan portal of interest in breathing and for our conversations about cutting edge Breathwork possibilities; Gay Hendricks for unwavering certainty about Conscious Breathing, and treasured communications about this work's value; Katie Hendricks for breathing harmony and grace everywhere; Stephen Elliott for prodigious, rigorous exploration and research embedded in a heart of gold; Peter Litchfield for diligence in dispelling misconceptions and revealing true breathing wisdom; Rabia Hayek for envisioning how one billion Breathers will breathe synchronously someday; Petri Berndston for thrilling philosophical Breathwork conversations; Carol Lampman for developing and teaching infant Breathwork; the late Leonard Orr for riding Breathwork's beginning wave and championing it through its crest.

Breathing gratitude and delight for those who contributed honest, insightful, creative, and encouraging feedback and suggestions about the manuscript or cover: Jessica Crutchfield, Suzanne Dion, Ilaria Luckovich, Dr. Ela Manga, Curtis Nielsen, Gretchen Steidle, Caroline Welch.

Breathing gratitude and exceptional appreciation for important book writing conversations that breathed energy into writing: Cynthia Bourgeault, Deborah Eggerton, Dawn Eidelman, Tim Ferriss, James Flaherty, Cheryl Richardson, and Holly Woods.

Breathing gratitude and joyous thankfulness for other Breathers who contributed information, encouragement, questions, wisdom, topics, cheerleading, and breathing: Mike Alexander, Adan and Ally Ayala, Kevin Barnett, Benedict Beaumont, Daniel Blum, Eno Breathe (program), Pete Craig, Sam Droege, Lisa Duva, Sharon Elsberry, Rob Fersh, Andy Freeman, Kathy Gabriel, Hope Gerecht, Becky Giles, Kathy Giles, Lauren Going, Amy Griffin, Wim Hof, Robert Holden, Jan Houbolt, Joey Jacobs, Ron Kraus, Lois Laynee, Sita Lozoff, John Luckovich, Peggy Mainor, Holly Margl, Karen Miller, Shelley Morhaim, Olivier Mortara, Jan Moylan, Susan Olesek, Deborah Ooten, Darriel Park, Ann Patricio, Louise Phipps-Senft, Eric Radom, Hope Rubin, Annie Sachs, Lawrence Schramm, Alexandra Smith, Laura Sweeney, Miko Take, Bill Tipper, Baya Voce, Alex Williams, Rachel Wohl, and more.

Breathing gratitude with a bow to respected colleagues, professors, and practitioners in science, health, and psychology whose conversations with me have enriched the book: Diana Fosha for creating a scholarly theory of radically transformative experientially-oriented therapy; Dr. Richard Schwartz for fascinating explorative conversations about self, essence, breathing, and integration; Stephen Porges for embodying relaxation, recognizing the primacy of breathing, and certainty about my writing this book; Christina Chambreau for seminal invitations and initiations into intuition; the late Rich Simon, founder of the groundbreaking Psychotherapy Networker Conferences, first coach for this book, whose redlining I was looking forward to—we miss you; Jon Dean at UCSD for thrilling, objective science explorations and deep humanity; Sita Severson for deep attuned listening, responsive wisdom, and intuition; Dr. Pippa Wheble for palpable excitement, encouragement, and extraordinary commitment to collaborating about accurate medical information; Dr. David Linden for discerning conversations about consciousness; and special gratitude to UCLA professor Jack Feldman for several generous, fascinating conversations about breathing and Breathwork, and innovative eureka-like cocreation of the Chapter 4 breathing cycle diagrams. It's an honor to work with you.

Breathing gratitude and ecstasy with all composers/singer-songwriters, and a quintessence tuning fork of them for composing the world I breathe and pray for: Ludwig van Beethoven, the Beatles, Bruce Springsteen, Animal Collective/Deakin, Laura Nyro.

Breathing gratitude and exhilaration with a few treasured coconspirators and journeyers:

Dan Siegel, you embody integration and continuous exploration about bringing wholeness and love to being, study, and practice. Our paths converged in the consilience of science, presence, integration, and the numinous through a Rumi poem. That exhilaration has guided our collaborations, talks, and walks ever since. I am awash in gratitude for your editing coaching, celebrating each step, and the honor of your foreword for this book. **Edward Sweeney**, lover of breathing and love, whose exquisite art breathed the sacred into the world. You bestowed brilliance, power, magic, and meaning, and my authentic self may never have been so unconditionally loved. **Jack Kornfield**, from the moment you enthusiastically stepped up to teach at "Breathwork: From the Science to the Samadhi," and supported this book from its inception, I have valued your friendship and vision—thus, it was profoundly meaningful to partner in polishing the Universal Breathing Declaration in the last hours of book editing. **Jennifer Welwood**, our shared commitment to awakening every moment has been inviolate and inspiring for over five decades. With compassionate attunement you held my journey with the *last breath* of three significant beloveds during the final nine months of the book's formation—sweetening the book's birth and *first breath*. **Jim Morningstar**, teacher of teachers, how am I so fortunate to have your partnership in birthing the GPBA, in advocating for excellence and high alignment in Breathwork? Our conversations—from our personal growth to the numinous—are eminently enriching. Your certainty about the book's essential importance blessed me through numerous critical junctures. **Patricia Waddell**, you neither need or want this attention—however, over decades you are there for every personal or professional conversation I ever want with you. Do you know how rare that is? It is beyond precious. **Roland Griffiths**, your humble, sincere, diligent search for truth, consciousness, and awakening gifted the world and my life. You and I were looking forward to this book being published, and though I miss hearing and seeing the words you would have offered, the words and breaths we shared are tuning forks of rapt attention on what really matters. **Russ Hudson**, wordmeister and steadfast, committed coconspirator of somatic, emotional, and cognitive presence for ourselves and students. We once said your presence strengthens my blood and my presence makes the air more breathable for you. You consistently expand my thinking, for which this book and the reading community are fortunate recipients. Every dharma dance and dharma duel with you is priceless.

Breathing gratitude, lifetime reverence, and infinities of words with *some* of my teachers who nourished my wholeness, inspired me, and empowered my dedication: Thalia Mara, the Elizabeth Cleaners Street School, Yogi S. A. A. Ramaiah, Jason Doty, Ram Dass, Norman Bradford, Priscilla Schmitt, Susan Anderson, and Sita.

Breathing gratitude and indescribable love with my family: My mother, Roberta, you modelled and supported brilliance and creativity, lived in bed for several months that I might be born, gave me breath, and loved me utterly. I can only hope to come close to your extraordinary writing. My father, Saul, you supported me being and doing whatever I desired, taught me to question, to learn, and to dare to dream. My brother Michael, you handed me a seminally important spiritual book one birthday in Laguna Beach, igniting a life-changing chain of events. My sister Jamie—our unshakable love, and your all-encompassing ingenious perspectives immersed me in expanded states of consciousness and love that indelibly abide within. My brother John, you eagerly, without complaint, run errands, procure exotic nourishment, and know the most perfect gifts. My sister Martha, your lifetime relationships with writers made you a writing and publishing coach beyond measure. My husband David, we read one another's college papers while we gestated and birthed Josh. I read your sublime writings still, and feel you beaming at me from beyond. My son Josh, I am infused with wonder by your coaching, food shopping, faith in me, and love. My magical nephews Samuel and Lewis, and brother-in-law Andrew: your selflessness in supporting my sister in supporting me, and carrying wood, cleaning, and preparing family celebrations with good cheer—you warmed my quivering writing heart. My beloved godson, second son, Wyatt Giles, you exemplify breathing love and joy with every person. Sybil Baldwin, for your love and consistently expressing how much you root for this book. My goddaughter Grace, overflowing gratitude for gracing us with care and magic.

Breathing gratitude and reverence for everything in this breathing world—humans, other animals, plants, the waters, the earth, the heat sources, the air—this is for all of you, and the wholeness and wonders that dwell within you.

With love,
Jessica

P.S. As research and experiential knowledge is rapidly accelerating in psychology, Breathwork, science, and consciousness, I offer sincere apologies for any incomplete, misunderstood, or incorrect information. Wholehearted apologies for incorrect representations of any Breather, group, or community—or insensitivity of language or concepts. I welcome insights and discoveries at breathworkandpsychotherapy@gmail.com.

Credits

Lyrics from "Good House" by Joshua Dibb licensed courtesy of Domino Publishing Company Ltd.

Annabel Laity, excerpts from "Breathe, You Are Alive!" from Thich Nhat Hanh, Breath, You Are Alive!: The Sutra on the Full Awareness of Breathing. Copyright © 2008 by the Plum Village Community of Engaged Buddhism, Inc. Reprinted with the permission of The Permissions Company, LLC on behalf of Parallax Press, Berkeley, California, parallax.org.

"Fire." Copyright © 1979 by Joy Harjo, from HOW WE BECAME HUMAN: NEW AND SELECTED POEMS: 1975–2001 by Joy Harjo. Used by permission of W. W. Norton & Company, Inc.

"For Calling the Spirit Back from Wandering the Earth in Its Human Feet," from CONFLICT RESOLUTION FOR HOLY BEINGS: POEMS by Joy Harjo. Copyright © 2015 by Joy Harjo. Used by permission of W. W. Norton & Company, Inc.

THE POEMS OF EMILY DICKINSON, edited by Thomas H. Johnson, Cambridge, Mass.: The Belknap Press of Harvard University Press, Copyright © 1951, 1955 by the President and Fellows of Harvard College. Copyright © renewed 1979, 1983 by the President and Fellows of Harvard College. Copyright © 1914, 1918, 1919, 1924, 1929, 1930, 1932, 1935, 1937, 1942, by Martha Dickinson Bianchi. Copyright © 1952, 1957, 1958, 1963, 1965, by Mary L. Hampson. Used by permission. All rights reserved.

"Breathe Deep" Written by Ryan O'Neal, Published by Wine And Song Music (BMI) obo Asteroid B 612. All rights reserved. Used by permission.

References

Abram, D. (2018). The commonwealth of breath. In L. Škof & P. Berndtson (Eds.), *Atmospheres of breathing*. SUNY Press.

Acosta, A., & Jimwani, Z. (2020, December 16). *Breathwork for healing racial trauma: A contemplative-based research journey*. Center for Contemplative Mind in Society. https://youtu.be/z4Lpz9U4yM8?si=9RYbn1-ll8HaLCRO

Agache, I., Miller, R., Gern, J. E., Hellings, P. W., Jutel, M., Muraro, A., Phipatanakul, W., Quirce, S., & Peden, D. (2019). Emerging concepts and challenges in implementing the exposome paradigm in allergic diseases and asthma: A Practall document. *Allergy*, 74(3), 449–463. https://doi.org/10.1111/all.13690

Agier, L., Basagaña, X., Maitre, L., Granum, B., Bird, P. K., Casas, M., Oftedal, B., Wright, J., Andrusaityte, S., de Castro, M., Cequier, E., Chatzi, L., Donaire-Gonzalez, D., Grazuleviciene, R., Haug, L. S., Sakhi, A. K., Leventakou, V., McEachan, R., Nieuwenhuijsen, M. . . . Siroux, V. (2019). Early-life exposome and lung function in children in Europe: An analysis of data from the longitudinal, population-based HELIX cohort. *Lancet Planetary Health*, 3(2), e81–e92. https://doi.org/10.1016/S2542-5196(19)30010-5

Aideyan, B., Martin, G., & Beeson, E. (2020). A practitioner's guide to breathwork in clinical mental health counseling. *Journal of Mental Health Counseling*, 42, 78–94.

Alkan, N., & Akis, T. (2013, August 15). Psychological characteristics of free diving athletes: A comparative study. *International Journal of Humanities and Social Science*, 3(15).

Allen, S. J., Watson, J. J., & Dawbarn, D. (2011). The neurotrophins and their role in Alzheimer's disease. *Current Neuropharmacology, 9*(4), 559–573. https://doi.org/10.2174/157015911798376190

Alshami, A. M. (2019). Pain: Is it all in the brain or the heart? *Current Pain and Headache Reports, 23*, 1–4. https://doi.org/10.1007/s11916-019-0827-4

American Psychiatric Association. (2013). *Diagnostic and statistical manual of mental disorders* (5th ed.).

Appelhans, B. M., & Luecken, L. J. (2006). Heart rate variability as an index of regulated emotional responding. *Review of General Psychology, 10*(3), 229–240. https://doi.org/10.1037/1089-2680.10.3.229

Art of Living. (2021). *Research on SKY breath meditation (SKY)*. https://www.artofliving.org/sudarshan-kriya

Ashhad, S., Kam, K., Del Negro, C. A., & Feldman, J. L. (2022). Breathing rhythm and pattern and their influence on emotion. *Annual Review of Neuroscience, 45*, 223–247. https://doi.org/10.1146/annurev-neuro-090121-014424

Ashley, S. L., Sjoding, M. W., Popova, A. P., Cui, T. X., Hoostal, M. J., Schmidt, T. M., Branton, W. R., Dieterle, M. G., Falkowski, N. R., Baker, J. M., Hinkle, K. J., Konopka, K. E., Erb-Downward, J. R., Huffnagle, G. B., & Dickson, R. P. (2020). Lung and gut microbiota are altered by hyperoxia and contribute to oxygen-induced lung injury in mice. *Science Translational Medicine, 12*(556). https://doi.org/10.1126/scitranslmed.aau9959

Bahá'u'lláh. (1857). *The hidden words of Bahá'u'lláh* (S. Effendi, Trans.). Bahá'í Reference Library. https://reference.bahai.org/en/t/b/HW/hw-20.html

Bahi, C., Irrmischer, M., Franken, K., Fejer, G., Schlenker, A., Deijen, J. B., & Engelbregt, H. (2024). Effects of conscious connected breathing on cortical brain activity, mood and state of consciousness in healthy adults. *Current Psychology, 43*, 10578–10589. https://rdcu.be/dCoiX

Balban, M. Y., Neri, E., Kogon, M. M., Weed, L., Nouriani, B., Jo, B., Holl, G., Zeitzer, J. M., Spiegel, D., & Huberman, A. D. (2023). Brief structured respiration practices enhance mood and reduce physiological arousal. *Cell Reports Medicine, 4*(1). https://www.cell.com/cell-reports-medicine/pdf/S2666-3791(22)00474-8.pdf

Bernard, O. (2020). *Breathing with orisha*. (Kindle ed.). Kìire Wellness.

Besnard, S., Denise, P., Cappelin, B., Dutschmann, M., & Gestreau, C. (2009). Stimulation of the rat medullary raphe nuclei induces differential responses in respiratory muscle activity. *Respiratory Physiology & Neurobiology, 165* (2–3). https://doi.org/10.1016/j.resp.2008.12.004

Bertin, M. (2017). *A 5-minute mindful breathing practice to restore your attention.* Mindful. https://www.mindful.org/5-minute-mindful-breathing-practice-restore-attention/

Bond, A. J. (2001). Neurotransmitters, temperament and social functioning. *European Neuropsychopharmacology, 11*(4), 261–274. https://doi.org/10.1016/S0924-977X(01)00094-3

Book Brigade: The Author Speaks. (2016, September 29). Mind: A journey to the heart of being human. *Psychology Today.* https://www.psychologytoday.com/us/blog/the-author-speaks/201609/mind-journey-the-heart-being-human

Bowen, M. (1986). *Family therapy in clinical practice.* Jason Aronson.

Bowlby, J. (1969). *Attachment and loss: Volume 1, attachment.* Basic Books.

Boyadzhieva, A., & Kayhan, E. (2021, June 29). Keeping the breath in mind: Respiration, neural oscillations, and the free energy principle. *Frontiers in Neuroscience, 15,* 647579. https://doi.org/10.3389/Ffnins.2021.647579

Brown, R. P., & Gerbarg, P. L. (2005a). Sudarshan Kriya yogic breathing in the treatment of stress, anxiety, and depression: Part I—neurophysiologic model. *Journal of Alternative and Complementary Medicine, 11*(2), 383–384.

Brown, R. P., & Gerbarg, P. L. (2005b). Sudarshan Kriya yogic breathing in the treatment of stress, anxiety, and depression: Part II—clinical applications and guidelines. *Journal of Alternative and Complementary Medicine, 11*(4), 711–717.

Brown, R. P., & Gerbarg, P. L. (2010). *First trial of breathing, movement, and meditation for PTSD, depression, and anxiety related to September 11th New York City World Trade Center attacks.* Lecture given at the annual meeting of the American Psychiatric Association, New Orleans, LA.

Brown, R. P., Gerbarg, P. L., & Muench, F. (2013, March). Breathing practices for treatment of psychiatric and stress-related medical conditions. *Psychiatric Clinics of North America, 36*(1), 121–140.

Buller, K. (2019). Trauma and breath: A clinical approach to trauma resolution utilizing breathwork. Academia. https://www.academia.edu/39338667/A_clinical_approach_to_trauma_resolution_utilizing_Breathwork

Bunzeck, N., Doeller, C. F., Dolan, R. J., & Duzel, E. (2012). Contextual interaction between novelty and reward processing within the mesolimbic system. *Human Brain Mapping, 33*(6), 1309–1324.

Calatayud, J., Vinstrup, J., Jakobsen, M. D., Sundstrup, E., Brandt, M., Jay, K., Colado, J. C., & Andersen, L. L. (2016). Importance of mind-muscle connection during progressive resistance training. *European Journal of Applied Physiology, 116*(3), 527–533. https://doi.org/10.1007/s00421-015-3305-7

Cao, Y., Chen, M., Dong, D., Xie, S., & Liu, M. (2020). Environmental pollutants damage airway epithelial cell cilia: Implications for the prevention of obstructive lung diseases. *Thoracic Cancer, 11,* 505–510. https://doi.org/10.1111/1759-7714.13323

Chaitanya, S., Datta, A., Bhandari, B., & Sharma, V. K. (2022). Effects of resonance breathing on heart rate variability and cognitive functions in young adults: A randomised controlled study. *Cureus, 14*(2), e22187.

Chan, P.-Y. S., Cheng, C.-H., Wu, Y.-T., Wu, C. W., Liu, H.-L. A., Shaw, F.-Z., Liu, C.-Y., & Davenport, P. W. (2018). Cortical and subcortical neural correlates for respiratory sensation in response to transient inspiratory occlusions in humans. *Frontiers in Physiology, 9.* https://doi.org/10.3389/fphys.2018.01804

Chevalier, G., Sinatra, S. T., Oschman, J. L., Sokal, K., & Sokal, P. (2012). Earthing: Health implications of reconnecting the human body to the earth's surface electrons. *Journal of Environmental and Public Health, 2012.* https://doi.org/10.1155/2012/291541

Chinagudi, S., Badami, S., Herur, A., Patil, S., GV, S., & Ankad, R. (2014a). Immediate effect of short duration of slow deep breathing on heart rate variability in healthy adults. *National Journal of Physiology, Pharmacy and Pharmacology, 4*(3), 233–235. https://njppp.com/fulltext/28-1399431673.pdf

Chinagudi, S., Patted S., Herur, A., Patil, S., GV, S., & Ankad, R. (2014b). Assessment of cognitive levels after short duration of slow deep breathing by Raven's Standard Progressive Matrices. *International Journal of Medical Science and Public Health, 3*(7), 842–844.

Ciarka, A., Vincent, J. L., & Van de Borne, P. (2007). The effects of dopamine on the respiratory system: Friend or foe? *Pulmonary Pharmacology and Therapeutics, 20*(6), 607–615. https://doi.org/10.1016/j.pupt.2006.10.011

Ciesla, M. C., Seven, Y. B., Allen, L. L., Smith, K. N., Gonzalez-Rothi, E. J., & Mitchell, G. S. (2022, January 1). Daily acute intermittent hypoxia enhances serotonergic innervation of hypoglossal motor nuclei in rats with and without cervical spinal injury. *Experimental Neurology, 347*, 113903. https://doi.org/10.1016/j.expneurol.2021.113903

Coherence. (2004). *Respire 1.* https://www.respire1.com

Cramer, H., Lauche, R., Klose, P., Langhorst, J., & Dobos, G. (2013). Yoga for schizophrenia: A systematic review and meta-analysis. *BMC Psychiatry, 13*, 1–12. https://doi.org/10.1186/1471-244X-13-32

Critchley, H. D., Nicotra, A., Chiesa, P. A., Nagai, Y., Gray, M. A., Minati, L., & Bernardi, L. (2015). Slow breathing and hypoxic challenge: Cardiorespiratory consequences and their central neural substrates. *PLOS ONE, 10*(5), e0127082. https://doi.org/10.1371/journal.pone.0127082

Crockett, J. E., Cashwell, C. S., Tangen, J. L., Hall, K. H., & Young, J. S. (2016). Breathing characteristics and symptoms of psychological distress: An exploratory study. *Counseling and Values, 61*, 10–27. https://doi.org/10.1002/cvj.12023

Cuncic, A. (2020). *An overview of coherent breathing.* Very Well Mind. https://www.verywellmind.com/an-overview-of-coherent-breathing-4178943

Currivan, J. (2022). *The story of Gaia: The big breath and the evolutionary journey of our conscious planet.* Inner Traditions/Bear.

Curtice, K. B. (2023, May 10). *How a single breathwork session uncovered my childhood trauma.* Oprah Daily. https://www.oprahdaily.com/life/health/a42867596/breathwork-unlocks-trauma/

D'Aquili, E. G., & Newberg, A. B. (1999). *The mystical mind: Probing the biology of religious experience.* Fortress Press.

Davidson, R. J. (2014, June 3). One of a kind: The neurobiology of individuality. *Cerebrum, 2014*(8). https://www.ncbi.nlm.nih.gov/pmc/articles/PMC4436197/

de Wit, P. A. J. M. & Cruz, R. M. (2021). Treating PTSD with connected breathing: A clinical case study and theoretical implications. *European Journal of Trauma & Dissociation, 5*(3), 100152. https://doi.org/10.1016/j.ejtd.2020.100152

Del Negro, C. A., Funk, G. D., & Feldman, J. L. (2018). Breathing matters. *Nature Reviews Neuroscience, 19*(6), 351–367. https://doi.org/10.1038/s41583-018-0003-6

Descilo, T., Vedamurtachar, A., Gerbarg, P. L., Nagaraja, D., Gangadhar, B. N., Damodaran, B., Adelson, B., Braslow, L. H., Marcus, S., & Brown, R. P. (2010). Effects of a yoga breath intervention alone and in combination with an exposure therapy for post-traumatic stress disorder and depression in survivors of the 2004 South-East Asia tsunami. *Acta Psychiatrica Scandinavica, 121*(4), 289–300. https://doi.org/10.1111/j.1600-0447.2009.01466.x

Edwards, S. (2014). Intuition as a healing modality: Historical and contemporary perspectives. *Journal of Psychology in Africa, 23*, 669–673. https://doi.org/10.1080/14330237.2013.10820686

Ehrmann, W., (2019, March 19). Body contact in breathwork. *Ideas by Wilfried*. https://wilfried-ehrmann-e.blogspot.com/2019/03.

Elliott, S., & Edmonson, D. (2006). *Coherent breathing: The definitive method—theory and practice.* Coherence Press.

Enaud, R., Prevel, R., Ciarlo, E., Beaufils, F., Wieërs, G., Guery, B., & Delhaes, L. (2020). The gut-lung axis in health and respiratory diseases: A place for inter-organ and inter-kingdom crosstalks. *Frontiers in Cellular and Infection Microbiology, 10*, 9. https://doi.org/10.3389/fcimb.2020.00009

Epel, E. S. (2020). The geroscience agenda: Toxic stress, hormetic stress, and the rate of aging. *Ageing Research Reviews, 63*, 101167. https://doi.org/10.1016/j.arr.2020.101167

Eric Davis Dental. (n.d.). *Tongue posture: What is proper tongue posture, and why is it so important?* https://www.ericdavisdental.com/faqs-and-blog/blog/tongue-posture-what-is-proper-tongue-posture-and-why-is-it-so-important/

Evans, K. C., Dougherty, D. D., Schmid, A. M., Scannell, E., McCallister, A., Benson, H., Dusek, J. A., & Lazar, S. W. (2009). Modulation of spontaneous breathing via limbic/paralimbic–bulbar circuitry: An event-related fMRI study. *NeuroImage, 47*(3), 961–971. https://doi.org/10.1016/j.neuroimage.2009.05.025

Evans, K. C., Shea, S. A., & Saykin, A. J. (1999). Functional MRI localisation of central nervous system regions associated with volitional inspiration in humans. *Journal of Physiology, 520*(Pt. 2), 383–392. https://doi.org/10.1111/j.1469-7793.1999.00383.x

Eyerman, J. (2013, Spring). A clinical report of holotropic breathwork in 11,000 psychiatric inpatients in a community hospital setting. *MAPS Bulletin Special Edition,* 24–27.

Eyerman, J. (2014). Holotropic breathwork: Models of mechanism of action. *Journal of Transpersonal Research, 6*(1), 64–72.

Farb, N. A. S., Segal, Z. V., Mayberg, H., Bean, J., McKeon, D., Fatima, Z., & Anderson, A. K. (2013). Mindfulness meditation training alters cortical representations of interoceptive attention. *Social Cognitive and Affective Neuroscience, 8*(1), 15–26. https://doi.org/10.1093/scan/nss066

Farb, N. A. S., Zuo, Z., & Price, C. J. (2023, June 23). Interoceptive awareness of the breath preserves attention and language networks amidst widespread cortical deactivation: A within-participant neuroimaging study. *Eneuro, 10*(6). https://www.ncbi.nlm.nih.gov/pmc/articles/PMC10295813/

Farber, S. (2012, November 21). *Szasz and beyond: The spiritual promise of the mad pride movement.* Mad in America. https://www.madinamerica.com/2012/11/szasz-and-beyondthe-spiritual-promise-of-the-mad-pride-movement/

Feldman, J. L., Del Negro, C. A., & Gray, P. A. (2013). Understanding the rhythm of breathing: So near, yet so far. *Annual Review of Physiology, 75*(1), 423–452. https://doi.org/10.1146/annurev-physiol-040510-130049

Feldman, J., & Huberman, A. (2022, January 10). *Dr. Jack Feldman: Breathing for mental and physical health and performance* [Video]. Huberman Lab. https://hubermanlab.com/dr-jack-feldman-breathing-for-mental-physical-health-and-performance/

Fincham, G., Strauss, C., & Cavanagh, K. (2023). Effect of coherent breathing on mental health and wellbeing: A randomised placebo-controlled trial. *Scientific Reports, 13,* 22141. https://www.nature.com/articles/s41598-023-49279-8

Fletcher, J. (2019, February 12). *4-7-8 Breathing: How it works, benefits, and uses.* Medical News Today. https://www.medicalnewstoday.com/articles/324417

Flics, D. (2021). *What meditation can't cure.* Lion's Roar: Buddhist Wisdom for Our Times. https://www.lionsroar.com/what-meditation-cant-cure/

Forsythe, P., Kunze, W., & Bienenstock, J. (2016). Moody microbes or fecal phrenology: What do we know about the microbiota-gut brain axis? *BMC Medicine, 14*(58). https://doi.org/10.1186/s12916-016-0604-8

Fosha, D. (2017). How to be a transformational therapist: AEDP harnesses innate healing affects to re-wire experience and accelerate transformation. In J. Loizzo (Ed.), *Advances in contemplative psychotherapy: Accelerating healing and transformation.* Routledge.

Fossella, T., & Welwood, J. (2011). Human nature, Buddha nature: An interview with John Welwood. *Tricycle: The Buddhist Review, 20*(3), 1–18.

Gendlin, E. T. (1982). *Focusing.* Bantam Books.

Gendlin, E. T. (1993). Three assertions about the body. *The Folio, 12*(1), 21–33. https://www.focusing.org/gendlin/docs/gol_2064.html

Gerbarg, P. L., Brown, R. P., Streeter, C., Katzman, M., & Vermani, M. (2019). Breath practices for survivor and caregiver stress, depression, and post-traumatic stress disorder: Connection, co-regulation, compassion. *OBM Integrative and Complementary Medicine, 4*(3). https://doi.org/10.21926/obm.icm.1903045

Gerritsen, R. J., & Band, G. P. (2018). Breath of life: The respiratory vagal stimulation model of contemplative activity. *Frontiers in Human Neuroscience, 12,* 393151.

Godek, D., & Freeman, A. M. (2022, September 26). *Physiology, diving reflex.* StatPearls. https://www.ncbi.nlm.nih.gov/books/NBK538245/

Gorman, P. (1995). *Moving 1000 pounds with 4 ounces.* Dr. Noel Bormann, Gonzaga University. https://connect.gonzaga.edu/bormann/moving-1000-pounds-with-4-ounces

Grof, S. (1996). *Realms of the human unconscious: Observations from LSD research.* Souvenir Press.

Grof, S. (2012). Revision and re-enchantment of psychology: Legacy of half a century of consciousness research. *The Journal of Transpersonal Psychology, 44*(2), 137–163.

Grof, S., & Grof, C. (Eds.). (1989). *Spiritual emergency: When personal transformation becomes a crisis.* Tarcher Perigee.

Hachmo, Y., Hadanny, A., Hamed, R. A., Daniel-Kotovsky, M., Catalogna, M., Fishlev, G., Lang, E., Polak, N., Doenyas, K., Friedman, M., & Zemel, Y. (2020). Hyperbaric oxygen therapy increases telomere length and decreases immunosenescence in isolated blood cells: A prospective trial. *Aging, 12*(22), 22445–22446. https://doi.org/10.18632/aging.202188

Hackett, D. A. (2020, December). Lung function and respiratory muscle adaptations of endurance- and strength-trained males. *Sports* (Basel), *8*(12), 160.

Hand, T. W., Vujkovic-Cvijin, I., Ridaura, V. K., & Belkaid, Y. (2016). Linking the microbiota, chronic disease and the immune system. *Trends in Endocrinology and Metabolism, 27*(12), 831–843. https://doi.org/10.1016/j.tem.2016.08.003

Hanh, T. N. (2005). Interrelationship. In *Call me by my true names: The collected poems of Thich Nhat Hanh.* Parallax Press.

Harinath, K., Malhotra, A. S., Pal, K., Prasad, R., Kumar, R., Kain, T. C., Rai, L., & Sawhney, R. C. (2004). Effects of hatha yoga and omkar meditation on cardiorespiratory performance, psychologic profile, and melatonin secretion. *Journal of Alternative and Complementary Medicine, 10*(2), 261–268.

Heck, D. H., Kozma, R., & Kay, L. M. (2019). The rhythm of memory: How breathing shapes memory function. *Journal of Neurophysiology, 122*(2), 563–571. https://doi.org/10.1152/jn.00200.2019

Herrero, J. L., Khuvis, S., Yeagle, E., Cerf, M., & Mehta, A. D. (2018). Breathing above the brain stem: Volitional control and attentional modulation in humans. *Journal of Neurophysiology, 119*(1), 145–159. https://doi.org/10.1152/jn.00551.2017

Heyda, A. (2000). An impact of the conscious connected breathing training on emotional states. *Healing Breath Journal, 5*(2), 9–18.

Intermountain Health. (2023, October 25). *The power of hugs and how they affect our daily health.* https://intermountainhealthcare.org/blogs/the-power-of-hugs-and-how-they-affect-our-daily-health

James, W. (1912). *Essays in radical empiricism.* Longman Green.

James, W. (1958). *The varieties of religious experience.* Mentor Books.

Jayaram, N., Rao, M. G., Narasimha, A., Raveendranathan, D., Varambally, S., Venkatasubramanian, G., & Gangadhar, B. N. (2013). Vitamin B12 levels and psychiatric symptomatology: A case series. *Journal of Neuropsychiatry and Clinical Neurosciences, 25*(2), 150–152.

Jeon, Y. K., Shin, M. J., Kim, C. M., Lee, B. J., Kim, S. H., Chae, D. S., Park, J. H., So, Y. S., Park, H., Lee, C. H., & Kim, B. C. (2018). Effect of squat exercises on lung function in elderly women with sarcopenia. *Journal of Clinical Medicine, 7*(7), 167. https://www.ncbi.nlm.nih.gov/pmc/articles/PMC6068941/

Jerath, R., & Barnes, V. (2009, January 5). Augmentation of mind-body therapy and role of deep slow breathing. *Journal of Complementary and Integrative Medicine, 6*(1).

Johnson, M. W., Griffiths, R. R., Hendricks, P. S., & Henningfield, J. E. (2019). Classic psychedelics: An integrative review of epidemiology, therapeutics, mystical experience, and brain network function. *Pharmacology and Therapeutics, 197,* 83–102. https://doi.org/10.1016/j.pharmthera.2018.11.010

Journey's Dream. (2021, March 16). *How your body helps with trauma resolution with Dr. Pat Ogden.* https://journeysdream.org/how-your-body-helps-with-trauma-resolution-with-dr-pat-ogden/

Kabat-Zinn, J. (2013). *Full catastrophe living: Using the wisdom of your body and mind to face stress, pain, and illness* (Rev. ed.). Bantam.

Kahn, S., Ehrlich, P., Feldman, M., Sapolsky, R., & Wong, S. (2020). The jaw epidemic: Recognition, origins, cures, and prevention. *Bioscience, 70*(9), 759–771. https://doi.org/10.1093/biosci/biaa073

Kanorewala, B. Z., & Suryawanshi, Y. C. (2022). The role of alternate nostril breathing (Anuloma Viloma) technique in regulation of blood pressure. *Asian Pacific Journal of Health Sciences, 9*(2), 48–52.

Katz, S., Arish, N., Rokach, A., Zaltzman, Y., & Marcus, E. L. (2018). The effect of body position on pulmonary function: A systematic review. *BMC Pulmonary Medicine, 18,* 1–16. https://doi.org/10.1186/s12890-018-0723-4

Kelly, G. (2021, May 3). *Neurohack your vision: A discussion on vision opti-*

mization with Meir Schneider, PhD. Qualia. https://www.qualialife.com/neurohack-your-vision-a-discussion-on-vision-optimization-with-meir-schneider-phd

Kjaer, T. W., Bertelsen C., Piccini, P., Brooks, D., Alving, J., & Lou, H. C. (2002). Increased dopamine tone during meditation-induced change of consciousness. *Cognitive Brain Research, 13*(2), 255–259. https://doi.org/10.1016/S0926-6410(01)00106-9

Kornfield, J. (2013). *Mirroring Meditation.* Workshop presented at Breathwork Immersion from Science to Sammadhi. Omega Institute.

Kromenacker, B. W., Sanova, A. A., Marcus, F. I., Allen, J. J. B., & Lane, R. D. (2018). Vagal mediation of low-frequency heart rate variability during slow yogic breathing. *Psychosomatic Medicine, 80*(6), 581–587. https://doi.org/10.1097/PSY.0000000000000603

Kubie, L. S. (1948). Instincts and homoeostasis. *Psychosomatic Medicine, 10*(1), 15–30.

LaComb, C. O., Tandy, R. D., Lee, S. P., Young, J. C., & Navalta, J. W. (2017). Oral versus nasal breathing during moderate to high intensity submaximal aerobic exercise. *International Journal of Kinesiology and Sports Science, 5*(1), 8–16.

Laing, R. D. (1983). *The Politics of Experience.* Pantheon.

Lee, D.-C. (2014, August). Leisure-time running reduces all-cause and cardiovascular mortality risk. *Journal of the American College of Cardiology, 64*(5), 472–481. https://www.ncbi.nlm.nih.gov/pmc/articles/PMC4131752/

Lee, L. X. (2018, September 18). *Hardwired for laziness? Tests show the human brain must work hard to avoid sloth.* University of British Columbia: UBC News. https://news.ubc.ca/2018/09/hardwired-for-laziness-tests-show-the-human-brain-must-work-hard-to-avoid-sloth/

Leggett, H. (2023, February 9). *"'Cyclic sighing'" can help breathe away anxiety.* Scope: Beyond the Headlines. https://scopeblog.stanford.edu/2023/02/09/cyclic-sighing-can-help-breathe-away-anxiety/

Litchfield, P. M., & Reamer, S. (2022). Embodied breathing habits: Aligning breathing mechanics with respiratory chemistry. *Journal of Holistic Healthcare and Integrative Medicine, 19*(2), 37–42.

Lloyd-Price, J., Abu-Ali, G., & Huttenhower, C. (2016). The healthy human microbiome. *Genome Medicine, 8,* 51. https://doi.org/10.1186/s13073-016-0307-y

Longden, E., Branitsky, A., Moskowitz, A., Berry, K., Bucci, S., & Varese, F. (2020). The relationship between dissociation and symptoms of psychosis: A meta-analysis. *Schizophrenia Bulletin, 46*(5), 1104–1113. https://doi.org/10.1093/schbul/sbaa037

Lowen, A. (1975). *Love and orgasm.* Collier Books.

Lowen, A. (1988). *Love, sex, and your heart.* Alexander Lowen Foundation.

Malik, A. S., & Amin, H. U. (2017). Chapter 1: Designing an EEG experiment. In A. S. Malik & H. U. Amin (Eds.), *Designing EEG experiments for studying the brain,* 1–30. Academic Press. https://doi.org/10.1016/B978-0-12-811140-6.00001-1

Mammen, M. J., & Sethi, S. (2016). COPD and the microbiome. *Respirology, 21*(4), 590–599. https://doi.org/10.1111/resp.12732

Manning, F., Dean, E., Ross, J., & Abboud, R. T. (1999). Effects of side lying on lung function in older individuals. *Physical Therapy, 79*(5), 456–466.

Marks-Tarlow, T. (2012). *Clinical intuition in psychotherapy: The neurobiology of embodied response.* W. W. Norton.

Matthiessen, P. (2008). *The snow leopard.* Penguin.

McCraty, R., Atkinson, M., & Bradley, R. T. (2004). Electrophysiological evidence of intuition: Part 1. The surprising role of the heart. *Journal of Alternative and Complementary Medicine, 10*(1), 133–143. https://doi.org/10.1089/107555304322849057

McCraty, R., Atkinson, M., Tomasino, D., & Bradley, R. T. (2009). The coherent heart: Heart–brain interactions, psychophysiological coherence, and the emergence of system-wide order. *Integral Review, 5*(2), 10–115.

McHugh, P., Aitcheson, F., Duncan, B., & Houghton, F. (2003). Buteyko breathing technique for asthma: An effective intervention. *Journal of the New Zealand Medical Association, 116*(1187), U710.

McKeown, P. (2004). *Close your mouth: Buteyko Clinic handbook for perfect health.* Buteyko Books.

McKeown, P. (2020, March 25). *Buteyko: Functional breathing as the foundation for physical, emotional, and spiritual health.* Interview by J. Dibb. The Breathwork Summit, The Shift Network.

Medical News Today. (2023, November 8). *How long can the average person hold their breath?* https://www.medicalnewstoday.com/articles/how-long-can-the-average-person-hold-their-breath#physical-effects

Melnychuk, M. C., Dockree, P. M., O'Connell, R. G., Murphy, P. R., Balsters, J. H., & Robertson, I. H. (2018). Coupling of respiration and attention via the locus coeruleus: Effects of meditation and pranayama. *Psychophysiology, 55*(9), e13091. https://doi.org/10.1111/psyp.13091

Menuet, C., Connelly, A. A., Bassi, J. K., Melo, M. R., Le, S., Kamar, J., Kumar, N. N., McDougall, S. J., McMullan, S., & Allen, A. M. (2020). Pre-Bötzinger complex neurons drive respiratory modulation of blood pressure and heart rate. *eLife, 9*, e57288. https://doi.org/10.7554/eLife.57288

Miller, A. (1997). *The drama of the gifted child: The search for the true self* (Rev. ed.). Basic Books.

Mills, J. (2006). Reflections on the death drive. *Psychoanalytic Psychology, 23*, 373–382. https://doi.org/10.1037/0736-9735.23.2.373

Montagu, A. (1986). *Touching: The human significance of the skin.* William Morrow Paperbacks.

Mourya, M., Mahajan, A. S., Singh, N. P., & Jain, A. K. (2009). Effect of slow- and fast-breathing exercises on autonomic functions in patients with essential hypertension. *Journal of Alternative and Complementary Medicine, 15*(7), 711–717.

Mutwa, V. C. (1997). *Zulu shaman: Dreams, prophecies, and mysteries (Song of the stars).* Destiny Books.

Nestor, J. (2020). *Breath: The new science of a lost art.* Riverhead Books.

Niemi-Pynttäri, J. A., Sund, R., Putkonen, H., Vorma, H., Wahlbeck, K., & Pirkola, S. P. (2013). Substance-induced psychoses converting into schizophrenia: A register-based study of 18,478 Finnish inpatient cases. *Journal of Clinical Psychiatry, 74*(1), 20155.

Nunez, P. L., Srinivasan, R., & Fields, R. D. (2015). EEG functional connectivity, axon delays and white matter disease. *Clinical Neurophysiology, 126*(1), 110–120. https://doi.org/10.1016/j.clinph.2014.04.003

Ogden, T. (1994). *Subjects of analysis.* Karnak Books.

Olsson, A. (2014). *Conscious breathing: Discover the power of your breath* (3rd ed.). Sorena AB.

O'Mahony, S. M., Clarke, G., Borre, Y. E., Dinan, T. G., & Cryan, J. F. (2015). Serotonin, tryptophan metabolism and the brain-gut-microbiome axis. *Behavioural Brain Research, 277*, 32–48. https://doi.org/10.1016/j.bbr.2014.07.027

O'Rourke, M. (2021, March 8). Unlocking the mysteries of long COVID. *The Atlantic*. https://www.theatlantic.com/magazine/archive/2021/04/unlocking-the-mysteries-of-long-Covid-19/618076

Ouspensky, P. D. (2001). *In search of the miraculous: Fragments of an unknown teaching*. Houghton Mifflin Harcourt.

Paine, W. (1984). *Tilling the soul*. Aurora Press.

Pal, G., Subramaniyam, V., & Madanmohan. (2004). Effect of short-term practice of breathing exercises on autonomic functions in normal human volunteers. *Indian Journal of Medical Research, 120*(2), 115–121.

Panneton, W. M., & Gan, Q. (2020). The mammalian diving response: Inroads to its neural control. *Frontiers in Neuroscience, 14*, 541224. https://doi.org/10.3389/fnins.2020.00524

Park, H., & Han, D. (2015). The effect of the correlation between the contraction of the pelvic floor muscles and diaphragmatic motion during breathing. *Journal of Physical Therapy Science, 27*(7), 2113–2115. https://doi.org/10.1589/jpts.27.2113

Perreau-Linck, E., Beauregard, M., Gravel, P., Paquette, V., Soucy, J.-P., Diksic, M., & Benkelfat, C. (2007). In vivo measurements of brain trapping of C-labelled α-methyl-L-tryptophan during acute changes in mood states. *Journal of Psychiatry and Neuroscience, 32*(6), 430–434.

Platteel-Deur, T. *The art of integrative therapy* (2009). Der Rheinländer.

Pomagam. (2022). *Ukraine Trauma-Resilience*. https://pomagam.pl/ukraineresilience

Popov, T. A. (2011). Human exhaled breath analysis. *Annals of Allergy, Asthma and Immunology, 106*(6), 451–456.

Porges, S. W. (2011). *The polyvagal theory: Neurophysiological foundations of emotions, attachment, communication, and self-regulation*. W. W. Norton.

Prescott, S. L., & Liberles, S. D. (2022). Internal senses of the vagus nerve. *Neuron, 110*(4), 579–599.

Rapozo, D. C. M., Bernardazzi, C., & de Souza, H. S. P. (2017). Diet and microbiota in inflammatory bowel disease: The gut in disharmony.

World Journal of Gastroenterology, 23(12), 2124–2140. https://doi.org/10.3748/wjg.v23.i12.2124

Ray, S. (1995). *Celebration of breath: How to survive anything and heal your body*. Celestial Arts.

Reynolds, G. (2018, November 20). Breathing through the nose may offer unique brain benefits. *New York Times*. https://www.nytimes.com/2018/11/20/well/mind/breathing-through-the-nose-may-offer-unique-brain-benefits.html

Rhinewine, J. P., & Williams, O. J. (2007). Holotropic breathwork: The potential role of a prolonged, voluntary hyperventilation procedure as an adjunct to psychotherapy. *Journal of Alternative and Complementary Medicine, 13*(7), 771–776. https://doi.org/10.1089/acm.2006.6203

Rilke, R. M. (1954). *Letters to a young poet* (Rev. ed., M. D. H. Norton, Trans.). W. W. Norton.

Riso, D. R., & Hudson, R. (1999). *The wisdom of the enneagram: The complete guide to psychological and spiritual growth for the nine personality types*. Bantam.

Roberts, B. (1993). *The experience of no-self: A contemplative journey*. State University of New York Press.

Rogers, C., & Kramer, P. D. (1995). *On becoming a person: A therapist's view of psychotherapy* (2nd ed.). Mariner Books.

Rossi, H. L. (2020, July 8). *Breath, the divine metaphor, becomes a hallmark of America's twin crises*. Religion News Service. https://religionnews.com/2020/07/08/breath-the-divine-metaphor/

Russo, M. A., Santarelli, D. M., & O'Rourke, D. (2017). The physiological effects of slow breathing in the healthy human. *Breathe, 13*(4), 298–309. https://doi.org/10.1183/20734735.009817

Ruth, A. (2015). The health benefits of nose breathing. *Nursing in General Practice*, 40–42.

Salmón, E. (2000). Kincentric ecology: Indigenous perceptions of the human-nature relationship. *Ecological Applications, 10*(5), 1327–1332. https://doi.org/10.2307/2641288

Sarkar, A. A. (2017, May 18). Functional correlation between breathing and emotional states. *MOJ Anatomy and Physiology, 3*(5), 157–158. https://doi.org/10.15406/mojap.2017.03.00108

Satir, V. (1988). *The new peoplemaking*. Science and Behavior Books.

Schachter, S. (2021, September 5). *The breath of life*. Ohr Torah Stone. https://ots.org.il/the-breath-of-life/

Schartner, M. M., Carhart-Harris, R. L., Barrett, A. B., Seth, A. K., & Muthukumaraswamy, S. D. (2017). Increased spontaneous MEG signal diversity for psychoactive doses of ketamine, LSD and psilocybin. *Scientific Reports, 7*(1), 46421. https://doi.org/10.1038/srep46421

ScienceDaily (2010, August 17). "Mitochondrial Eve": Mother of all humans lived 200,000 years ago. https://www.sciencedaily.com/releases/2010/08/100817122405.htm.

Schmidt, J. E., Carlson, C. R., Usery, A. R., & Quevedo, A. S. (2009). Effects of tongue position on mandibular muscle activity and heart rate function. *Oral Medicine, 108*(6), 881–888. https://doi.org/10.1016/j.tripleo.2009.06.029

Schwartz, R. C. (2001). *Introduction to the internal family systems model*. Trailheads.

Schwartz, R. C. (2021). *No bad parts: Healing trauma and restoring wholeness with the internal family systems model*. Sounds True.

Selo, A. M. F. (1954). Breath and prayer in ancient and modern times. *Life of the Spirit* (1946–1964), 9(98), 53–62.

Shah, S. (n.d.). *Ujjayi breathing for yoga, meditation and better sleep*. Art of Living. https://www.artofliving.org/us-en/breathwork/pranayama/ujjayi-breathing

Sharma, S. K., Kala, N., & Telles, S. (2021, November 16). Volitional yoga breathing influences attention and anxiety: An exploratory randomized crossover study. *Complementary Medicine Research, 29*(2), 120–126. https://doi.org/10.1159/000519715

Shatz, C. J. (1992). The developing brain. *Scientific American, 267*(3), 60–67. https://doi.org/10.1038/scientificamerican0992-60

Shibata, T., Yamagata, H., Uchida, S., Otsuki, K., Hobara, T., Higuchi, F., Abe, N., & Watanabe, Y. (2013). The alteration of hypoxia inducible factor-1 (HIF-1) and its target genes in mood disorder patients. *Progress in Neuro-psychopharmacology and Biological Psychiatry, 43*, 222–229. https://doi.org/10.1016/j.pnpbp.2013.01.003

Siegel, D. J. (1999). *The developing mind: Toward a neurobiology of interpersonal experience*. Guilford Press.

Siegel, D. J. (2007). *The mindful brain: Reflection and attunement in the cultivation of well-being*. W. W. Norton.

Siegel, D. J. (2012). *The developing mind: How relationships and the brain interact to shape who we are* (2nd ed.). Constable and Robinson.

Siegel, D. J. (2016). *Mind: A journey to the heart of being human*. W. W. Norton.

Siegel, D. J. (2018). *Aware: The science and practice of presence*. TarcherPerigee.

Sinclair, D. A. (2020, January 9). *Four lifestyle interventions I do to maximize my healthspan*. Lifespan. https://lifespanbook.com/4-interventions/

Singh, M. (2021). *Bhastrika Pranayama: How to do Bhastrika and its benefits*. Art of Living. https://www.artofliving.org/in-en/yoga/breathing-technique/bhastrika-pranayam

Slavich, G. M. (2020). Social safety theory: A biologically based evolutionary perspective on life stress, health, and behavior. *Annual Review of Clinical Psychology, 16*(1), 265–295. https://doi.org/10.1146/annurev-clinpsy-032816-045159

Šmejkal, V., Druga, R., & Tintěra, J. (1999). Control of breathing and brain activation in human subjects seen by functional magnetic resonance imaging. *Physiological Research. 48*(1), 21–25.

Song, H.-S., & Lehrer, P. M. (2003). The effects of specific respiratory rates on heart rate and heart rate variability. *Applied Psychophysiology and Biofeedback, 28*(1), 13–23.

Sonnier, S. (2021, October 20). *Three exercises to strengthen your pelvic floor*. UT Health Houston. https://www.utphysicians.com/three-exercises-to-strengthen-your-pelvic-floor/

Squire, L. R., & Kandel, E. R. (2009). *Memory: From mind to molecules*. Roberts.

Steffen, P. R., Austin, T., DeBarros, A., & Brown, T. (2017). The impact of resonance frequency breathing on measures of heart rate variability, blood pressure, and mood. *Frontiers in Public Health, 5*, 222. https://doi.org/10.3389/fpubh.2017.00222

Streeter, C. C., Gerbarg, P. L., Brown, R. P., Scott, T. M., Nielsen, G. H., Owen, L., Sakai, O., Sneider, J. T., Nyer, M. B., & Silveri, M. (2020). Thalamic gamma-aminobutyric acid level changes in major depressive disorder after a 12-week Iyengar yoga and coherent breathing intervention. *Journal of Alternative and Complementary Medicine, 26*(3), 190–197. https://doi.org/10.1089/acm.2019.0234

Strigo, I. A., & Craig, A. D. (2016). Interoception, homeostatic emotions and sympathovagal balance. *Philosophical Transactions of the Royal Society B: Biological Sciences, 371*(1708), 20160010. https://doi.org/10.1098/rstb.2016.0010

Tang, Y.-Y., Lu, Q., Geng, X., & Posner, M. I. (2010). Short-term meditation induces white matter changes in the anterior cingulate. *Proceedings of the National Academy of Sciences of the United States of America, 107*(35), 15649–15652. https://doi.org/10.1073/pnas.1011043107

Telles, S. (2023). *Volitional breathing: Subtle modifications in the breath and their applications in health.* Interview by J. Dibb. Breathwork Summit, The Shift Network. https://breathworksummit.com/program/52820

Telles, S., Nagarathna, R., & Nagendra, H. R. (1994). Breathing through a particular nostril can alter metabolism and autonomic activities. *Indian Journal of Physiology and Pharmacology, 38*(2), 133–137.

Tibetan Buddhist Encyclopedia. (n.d.). *The Buddhist tradition of breath meditation.* https://www.tibetanbuddhistencyclopedia.com/en/index.php?title=The_Buddhist_Tradition_of_Breath_Meditation

Torres, G. (2023, June 28). Instagram post. https://www.instagram.com/gabestorres

Tsubamoto-Sano, N., Ohtani, J., Ueda, H., Kaku, M., Tanne, K., & Tanimoto, K. (2019). Influences of mouth breathing on memory and learning ability in growing rats. *Journal of Oral Science, 61*(1), 119–124. https://doi.org/10.2334/josnusd.18-0006

Twal, W. O., Wahlquist, A. E., & Balasubramanian, S. (2016). Yogic breathing when compared to attention control reduces the levels of pro-inflammatory biomarkers in saliva: A pilot randomized controlled trial. *BMC Complementary and Alternative Medicine, 16*(1). https://doi.org/10.1186/s12906-016-1286-7

University of British Columbia. (2020, July 8). *Hearing persists at the end of life.* Neuroscience News. https://neurosciencenews.com/hearing-death-16620/

van der Kolk, B. A. (2014). *The body keeps the score: Brain, mind, and body in the healing of trauma.* Viking.

Venkateswar, P. & Parvathisam, S. (2022). Breathing your way to better brain function: The role of respiration in cognitive performance. *Journal of Pharmaceutical Negative Results,* 8214-8219. https://doi.org/10.47750/pnr.2022.13.S07.992

Vimal, R. L. P. (2010). On the quest of defining consciousness. *Mind and Matter, 8,* 93–121.

Vranich, B. (2016). *Breathe: The simple, revolutionary 14-day program to improve your mental and physical health.* St. Martin's.

Wang, J., Song, R., Dove, A., Qi, X., Ma, J., Laukka, E. J., Bennett, D. A., & Xu, W. (2021, September 30). Pulmonary function is associated with cognitive decline and structural brain differences. *Alzheimer's Dementia, 18,* 1335–1344. https://doi.org/10.1002/alz.12479

Watts, R. D. (2022, February 28). *Can magic mushrooms unlock depression? What I've learned in the 5 years since my TEDx talk.* Medium. https://medium.com/@DrRosalindWatts/can-magic-mushrooms-unlock-depression-what-ive-learned-in-the-5-years-since-my-tedx-talk-767c83963134

Weber, G. (2015, September 5). *Are our mystical experiences psychotic? . . . Key indicators.* Happiness Beyond Thought: A Practical Guide to Awakening. http://happinessbeyondthought.blogspot.com/2015/09/are-our-mystical-experiences.html

Wehrwein, E. A., Johnson, C. P., Charkoudian, N., Wallin, B. G., & Joyner, M. J. (2012). A single, acute bout of yogic breathing reduces arterial catecholamines and cortisol. *FASEB J, 26*(S1), 893.16. https://doi.org/10.1096/fasebj.26.1_supplement.893.16

Weil, A. (n.d.). *4-7-8 Breathing: Health benefits and demonstration.* Weil. https://www.drweil.com/videos-features/videos/the-4-7-8-breath-health-benefits-demonstration/

Wells, R. E., Collier, J., Posey, G., Morgan, A., Auman, T., Strittmatter, B., Magalhaes, R., Adler-Neal, A., McHaffie, J. G., & Zeidan, F. (2020). Attention to breath sensations does not engage endogenous opioids to reduce pain. *Pain, 161*(8), 1884–1893. https://doi.org/10.1097/j.pain.0000000000001865

Wild, C. P. (2005). Complementing the genome with an "exposome": The outstanding challenge of environmental exposure measurement in molecular epidemiology. *Cancer Epidemiology, Biomarkers and Prevention, 14*(8), 1847–1850. https://doi.org/10.1158/1055-9965.epi-05-0456

Wilson, E. O. (1984). *biophilia: the human bond with other species.* Harvard University Press.

Yackle, K., Schwarz, L. A., Kam, K., Sorokin, J. M., Huguenard, J. R., Feldman, J. L., Luo, L., & Krasnow, M. A. (2017). Breathing control center neurons that promote arousal in mice. *Science, 355*(6332), 1411–1415. https://doi.org/10.1126/science.aai7984

Yang, C. F., & Feldman, J. L. (2018). Efferent projections of excitatory and inhibitory preBötzinger Complex neurons. *Journal of Comparative Neurology, 526*(8), 1389–1402. https://doi.org/10.1002/cne.24415

Yoo, E., & Roberts, J. (2024). Differential effects of air pollution exposure on mental health: Historical redlining in New York State. *Science of The Total Environment, 948.* https://doi.org/10.1016/j.scitotenv.2024.174516.

Zelano, C., Jiang, H., Zhou, G., Arora, N., Schuele, S., Rosenow, J., & Gottfried, J. A. (2016). Nasal respiration entrains human limbic oscillations and modulates cognitive function. *Journal of Neuroscience, 36*(49), 12448–12467. https://doi.org/10.1523/JNEUROSCI.2586-16.2016

Zhan, Q., Buchanan, G. F., Motelow, J. E., Andrews, J., Vitkovskiy, P., Chen, W. C., Serout, F., Gummadavelli, A., Kundishora, A., Furman, M., Li, W., Bo, X., Richerson, G. B., & Blumenfeld, H. (2016). Impaired serotonergic brainstem function during and after seizures. *Journal of Neuroscience, 36*(9), 2711–2722. https://doi.org/10.1523/JNEUROSCI.4331-15.2016

Index

In this index, *f* denotes figure and *n* denotes footnote.

12 Pillars of Breathwork, 169
5P Process, 314–321

abandonment, 178, 195, 202, 256
Abbagnano, A., 56
Abram, D., 19–20
Accelerated Breathing, 155–157
  See also Bhastrika, Kapalabhati; cyclical hyperventilation
Accelerated Experiential Dyadic Therapy (AEDP), 200
The Accidental Mind (Linden), 14
acetylcholine (Ach), 67, 84, 86
Acosta, A., 38–39, 41
acute intermittent hypoxia (AIH), 136–137
adrenaline. *See* epinephrine
AEDP. *See* Accelerated Experiential Dyadic Therapy (AEDP)
African traditions and wisdom, 40–41
air hunger, 116–118, 129, 147, 274
air quality, 181, 186
alchemy. *See* joy/gratitude/generativity/possibility/alchemy/vision
alignment/willingness/integrity/sacredness, 234–235

aliveness/power/confidence/immediacy, 232–233
All Together in One Breath, 12; physiological dynamics, 83–87
alternate nostril breathing, 124–126, 132
anger and rage, 215–218
anger breathing practices, 351
Annals of Allergy, Asthma and Immunology, 106
ANS. *See* autonomic nervous system (ANS)
antidepressants and anti-anxiety medications, 173, 255
anxiety and breathing practices, 121, 128, 249–255, 351
The Art of Integrative Therapy (Platteel-Deur), 200
Assagioli, R., 326
asthma, 279–280
Asthma Pranayama. *See* Respiratory Healing Pranayama (RHP)
Attachment, 343. *See* aversion, judgment, attachment, or fear orientations
attachment theory, 23, 192, 213, 217, 226, 277, 281, 315

attunement, 307
See also responsiveness/nurturing/kindness/attunement, 5P Process,
authentic breathing, 266, 307, 312–314
authentic self, 309–314
autonomic nervous system (ANS), 66, 71–72
aversion, judgment, attachment, or fear orientations, 316–317
awakeness/guidance/connectivity/wisdom, 240–242
awareness. *See* clarity/awareness/curiosity/learning; Wheel of Awareness
awareness and mindfulness (Group 2 Practices). *See* Group 2 Practices

Babaji's Kriya Yoga, 95, 103, 141
back of the body, 110
Baker, L., 11
BBTRS (Biodynamic Breathwork and Trauma Release System), 33
beauty. *See* depth/mystery/intimacy/beauty
being. *See* peace/unity/being/harmony
Bernardi, L., 142
Berndtson, P., 25, 43
Bertin, M., 47
Bhastrika (Bellows Breath), 132, 133–134
See also Accelerated Breathing
Biodynamic Breathwork and Trauma Release System (BBTRS), 33
biographies, breathing, 91–101
biophilia hypothesis, 181

bipolar disorder, 173, 269–270
bliss states, 57
Blue, M., 56, 60
body positions, 112–116
body wave, 206–207
Boisgontier, M., 305, 306
Booker, K., 39–40
Bostock, R., 179–180
boundaries and boundlessness relationship, 312–315
Box Breathing, 33, 54, 123
brain anatomy, 65–72, 75–77, 79, 80, 82–83
See also vagus nerve (VN) and the polyvagal response
brain stem, sympathetic, and parasympathetic control of respiration, 69–72
brain waves, 75–77
Breath (Nestor), 106, 124, 125
breath, spiritual lineages of culture and language of, 16–20
breath cycles, in Group 5 process, 197–198
breathing cycle, 70*f*
See also preBötzinger Complex (preBötC)
Breathees, xxvi, 171–174, 175–188
considerations for Breathwork readiness, 171–174
definition xxvi
Breathers, xxvi, 34, 42, 44, 103, 134, 146, 169, 176, 196, 349
breathing
anatomy of, 62–63
benefits of, 27
control of, 69
defined, 60
factors affecting, 282–283

physiology of, 61–62, 63–65, 78, 83–87
types and modulators, 73f
See also *specific type of breathing*
breathing biographies, 91–101
guidance for creating, 100–101
Breathing-centered world, 348–350
breathing kit protocol, 169
breathing rates, 26, 28, 49–50, 55, 80
See also overbreathing; rapid breathing; underbreathing
breathing ratios, 141–143
breathing recovery sitting practice, 51
breathing touch, 201–203, 280
breathlessness. See consciousness and breathlessness, expanded states of; Embodied Novelty Breathing (ENB)
Breath Liberation Society, 38
Breathplay, 42, 43
breath quality, awareness of, 5
breath retention, 122–123
Breathwork
  benefits of, 26–27, 230–231, 282, 283, 302–303, 334
  defined, 4, 26, 43
  five groups of, 44–59
  five groups for addressing trauma, 268–269
  future of, 282, 288-289, See also Conscious Responsive Breathing
  with individuals and groups, 178–181
  and integration into other therapies, 187–188, 192–193
  and integration into treatment sessions, 31–32, 177–181
  personal experience in five groups of, 58–59
  for psychological distress (anxiety, depression, trauma, and psychopathologies), 247–272
  transformational pathways, 195–196
  in war zones, 32–33
  in water, 184–185
  See also Human Potential Breathwork; *specific practices*
Breathworkers
  best practices and safety in Breathwork for trauma, 256–261, 262–264
  defined, xxv–xxvi, 43
  discernment during breathlessness by, 226
  as essential workers, 40, 43, 188, 287
  evaluating readiness by, 171–174
  filtering identities of, x–xi
  flow of applications used by, 244–247
  as mirrors of unconditional love, 308
  presence and orientations of, 193–196, 199–200
  safety and structural supports for facilitation, 175–188
  self-care for, 188–190, 244
  training of the future, 288–289
breathwork positions, 112–116, 230–
Breathwork Practices for Wholeness, 146–169
Breathwork spectrum, 26
Breggin, P., 269

388 | Index

Brown, R., 28, 29
Bryant, C., 38, 41
Buhner, S., 332
Buller, K., 289
Bumblebee Breath, 44, 133
Buteyko, K., 50, 116, 117
Buteyko Breathing, 50–51, 116, 119

Cade, M., 49
carbon dioxide
  air hunger and, 117
  anxiety and, 121, 128
  exhalations and, 86
  gas exchange and, 63–64
  mouth versus nasal breathing, 130
  overbreathing and, 118–119, 135, 136
  pH and, 65
  tolerance for (reduced sensitivity to), 116, 117
  underbreathing and, 120, 137
catharsis, 180, 213–215, 267, 276
CB. *See* Conscious Breathing (CB)
CCB. *See* Conscious Connected Breathing (CCB)
cellular respiration and energy exchange, 61–62
centers of energy flow, 11, 14, 220, 296, 299, 320, 327
  defined, 11
central nervous system (CNS), 65–66
  See also brain anatomy
cephalic brain, 10
chanting, 210–211
Chavez, J., 333
Cheng Man-Ch'ing, 319
clarity/awareness/curiosity/learning, 239–240

CNS. *See* central nervous system (CNS)
COAL (curiosity, openness, acceptance, love), xvii
cognitive task performance, 80, 81
Coherent Breathing, 27–29, 33, 49–50, 141–142, 143, 173
collective trauma, 263–264
The Commonwealth of Breath (Abram), 19
concentration camp survivor's narrative, 262–263
confidence. *See* aliveness/power/confidence/immediacy
connected breathing, 120–122
connectivity. *See* awakeness/guidance/connectivity/wisdom
conscious breath holding. *See* breath retention
Conscious Breathing (CB)
  author's experience in discovering, 98–99
  benefits of, 10-11, 26-27, 79–83, 98, 130–131, 249, 256, 261–262
  cultivation of integrated presence through, 10, 11–12, 21–22
  defined, 4
  effects of, 26–27, 299–301
  intraconnection and, 297
  intuition and, 322
  possible reasons for helpfulness of, xii–xiii, xiv
  SEC and, 273–282
  SNS and, 74
  unification with nature through, 20–21
  See also Breathwork; Breathwork Practices for Wholeness

Conscious Connected Breathing (CCB), 54, 57, 121, 123
conscious deep rapid breathing, 131–134
consciousness, indefinite meaning of, 4–5
consciousness and cessation of breathing, expanded states of, 224–226
consciousness and psychological development, 230–243
Conscious Responsive Breathing (CRB), 282–287
conscious slow deep breathing, 131
conscious volitional overbreathing, 58
consent agreements, 201–202
contact without pressure, 319
    See also touch
control pause (CP), 117–118
coregulation, 250–251
    See also enhanced co-empowerment and relational modeling; responsiveness/ nurturing/kindness/attunement; sitters
countertransference and transference, 226–230
CP. See control pause (CP)
Credo Mutwa, V., 17
culture and languages, breath and spiritual lineages of, 16–20
curiosity. See clarity/awareness/ curiosity/learning
cyclical hyperventilation, 54, 137
    See also Accelerated Breathing
cyclical sighing, 54, 157, 253

DA. See dopamine (DA)
Daniels, David, 11

Daniels, Denise, 11
Dansby, B., 305
Davis, H., 251
Deci, E., 284
deep breathing
    benefits of, 12, 131–132, 174, 256, 276
    effects of, 96, 172, 258–259, 276
    See also Coherent Breathing; Conscious Breathing
depression and breathing practices, 249–255, 351
depth and human potential (Group 5 Practices). See Group 5 Breathing Practices (or Group 5 Breathwork)
depth/mystery/intimacy/beauty, 237–239
development, as a breathwork pathway, 195
development, human. See Group 4 Practices
diaphragm
    and breathing practices, 104–106, 259
    description of, 62, 104
disaster and social trauma, 264
discernment, 226, 342, 343–344
    See also self-honesty
dis-ease and illnesses. See drug and alcohol detoxification; physical illnesses; psychopathologies; trauma survivors
dissociation. See sleepiness, dissociation, and expanded states of consciousness
dissociative disorders, 271
the Divine, breathing and, 16–20, 164, 238, 242, 247

DMT, 332–333
Dobosz, N., 33
dopamine (DA), 57, 68, 127, 132, 313
Doty, J., 97
droning, 209–210
drug and alcohol detoxification, 276–277

ecopsychology, 181
Edmonson, D., 28
Edwards, S., 326
Ehrmann, W., 266
Einstein, A., xvii, 310–311
Elliott, S., 27, 49, 141–142, 143, 160–161
embodied integration, 219–221
Embodied Novelty Breathing (ENB), 165–169, 242, 327
emotional awareness, inquiries to support, 219–220
emotional regulation, 300
　Breathwork and, xviii, 13, 26, 54, 255, 266–267, 275, 352
　rhythmic sounds and, 260
　See also heart intuition
emotions, 211–218
　See also heart center; somatic–emotional–cognitive continuum (SEC continuum)
empowerment. See enhanced co-empowerment and relational modeling
ENB. See Embodied Novelty Breathing (ENB)
energy
　the body as, 164
　breathing practices, 352
　defined, 293, 302
　degree of probability and, 293
　effects of breath rates on, 26, 132, 156
　Group 4 Practices and, 240
　Group 5 Practices and, 197–198
　See also somatic–emotional–cognitive continuum (SEC continuum); tetany; vibration
energy exchange. See cellular respiration and energy exchange
enhanced co-empowerment and relational modeling, 194–195
Enhanced Focus Breathing, 157–159
Enneagram, 11
epinephrine, 67, 74, 84, 86
equanimity breath, 46
equilibrium breathing practices, 352
Erickson, M., 323
essence as a breathwork pathway, 196
essence/essences, 195–196, 230, 231
　See also value/personal essence/radiance/manifestation
ethics, 175–177, 193–196
　See also consent agreements
exhalation, 86–87, 142
　See also expiration
Exhale (Bostock), 179
expanded states of consciousness, xiii, 83, 122, 171, 175, 255, 287, 322–346,
See also Group 5 Breathing Practices, expanded states of consciousness and; sleepiness, dissociation, and expanded states of consciousness
The Experience of No Self (Roberts), 345

experiencing versus feeling, 194
expiration, 69, 70–71
   See also exhalation
exposome, 78–79
expression breathing practices, 354
exquisite energetic contact, 319
extended inspiration, 166–167
eye contact and eye gazing, 199–200
eye positions, 115–116

FACES flow, xv
fast breathing, 132, 264
   See also rapid breathing
fatigue breathing practices, 352
fear, 118
   See also aversion, judgment, attachment, or fear orientations; phobic stir
Feldman, J., 47, 128, 137, 298
FFCB. *See* Form and Formlessness Communion Breathing (FFCB)
Fincham, G., 143
first breath, the importance of, xi, 3, 5, 91, 304, 348
5P Process, 314–321
flashbacks, 260–261
Flics, D., 341–342
flow states, 167-168, 208, 286
   See also Embodied Novelty Breathing (ENB)
Floyd, G., 22
focus breathing practices, 352
Focusing (Gendlin), 12
Form and Formlessness Communion Breathing (FFCB), 164–165
Fosha, D., 200
four ounces of pressure, 319
Framingham Heart Study, xix

Frankl, V., 188
Freud, S., 192, 307

gas exchange and filtering, 63–64
Gendlin, E., 8, 12, 192
generativity. *See* joy/gratitude/generativity/possibility/alchemy/vision
Gerberg, P., 28, 29
gleeful aliveness, 284
glial cells, 66
Global Professional Breathwork Alliance (GPBA), xxi–xxii, 43, 58, 175, 181, 201, 288
God Instinct, 13, 14
   See also the Divine, breathing and
Going, L., 336
gratitude. See joy/gratitude/generativity/possibility/alchemy/vision
Griffiths, R., 333, 337
Grof, C., 271
Grof, S., 192, 243–244, 271, 278
Group 5 Breathing Practices (or Group Five Breathwork)
   about, 52–58
   applications for asthma—narrative, 279–280
   applications for cancer, examples, 274–275
   applications in physical and mental healing—narrative, 275–278
   components and processes, 190–230
   for cultivating authentic self, 310
   expanded states of consciousness and, 30, 52–54, 56–58, 135, 138, 211

Group 5 Breathing Practices (or
    Group Five Breathwork)
    (*continued*)
  facilitator ration to participants
      and, 179, 180
  flow of applications, example,
      244–247
  group Breathwork sessions, 179,
      180
  hyperventilation in, 135–136
  intuition and, 325
  and online Breathwork, 182
  and psychopathologies, 269
  surgery and, 174
  for trauma healing, 267–268
  water Breathwork and, 185
  See also Conscious Responsive
      Breathing (CRB); Human
      Potential Breathwork
Group 4 Breathing Practices,
    51–52, 231–243, 267, 269
Group 3 Breathing Practices,
    49–51, 267
Group 2 Breathing Practices,
    47–48, 266–267
Group 1 Breathing Practices,
    45–46, 266
guidance. *See* awakeness/guidance/
    connectivity/wisdom
Gurdjieff, G., 18, 151
gut feelings. *See* somatic intuition

Hakuin Ekaku, 345–346
Handy-Kendi, A., 37
Hari, J., 250
harmony. *See* peace/unity/being/
    harmony
Haworth, J., 189
Hayek, R., 43

head center, 9
healing, as a breathwork pathway,
    195
healing and therapeutic (Group
    3 Practices). *See* Group 3
    Practices
health issues, 171–174
  See also physical illnesses;
      psychopathologies
heart center, 9
heart intuition, 325–326, 329–330
heart pumps, 203–205
heart rate variability (HRV), 12,
    28, 29, 74–75, 79, 85, 86, 87,
    141, 142, 157, 267, 283
Heyda, A., 213, 275–276
Hoffberger, R., 284
Holotropic Breathwork, 30, 58, 83,
    140, 179
Huberman, A., 47, 54, 137
Hudson, R., 231
human development (Group
    4 Practices). *See* Group 4
    Practices
Human Potential Breathwork
  about, 30–32
  frequent use of, 58
  processes, 196–224
  states of consciousness and, 57,
      224–226, 230–243
  transference and countertrans-
      ference, 226–230
  See also Group 5 Breathing
      Practices (or Group Five
      Breathwork)
Huslage, M., 335–336
hygiene, 186–187
hyperoxia, 138
hyperoxic hypoxic paradox, 138

hyperventilation, 135–136, 137, 138, 174
   See also overbreathing
hypocapnia, 129, 130, 136
hypoventilation, 136
   See also underbreathing
hypoxia, 136–138, 184

IFS. *See* Internal Family Systems (IFS)
immediacy. *See* aliveness/power/confidence/immediacy
inhalation, physiology of, 83–84, 86
The Inner Work of Racial Justice (Magee), 36
insight intuition (from head center), 326, 330–331
inspiration, 70, 71, 80
   See also extended inspiration; inhalation, physiology of
Inspiration Consciousness School, xxi, 58, 175–176, 179, 183, 228, 313, 333
integrated (three-centered) intuition, 327–328
integrating Breathwork and psychotherapy, xii, xv, 4, 23–24, 27, 31-32, 174, 177–178, 191–193, 230–231, 287–288
integration, xiv, 8–13, 15
   See also embodied integration; Wheel of Awareness
Integrative Breathing, xii, 6, 30–32, 43, 59, 83, 226, 228, 250, 252, 259, 269, 276, 331, 335
integrity. *See* alignment/willingness/integrity/sacredness

intelligence. *See* head center
intention, in Group 5 process, 196–197
interconnection, 294, 296
Internal Family Systems (IFS), 187, 192
interoception, 14–15, 47, 72, 283
intersectionality. *See* marginalization, breathwork and
intimacy. *See* depth/mystery/intimacy/beauty
intraconnection, 294, 296–297
intuition, 322–331
Intuitive Center, 13–14

James, W., 52–53, 344
Johnson, B., 29
Jones, E., 140
Journal of Alternative and Complementary Medicine, 29
joy and fulfillment, 312–323
joy/gratitude/generativity/possibility/alchemy/vision, 242–243
judgment. *See* aversion, judgment, attachment, or fear orientations
Jung, C., 151, 192, 278, 326

Kabat-Zinn, J., 192, 272
Kapalabhati Breathing (Breath of Fire), 133
   See also Accelerated Breathing
"Keeping the Breath in Mind" (Boyadzhieva & Kayhan), 283
Killen, J., 11
kindness. *See* responsiveness/nurturing/kindness/attunement

knowing, inquiries to support, 220
Kornfield, J., 47, 52, 134
Kraus, A., 262–263
Kubie, L., 305–306

Laing, R. D., 269
Lampman, C., 30
Laning, K., 336
LaPierre, A., 262
Leading From Within (Steidle), 29
learning. *See* clarity/awareness/curiosity/learning
Lefort, R., 340
left nostril breathing, 125
Lehrer, P., 142
Levine, P., 262
life force, 110, 112, 118, 119, 121, 138–140, 147, 153, 155-166, 181, 191, 195, 198, 207, 210, 215, 222, 285–287, 304, 306–314
life purpose, 191
Linden, D., 14
Litchfield, P., 116, 130, 138, 274, 285
Lost Connections (Hari), 250
Lowen, A., 106
lungs, 28, 63–64, 69–71, 72, 77–78, 84–85, 94, 104–106, 113, 114, 120, 122, 123, 126, 127, 128, 136, 157, 159, 184, 253, 280, 299

Magee, R., 36–37
mammalian diving reflex, 185
Manga, E., 41
manifestation. *See* value/personal essence/radiance/manifestation

marginalization, breathwork and, 34–42
Marks-Tarlow, T., 323
masks, 186–187
Matrika Pranayama, 140, 143, 149–151, 232
  See also Enhanced Focus Breathing
McConnell, S., 187
McCraty, R., 75, 325–326
McKeown, P., 50, 116, 119, 127, 130
medication usage, 173–174, 255
meditation, 82, 267, 337, 345
  See also mindfulness meditation
memory, olfactory system and, 81
mental well-being, screening for, 174
mice, mindfully meditating 47
microbiome, 77–78
Miller, A., 192
Mills, J., 307
the mind, defined, 11, 273–274, 297, 330
mindful awareness, xvii
mindfulness. *See* awareness and mindfulness (Group 2 Practices)
mindfulness breathing practice, simple, 48
mindfulness meditation, 47, 54
mirror, use of, 200
mirroring, 199
mirroring breath, 52
Montagu, A., 305
Morningstar, J., xxi, 13, 43,
mouth and tongue placement, 107–109
mouth breathing, 108, 119, 127–131, 174

movement, 111–112, 115, 217–218, 230–242, 253–254, 259
movement and touch, 203–208
music, 211, 266
mystery. *See* depth/mystery/intimacy/beauty
mystical experiences breathing practices, 353
  See also transpersonal, spiritual, and mystical experiences
mystical states, 223

nasal breathing, 81, 117, 124–125, 174
nasal decongestion exercise, 126–127
NE (norepinephrine), 67–68
nectar, 107–108
Nestor, J., 28, 106, 116, 124, 125, 140
neurotransmitters, 67–68
Newberg, A., 344
Newton, I., xvi
Nhat Hanh, T., 43, 46
noise levels, 180–181, 246, 282
The Noonday Demon (Solomon), 250
norepinephrine (NE), 67–68
nose breathing. *See* nasal breathing
nose breathing—mouth breathing comparison, 130
novelty, in breathing, 286
  See also Embodied Novelty Breathing (ENB)
nurturing. *See* responsiveness/nurturing/kindness/attunement

O'Donohue, J., xii
Ogden, P., 215, 258–259
olfactory stimulation, 259–260, 265

olfactory system, 14, 57, 67, 81
Oliver, M., 5, 44
Olsson, A., 116, 124
OluDaré, B., 19, 40, 41
online Breathwork, 182–184
optimal breathing, 102–144
  air hunger in, 116–118
  breathing ratios, 141–143
  connected breathing and breath retention, 120–123
  life force, tingling, tetany, and vibration, 138–140
  overbreathing and underbreathing, 118–120
  physical components of, 104–116
  practice and integration of, 144
  practice of unifying, 110–112
  spectrum of breathing depth and speed, 131–138
othering, 34–35
  See also marginalization, breathwork and
outdoor Breathwork, 181–182
overbreathing
  about, 118–119, 147, 159
  anxiety and, 254
  effects of, 55, 129–130, 174, 187
  emotions and, 117
  Group 5 Practices and, 58
  tetany and, 139
  See also hyperventilation
The Oxygen Advantage (Buteyko), 50
oxygenation, 25–26, 61–62

parasympathetic nervous system (PSN), 66, 72, 74
  See also brain stem, sympathetic, and parasympathetic control of respiration

Patterson, J., 38, 41
peace/unity/being/harmony, 233–234
pelvic floor muscles (PFM), 112
pendulation, 33, 257
peripheral nervous system (PNS), 66
personal and spiritual development breathing practices, 353
personal essence. *See* essences; value/personal essence/radiance/manifestation
PFM. *See* pelvic floor muscles (PFM)
pH, 64–65
phobic stir, 305–308
physical and psychological relatedness in wellbeing, Breathwork for, 273–279
physical illnesses, 136–137, 139–140, 275–276, 279–280
See also health issues
physician training, 26
PI. *See* postinspiration (PI) periods
Plane of Possibility, xvi
Plane of Possibility, Conscious Breathing, and Breathwork, 167, 293–303
Plane of Possibility Practitioners Presence Process (the 5P Process), 314–321
Platteel-Deur, T., 200
Pneumanity Breathwork, 41
PNS (peripheral nervous system), 66
polyvagal response, 131, 135, 177, 216, 256, 259, 260, 262, 265, 299

See also vagus nerve (VN) and the polyvagal response
Polyvagal Theory, 73, 299
Porges, S., 72, 256, 299
possibility. *See* joy/gratitude/generativity/possibility/alchemy/vision
postinspiration (PI) periods, 69–70
postures, 112–116
power. *See* aliveness/power/confidence/immediacy
The Power of Breathwork (Patterson), 38
pranayama practices, 16, 108, 129, 143, 149–151, 159–162
preBötzinger Complex (preBötC), 69, 70, 71, 72, 83–84
pregnancy, Breathwork readiness and, 171–172
presence
Breathworker presence orientation, 192–194, See also 5P Process
integrated embodied presence, See SEC continuum
three-centered presence, 8–13
See also attunement
psilocybin, 57, 68, 331–332, 333, 335
psoas muscle and breathing, 114
PSN. *See* parasympathetic nervous system (PSN)
psychedelics, 331–337
psychopathologies
Breathwork for, 268–272, 277–278
Breathwork readiness and, 172, 173

mystical experiences versus, 342, 344
See also anxiety and breathing practices; depression and breathing practices; schizophrenia
psychophysiologic nature of breathing, 102, 110, 116, 118, 121, 129, 137, 139, 274, 285, 299, 305
psychotherapy, definition and evolution of, 191–192, 289–290
PTSD, 28, 172–173, 267
See also trauma survivors
purpose, of life, 191

Qigong, 107, 121
quantum physics, xv–xvi
Quintessence Breathing (QB), 151–155

race or skin color, 36*n*
racial healing breathwork, 36–42
radiance. See value/personal essence/radiance/manifestation
Ramaiah, S., 141
rapid breathing, 82, 121, 129–130, 132, 174
See also conscious deep rapid breathing
Receiving Breathing, 146–149
refugees, Breathwork and, 33
regulation breathing practices, 354
See also emotional regulation
relational modeling. See enhanced co-empowerment and relational modeling
relative conditions, 316

relaxation and resetting (Group 1 Practices). See Group 1 Practices
relaxation breathing practices, 354
release of tension breath, 46
repetition syndrome, 257
resiliency breathing practices, 354
resonant breathing. See Coherent Breathing
respiration, defined, 60
respiratory anatomy, 62–63
respiratory cycle, 70*f*
See also preBötzinger Complex (preBötC)
Respiratory Healing Pranayama (RHP), 159–160
respiratory health breathing practices, 353
respiratory issues, Breathwork readiness and, 172
respiratory sinus arrhythmia (RSA), 49
responsiveness/nurturing/kindness/attunement, 235–236
rhythmic sounds, 260
right nostril breathing, 125
Rilke, R., 339, 341
Roberts, B., 345
RSA. See respiratory sinus arrhythmia (RSA)
Ryan, R., 284

sacredness. See alignment/willingness/integrity/sacredness
Samadhi, 224–225
Schachter, S., 17
schizophrenia, 125, 172, 269, 333

Schneiderian symptoms, 278
Schwartz, R., 187
Science Instinct, 14
SEC continuum. *See* somatic–emotional–cognitive continuum (SEC continuum)
sedentary behaviors, 305
seizure disorders, 174
self-care, 188–190
self-determination theory, 283–284
Self-Healing Breathing, 162–163
self-honesty, 324
senses, Intuitive Center and, 14
  See also olfactory system
sensory implications of motor action (SIMA), xii, 300
serotonin, 68, 84, 86, 201
shaking. *See* vibration
Shankar, R., 29
Siegel, D., 11, 61, 166, 192, 293, 294, 297, 298, 300, 339
sighing, 128–129
  See also cyclical sighing
SIMA process (sensory implication of motor action), xii, 300
simple mindfulness breathing practice, 48
Sinclair, D., 136
Sirota, K., 31–32
Sitali Pranayama, 129
sitters, 179
SKY. *See* Sudarshan Kriya Yoga (SKY)
sleep breathing practices, 353
sleepiness, dissociation, and expanded states of consciousness, 221–224

Sleep Pranayama, 160–162
slow breathing, 29, 47, 74, 76, 264–265
  See also conscious slow deep breathing
slow deep breathing, 12, 131–132
smell, sense of, 14
  See also olfactory system
SNS. *See* sympathetic nervous system (SNS)
social and disaster trauma, 264
Solomon, A., 250
somatic awareness, inquiries to support, 219
somatic center, 8
somatic–emotional–cognitive continuum (SEC continuum), 11, 15, 273–281, 312
  See also integrated (three-centered) intuition
somatic intelligence, 218
somatic intuition, 324–325, 328
sound, in breathwork, 208–211, 260
  See also noise levels; sighing
spaces, for Breathwork, 181–186
Spectrum of Wellness, Nutrients and Medicine 281*f*
Spiegel, D., 54
spinal positions during Breathwork, 104, 110, 112–114, 259
  See also breathwork positions
spiritual and personal development breathing practices, 353
spiritual bypass and other cautions, 342
spiritual center, 13, 14
spiritual emergencies, 271–272

spiritual experiences. *See* transpersonal, spiritual, and mystical experiences
spontaneous movement, 111, 207–208
Starting Your Own High School (Elizabeth Cleaners Street School People), 95
Steidle, G., 29
Strassman, R., 332–333, 337
stress breathing practices, 353–354
Sudarshan Kriya Yoga (SKY), 29–30
Sun Lun Sayadaw, 134–135
surgery, 174
sympathetic nervous system (SNS), 66, 71, 74
　See also brain stem, sympathetic, and parasympathetic control of respiration
Szasz, T., 269

Tamil Yoga Siddha, 160, 161
Tao Te Ching, 16–17
The Teachers of Gurdjieff (Lefort), 340
Teilhard de Chardin, P., xxiii
Telles, S., 55, 58, 102–103, 125, 132–133, 180, 269, 335
Teresa of Avila, Saint, 344
tetany, 139–140, 224–225
Theragatha Verse 548, 18
Therapist-Breathworkers. *See* Breathworkers
three-centered (integrated) intuition, 327–328
three-centered presence, 8–13
　See also somatic–emotional–cognitive continuum (SEC continuum)

three-centered process exploration, 219–224
Tonglen, 51–52
tongue and mouth placement, 107–109
toning, 210
Tonkov, G., 33
Torres, G., 348–349
touch. *See* breathing touch; movement and touch
trachea, 63
Transcendence Breathwork, 37
transference and countertransference, 226–230
Transformational Breath, 30, 58, 83
transient hypofrontality, and Breathwork
　benefits, 53, 213
　defined, 53
　effects, 135, 213
transpersonal, spiritual, and mystical experiences, 338–347
　See also mystical experiences breathing practices; mystical states
"Trauma and Breath" (Buller), 289
Trauma and the Body (Ogden), 258
trauma survivors, 28, 29, 30–31, 33, 172–173, 255–268
tremoring. *See* vibration
triune brain, 10

Ujjayi breath, 29
Ujjayi Pranayama, 108–109
unconditional positive regard, mirroring, and eye contact, 199–200
unconscious breath holding, 121

underbreathing, 119–120
  See also hypoventilation
unifying optimal breathing practice, 110–112
unity. See peace/unity/being/harmony
Universal Breathing Declaration, xxii, 349

vagus nerve (VN) and the polyvagal response, 72–74, 256, 262, 299
value/personal essence/radiance/manifestation, 236–237
van der Kolk, B., 260
vibration, 138–139, 206
Vimal, R., 4
Vipassana, 48
virtual Breathwork, 182–184
vision. See joy/gratitude/generativity/possibility/alchemy/vision
vitamin B_{12} deficiency, 278–279
VN. See vagus nerve (VN) and the polyvagal response

Walsh, M., 33, 58, 208
Watts, R., 334

Weber, G., 344
Weil, A., 47, 128, 190
wellness. See mental well-being, screening for; Spectrum of Wellness
Wells, A., 228–229
Welwood, J., 325, 342
Wheble, P., 337
Wheel of Awareness, xv–xvi, 297–299
Wiggins, S., 296
Wild, C., 78–79
willingness. See alignment/willingness/integrity/sacredness
Wilson, E., 181
Wind in My Hair (Hoffberger), 284
wisdom. See awakeness/guidance/connectivity/wisdom; head center; intuition
Wisdom of the Enneagram (Hudson), 231
world map and breathing practices, 53f

Zeidan, F., 283
Zulu Shaman (Mutwa), 17

About the Author

Through lifelong exploration of pathways for physical and psychological health and development, awakened consciousness, and living from love, **Jessica Dibb's** work centers conscious breathing—synthesizing depth psychology; consciousness studies; science; individualized spirituality; somatic, emotional, and cognitive energy; and wholeness. Extensively trained in ballet and yoga, during pre-med studies at UC Irvine, she had an epiphany: Breathing is a universal and unifying medicine in every situation, for everyone.

Jessica advocates rigorous training and ethical standards that support powerful, safe, multidimensional, and nuanced Breathwork to access our deepest potential. She founded a 1200+ hour Breathwork and Psychospiritual Facilitation Program at Inspiration Consciousness School, is the Global Professional Breathwork Alliance founding codirector and ethics chair, and has created Breath Immersion–From Science to Samadhi conferences.

Jessica develops innovative processes for embodying psychospiritual wholeness using Breathwork with established and emergent wisdom teachings to cultivate presence, wisdom, and love throughout our lifespan—in relationship with all life and this breathing planet.